THE LAST TWELVE VERSES

OF THE GOSPEL ACCORDING TO

S. MARK

THE
LAST TWELVE VERSES

OF THE GOSPEL ACCORDING TO

S. MARK

BY

JOHN W. BURGON B.D.

WIPF & STOCK · Eugene, Oregon

Wipf and Stock Publishers
199 W 8th Ave, Suite 3
Eugene, OR 97401

The Last Twelve Verses of the Gospel According to Mark
By Burgon, John
Softcover ISBN-13: 979-8-3852-1241-5
Hardcover ISBN-13: 979-8-3852-1242-2
eBook ISBN-13: 979-8-3852-1243-9
Publication date 1/5/2024
Previously published by James Parker and Co., 1871

This edition is a scanned facsimile of the original edition published in 1871.

ἀμὴν γὰρ λέγω ὑμῖν,
ἕως ἂν παρέλθῃ ὁ οὐρανὸς καὶ ἡ γῆ,
ἰῶτα ἓν ἢ μία κεραία οὐ μὴ παρέλθῃ ἀπὸ τοῦ νόμου,
ἕως ἂν πάντα γένηται.

εὐκοπώτερον δέ ἐστι
τὸν οὐρανὸν καὶ τὴν γῆν παρελθεῖν,
ἢ τοῦ νόμου μίαν κεραίαν πεσεῖν.

ὁ οὐρανὸς καὶ ἡ γῆ παρελεύσονται,
οἱ δὲ λόγοι μου οὐ μὴ παρέλθωσι.

καὶ ἐάν τις ἀφαιρῇ
ἀπὸ τῶν λόγων βίβλου τῆς προφητείας ταύτης,
ἀφαιρήσει ὁ Θεὸς τὸ μέρος αὐτοῦ
ἀπὸ βίβλου τῆς ζωῆς,
καὶ ἐκ τῆς πόλεως τῆς ἁγίας,
καὶ τῶν γεγραμμένων ἐν βιβλίῳ τούτῳ.

This is a facsimile of the CODEX VATICANUS (B), showing space left for Mark 16:9-20

This is a facsimile of the CODEX SINAITICUS showing Mark 16:2 - Luke 1:18

INTRODUCTION, by Dr. Edward F. Hills 17

CONTENTS.

DEDICATION . . . . p. 73
PREFACE . . . . p. 75

CHAPTER I.

THE CASE OF THE LAST TWELVE VERSES OF S. MARK'S GOSPEL, STATED.

These Verses generally suspected at the present time. The popularity of this opinion accounted for . . . . . . p. 79

CHAPTER II.

THE HOSTILE VERDICT OF BIBLICAL CRITICS SHEWN TO BE QUITE OF RECENT DATE.

Griesbach the first to deny the genuineness of these Verses —Lachmann's fatal principle the clue to the unfavourable verdict of Tischendorf of Tregelles , of Alford ; which has been generally adopted by subsequent Scholars and Divines .— The nature of the present inquiry explained . . p 83

CHAPTER III.

THE EARLY FATHERS APPEALED TO, AND OBSERVED TO BEAR FAVOURABLE WITNESS TO THESE VERSES.

Patristic evidence sometimes the most important of any —The importance of such evidence explained —Nineteen Patristic witnesses to these Verses, produced —Summary . . . p. 97

CHAPTER IV.

THE EARLY VERSIONS EXAMINED, AND FOUND TO YIELD UNFALTERING TESTIMONY TO THE GENUINENESS OF THESE VERSES.

The Peshito,—the Curetonian Syriac,—and the Recension of Thomas of Hharkel —The Vulgate --and the Vetus Itala the Gothic —and the Egyptian Versions —Review of the Evidence up to this point . . . . p. 110

CHAPTER V.

THE ALLEGED HOSTILE WITNESS OF CERTAIN OF THE EARLY FATHERS PROVED TO BE AN IMAGINATION OF THE CRITICS.

The mistake concerning Gregory of Nyssa —The misconception concerning Eusebius —The oversight concerning Jerome also concerning Hesychius of Jerusalem, (or else Severus of Antioch) —and the mis-statement concerning Victor of Antioch . p 116

CHAPTER VI.

MANUSCRIPT TESTIMONY SHEWN TO BE OVERWHELMINGLY IN FAVOUR OF THESE VERSES.—PART I.

S. Mark xvi. 9—20, contained in every MS. in the world except two,— Irrational claim to Infallibility set up on behalf of Cod. B and Cod. ℵ —These two Codices shewn to be full of gross Omissions —Interpolations —Corruptions of the Text ,—and Perversions of the Truth —The testimony of Cod. B to S. Mark xvi. 9—20, shewn to be favourable, notwithstanding . p. 148

CHAPTER VII.

MANUSCRIPT TESTIMONY SHEWN TO BE OVERWHELMINGLY IN FAVOUR OF THESE VERSES.—PART II.

The other chief peculiarity of Codices B and ℵ (viz. the omission of the words ἐν Ἐφέσῳ from Ephes. i. 1) considered.—Antiquity unfavourable to the omission of those words —The Moderns infelicitous in their attempts to account for their omission —Marcion probably the author of this corruption of the Text of Scripture —Other peculiarities of Codex ℵ disposed of, and shewn to be errors p. 169

CHAPTER VIII.

THE PURPORT OF ANCIENT SCHOLIA AND NOTES IN MSS. ON THE SUBJECT OF THESE VERSES, SHEWN TO BE THE REVERSE OF WHAT IS COMMONLY SUPPOSED.

Later Editors of the New Testament the victims of their predecessors' inaccuracies. — Birch's unfortunate mistake — Scholz' serious blunders —Griesbach's sweeping misstatement —The grave misapprehension which has resulted from all this inaccuracy of detail

CONTENTS. 13

Codex L .—*Ammonius not the author of the so-called "Ammonian" Sections* —*Epiphanius* —" *Cæsarius*," *a misnomer.*— " *The Catenae*" *misrepresented* . . . p. 194

CHAPTER IX.

INTERNAL EVIDENCE DEMONSTRATED TO BE THE VERY REVERSE OF UNFAVOURABLE TO THESE VERSES.

The "Style" and "Phraseology" of these Verses declared by Critics to be not S. Mark's.—*Insecurity of such Criticism* .—*The "Style" of chap.* xvi. 9—20 *shewn to be the same as the style of chap.* i. 9—20 —*The " Phraseology" examined in twenty-seven particulars, and shewn to be suspicious in none* —*but in twenty-seven particulars shewn to be the reverse* .—*Such remarks fallacious* — *Judged of by a truer, a more delicate and philosophical Test, these Verses proved to be most probably genuine* . . . . p. 216

CHAPTER X.

THE TESTIMONY OF THE LECTIONARIES SHEWN TO BE ABSOLUTELY DECISIVE AS TO THE GENUINENESS OF THESE VERSES.

The Lectionary of the East shewn to be a work of extraordinary antiquity —*Proved to be older than any extant MS. of the Gospels, by an appeal to the Fathers* —*In this Lectionary, (and also in the Lectionary of the West,) the last Twelve Verses of S. Mark's Gospel have, from the first, occupied a most conspicuous, as well as most honourable place* —*Now, this becomes the testimony of ante-Nicene Christendom in their favour, and is therefore decisive* . p. 271

CHAPTER XI.

THE OMISSION OF THESE TWELVE VERSES IN CERTAIN ANCIENT COPIES OF THE GOSPELS, EXPLAINED AND ACCOUNTED FOR.

The Text of our five oldest Uncials proved, by an induction of instances, to have suffered depravation throughout by the operation of the ancient Lectionary system of the Church ,.—*The omission of S. Mark's "last Twelve Verses," (constituting an integral Ecclesiastical Lection,) shewn by an appeal to ancient MSS. to be probably only one more example of the same depraving influence This solution of the problem corroborated by the language of Eusebius and of Hesychius* ; *as well as favoured by the "Western" order of the Gospels* . . . . . p. 292

CHAPTER XII.

GENERAL REVIEW OF THE QUESTION: SUMMARY OF THE EVIDENCE; AND CONCLUSION OF THE WHOLE SUBJECT.

This discussion narrowed to a single issue .—That S. Mark's Gospel was imperfect from the very first, a thing altogether incredible :— But that at some very remote period Copies have suffered mutilation, a supposition probable in the highest degree —Consequences of this admission —Parting words . . . p. 323

APPENDIX (A).

On the Importance of attending to Patristic Citations of Scripture.—*The correct Text of* S. LUKE ii. 14, *established* 337

APPENDIX (B).

EUSEBIUS "ad Marinum" *concerning the reconcilement of* S. Mark xvi. 9 *with* S. Matthew xxviii. 1 345

APPENDIX (C).

Proof that HESYCHIUS *is a Copyist only in what he says concerning the end of S. Mark's Gospel* 347

APPENDIX (D).

Some account of VICTOR OF ANTIOCH'S *Commentary on S. Mark's Gospel; together with a descriptive enumeration of MSS. which contain Victor's Work* 349

APPENDIX (E).

Text of the concluding Scholion of VICTOR OF ANTIOCH'S *Commentary on S. Mark's Gospel; in which Victor bears emphatic Testimony to the Genuineness of "the last Twelve Verses"* 368

APPENDIX (F).

On the relative antiquity of the CODEX VATICANUS (B), *and the* CODEX SINAITICUS (א) 371

APPENDIX (G).

*On the (so-called) "*Ammonian*" Sections and on the* Eusebian Canons: *a Dissertation. With some account of the Tables of Reference occasionally found in Greek and Syriac MSS.* 375

APPENDIX (H).

On the Interpolation of the Text of Codex B *and* Codex ℵ, *at* S. Matthew xxvii. 48 *or* 49   393

POSTSCRIPT   399

L'Envoy.

F. H. SCRIVENER on Mark 16:9-20 (p 407)

BISHOP WORDSWORTH'S COMMENDATION (p 415)

CANON COOK'S REMARKS (p 415)

Subjoined, for convenience, are "the Last Twelve Verses."

Ἀναστὰς δὲ πρωῒ πρώτῃ σαββάτου ἐφάνη πρῶτον Μαρίᾳ τῇ Μαγδαληνῇ, ἀφ' ἧς ἐκβεβλήκει ἑπτὰ δαιμόνια. ἐκείνη πορευθεῖσα ἀπήγγειλε τοῖς μετ' αὐτοῦ γενομένοις, πενθοῦσι καὶ κλαίουσι. κἀκεῖνοι ἀκούσαντες ὅτι ζῇ καὶ ἐθεάθη ὑπ' αὐτῆς ἠπίστησαν.

Μετὰ δὲ ταῦτα δυσὶν ἐξ αὐτῶν περιπατοῦσιν ἐφανερώθη ἐν ἑτέρᾳ μορφῇ, πορευομένοις εἰς ἀγρόν. κἀκεῖνοι ἀπελθόντες ἀπήγγειλαν τοῖς λοιποῖς· οὐδὲ ἐκείνοις ἐπίστευσαν.

Ὕστερον ἀνακειμένοις αὐτοῖς τοῖς ἕνδεκα ἐφανερώθη, καὶ ὠνείδισε τὴν ἀπιστίαν αὐτῶν καὶ σκληροκαρδίαν, ὅτι τοῖς θεασαμένοις αὐτὸν ἐγηγερμένον οὐκ ἐπίστευσαν. Καὶ εἶπεν αὐτοῖς, "Πορευθέντες εἰς τὸν κόσμον ἅπαντα, κηρύξατε τὸ εὐαγγέλιον πάσῃ τῇ κτίσει. ὁ πιστεύσας καὶ βαπτισθεὶς σωθήσεται· ὁ δὲ ἀπιστήσας κατακριθήσεται. σημεῖα δὲ τοῖς πιστεύσασι ταῦτα παρακολουθήσει· ἐν τῷ ὀνόματί μου δαιμόνια ἐκβαλοῦσι· γλώσσαις λαλήσουσι καιναῖς· ὄφεις ἀροῦσι· κἂν θανάσιμόν τι πίωσιν, οὐ μὴ αὐτοὺς βλάψει· ἐπὶ ἀρρώστους χεῖρας ἐπιθήσουσι, καὶ καλῶς ἕξουσιν."

Ὁ μὲν οὖν Κύριος, μετὰ τὸ λαλῆσαι αὐτοῖς, ἀνελήφθη εἰς τὸν οὐρανὸν, καὶ ἐκάθισεν ἐκ δεξιῶν τοῦ Θεοῦ· ἐκεῖνοι δὲ ἐξελθόντες ἐκήρυξαν πανταχοῦ, τοῦ Κυρίου συνεργοῦντος, καὶ τὸν λόγον βεβαιοῦντος διὰ τῶν ἐπακολουθούντων σημείων. Ἀμήν.

(9) Now when JESUS was risen early the first day of the week, He appeared first to Mary Magdalene, out of whom He had cast seven devils. (10) And she went and told them that had been with Him, as they mourned and wept. (11) And they, when they had heard that He was alive, and had been seen of her, believed not. (12) After that He appeared in another form unto two of them, as they walked, and went into the country. (13) And they went and told it unto the residue: neither believed they them. (14) Afterward He appeared unto the eleven as they sat at meat, and upbraided them with their unbelief and hardness of heart, because they believed not them which had seen Him after He was risen. (15) And He said unto them, "Go ye into all the world, and preach the Gospel to every creature. (16) He that believeth and is baptized shall be saved; but he that believeth not shall be damned. (17) And these signs shall follow them that believe; In My Name shall they cast out devils; they shall speak with new tongues; (18) they shall take up serpents; and if they drink any deadly thing, it shall not hurt them; they shall lay hands on the sick, and they shall recover."

(19) So then after the LORD had spoken unto them, He was received up into Heaven, and sat on the Right Hand of GOD. (20) And they went forth, and preached every where, the LORD working with them, and confirming the word with signs following. Amen.

INTRODUCTION
BY
EDWARD F. HILLS, A. B. (Yale), Th. D. (Harvard)

CHAPTER ONE
DEAN BURGON AND THE TRADITIONAL TEXT

Every faithful Christian must reckon seriously with the teaching of Christ concerning the providential preservation of Scripture. Our Lord evidently believed that the Old Testament Scriptures had been preserved in their original purity from the time of their first writing down to His own day and that this providential preservation would continue until the end of the ages. There are two passages especially which clearly indicate this. The first is Matt. 5:18, *Till heaven and earth pass away, one jot or one tittle shall in no wise pass from the law until all be fulfilled.* And the second is Luke 16:17, *It is easier for heaven and earth to pass away, than one tittle of the law to fail.* Here Jesus attributes greater stability to the text of the Old Testament than to the heavens and the earth. Calvin has well explained these words of Christ thus, "There is nothing in the law that is unimportant, nothing that was put there at random; and so it is impossible that a single letter shall perish."

Christ also promised that the same divine providence which had preserved the Old Testament would preserve the New Testament too. In the concluding verses of the Gospel of Matthew we find His "Great Commission" not only to the twelve apostles but also to His Church throughout all ages, *go ye therefore and teach all nations.* Implied in this solemn charge is the promise that through the working of God's providence the Church will always be kept in possession of an infallible record of Christ's words and works. And, similarly, in His discourses on the last things He assures His disciples that His words not only shall certainly be fulfilled but shall remain available for the comfort of His people during that troubled period which shall precede His second coming. In other words, that they shall be preserved until that time. *Heaven and earth shall pass away, but My words shall not pass away* (Matt. 24:35; Mark 13:31; Luke 21:33). Likewise the Word of Christ is to be the foundation of Christian character down through the ages (Matt. 7:24-27) and the standard by which all men shall be judged at the last day (John 12:48).

Thus it is the promise of Christ that a trustworthy text of the sacred New Testament books shall always be preserved in His Church down through the ages until the last day. How has this promise been fulfilled? By what special working of His divine providence has Christ kept this promise? Many scholars have endeavored to answer this question, but none have succeeded better than J.W. Burgon (1813-1888), Dean of Chichester. The following paragraphs, therefore, present a summary of Burgon's views concerning the New Testament text.

1. *The Life and Character of Burgon*

Most of Burgon's adult life was spent at Oxford, as Fellow of Oriel College and then as vicar of St. Mary's (the University Church) and Gresham Professor of Divinity. During his last twelve years he was Dean of Chichester. His father was an English Turkey merchant and his mother a native of Smyrna of Austrian and Greek extraction. It was from this foreign blood, no doubt, that Burgon derived his warm and enthusiastic nature, not typically English, which expressed itself in a lively literary style. In theology he was a High-church Anglican, strenuously upholding the doctrine of baptismal regeneration but opposing the ritualism into which even in his day the High-church movement had begun to decline. Throughout his life he remained unmarried, but, like many other celibates, he is said to have been unusually fond of children. As for his learning, even his adversaries acknowledged that it was very great.

The thing about Burgon, however, which lifts him out of his nineteenth century English setting and endears him to the hearts of earnest Christians of other lands and other ages is his steadfast defence of the Scriptures as the infallible Word of God. He strove with all his power to arrest the modernistic currents which during his lifetime had begun to flow within the Church of England, continuing his efforts with unabated zeal up to the very day of his death. With this purpose in mind he labored mightily in the field of New Testament textual criticism.

In 1860, while temporary chaplain of the English congregation at Rome, he made a personal examination of *Codex B*, and in 1862 he inspected the treasures of St. Catherine's Convent on Mt. Sinai. Later he made several tours of European libraries, examining and collating New Testament manuscripts wherever he went. It is on the strength of these labors that K. W. Clark (1950)[1] ranks him with Tregelles and Scrivener as one of the "great contemporaries" of Tischendorf. And Rendel Harris (1908) had high praise for Burgon's great Index of New Testament quotations in the Church Fathers, which was deposited in the British Museum at the time of his death but has never been published. It is possible," Harris said, "to object to many of his references and to find fault with some of the texts which he used, but I only wish that I possessed a transcript of those precious volumes."[2]

Burgon was amassing all these materials for a definitive work in which he would defend the *Traditional Text*. This was Burgon's name for that type of text which is found in the vast majority of the extant Greek New Testament manuscripts, which was adopted by Protestants at the time of the Reformation and used by them universally for more than three hundred years, and which forms the basis of the King James Version and other early Protestant translations. Unfortunately, however, Burgon did not live to complete his project. The fragments of it, which he left at his death, were pieced together by his friend E. Miller, and published in 1896 in two volumes entitled *The Traditional Text of the Holy Gospels*[3] and *The Causes of the Corruption of the Traditional Text*.[4] That Burgon died before he could finish his *opus magnum* is a matter of deep regret, but enough of it survives in Miller's volumes to convey to us Burgon's fundamental ideas, together with the arguments by which he supported them. And these same basic concepts had been expressed in two earlier books which had won him fame as a textual critic, namely, *The Last Twelve Verses of Mark* (1871),[5] a defence of this portion of the New Testament text, and *The Revision Revised* (1883),[6] a reprint of three articles in the *Quarterly Review* against the Revised Version of 1881, together with a reply to a pamphlet by Bishop Ellicott against these three articles. Such, then, were the publications in which Burgon laid down the principles of consistently Christian New Testament textual criticism and elaborated them with considerable fullness. Of all the great textual critics of the nineteenth century Burgon alone was consistently Christian.

2. Dean Burgon the Champion of the Traditional (Byzantine) Text

According to Kenyon (1940),[7] there are about 4,489 Greek New Testament manuscripts known to be extant. Of these 170 are papyrus fragments, dating from the second century to the seventh; 212 are uncial (capital letter) manuscripts, dating from the fourth century to the tenth; 2,429 are minuscule (small letter) manuscripts dating from the ninth century to the sixteenth; and 1,678 are lectionaries (lesson books for public reading containing extracts from the New Testament). K.W. Clark (1950)[8] gives figures which agree very closely with those of Kenyon. He places the total number of extant Greek manuscripts at about 4,500. About three out of four of the minuscules, he continues, contain only the Gospel text, and one third of these are fragmentary. There are about 350 manuscripts available for Acts and the Catholic Epistles, over 600 for the Pauline Epistles, and less than 250 for the Apocalypse. Clark reckons the lectionary manuscripts at more than 1,600. Of these about 1,200 contain lessons from the Gospels and 300 lessons from the Epistles, the remainder containing few canonical quotations of any sort.

The vast majority of these extant Greek New Testament manuscripts agree together very closely, so closely, indeed, that they may fairly be said to contain the same New Testament text. This *majority* text is usually called the *Byzantine* text by modern textual critics. This is because all modern critics acknowledge that this was the Greek New Testament text in general use throughout the greater part of the Byzantine Period (312-1453). For many centuries before the Protestant Reformation this Byzantine text was the text of the entire Greek Church and for more than three centuries after the Reformation it was the text of the entire Protestant Church. Even today it is the text which most Protestants know best, since the King James Version and other early Protestant translations were made from it.

Burgon was an ardent defender of this Byzantine text found in vast majority of the Greek New Testament manuscripts. He gave to this text the name *Traditional Text*, thus indicating his conviction that this was the true text which by a perpetual tradition had been handed down generation after generation without fail in the Church of Christ from the days of the apostles onwards. Burgon believed this because he believed that it was *through the Church* that Christ had fulfilled His promise always to preserve for His people a true New Testament text. The Byzantine text, he maintained, is the true text because it is that form of the Greek New Testament which is known to have been used in the Church of Christ in unbroken succession for many centuries, first in the Greek Church and then in the Protestant Church. And all orthodox Christians, all Christians who show due regard for the divine inspiration and providential preservation of Scripture, must agree with Burgon in this matter. For in what other way can it be that Christ has fulfilled His promise always to preserve in His Church the true New Testament text?

3. *Burgon's Condemnation of Manuscripts B, Aleph and D*

Although the vast majority of the extant Greek New Testament manuscripts contain the Byzantine (Traditional) text and thus agree with one another very closely, there is a relatively small majority of the manuscripts that disagree sharply both with the majority and also with each other. Since the days of Griesbach (1796) it has been customary to divide the manuscripts of this non-Byzantine minority group into two principal groups or *families,* namely, the Western family and the Alexandrian family. The most noteworthy member of the Western family is *D*, a sixth century manuscript containing the Gospels and Acts, which was presented to Cambridge University by Theodore Beza in 1581. Two other important members of the Western family are the Old Latin and the Old Syriac versions. In the Alexandrian family of New Testament documents are included the two oldest complete (or nearly complete) manuscripts of the entire New Testament. These are *B* (*Codex Vaticanus*), a fourth century manuscript which has been the property of the Vatican Library at least since 1481, and *Aleph* (*Codex Sinaiticus*), a somewhat later manuscript discovered by Tischendorf at Mt. Sinai and now domiciled at the British Museum. About 25 other manuscripts have been assigned to the Alexandrian family as well as the Egyptian (Coptic) versions.

Since the days of Griesbach also it has been customary for textual critics to side either with the Western family of New Testament manuscripts or with the Alexandrian and to say rather harsh things about the documents on which the critics on the opposite side are pinning their hopes. Thus A. C. Clark (1933) maintained that the Western text was the original and that the Alexandrian text had been formed out of the Western text during the third century by an abbreviator, who "adopted the rough and ready method of striking out lines in his model, botching from time to time to produce a construction."[9] J. H. Ropes (1926), on the other hand, took a diametrically opposite view of the matter. The Alexandrian text, he insisted, was the original text. The Western text was an intentional rewriting of this original text, "made before, and perhaps long before, the year 150, by a Greek-speaking Christian who knew something of Hebrew, in the East, perhaps in Syria or Palestine."[10]

Since all the non-Byzantine New Testament manuscripts have been condemned by some noted modern critic or other, no scholar ought to be offended at Burgon's treatment of this minority group. He also condemned these non-Byzantine texts in strongest terms, deeming them depraved, far inferior, that is, to the Byzantine (true) text found in the vast majority of the Greek New Testament manuscripts. "By far the most depraved text is that exhibited by *Codex D*."[11] And concerning *B* and *Aleph* his remarks are similar. "As for the origin of these two curiosities, it can perforce only be divined from their contents. That they exhibit fabricated texts is demonstrable. No amount of honest copying—persevered in for any number of centuries,—could by possibility have resulted in two such documents. Separated from one another in actual date by 50, perhaps by 100 years, they must needs have branched off from a common corrupt ancestor, and straightway become exposed to fresh depraving influences."[12]

Burgon regarded the exceptional age of B and *Aleph* as a proof not of their goodness but of their badness. If they had been good manuscripts, they would have been read to pieces long ago. "We suspect that these two manuscripts are indebted for their preservation, *solely to their ascertained evil character;* which has occasioned that the one eventually found its way, four centuries ago, to a forgotten shelf in the Vatican Library; while the other, after exercising the ingenuity of several generations of critical Correctors, eventually (viz. in A.D. 1844) got deposited in the waste-paper basket of the Convent at the foot of Mount Sinai. Had B and *Aleph* been copies of average purity, they must long since have shared the inevitable fate of books which are freely *used* and highly prized; namely, they would have fallen into decadence and disappeared from sight."[13]

Thus the fact that B and *Aleph* are so old is a point against them, not something in their favor. It shows that the Church rejected them and did not read them. Otherwise they would have worn out and disappeared through much reading. Burgon has been accused of sophistry in arguing this way, but certainly his suggestion cannot be rejected by naturalistic critics as impossible. For one of their "own poets", Kirsopp Lake (1928), favored the idea that the scribes "usually destroyed their exemplars when they had copied the sacred books."[14] If Lake could believe this, why may not orthodox Christians believe that many ancient Byzantine manuscripts have been worn out with much reading and copying? And conversely, why may we not believe that B, *Aleph* and the other ancient non-Byzantine manuscripts have survived unto the present day simply because they were rejected by the Church and *not* used?

4. *How False Readings Originated*

Burgon attributed the false readings present in B, *Aleph*, D and the other non-Byzantine manuscripts to two principal causes. The first of these was the deliberate falsification of the New Testament Scriptures by heretics during the second and third centuries. The second was the doubtless well meant but nevertheless disastrous efforts of certain learned Christians during this same early period to improve the New Testament text through the use of conjectural emendation. In support of these contentions Burgon brought forth a number of quotations from the writings of the Church Fathers, and these we will do well to consider briefly.

(a) Heresy in B, Aleph, D and the Other Non-Byzantine Manuscripts

According to the testimony of many ancient ecclesiastical writers, the influence of heretics on the transmission of the New Testament text was very considerable. Eusebius (c. 320), for example, gives the following extract from an earlier unnamed Christian Father, who lived about 200 A.D. and wrote against the heresy of Artemon, which claimed, according to Eusebius, "that the Savior was a mere man."[15]

> Wherefore they (these heretics) have not feared to lay hands upon the divine Scriptures under pretense of correcting them. That I bring no false accusation anyone who wishes may easily convince himself. He has but to compare the copies belonging to these persons severally; then, to compare one with another; and he will discover that their discrepancy is extraordinary. For the copies of Asclepiades do not agree with those of Theodotus . . . Again the copies of Hermophilus do not agree with these. As for the copies of Apolloniades, they even contradict one another . . . As for their denying their guilt, the thing is impossible, seeing that the copies were written in their own hand; and they did not receive the Scriptures in this condition from their teachers, nor can they show the originals from which they made their copies.[16]

Celsus (c. 175), the Platonist, one of the earliest writers against Christianity, accused the Christians of corrupting the Gospel text. Origen (c. 248), however, denied this, insisting that only the heretics Marcion, Valentinus and Lucian had been guilty of such impiety.

> He (Celsus) says, that certain of the Christian believers . . . have corrupted the Gospel from its original integrity, to a threefold, and fourfold, and manyfold degree, and have remodeled it, so that they might be able to answer objections. Now I know of no others who have altered the Gospel, except the followers of Marcion, and those of Valentinus, and, I believe, also those of Lucian.[17]

Jerome (c. 385) also speaks of the damage to the New Testament text by heretics.

> I speak of Marcion and Basilides and all the heretics who have torn the Old Testament. Yet we might have borne this somehow, if at least they had kept their hands off the New . . . But now, since they have wasted the Gospels and have appropriated to themselves the Epistles of Christ's Apostles, I wonder how they dare to claim for themselves the name Christian.[18]

Burgon adduced many other passages from the Fathers of the same purport, but these need not be mentioned here. The three cited above are amply sufficient to prove his point, that the New Testament text must have received hard usage at the hands of heretics, especially during the second and third centuries.

The following are samples of the heretical corruptions which Burgon found in *B, Aleph, D*, etc.:

(1) Matt 24:36, add *neither the Son* after the word *heaven*.
(2) Mark 1:1, omit *the Son of God*.
(3) Luke 23:42, *Jesus* instead of *Lord*.
(4) John 1:34, *Chosen One of God* instead of *Son of God*.
(5) John 3:13, omit *which is in heaven*.
(6) John 6:69, *Holy One of God* instead of *Son of God*.
(7) John 9:35, *Son of man* instead of *Son of God*.
(8) 1 Tim. 3:16, *who (which) was manifest in the flesh* instead of *God was manifest in the flesh*.

(b) Conjectural Emendation a Source of False Readings

Among a certain class of present day New Testament textual critics a tremendous emphasis is placed upon the skill which early Christians of Alexandria are thought to have possessed in matters of textual criticism. Alexandria, it is said, was a city which specialized in textual criticism. Therefore the Alexandrian Christians probably excelled in this department, and the texts of *B* and *Aleph*, which seem to have originated in Alexandria, are probably very good texts. There are weak links, however, in this chain of reasoning. The skill which the pagan scholars of the Alexandrian library exercised in the realm of textual criticism was probably not automatically transferred to the Alexandrian Christian community. On the contrary, the early Christians of Alexandria were probably much influenced by the heretics who flourished there and who are known to have corrupted the New Testament text, by Basilides, for example, and Valentinus and their disciples. Morever, the only Alexandrian Christian of whose New Testament textual criticism we have specimens is Origen, and his decisions in this field seem fanciful rather than sound.

Burgon refers us to an outstanding example of Origen's New Testament textual criticism. In his comment on Matt. 19:17-21 (Jesus' reply to the rich young man)[19] Origen reasons that Jesus could not have concluded his list of God's commandments with the comprehensive requirement, *Thou shalt love thy neighbor as thyself.* For the reply of the young man was, *All these things have I kept from my youth up,* and Jesus evidently accepted this statement as true. But if the young man had loved his neighbor as himself, he would have been perfect, for Paul says that the whole law is summed up in this saying, *Thou shalt love thy neighbor as thyself.* But Jesus answered, *If thou wilt be perfect, etc.,* implying that the young man was not yet perfect. Therefore, Origen argued, the commandment, *Thou shalt love thy neighbor as thyself,* could not have been spoken by Jesus on this occasion and was not part of the original text of Matthew. This clause, he believed, was added by some tasteless scribe.

Thus it is clear that this renowned Father was not content to abide by the text which he had received but freely indulged in the boldest sort of conjectural emendation. In the very passage in which he speaks most fully concerning his critical work on the Old Testament text he gives us this specimen of his handling of the New. It is likely, morever, that there were other Christian scholars at Alexandria who were even less restrained in their speculations than Origen. These well meaning but misguided critics evidently deleted many readings from the original New Testament text, thus producing the abbreviated text found in *B* and *Aleph* and in other manuscripts of their type.

5. Burgon's View of the History of the New Testament Text

In his *Revision Revised* Burgon gives his reconstruction of the history of the New Testament text in the vivid style that was habitual to him. "Vanquished by *THE WORD Incarnate,* Satan next directed his subtle malice against *the Word written.* Hence, as I think, — *hence* the extraordinary fate which befell certain early transcripts of the Gospel. First, heretical assailants of Christianity, — then, orthodox defenders of the Truth, — lastly and above all, self constituted Critics . . . such were the corrupting influences which were actively at work throughout the first hundred years after the death of S. John the Divine. Profane literature has never known anything approaching to it, — can show nothing at all like it. Satan's arts were defeated indeed through the Church's faithfulness, because, — (the good Providence of God has so willed it,) — the perpetual multiplication in every quarter, of copies required for Ecclesiastical use — not to say the solicitude of faithful men in diverse regions of ancient Christendom to retain for themselves unadulterated specimens of the inspired Text, — proved a sufficient safeguard against the grosser forms of corruption. But this was not all.

"The Church, remember, hath been from the beginning the 'Witness and Keeper of Holy Writ.' Did not her Divine Author pour out upon her in largest measure, 'the SPIRIT of truth;' and pledge Himself that it should be that SPIRIT'S special function to *'guide' her children 'into all the Truth'?* . . . That by a perpetual miracle, Sacred Manuscripts would be protected all down the ages against depraving influences of whatever sort, — was not to have been expected; certainly, was never promised. But the Church, in her collective capacity, hath nevertheless — as a matter of fact — been perpetually purging herself of those shamefully depraved copies which once everywhere abounded within her pale: retaining only such an amount of discrepancy in her Text as might serve to remind her children that they carry their 'treasure in earthen vessels,' — as well as to stimulate them to perpetual watchfulness and solicitude for the purity and integrity of the Deposit. Never, however, up to the present hour, hath there been any complete eradication of all traces of the attempted mischief, — any absolute getting rid of every depraved copy extant. These are found to have lingered on anciently in many quarters. *A few such copies linger on to the present day.* The wounds were healed, but the scars remained, — nay, the scars are discernible still.

"What, in the meantime, is to be thought of those blind guides — those deluded ones — who would now, if they could, persuade us to go back to those same codices of which the Church hath already purged herself?"[20]

Burgon's reconstruction of the history of the New Testament text is not only vividly expressed but eminently biblical and therefore true. For if the true New Testament text came from God, whence came the erroneous variant readings ultimately save from the evil one. And how could the true text have been preserved save through the providence of God working through His Church? No doubt most Christians, not being High-church Anglicans, will place less emphasis than Dean Burgon did on the organized Church, and more emphasis on the providence of God working *through* the Church, especially the *Greek* Church. But this possible defect in Burgon's presentation does not in any essential way affect the eternal validity of his views concerning the New Testament text. They are eternally valid because they are consistently Christian. In elaborating these views Burgon, unlike most other textual critics, was always careful to remember that the New Testament is not an ordinary book but a *special* book, a book which was written under the infallible inspiration of the Holy Spirit, a book whose text Christ has promised to preserve in His Church down through the ages.

6. *The Canon and Text of the New Testament*

The essential soundness of Burgon's views is most readily seen when we compare the history of the New Testament canon with the history of the New Testament text, and, therefore, it is to this task that we must now address ourselves.

Why did the Christian Church receive the twenty-seven New Testament books and these only as her canonical New Testament Scripture? Harnack (1914)[21] and other noted students of the New Testament canon have asked this question repeatedly and have endeavored to answer it in their own fashion. But, as Greijdanus (1927)[22] and Grosheide (1935)[23] point out, this question can be satisfactorily answered only on the basis of Christian faith. And when we look with the eye of faith upon the history of the New Testament canon, then we see in that history a mighty conflict between God and Satan, between the Holy Spirit on the one hand and the spirit of darkness on the other. First God gave to His Church the twenty-seven New Testament books through the inspiration of the Holy Spirit, and then through the Spirit also He began to lead the Church into a recognition of these books as her canonical New Testament Scripture. During the second century, however, Satan endeavored to confuse the Church by raising up deceitful men who wrote pseudonymous works, falsely claiming to be apostolic. These satanic devices hindered and delayed the Church's recognition of the true New Testament canon but could not prevent it. Soon after the beginning of the fifth century the opposition of the devil was completely overcome. Under the leading of the Holy Spirit the Church was guided to receive only the twenty-seven New Testament books as canonical and to reject all others.

Dean Burgon believed that the history of the New Testament text was similar to the history of the New Testament canon, and all orthodox Christians will do well to agree with him in this, for a study of the New Testament manuscripts bears him out. In other words, during the early Christian centuries Satan directed his assault not only upon the New Testament canon but also upon the New Testament text. No sooner had the New Testament books been given to the Church through the inspiration of the Holy Spirit than the spirit of darkness began his endeavors to corrupt their texts and render them useless. But in these efforts also the evil one failed to attain his objective. In regard to the New Testament text as well as in regard to the New Testament canon God bestowed upon His Church sufficient grace to enable her to overcome all the wiles of the devil. Just as God guided the Church to reject, after a period of doubt and conflict, all non-canonical writings and to receive only the true canonical New Testament books, so God guided the Church during this same period of doubt and conflict, to reject false readings and to receive into common usage the true New Testament text.

For an orthodox Christian Burgon's view is the only reasonable one. If we believe that God gave the Church guidance in regard to the New Testament books, then surely it is logical to believe that God gave the Church similar guidance in regard to the text which these books contained. Surely it is very inconsistent to believe that God guided the Church in regard to the New Testament canon but gave the Church no guidance in regard to the New Testament text. But this seems to be just what many modern Christians do believe. They believe that all during the medieval period and throughout the Reformation and post-Reformation era the true New Testament text was lost and that it was not regained until the middle of the nineteenth century, when Tischendorf discovered it in the Sinaitic manuscript *Aleph* and Westcott and Hort found it in the Vatican manuscript *B*. Such inconsistency, however, is bound to lead to a scepticism which deprives the New Testament text of all authority. If we must believe that the true New Testament text was lost for fifteen hundred years, how can we be certain that it has now been found? What guarantee have we that either *B* or *Aleph* contain the true text? How can we be sure that Harris (1908), Conybeare (1910), Lake (1941), and other radical critics are not correct in their suspicions that the true New Testament text has been lost beyond possibility of recovery?

7. *Burgon's Rejection of Contemporary New Testament Textual Criticism*

Burgon, therefore, was right in utterly rejecting the claims of Tischendorf (1815-74), Tregelles (1813-75), Westcott (1825-1901), Hort (1828-1892), and other contemporary scholars, who insisted that as a result of their labors the true New Testament text had at last been discovered after having been lost for well nigh fifteen centuries. "And thus it would appear," he remarks ironically, "that the Truth of Scripture has run a very narrow risk of being lost for ever to mankind. Dr. Hort contends that it more than half lay *perdu* on a forgotten shelf in the Vatican Library; — Dr. Tischendorf that it had been deposited in a waste-paper basket in the convent of S. Catherine at the foot of Mount Sinai; — from which he rescued it on the 4th of February, 1859; — neither, we venture to think, a very likely circumstance. We incline to believe that the Author of Scripture hath not by any means shown Himself so unmindful of the safety of the Deposit, as these distinguished gentlemen imagine."[24]

In another place Burgon expresses himself still more vigorously along the same lines. "I am utterly disinclined to believe — so grossly improbable does it seem — that at the end of 1800 years 995 copies out of every thousand, suppose, will prove untrustworthy; and that the one, two, three, four or five which remain, whose contents were till yesterday as good as unknown, will be found to have retained the secret of what the Holy Spirit originally inspired. I am utterly unable to believe, in short, that God's promise has so entirely failed, that at the end of 1800 years much of the text of the Gospel had in point of fact to be picked by a German critic out of a waste-paper basket in the convent of St. Catherine; and that the entire text had to be remodeled after the pattern set by a couple of copies which had remained in neglect during fifteen centuries, and had probably owed their survival to that neglect; whilst hundreds of others had been thumbed to pieces, and had bequeathed their witness to copies made from them."[25]

According to Burgon, the fundamental mistake of contemporary New Testament textual critics was that they ignored the unique character of the New Testament text. They would not recognize that they were dealing with a book that was different from all other books, in short, with a divinely inspired and providentially preserved book. "That which distinguishes Sacred Science from every other Science which can be named is that it is Divine, and has to do with a Book which is inspired, and not regarded upon a level with the Books of the East, which are held by their votaries to be sacred. It is chiefly from inattention to this circumstance that misconception prevails in that department of Sacred Science known as 'Textual Criticism.' Aware that the New Testament is like no other book in its origin, its contents, its history, many critics of the present day nevertheless permit themselves to reason concerning its Text, as if they entertained no suspicion that the words and sentences of which it is composed were destined to experience an extraordinary fate also. They make no allowances for the fact that influences of an entirely different kind from any with which profane literature is acquainted have made themselves felt in this department, and therefore that even those principles of Textual Criticism which in the case of profane authors are regarded as fundamental are often out of place here."[26]

We see here the fundamental difference between Burgon's approach to the problem of the New Testament text and that adopted by his contemporaries, especially Westcott and Hort. In matters of textual criticism, at least, these latter scholars followed a *naturalistic* method. They took particular pride in handling the text of the New Testament just as they would the text of any other ancient book. "For ourselves," Hort declared, "we dare not introduce considerations which could not reasonably be applied to other ancient texts, supposing them to have documentary attestation of equal amount, variety, and antiquity."[27]

Burgon, on the other hand, followed a *consistently Christian* method of New Testament textual criticism. He believed that the New Testament had been divinely inspired and providentially preserved, and when he came to the study of the New Testament text, he did not for one instant lay this faith aside. On the contrary, he regarded the divine inspiration and providential preservation of the New Testament as two fundamental facts which must be taken into account in the interpretation of the details of New Testament textual criticism, two basic verities which make the textual criticism of the New Testament different from the textual criticism of any other book.

CHAPTER TWO
ALTERNATIVE VIEWS OF THE PRESERVATION OF THE NEW TESTAMENT

As we have seen, Burgon believed that it was through the usage of the Church that Christ fulfilled His promise always to preserve the New Testament text in its purity. By His Holy Spirit Christ guided His Church to reject false readings and to receive into common usage the true New Testament text. This divine guidance, moreover, centered in the Greek Church, because it was this Church especially that actually used the *Greek* New Testament text. Such was Burgon's view of the history of the New Testament text. There are, however, many orthodox Christians who cannot see their way clear to agree with Burgon. It is necessary, therefore, to devote some space to a consideration of *their* theories. How do *they* think that Christ fulfilled His promise always to preserve a pure New Testament text? A realization of the inadequacy of these alternative views will dispose us more than ever to follow Burgon.

1. *The Alleged Agreement of All the New Testament Manuscripts in Matters of Doctrine. Is This a Fulfillment of Christ's Promise?*

In dealing with the problems of the New Testament text most conservatives place great stress on the amount of agreement alleged to exist among the extant New Testament manuscripts. These manuscripts, it is said, agree so closely with one another in matters of doctrine that it does not make much difference which manuscript you follow. The same essential teaching is preserved in them all. This reputed agreement of all the extant New Testament manuscripts in doctrinal matters is ascribed to divine providence and regarded as the fulfillment of the promise of Christ always to preserve in His Church a trustworthy New Testament text.

This is the thought that was emphasized by Richard Bentley (1713) in his celebrated reply to the free-thinker, Anthony Collins, who alleged that New Testament textual criticism had made the sacred text uncertain. This charge, Bentley rejoined, was baseless. "The real text of the sacred writers does not now (since the originals have been so long lost) lie in any single manuscript or edition, but is dispersed in them all. 'Tis competently exact indeed even in the worst manuscript now extant; choose as awkwardly as you can, choose the worst by design, out of the whole lump of readings . . . Make your 30,000 (variant readings) as many more, if numbers of copies can ever reach that sum: all the better to a knowing and serious reader, who is thereby more richly furnished to select what he sees genuine. But even put them into the hands of a knave or a fool, and yet with the most sinistrous and absurd choice, he shall not extinguish the light of any one chapter, nor so disguise Christianity but that every feature of it will still be the same."[1]

Since the days of Bentley countless conservative scholars have adopted this same apologetic approach to the study of the New Testament text. New Testament textual criticism, they have affirmed, can do no harm to the Christian faith, because the special providence of God has brought it to pass that the differences which exist among the extant New Testament manuscripts do not affect any essential point of doctrine. This type of apologetic approach, however, to the problem of the New Testament text is full of dangers. At first sight it seems reassuring, but soon it involves the Christian in a morass of inextricable difficulties.

In the first place, this theory, that the special providence of God has so operated as to exclude from all the extant New Testament manuscripts all variant readings which involve important points of doctrine, presupposes an extremely mechanical and unhistorical conception of the providential preservation of Scripture. According to this theory, God in some mechanical way must have prevented heretical scribes from inserting into the New Testament manuscripts which they were copying readings that favored their false views. Or, if God did now and then allow an heretical reading to creep into a manuscript, He must have quickly brought about the destruction of that manuscript before the false reading could be transferred to another manuscript and thus propagated. The testimony of history indicates, however, that God's providential preservation of Scripture did not function in any such mechanical fashion but organically through the Church. Heretical readings were invented and did circulate for a time, but they were rejected by the Church under the guidance of God.

In the second place, it does not seem to be true that in the New Testament manuscripts there are no various readings which involve cardinal Christian doctrines. On the contrary, in a few manuscripts at least, readings occur which appear even to call in question the deity of Christ. One of these readings is found in Luke 18:18-19. Here the rich young ruler asks Jesus, *Good Master, what shall I do that I may inherit eternal life?* and Jesus replies, *Why callest thou Me good? No one is good except one, God.* According to this reading (which seems to be found in all the Greek manuscripts) Jesus need not be interpreted as denying His deity. He is merely reproving the young man for his fulsomeness in addressing as *good* one whom he regarded as a mere man. "Why do you," Jesus replies, "who take me for an ordinary mortal like yourself, call me good? Only God is essentially good." In the Latin of *Codex D*, however, there is another reading. According to this manuscript, Jesus says, *no one is good except one, God the Father.* As Rendel Harris (1891)[2] has pointed out, here we do have a variant reading which affects the most basic doctrine of the Christian faith, namely, that of the holy Trinity. According to this reading, Jesus actually does disclaim deity, attributing essential goodness only to God the Father.

This same reading, *no one is good except one, God the Father,* is found in Justin Martyr, Clement of Alexandria and Origen, as well as in certain manuscripts of the Armenian version and the Old Latin manuscript *e* (in Matthew's parallel account). C. A. Phillips[3] regarded it as genuine. All orthodox Christians, however, will of course reject it. Rendel Harris[4] may have been right in attributing this reading to Marcion (c. 144), since it seems to have been favored by this arch-heretic. Or it may be that Burgon[5] was correct in crediting the great gnostic leader Valentinus (c. 140) with the invention of it, seeing that it appears to have been advocated by him and by his disciple

Ptolemaeus and to have been much in vogue among the Marcosians, the Naasenes and other gnostic sects.

In the manuscripts are found other variant readings also which, if accepted as genuine, would seem to cast some reflection upon Christ's person and work. In the Sinaitic Syriac manuscript, for example, Matt. 1:16 reads: *Jacob begat Joseph; Joseph to whom was betrothed Mary the Virgin, begat Jesus called the Messiah.* Mrs. A. S. Lewis (1913),[6] the discoverer of the Sinaitic Syriac manuscript, regarded this reading as the true reading. She argued, moreover, that even so the testimony of Matthew to the virgin birth is not weakened, since the word *begat* is used here in a purely legal sense. It does seem, however, that here she was a bit carried away by her zeal for her precious manuscript. If in this passage the reading of the Sinaitic Syriac were the true reading, then surely the witness of Matthew to the virgin birth of Christ would be somewhat obscured. A difficulty would arise in the exposition of that doctrine that had not been present previously. Ground would be given for the charge that here Matthew had been affected by the Ebionite doctrine that Jesus was a naturally born man.

The same sort of variant reading is found in Luke's narrative of the baptism of Jesus (Luke 3:22). Here instead of, *Thou art my beloved Son: in Thee I am well pleased,* D, certain Old Latin manuscripts, Justin Martyr and Clement of Alexandria read, *Thou art my Son; this day have I begotten Thee.* If we should follow Streeter (1924)[7] in accepting this reading as genuine, then we would leave room for the accusation that Luke was inclined to the adoptionist view that Jesus became the Son of God at His baptism. And similarly, in Luke's account of the Lord's Supper (Luke 22:17-20) D and certain Old Latin manuscripts omit all reference to the vicarious atonement. If we should agree with Chadwick (1957)[8] and a long line of earlier critics in favoring this shorter text, then we should be obliged to admit that the doctrine of the Lord's Supper in Luke is very different from that presented in the other Gospels.

In Matt. 13:35 *Aleph* and certain manuscripts of the "Caesarean" family ascribe to Isaiah a quotation from Psalm 78.

If we agree with Tischendorf[9] and Hort[10] in regarding this as the true reading, then we have here a contradiction in the sacred text which can hardly be explained away and which does have an important bearing on our doctrine of holy Scripture. And in 1 Cor. 15:51 also, that very significant passage in which the apostle Paul discloses the mystery of the resurrection of the saints, it does make a difference for Christian doctrine which one of the variant readings we adopt. Here *B* and the vast majority of the Greek New Testament manuscripts read: *We shall not all sleep, but we shall all be changed.* But *Aleph, A, C, F* and *G* read: *We shall all sleep, but we shall not all be changed.* And *D* reads: *We shall all rise, but we shall not all be changed.* And the Chester Beatty Papyrus has this reading: *We shall not all sleep, nor shall we all be changed.*

In view of the foregoing examples, and still others that might be adduced, conservative scholars ought not to keep on saying that there are no variant readings in the New Testament manuscripts which affect basic Christian doctrines. This type of apologetic approach, which Bentley advocated so vigorously, can be maintained only by moving in a modernistic direction, that is to say, by denying that the doctrines of the deity of Christ, the vicarious atonement, the inerrancy of Scripture, and the resurrection of the saints are actually basic Christian doctrines. But even this retreat would not bring us into any position of security. For new manuscripts may yet be discovered with new variant readings in still other areas of Christian truth, and these doctrines also would have to be declared non-basic.

Instead of repeating, parrot-like, Bentley's saying that it makes no difference for doctrine which of the extant New Testament manuscripts one chooses to follow, orthodox Christians ought to take the very opposite course. They ought to maintain with Burgon that it sometimes makes a great deal of difference in matters of doctrine whether we hold to the Byzantine text found in the vast majority of the extant manuscripts of the Greek New Testament or whether we prefer the readings of non-Byzantine texts found in the manuscripts of the minority group. The vast majority of the extant Greek New Testament manuscripts do agree with one another not only doctrinely but in every other way. It is through these manuscripts that Christ has fulfilled His promise to preserve in His Church a trustworthy New Testament text. The manuscripts of the minority group, on the other hand, and of many of the ancient versions are not trustworthy exhibitions of the New Testament text. They differ widely both from the manuscripts of the majority group and also from each other, and sometimes these differences involve serious doctrinal errors. In short, the New Testament text has not been trustworthily preserved in *all* the New Testament manuscripts without exception but only in the Byzantine text found in the *vast majority* of the Greek New Testament manuscripts. It is this text that represents the usage of the Greek speaking Church, the providentially appointed guardian of the *Greek* New Testament. It was this text that was handed down from the Greek Church to the Protestant Reformers in the days of the Reformation.

2. The True Reading Preserved In At Least One of the Extant Manuscripts. Is This an Adequate Fulfillment of Christ's Promise?

Many conservative scholars seem to feel that God's providential care over the New Testament text is adequately defined by the saying that the true reading has been preserved in at least one of the extant New Testament manuscripts. Theodore Zahn (1909) gave expression to this point of view in the following words: "Though the New Testament text can be shown to have met with varying treatment, it has never as yet been established from ancient citations, nor made really probable on internal grounds, that a single sentence of the original text has disappeared altogether from the text transmitted in the Church, that is, from all the manuscripts of the original and of the ancient translations."[11] In other words, the true reading is always to be found in some one or other of the extant manuscripts. The only question is, which one?

Zahn's doctrine also seems to be comforting at first glance, but on closer analysis this comfort soon disappears. Has the special providence of God over the New Testament text done no more than to preserve the true readings somewhere, that is to say, in some one or other of the great variety of New Testament manuscripts now existing in the world? If Christ has done no more than this, how can it be said that He has fulfilled His promise always to preserve in His Church the true New Testament text? How can His people ever be certain that they have the true New Testament text? For not all the extant New Testament manuscripts have yet been discovered. No doubt many of them still remain in the obscurity into which they were plunged centuries ago, concealed in holes, ruins, and other unknown places. How can we be sure that many true readings are not hiding in these undiscovered manuscripts? And even if this is not the case, how can we be certain which of the known manuscripts contain the true reading in places in which these manuscripts differ?

Zahn was on the right track in the first part of his statement quoted above, namely, that not a single sentence of the original text has disappeared from the text transmitted in the Church. To this sentiment every orthodox Christian will surely say *Amen*. Zahn got off the track, however, when he went on to define the text transmitted in the Church as the text found in *all* the manuscripts of the original and in the ancient versions. The text transmitted in the Church is not the text found in *all* the New Testament manuscripts but only the Byzantine text found in the *vast majority* of the Greek New Testament manuscripts. The non-Byzantine texts found in the minority of the Greek New Testament manuscripts and in many of the ancient versions are not texts *transmitted* in the Church but texts *rejected* by the Church. In places in which these non-Byzantine texts differ from the Byzantine text of the majority of the Greek New Testament manuscripts they contain almost invariably not true readings but errors. Only when we follow the text of the majority of the Greek manuscripts, do we know that we have in our hands a trustworthy New Testament text. This is the text that was used down through the centuries by the Greek speaking Church, the providentially appointed guardian of the *Greek New Testament*.

3. Is Naturalistic New Testament Textual Criticism a Fulfillment of Christ's Promise Always to Preserve In His Church the True New Testament Text?

Many conservatives have adopted the belief that it is through textual criticism, and especially through the textual criticism of Westcott and Hort, that Christ has fulfilled His promise always to preserve in His Church the true New Testament text. In regard to this matter J. H. Skilton (1946) writes as follows: "Textual criticism, in God's providence, is the means provided for ascertaining the true text of the Bible."[12] And half a century earlier Dr. B. B. Warfield (1893) expressed himself in a very similar manner. "In the sense of the Westminster Confession, therefore, the multiplication of copies of the Scriptures, the several early efforts towards the revision of the text, the raising up of scholars in our own day to collect and collate manuscripts, and to reform them on scientific principles — of our Tischendorfs and Tregelleses, and Westcotts and Horts — are all parts of God's singular care and providence in preserving His inspired Word pure."[13]

Is this really true? Did God use Tischendorf, Tregelles, and, above all, Westcott and Hort as His instruments to restore (late in the nineteenth century) the true New Testament text after it had been lost for almost fifteen hundred years? The history of New Testament textual criticism since 1881 (the year in which these latter two scholars published their *New Testament in Greek*) hardly justifies this conclusion. Westcott and Hort, to be sure, made confident claims as to the results which they had achieved by their methods. As a consequence of their labors, they asserted, the New Testament text was no longer a matter of doubt. "The amount of what can in any sense be called substantial variation . . . can hardly form more than a thousandth part of the entire text."[14] Modern critics, however, do not concede to these distinguished scholars the great success which they claimed for themselves. "We can all remember," declares K. W. Clark (1950), "the confident statement of Hort that 'substantial variation . . . can hardly form more than a thousandth part of the entire text'. This thousandth part would be equivalent to a solid block of twenty-one lines, or less than half a page in the Oxford textus receptus, and we can hardly agree with so sanguine a view."[15]

Other scholars have been still more emphatic in their rejection of Westcott and Hort's claims to have recovered the true New Testament text. As early as 1908 Rendel Harris declared that the New Testament text had not in any way been settled but was "more than ever, and perhaps finally, unsettled."[16] Two years later F. C. Conybeare gave it as his opinion that "the ultimate (New Testament) text, if there ever was one that deserves to be so called, is for ever irrecoverable."[17] And in 1941 Kirsopp Lake, after a lifetime spent in the study of the New Testament text, delivered the following judgment: "In spite of the claims of Westcott and Hort and of von Soden, we do not know the original form of the Gospels, and it is quite likely that we never shall."[18] F. G. Kenyon (1937) also, another lifelong student of the New Testament text, came to the conclusion that the text of the New Testament had not been as accurately transmitted as the texts of other books. "So long as Christianity was at best tolerated and at worst persecuted, the transcription and circulation of the Scriptures were exposed to difficulties from which pagan literature was free."[19] In the hands, therefore, of these distinguished twentieth century scholars textual criticism has *not* proved to be a God-given instrument for the restoration of the original New Testament text. On the contrary, the most recent textual criticism has led its practitioners to the conclusion that this original text is irrecoverable.

Thus the sceptical trend of New Testament textual criticism since the days of Westcott and Hort makes it very difficult indeed to believe that these two scholars were God's chosen vessels in the work of restoring the New Testament text. But there are even more basic considerations which make it impossible for an orthodox Christian ever to suppose this. As has already been observed, in the working out of their theory Westcott and Hort followed an essentially naturalistic method. Indeed, they prided themselves on treating the text of the New

Testament as they would that of any other book, making little or nothing of inspiration and providence. "For ourselves," Hort wrote, "we dare not introduce considerations which could not reasonably be applied to other ancient texts, supposing them to have documentary attestation of equal amount, variety, and antiquity."[20] Here, however, Hort was basically wrong. The Christian knows by faith that the Bible is not an ordinary book. The Bible is a unique book, a divinely inspired and providentially preserved book. Therefore, to ignore, as Westcott and Hort did, the divine inspiration and providential preservation of the New Testament and to treat its text like the text of any other book is to be guilty of a fundamental error which is bound to lead to erroneous conclusions.

Thus the theories of Westcott and Hort as well as the skeptical attitudes of subsequent scholars all alike involve the denial of the orthodox Christian faith. They all require the orthodox Christian, as soon as he enters the province of New Testament textual criticism, to lay aside his faith in the divine inspiration and providential preservation of the New Testament and to treat its sacred text as if it were the text of an ordinary ancient book. And when the orthodox Christian does this, he must pay the penalty of his sin. He must forfeit all his certainty as to the trustworthiness of the extant New Testament text. For the extant text of an ordinary book can never be proved *certainly* trustworthy. At best it can be regarded only as *probably trustworthy*. Thus to treat the text of the New Testament like the text of an ordinary book is necessarily to come to the conclusion that the extant New Testament text is only *probably* trustworthy. And the farther the orthodox Christian proceeds on this pathway of naturalism, the fainter this probability becomes. Naturalistic textual criticism frequently marks the beginning of a general breakdown of his orthodox Christian faith. Hence the danger of it.

Conclusion

We have examined various alternative views which conservative scholars have offered as substitutes for Burgon's view and have found these alternatives inadequate and erroneous.

We conclude, therefore, that Burgon and all the other earnest Christian souls who have thought as he did have been correct. It was through the usage of the Church, and especially the Greek speaking Church, that Christ fulfilled His promise always to preserve the true New Testament text. By His Holy Spirit Christ guided His Church to reject false readings and to receive into common use this true text. Thus the Byzantine text found in the vast majority of the Greek New Testament manuscripts must be the true text, since it was this text which was used by the whole Greek Church for many centuries before the Reformation and by the whole Protestant Church for at least three centuries thereafter.

All orthodox Christians are bound to take this view of the history of the New Testament text, for it is only in this way that they can make intelligible to themselves and others their God-given faith in the trustworthiness of the extant New Testament text. It is only on the basis of this view that they can explain why they are certain that the extant New Testament text is a trustworthy representation of the original New Testament text. It is only along these lines that they can show why this is necessarily so.

44

CHAPTER THREE

DEAN BURGON IN THE LIGHT OF RECENT RESEARCH

It may be that certain orthodox Christians who have read the foregoing pages will reason thus within themselves. "Burgon's views seem very reasonable and much more in accord with the fundamentals of our Christian faith than the theories of Westcott and Hort and other naturalistic textual critics. It is certainly much more reasonable to believe with Burgon that the true New Testament text has been preserved in the vast majority of the New Testament manuscripts than to suppose with Westcott and Hort that the true text is hardly to be found any place save in *Codex B*, now securely locked up in the library of the pope. Who but those with Roman Catholic sympathies could ever be pleased with the notion that God preserved the true New Testament text in secret for almost one thousand years and then finally handed it over to the Roman pontiff for safe keeping? Surely every orthodox Protestant will prefer to think with Burgon that God preserved the true text of the *Greek* New testament in the usage of the Greek speaking Church down through the centuries and then at length delivered it up intact to the Protestant reformers. Burgon's views, in short, seem eminently reasonable and in accord with our orthodox Christian faith. We feel inclined to adopt them, but how about the facts? Are Burgon's views in agreement with the facts?"

The answer to this question is an unqualified *yes*. The evidence now available is amply sufficient to support the orthodox view that regards the Byzantine text as the authentic New Testament text and is even greater now than it was in Burgon's day. There is now greater reason than ever to believe that the Byzantine text, which is found in the vast majority of the Greek New Testament manuscripts and which was used well nigh universally throughout the Greek Church for many centuries is a faithful reproduction of the original New Testament and is the divinely appointed standard by which all New Testament manuscripts and all divergent readings must be judged. No non-Byzantine reading may be regarded as possibly or probably true which in any way detracts from the divine fullness of the doctrine contained in the Byzantine text. For it is in the Byzantine text that Christ has fulfilled His promise always to preserve in His Church the true New Testament text.

In the paragraphs which follow a summary is given of the evidence that has accumulated since Burgon's day in support of the authenticity of the Byzantine text.

1. The Freer Manuscript of the Gospels *(Codex W)*

Until the beginning of the twentieth century the best manuscript evidence for the early existence of the Byzantine text was found in *Codex Alexandrinus (Codex A)*. This venerable codex, which (in the opinion of experts) dates from the fifth century, has played a very important role in the history of New Testament textual criticism. It was given to the King of England in 1627 by Cyril Lucar, Patriarch of Constantinople, and for many years was regarded as the oldest extant New Testament manuscript. In the Gospels it agrees generally with the Byzantine text found in the majority of the Greek New Testament manuscripts. In the other New Testament books it is generally considered to agree most closely with the Alexandrian type of text found in *B* and *Aleph*.

Thus in the Gospels *Codex A* bears witness to the early existence of the Byzantine text. There are two points, however, at which this testimony can bear strengthening. In the first place, most of the Gospel of Matthew is missing from *Codex A*, and in the second place, the Byzantine text found in the Gospel section of *Codex A* is not the purest form of the Byzantine but is corrupted here and there by Alexandrian and Western readings. It was a remarkable manifestation of God's special providence, therefore, that in 1906 another ancient witness was discovered which did strengthen the testimony of *Codex A* at precisely these points.

This welcome addition to the evidence for the antiquity of the Byzantine text is the Freer Manuscript of the Gospels *(Codex W)*, named after Charles L. Freer of Detroit, who purchased it in 1906 from an Arab dealer at Gizeh, near Cairo. It is now housed in the Freer Gallery of Art in Washington, D.C. In 1912 it was edited by H. A. Sanders, with a separate complete facsimile.[1] It contains the four Gospels in the Western order, Matthew, John, Luke, Mark. In John and the first third of Luke the text is Alexandrian in character. In Mark the text is of the Western type in the first five chapters and of a mixed "Caesarean" type in the remaining chapters. The especial value of W, however, lies in Matthew and the last two thirds of Luke. Here the text is Byzantine and not only Byzantine but of a purer Byzantine type than that of *Codex A*. According to Sanders, these Byzantine portions of W contain the same type of text as that found in *Omega, V*, and S, Byzantine manuscripts of the eighth, ninth, and tenth centuries.

The discovery of W tends to disprove the thesis of Hort that the Byzantine text is a fabricated text which was put together in the fourth century by a group of scholars residing at Antioch. For *Codex W* is a very ancient manuscript. B. P. Grenfell regarded it as "probably fourth century."[2] Other scholars have dated it in the fifth century. Whichever of these dates is accepted, the fact remains that W is one of the oldest complete manuscripts of the Gospels in existence, probably of the same age as *Aleph*. Moreover, W seems to have been written in Egypt, since during the first centuries of its existence it seems to have been the property of the Monastery of the Vinedresser, which was located near the third pyramid. If the Byzantine text had been invented at Antioch in the fourth century, how would it have found its way into Egypt and thence into *Codex W* so soon thereafter? Why would the scribe of W, writing in the fourth or early fifth century, have adopted this new fabricated text in Matthew and Luke in preference to other texts which (according to Hort's hypothesis) were older and more familiar to him? Thus the presence of the Byzantine text in W indicates that this text is a very ancient text and that it was known in Egypt before the fourth century.

2. The Evidence of the Papyri

Since the death of Burgon an entirely new field of New Testament textual study has been opened up through a series of discoveries of New Testament papyrus manuscripts. These discoveries began with the explorations of B. P. Grenfell and A. S. Hunt between the years 1896-1906. Almost all of them have been made in Egypt, since this is almost the only place dry enough to preserve so perishable a material as papyrus (an ancient type of paper made from the fibrous pith of the papyrus plant). According to the recent lists of Metzger (1949)[3] and Aland (1957),[4] the New Testament papyri now number 68 and range in date all the way from the second to the eighth century. A few of them are manuscripts of considerable size, but most of them are only small fragments.

(a) The Proper Interpretation of the
New Testament Papyri

In interpreting the meaning of the New Testament papyri for the history of the New Testament text much false reasoning has been employed. It has been assumed that the status of the New Testament text as it appears in these few surviving papyri is a reliable indication of the status of the New Testament text in the days in which these papyri were written. And on the basis of this false assumption erroneous conclusions have been drawn regarding the Byzantine text. For example, because there are 23 third century papyri and none of these contains a distinctively Byzantine text, it has been argued that the Byzantine text was not in existence as early as the third century. And similarly, because out of the 15 papyri stemming from the fourth century not one is found with a preponderantly Byzantine text, it has again been assumed that the Byzantine text did not yet exist at the time in which these papyri were written, or at least was not known in the place in which they were written.

The inconsequential character of such reasoning, however, becomes apparent when we pass from these early papyri to those that date from the sixth to the eighth century. There are 29 of these later papyri, and of these also there seems to be none that can be proved to be Byzantine in its textual affiliation. If, therefore, we should apply to these later papyri the same mode of reasoning that has been followed in the case of the earlier papyri, we should be obliged to conclude that as late as the eighth century the Byzantine text had not begun to exist.

But this conclusion would be false. For *Codex W* proves that the Byzantine text existed as early as the fifth century and seemingly was well known at that time in Egypt, the land in which most of the papyri appear to have been written. And the New Testament quotations of the post-Nicene Church Fathers demonstrate that the Byzantine text was in existence as early as the last half of the fourth century. According to von Soden (1907),[5] Byzantine readings are found in the writings of Athanasius (293-373), Didymus (313-398), and Cyril (d. 444), all of whom lived at Alexandria. This would indicate that the Byzantine text was known in Egypt in the days of these illustrious Fathers.

There is a better way to account for the absence of distinctively Byzantine texts from the New Testament papyri which have thus far been discovered. We must remember that these papyrus relics do not come to us fresh from the early Christian centuries packed, as it were, in ice. On the contrary, the Greek New Testament papyri were probably well picked over during the middle ages by Christians who could read Greek. The 68 papyrus fragments on hand today are merely part of the chaff that was left after this sifting process had taken place. They are remnants of papyrus manuscripts which were rejected by medieval Christians because they contained texts of which these Christians did not approve. Because they were rejected they were not used, and because they were not used they experienced less wear and tear, and thus it is that portions of them have survived until the present day. And conversely, the New Testament papyri containing texts which met the approval of these medieval Christians were undoubtedly worn out very quickly through continual reading and handling. Thus it is likely that relatively few fragments of these approved manuscripts are still extant and for this reason have not yet been discovered.

Such considerations as these give us a true understanding of the history of the New Testament papyri. Without doubt the early Christian centuries produced many papyrus manuscripts which were Byzantine in their text type. But the Byzantine text was the text which was used by the Greek Church well nigh universally during the middle ages. That this was so even in Egypt seems sufficiently indicated by the Byzantine readings which appear in the margins (and texts) of the manuscripts of the Coptic versions. Since, then, medieval Christians conversant with Greek regarded the Byzantine text as the true text, it is natural that they made use of the papyri that contained this text and rejected the non-Byzantine papyri. Thus it was the Byzantine papyri tended to wear out and disappear and that only the non-Byzantine papyri (which had been rejected and left unread) survived to bequeath their remains to posterity.

If there are Byzantine papyri still extant and if in the future some of these should come to light, so much the better. But in the meantime, the orthodox Christian is not at all distressed over the fact that no such papyri have yet been discovered. This is just what a proper interpretation of the New Testament papyri would lead him to expect. This is not at all the most important thing to observe concerning the 68 New Testament papyri that have already been discovered. It is far more vital to perceive that in spite of the non-Byzantine character of these papyri much can be found in them both for the antiquity and the authenticity of the Byzantine text. That this is a fact will become evident in the following discussion of the Chester Beatty Papyri and Papyrus Bodmer II.

(b) The Chester Beatty Papyri

The Chester Beatty Papyri is the designation usually given to a collection of portions of eleven papyrus codexes containing parts of nine Old Testament books, fifteen New Testament books, and two non-canonical books. The greater part of this collection was purchased by Chester Beatty from native Egyptian dealers during the years 1930-35, but substantial portions of it were acquired during this same period by the University of Michigan. These papyri were edited by F. G. Kenyon between the years 1933 and 1937.[6] The New Testament section includes Pap. 45 (portions of 30 leaves of a codex which originally contained all four Gospels and Acts), Pap. 46 (86 leaves of a codex of the Pauline Epistles), and Pap. 47 (10 leaves of a codex of Revelation). According to the judgment of experts, Pap. 45 and Pap. 46 were written in the first half of the third century and Pap. 47 in the second half.

At the time of their publication the Chester Beatty Papyri were hailed as the most important discovery of the twentieth century in the department of New Testament textual criticism. Many studies have been made concerning the texts of these papyri, and the general concensus of opinion seems to be as follows: In Mark the text is of the "Caesarean" type (the type of text which Origen is thought to have used at Caesarea during the second quarter of the third century). In the rest of the Gospels, according to Aland (1957)[7] and Klijn (1957),[8] the text is a mixture of Alexandrian, Caesarean, and Western readings. In Acts and the Pauline Epistles the text is still mixed, but there is greater agreement with the Alexandrian text found in *B* and *Aleph*.

From an orthodox Christian point of view one of the most important features of the text of the Chester Beatty Papyri is the support which they give to the Byzantine text. In these papyri are to be found many Byzantine readings which previously had been regarded as late readings. Twenty-six of these Byzantine readings occur in the Gospel section of the Chester Beatty Papyri, eight in Acts, and 31 in the Pauline Epistles. It is true that critics have endeavored to explain these Byzantine readings away by alleging that they are not really Byzantine readings but Caesarean readings which were later incorporated into the Byzantine text, but this explanation falls down in Acts and the Pauline Epistles, for there is no evidence that there ever was a Caesarean text in these areas.

Zuntz (1953) admits that there are Byzantine readings in the Chester Beatty Papyri and under the pressure of this ancient testimony seems on the point of giving up the notion that any considerable portion of the readings of the Byzantine text are late readings. "Are all the Byzantine readings ancient? In the cognate case of the Homeric tradition C. Pasquali answers the same question in the affirmative; and, indeed, it seems to me unlikely that the Byzantine editors ever altered the text without manuscript evidence. They left so many hopelessly difficult places unassailed. Their method, I submit, was selection rather than conjecture."⁹

Zuntz, it is true, vehemently disclaims any thought of defending the Byzantine text. "We are not," he says, "going to resume the hopeless fight of Dean Burgon. The Byzantine text is the latest text, and it is both natural and evident that it contains the largest proportion of corruptions." Nevertheless, however reluctantly, Zuntz has given material aid to the cause for which Burgon stood by admitting that all the readings of the Byzantine text are ancient readings. Once this is admitted, the critical hypothesis that the Byzantine text was the creation of editors becomes hard indeed to maintain. It would have to be assumed that before these editors began their work of creating the Byzantine text they took the trouble to assemble a vast collection of variant readings, examining for this purpose all the manuscripts then extant and selecting readings now from this source and now from that. Only in this way could be explained the appearance of Byzantine readings in almost every type of ancient text. But this is to ascribe incredibly modern procedures to these assumed ancient editors. Surely the agreements of the Byzantine text with ancient non-Byzantine texts are much more easily explained by regarding the Byzantine text as the original text and these non-Byzantine text as departures from it.

(c) Papyrus Bodmer II

We come now to one of the most striking recent developments in the field of New Testament studies. We refer, of course, to Professor V. Martin's publication, late in the year 1956, of Papyrus Bodmer II,[10] an ancient papyrus manuscript containing the first fourteen chapters of John's Gospel. Expert paleographers agree in assigning this manuscript to the beginning of the third century. It was written, they believe, about the year 200 A.D. According to Wilhelm Schubart, a great authority in this field, the beginning of it makes an impression of still greater age.[11] Thus Papyrus Bodmer II enjoys the distinction of being the oldest New Testament manuscript now known, preceding by a few years even the Chester Beatty Papyri. Hence its great importance for the history of the New Testament text.

As its name implies, this manuscript is the property of the Bodmer Library in Geneva, Switzerland. According to Kurt Aland (1957),[12] it is part of a collection of more than fifty papyrus documents which was purchased in 1954 by the Bodmer Library from E. N. Adler of London. In his edition of Papyrus Bodmer II, however, Professor Martin tells us very little concerning the discovery and recent history of this manuscript. In the effort to supply this deficiency in Martin's presentation the present writer addressed a letter of inquiry to the Bodmer Library and received the following answer:

August 6, 1957

We have received your letter of the first of the current month and understand very well the questions which disturb you. Unfortunately, we ourselves have not been able to obtain any precise information concerning the discovery of the *St. John.* We think that it comes certainly from the Middle East, perhaps from Lebanon, Egypt, or North Africa, (the only places in which the preservation of papyrus is possible, due to the dry climate). We can only tell you that it was purchased at Geneva by M. Bodmer. The numerous intermediaries are themselves ignorant of the exact source. And so we ourselves have given up looking for it.

We regret very much not to be able to give you a more satisfactory answer and beg you to accept, Monsieur, the expression of our best regards.

O. Bongard, Secretary

Apparently, therefore, the manner in which this manuscript made its way from its ancient resting place to Geneva and the Bodmer Library is a mystery that defies all investigation.

The researches of Martin[13] and of A. Klijn (1957)[14] have led them to conclude that Papyrus Bodmer II belongs to the Alexandrian family of New Testament manuscripts. It agrees, they believe, quite closely with the text of *Aleph* and to a lesler degree with the text of *B*. This agreement of Papyrus Bodmer II with *Aleph* and *B*, however is far from perfect. It contains a number of instances of agreement with the Western text found in *D* and in the Latin versions. Aland considers the Western element in this ancient manuscript sufficiently strong to warrant the hypothesis that its text is a "mixed" text, partly Western partly Alexandrian,[15] and Filson (1957)[16] sums up the situation with the observation that Papyrus Bodmer II does not agree consistently with any of the other ancient manuscripts.

According to Aland,[17] the number of corrections in Papyrus Bodmer II is unusually large, totalling 269. No doubt many of these corrections were occasioned by careless mistakes on the part of the original scribe, but even after corrections of obvious errors and peculiar readings have been eliminated, at least 35 very significant examples still remain, and these have been listed by Klijn.[18] This scholar remarks that in most of these 35 instances the original reading was clearly of the Western variety and that the corrections were added for the purpose of bringing these Western readings into conformity with the Alexandrian type of New Testament text. This observation, however, does not do justice to all the facts. For in addition to those instances in which the original text of Papyrus Bodmer II agrees with the Western authorities and the correction with the Alexandrian, there are 5 cases in which precisely the opposite situation prevails. The original reading agrees with that form of the Alexandrian text found in *B*, while the correction is Western in character. And beside this, there are 2 places in which the original reading of Papyrus Bodmer II agrees only with the Byzantine text, the correction being Western or Alexandrian in character, and also one passage in which the original reading is Alexandrian but the correction exclusively Byzantine.

The evidence, then, of the corrections in Papyrus Bodmer II effectively refutes the hypothesis of Hort and others that the text found in *B* and *Aleph* is a "Neutral" text of exceptional purity in which errors have found almost no lodging place. Quite to the contrary, these corrections support the contention of Hoskier (1914) that Hort's "Neutral" text is "a doctored text, plainly, indubitably doctored."[19] In these corrections we see the "Neutral" text being "doctored" before our eyes. Here, in short, we see the ancient scribes of Alexandria at their work, remodeling the original New Testament text down to the last detail and disputing among themselves as to the proper way in which this should be done. It was evidently in this capricious, haphazard fashion (not in any systematic manner) that the "Neutral" text was produced.

If the "Neutral" text of B and *Aleph* and their ancient relative, Papyrus Bodmer II, is a "doctored" text, what was the original New Testament text like? Papyrus Bodmer II helps to answer this question also. Although this early manuscript agrees often with Aleph and other manuscripts of the Alexandrian family, it also contains a number of agreements with the Byzantine text in places in which this text stands alone without any support from the Alexandrian and Western texts. To be precise, Papyrus Bodmer II contains thirteen percent of all the alleged late readings of the Byzantine text in the area which it covers (18 out of 138). Thirteen percent of the Byzantine readings which most critics have regarded as late have now been proved by Papyrus Bodmer II to be early readings. This remarkable circumstance constitutes additional proof that the Byzantine text, contrary to current critical opinon, is not a late text but an early one and therefore on the ground of age, as well as on other grounds, may rightly be regarded as the original text.

Certainly the agreements of Papyrus Bodmer II with the Byzantine text (like those of the Chester Beatty Papri) help to refute the contention of Hort and other famous critics that the Byzantine text was created by editors out of previously existing texts. Modern defenders of Hort's theory must maintain that these assumed editors selected their readings from a vast varity of early texts. Only in this way can they explain how Byzantine readings which Hort regarded as late have been found to exist some in Papyrus Bodmer II, some in the Chester Beatty Papyri, and some in almost every other ancient New Testament document. The makers of the Byzantine text must have gathered together a tremendous number of New Testament manuscripts of many different text-types and then have wandered over this large collection more or less at random, choosing a reading now from this manuscript and now from that, omitting, quite unaccountably, many Western readings which contain interesting additions to the sacred text.

There is surely a much more reasonable way of explaining why each non-Byzantine text (including Papyrus Bodmer II) contains Byzantine readings not found in other non-Byzantine texts. If we regard the Byzantine text as the original text, then it is perfectly natural that each non-Byzantine text should agree with the Byzantine text in places in which the other non-Byzantine texts have departed from it.

3. The Testimony of the Peshitta

Since the Christological controversies of the fifth century, the Syrian Church has been divided into several rival sects, the most important of which are the Nestorians and the Monophysites. The Nestorians are followers of Nestorius (d. 451), bishop of Constantinople, who was accused of teaching that in Christ there are not only two natures but also two persons. The Monophysites (*monos,* one and *physis,* nature) hold to the doctrines of Eutyches (c. 448), one of the chief opponents of the Nestorians, who asserted not only that Christ was one person but also His divine and human natures were so fused together as to be one.

Although the Nestorians and Monophysites and other Syrian sects are fiercely divided in matters of Christology, they have always been united in their common use of the *Peshitta* as their authoritative Scripture. This is a very ancient translation of the Old and New Testaments into Syriac. Why it was given the title *Peshitta* (Simple) is not known. Its contents in the Old Testament are about the same as those of the Hebrew Old Testament, but in the New Testament it does not include the minor Catholic Epistles (2 Peter, 2 and 3 John, and Jude) and Revelation. Up until the latter part of the nineteenth century the Peshitta was generally regarded as the oldest translation of the New Testament into Syriac, a second century date being assigned to it.

In text the Peshitta agrees closely with the Byzantine family of New Testament manuscripts. Just how close this agreement is, however, has not yet been determined. Souter (1912)[20] has stated that "the Peshitta Syric rarely witnesses to anything different from what we find in the great bulk of Greek manuscripts." Metzger (1950)[21] would question this assertion somewhat on the basis of the thorough examination which Gwilliam (1903)[22] made of Matt. 1-14. Here Gwilliam discovered a considerable non-Byzantine element in the Peshitta, and C. S. C. Williams (1954), taking cognizance of this, has revised Souter's statement, asserting merely that 'the Peshitta Syriac often witnesses to something akin to what we find in the great bulk of Greek manuscripts."[23] But in spite of these modifications, all scholars still seem to agree that the Peshitta frequently supports the Byzantine text. If, therefore, the Peshitta actually does date from the second century, it remains an outstanding witness to the antiquity of the Byzantine text and consequently to the falsity of Hort's theory that this text is a late text.

Burkitt (1904) advanced an hypothesis which did away with this testimony of the Peshitta to the Byzantine text. He maintained that the Peshitta did not exist before the fifth century, since it was "the result of a revision made and promulgated by Rabbula, bishop of Edessa from 411-435 A.D."[24] Burkitt's hypothesis has been generally adopted by modern scholars and, like Westcott and Hort's theories, has frequently been asserted as an established fact, but there is a difficulty involved in it of which Burkitt himself was well aware. This is the fact that the Peshitta is regarded as authoritative Scripture by both the Nestorians and the Monophysites. It is hard to see how this could have come to pass on the hypothesis that Rabbula was the author and chief promoter of the Peshitta. For Rabbula was a decided Monophysite and a determined opponent of the Nestorians. It is almost contrary to reason, therefore, to suppose that the Nestorian Christians would adopt so quickly and so unanimously the handiwork of their greatest adversary.

Due to this historical difficulty Burkitt's hypothesis was rejected by such competent scholars as A. Mingana (1915)[25] and A. C. Clark (1933).[26] Its complete overthrow, however, seems to have been accomplished in recent years by the researches of A. Voobus, who has published his results in several important monographs on the origin and early use of the Peshitta. In his first work (1947)[27] Voobus not only denies that Rabbula was the author of the Peshitta but even contends that he did not use it at all. In a second study (1948)[28] Voobus controverts Burkitt's statement that after the time of Rabbula only the Peshitta was used by Syriac writers. Burkitt, he says, made this assertion on insufficient grounds. And in a third treatment of the same subject (1951)[29] he disputes Burkitt's dictum, "before Rabbula no traces of the Peshitta." Voobus finds traces of the Peshitta in an Armenian translation of a writing by Aitallaha, bishop of Edessa, who died about 346. This work was not known until 1911 and so was not available to Burkitt at the time he formulated his theory.

If Voobus is correct in his findings (and these have been accepted at least in part by M. Black (1951)[30] and other authorities in this field), and especially if he is right in his contention that the Peshitta was not unanimously accepted by Syrian Christians until after the fifth century, then there is only one theory which can explain how both the Nestorians and the Monophysites came to receive it as their official text. This is the traditional view that the Peshitta was made in the second century and is the oldest Syriac version. The other Syriac versions (the Diatessaron and the so-called Old Syriac) were foreign importations which may for a time have eclipsed the Peshitta in popularity but never drove it out of circulation altogether. In the sixth century, after the Nestorians and Monophysites had broken off relations with the Greek Church, both groups returned to this ancient version, which they knew to have been the text of their fathers. Indeed, they vied with each other in doing so, for in this way each party sought to demonstrate that they were the ones who were truly orthodox. Thus recent studies of the Peshitta tend to re-establish it as the oldest of the ancient versions and thus as a very important witness to the antiquity of the Byzantine text from which it was made.

4. Origen and the Ante-Nicene Fathers

One of the arguments advanced by Hort and other naturalistic critics against the early existence and thus against the genuineness of the Byzantine text is the alleged fact that "distinctively" Byzantine readings are never found in the New Testament quotations of Origen and other second and third century Church Fathers. In other words, it is alleged that these ante-Nicene Fathers never agree with the Byzantine text in places in which it stands alone in opposition to both the Western and Alexandrian text types. If this alleged fact were actually a fact, it would, to be sure, constitute a difficulty for the defenders of the Byzantine text. Happily, however, it is not a fact at all, as anyone can determine for himself by scanning the appartus of Tischendorf. For example, in the first fourteen chapters of the Gospel of John (that is, in the area covered by Papyrus Bodmer II) out of 52 instances in which the Byzantine text stands alone Origen agrees with the Byzantine text 20 times and disagrees with it 32 times. Thus the assertion of the critics that Origen knew nothing of the Byzantine text becomes difficult indeed to maintain. On the contrary, these statistics suggest that Origen was familiar with the Byzantine text and frequently adopted its readings in preference to those of the Western and Alexandrian texts.

Naturalistic critics, it is true, have made a determined effort to explain away the "distinctively" Byzantine readings which appear in the New Testament quotations of Origen (and other ante-Nicene Fathers). It is argued that these Byzantine readings are not really Origen's but represent alterations made by scribes who copied Origen's works. These scribes, it is maintained, revised the original quotations of Origen and made them conform to the Byzantine text. The evidence of Papyrus Bodmer II, however, indicates that this is not an adequate explanation of the facts. Certainly it seems a very unsatisfactory way to account for the phenomena which appear in the first fourteen chapters of John. In these chapters 5 out of the 20 "distinctively" Byzantine readings which occur in Origen occur also in Papyrus Bodmer II. These 5 readings at least must have been Origen's readings, not those of scribes who copied Origen's works, and what is true of these 5 readings is probably true of the other 15, or at least of most of them.

The complex character of the New Testament quotations of Origen and the other ante-Nicene Fathers can be most satisfactorily explained by supposing that, although during the second and third centuries the true (Byzantine) New Testament text was not unknown in the larger cities, it was preserved throughout this early period mainly in the rural regions and the small towns. From very earliest times it has always been the tendency of country folk to preserve unaltered the heritage handed down to them from previous generations. Christians residing in these localities, therefore, would be prompted by their customary conservatism to reproduce without change the New Testament text which they had received from their fathers. The relative seclusion also of these country districts would serve to protect the transmission of the New Testament from disturbing influences from without.

If during the ante-Nicene period the true New Testament text was preserved mainly in the country districts and the smaller towns, where did the false texts originate? In order to answer this question correctly it is necessary to bear in mind that the variant readings in the extant New Testament manuscripts do not consist in careless blunders which have slowly accumulated during the course of many ages. Quite to the contrary, these variants came into being not gradually but suddenly during the century that followed the writing of the New Testament. And because these variants appeared so suddenly as this, they could not to any large extent have been the result of mere careless copying but must have been created deliberately. It was this that Dean Burgon (1882)[31] insisted upon, and many modern scholars have agreed with him. Thus Ropes (1926)[32] believed that the variants of the Western text were the creation of a single second century editor, and A. C. Clark (1933)[33] held almost the same opinion concerning the variants of the Alexandrian text. And Colwell (1952) has expressed himself along similar lines. "The first two Christian centuries witnessed the creation of the large majority of all variations known to scholars today . . . In the manuscripts of the New Testament most variations, I believe, were made deliberately."[34]

If, then, the variations in the extant New Testament manuscripts were created not gradually and accidentally but suddenly and deliberately, where were they created? In the big cities, most probably, and especially in the two great capitals, Rome and Alexandria. Citified Christians, accustomed as they were to constant movement and variety in their everyday life, would be much less opposed than their rural brethren to the introduction of novel readings into the New Testament text. Thus it was in the cities rather than in the country that heretics stood the best chance of gaining acceptance in orthodox Christian circles for their revisions of the New Testament Scriptures. And, as we have seen, there were at Alexandria and Rome especially no lack of gnostics and other false teachers to take advantage of this exceptional opportunity. And in the cities also much other damage was evidently done by educated scribes who thought themselves competent to correct the original New Testament text and improve its style.

Thus during the second and third centuries the true New Testament text labored under a temporary disadvantage in its struggle against the false texts which had come into existence during this period. The true text circulated mainly among the humbler Christians of the rural areas. The false texts, on the other hand, having originated in Rome and Alexandria and other big cities and having achieved great popularity in the Christian communities of these large urban centers, enjoyed enormous prestige. Small wonder, therefore, that the ante-Nicene Fathers appear to have been somewhat affected by this general situation. They seem often to have fallen in with the usage of the big city churches, especially the Roman and Alexandrian churches, preferring the false readings of the corrupt city texts to the genuine readings of the true text. To acknowledge this weakness on the part of the ante-Nicene Fathers, however, is far from admitting the claim of Hort and other naturalistic critics that these ancient ecclesiastical writers knew nothing of the true (Byzantine) text. The facts indicate that the Fathers of the second and third century were familiar with the true text even though they did not always choose to follow it.

5. The Post-Nicene Fathers

After the middle of the fourth century there appeared in the Greek Church a general trend toward the Byzantine (true) text. This tendency, it seems, first manifested itself in Antioch and Asia Minor. According to the researches of Hort, von Soden, and other modern scholars, the Byzantine text was used in Antioch and its vicinity by Diodorus (died c. 394), Chrysostom (345-407), Theodore of Mopsuestia (c. 350-428), and Theodoret (397-457). And this same text is also found in the writings of the three great Cappadocian Fathers (natives of the province of Cappadocia in Asia Minor), namely, Basil (330-379), Gregory Nazianzen (329-390), and Gregory of Nysa (d. 394).

Hort had an explanation for this use of the Byzantine text by Chrysostom and these other fourth century Fathers of Antioch and Asia Minor.[35] He believed that the Byzantine text originated at Antioch as the result of two "authoritative revisions" of the New Testament text which were completed there beween the years 250 and 350. Hort further conjectured that the ancient scholar and martyr Lucian (d. 312) may have been the leader in the first of these "authoritative revisions." In other words, Hort's theory was that the Byzantine text was created at Antioch and imposed upon the Church there by ecclesiastical authority. History, however, makes no mention of any such revision (or revisions) of the New Testament text as Hort postulated, and this silence constitutes a formidable objection against his theory. As Kenyon (1912) truly remarked, "We know the names of several revisers of the Septuagint and the Vulgate, and it would be strange if historians and Church writers had all omitted to record or mention such an event as the deliberate revision of the New Testament in its original Greek."[36]

Kenyon's recognition of the weakness of this aspect of Hort's theory led him to modify it as follows: "It seems probable," he wrote, "that the Syrian revision was rather the result of a tendency spread over a considerable period of time than of a definite and authoritative revision or revisions, such as produced our English Authorized and Revised Versions. We have only to suppose the principle to be established in Christian circles in and about Antioch, that in the case of divergent readings being found in the texts copied, it was better to combine both than to omit either, and that obscurities and roughness of diction should be smoothed away as much as possible . . . The point is that the Syrian revision was a long-continued process, not a single act." But if the Byzantine text just drifted into being in this gradual manner without being sponsored by any ecclesiastical authority, it is hard to see what could have given it that impetus which enabled it to supplant both the scholarly Alexandrian text and the popular Western text and ultimately to win for itself well nigh universal acceptance within the Greek Church. Moreover, the Byzantine text is much too definite an entity to have been produced by a tendency or a trend.

Thus naturalistic critics are unable to explain either how the Byzantine text originated or what there was about it that won for it the supremacy over all other texts and caused it to become the text of the whole Greek Church during the greater part of the Byzantine Period (312-1453). Why, then, may we not explain these historical phenomena along the lines laid down by Burgon and other orthodox scholars?

It is because the Byzantine text is the true text that it gained its victory over other texts. During the second and third centuries, mainly in big cities such as Rome and Alexandria, this true text was seriously corrupted both by heretics, who altered it into conformity with their false doctrines, and by officious scribes, who thought themselves capable of improving its literary style. Yet even in those first chaotic centuries God in His providence was preserving the true New Testament text, mainly (it would seem) in the rural regions and in the small towns. And it was to this text that the whole Greek Church returned after the middle of the fourth century. Due to the theological controversies of this period the Church arrived at maturity in doctrinal matters and thus awoke to a deeper appreciation of the doctrinal richness and perfect orthodoxy of the Byzantine (true) text. It was this awakening which produced that unmistakable trend toward the Byzantine text which began during the latter part of the fourth century and then rapidly gathered momentum until it finally resulted in the complete triumph of the Byzantine (true) text over all its rivals. And all this came to pass under the guidance of the Holy Spirit.

Thus it was that God used the Greek Church (in spite of its manifest sins and shortcomings) to preserve for posterity the true text of the Greek New Testament. Thus it was that the true New Testament text was handed down in the Greek Church in unbroken succession from the days of the apostles to the days of the Protestant Reformation and then became available to all men everywhere *via* the King James Version and other early Protestant translations. But when we say that the Holy Spirit guided the Greek Church to preserve the true New Testament text, we do not wish to be misunderstood. We are not speaking of the Church as an organization but of the Church as an *organism*. We do not mean that in the latter part of the fourth century the Holy Spirit guided Chrysostom and the other bishops to the true text and that then these bishops issued decrees for the guidance of the common people. Investigations indicate that the Holy Spirit's guidance worked in precisely the opposite way. The trend toward the Byzantine (true) text began with the common people, the rank and file, and then rapidly built up such strength that Chrysostom and the other leaders were carried along with it. Chrysostom, for example, does not seem to have initiated this trend, for a study (1931)[37] by J. Geerlings and S. New appears to indicate that Chrysostom did not always use the Byzantine text.

6. The Medieval Period

Herman von Soden (1907), Professor of New Testament at the University of Berlin, made the most extensive study of the Byzantine text that has ever yet been undertaken.[38] He called the Byzantine text the K (Common) text, thereby indicating that it is the text most commonly found in the New Testament manuscripts. He divided the Byzantine manuscripts into three classes, K^1, K^x, and K^r. The manuscripts in the K^1 class (as the numeral 1 implies) he regarded as containing the earliest form of the

Byzantine text. Among the best representatives of this class he placed *Omega* (8th or 9th century), *V* (9th century), and *S* (10th century). The K^r he considered to be a revision of the *K* (Byzantine) text made in the eleventh or twelfth centuries (the letter *r* signifying *revision*). In between the K^1 manuscripts and the K^r in point of time von Soden located the great majority of the Byzantine manuscripts. These he named K^x (the letter *x* signifying *unknown*) to indicate that the small differences which distinguish them from each other have not yet been thoroughly studied. Thus, according to von Soden, the K^x text was derived from the K^1 text, and the K^r text was derived from the K^x.

The principal results of von Soden's study have been confirmed by more recent research. He was evidently right in regarding the K^1 as the oldest form of the Byzantine text, for H. A. Sanders (1912) found the Byzantine text which the ancient manuscript W (4th or 5th century) contains in Matthew and the last part of Luke to be of this type. And von Soden was correct also in his insistence on the essential unity of the Byzantine text. The K^1, K^x, and K^r are all varieties of one basic text and agree with one another very closely. Additional evidence that this is a fact is to be found in a study of the Byzantine text published by Kirsopp Lake in the *Harvard Theological Review* (1928).[39]

Lake and his associates made a careful examination in the eleventh chapter of Mark of all the manuscripts on Mt. Sinai, at Patmos, and in the Patriarchal Library and the collection of St. Saba at Jerusalem. On the basis of this examination Lake was even disposed to deny that the K^1 and K^r texts are really distinct from the K^x text (which Lake preferred to call the *Ecclesiastical text*). Also in a later article published in *Memorial Lagrange* (1940) Lake speaks again of the close agreement existing among the Byzantine manuscripts classified as K^1 and K^x by von Soden. "K^1 and K^x each show a certain amount of individual variation by which they can be identified — but it is surprisingly little. The scribes who were responsible for the variations in the Byzantine text introduced remarkably few and unimportant changes. They shunned all originality."[40]

Thus recent researches in the Byzantine text do confirm the views of Burgon concerning it. The Byzantine text contained in the ancient manuscript W (4th or 5th century) did triumph over all other text types and is now found in the vast majority of the Greek New Testament manuscripts. The vast horde of manuscripts which contain the Byzantine text do agree with one another very closely, the variations which exist among them being merely sufficient to prove that they do indeed represent the well nigh unanimous usage of the Greek Church and were not the result of mass production on the part of just a few scribes.

There is evidence that the triumphal march of the Byzantine text met with resistance in certain quarters. There were some scribes and scholars who were reluctant to renounce altogether their faulty Western, Alexandrian, and Caesarean texts. And so they compromised by following sometimes their false texts and sometimes the true (Byzantine) text. Thus arose those classes of mixed manuscripts observed by von Soden, which he calls K^a, K^i, *Pi*, etc.[41] This would explain also the non-Byzantine readings which Colwell (1933)[42] and his associates claim to find in certain portions of the lectionary manuscripts. And if J. N. Birdsall (1956)[43] is right in his contention that Photius (815-897), Patriarch of Constantinople, customarily used the Caesarean text, this too must be regarded as a belated effort on the part of this learned churchman to keep up the struggle against the Byzantine text. His endeavor, however, was in vain. Long before his time the God-guided preference of the common people for the true (Byzantine) text had brought this text into general use throughout the Greek Church.

7. Conclusion

Thus the evidence which has accumulated since Burgon's day is amply sufficient to justify the view held by him and by all consistently orthodox Christians, namely, that it was through the usage of the Church that Christ has fulfilled His promise always to preserve the true New Testament text, and that therefore the Byzantine text found in the vast majority of the Greek New

Testament manuscripts is that true text. To reject this view is to act unreasonably. It is to fly in face of the facts.

Those, moreover, who reject this orthodox view of the New Testament text have rejected not merely the facts but also the promise of Christ always to preserve the true New Testament text and the doctrines of the divine inspiration and providential preservation of Scripture implied in this promise. Has Christ kept this promise or has He not? If we believe this promise, then we must do as Burgon and other orthodox Christians have done. Like Burgon, we must allow this promise to guide us in our dealings with the New Testament text. We must interpret all the data of New Testament textual criticism in the light of this promise. It is just here, however, that many Christians are fatally inconsistent. They say that they believe in the promise which Christ has given always to preserve the true New Testament text, but in practice they ignore this promise and treat the text of the New Testament exactly like the text of an ordinary book concerning which no such promise has been made. Thus they are guilty of a basic unfaithfulness. In their efforts to be pleasing to naturalistic critics they themselves have lapsed into unbelief. They have undermined their own faith and deprived themselves of all ground for confidence in the infallibility of the Bible. For if the New Testament is just an ordinary book, then the trustworthiness of its text is, at best, only a *probability*, never a *certainty*.

Dean Burgon has a message for these waverers and for all who desire to attain unto a firmer faith. In his controversy with the revisionists of 1881 Burgon stood forth as the uncompromising champion of the King James (Authorized) Version. "As a companion in the study and for private edification: as a book of reference for critical purposes, especially in respect of difficult and controverted passages: — we hold that a revised edition of the Authorized Version of our English Bible (if executed with consummate ability and learning) would at any time be a work of inestimable value. The method of such a performance, whether by marginal Notes or in some other way, we forbear to determine. But certainly only as a handmaid is it to be desired.

As something *intended to supersede* our present English Bible, we are thoroughly convinced that the project of rival Translation is not to be entertained for a moment. For ourselves we deprecate it entirely."[44]

Burgon's main purpose, however, was to defend the Byzantine (Traditional) text of the Greek New Testament upon which the King James Version is based. He was removed from earth, it is true, before he could complete his grand design, but even before his death he had in great measure accomplished his purpose. Christians who desire to study the problems of the New Testament text should make every effort to procure Dean Burgon's works for their own possession. From him they will learn what it is to take first the standpoint of faith and then to deal faithfully and conscientiously with all the pertinent facts.

TABLE

Distinctively Byzantine Readings in Papyrus Bodmer II.

John 1:32   ōsei with K M P U X Delta Pi many others fam 1 fam 13 700 W.

John 3:24   o ante iō. with A L Delta Pi others very many fam 1 fam 13 700 W Theta Origen.

John 4:14   dipsēsē with Lambda Pi many others 118 209 700 W Origen.

John 4:51   kai apēggeilan with A C Gamma Delta Lambda others very many fam 13 700 W Theta.

John 5:8   egeirai with U V Gamma Delta many others 118 209 700.

John 6:10   ōsei with A Gamma Delta Lambda many others fam 1 fam 13 700 Theta.

John 6:57   zēsetai with Gamma Delta Lambda others very many fam 1 700 W.

John 7:3   theorēsōsi with X Gamma Lambda Pi others very many fam 1 fam 13 700 Theta.

John 7:39   agion post pneuma with L N X Gamma Delta Lambda fam 1 fam 13 W 700 Origen int.

            oudepō with L T X Gamma Delta Lambda Pi others very many fam 1 fam 13 700 W Origen.

John 8:41   ou gegenēmetha with C X Gamma Delta Lambda Pi many others fam 1 fam 13 700 W Theta Origen.

John 8:48   eipon with L X Gamma Delta Lambda Pi fam 1 fam 13 700.

John 8:55   kai ean with A C L X Gamma Delta Pi many others fam 1 fam 13 700 Theta.

John 9:23   eipon with A L X many others fam 1 fam 13 700 W Theta.

John 10:38   pisteusate with A E G H M S X Gamma Lambda others very many Pap. 45 118 209 fam 13 700.

John 12:36   eōs with X Gamma Delta Lambda Pi others very many fam 1 fam 13 700.

John 12:44   all'with A X Gamma Lambda Pi others very many fam 1 fam 13 700 Theta.

John 14:17   auto post ginōskei with A X many others fam 1 fam 13 700 Theta.

In the preparation of this table the following sources were consulted:

Tischendorf....................N. T. Graece, Editio Octava.

von Soden......................Die Schriften des N. T., Text und Apparat.

H. A. Sanders................The Washington MS of the Four Gospels.

G. Beermann und
C. R. Gregory................Die Koridethi Evangelien.

K. Lake...........................Codex 1 of the Gospel and Its Allies.

W. H. Ferrar and
T. K. Abbott..................A Collation of Four Important MSS of the Gospels.

H. C. Hoskier................Collation of the Greek Cursive Codex Evangelium 604 (700).

NOTES
ABBREVIATIONS

Berlin..........Die Griechischen Christlichen Schriftsteller, Preussisch. Akademie der Wissenschaften.
HTR..........Harvard Theological Review (Harvard University Press).
JBL...........The Journal of Biblical Literature.
JTS............The Journal of Theological Studies (Oxford University Press).
LCL..........The Loeb Classical Library.
MPL..........Migne Patrologiae Cursus Completus, Series Latina.
NTS..........New Testament Studies (Cambridge University Press).
TS..............Texts and Studies (Cambridge University Press).
ZNW.........Zeitschrift fur die neutest. Wissenschaft.

CHAPTER ONE

Note 1. New Testament Manuscript Studies, Parvis & Wikgren, Chicago: University of Chicago Press, Copyright 1950 by the University of Chicago, p. 9.

Note 2. Side Lights on New Testament Research, by J. Rendel Harris, London: James Clarke & Co., 1908, p. 22.

Note 3. The Traditional Text of the Holy Gospels, London: George Bell & Sons, 1896.

Note 4. The Causes of the Corruption of the Traditional Text of the Holy Gospels, London: George Bell & Sons, 1896.

Note 5. The Last Twelve Verses of the Gospel According to Mark, London: James Parker & Co., 1871.

Note 6. The Revision Revised, London: John Murray, 1883.

Note 7. Our Bible and the Ancient Manuscripts, New York, 1940, pp. 105-106.

Note 8. New Testament Manuscript Studies, Parvis & Wikgren, pp. 4-5.

Note 9. The Acts of the Apostles, by A. C. Clark, Oxford: Clarendon Press, 1933, p. viii.

Note 10. The Beginnings of Christianity, vol. 3, by J. H. Ropes, London: Macmillan, 1926, p. ccxliv.

Note 11. Revision Revised, p. 12.

Note 12. Idem, p. 318.

Note 13. Idem, p. 319.

Note 14. HTR, vol. 21 (1928), pp. 347-349.

Note 15. Eusebius, H. E., LCS, vol. 1, p. 516.

Note 16. Idem, pp. 522-524.

Note 17. Berlin, Origenes Werke, vol. 1, p. 156.

Note 18. MPL, vol. 26, col. 589.

Note 19. Berlin, Origenes Werke, vol. 10, pp. 385-388.
Note 20. Revision Revised, pp. 334-335.
Note 21. The Origin of the New Testament, New York, 1925, pp. 2-3.
Note 22. Schriftgeloof en Canoniek, Kampen, 1927, pp. 76-77.
Note 23. Algemeene Canoniek van het Nieuwe Testament, Amsterdam, 1935, pp. 206-207.
Note 24. Revision Revised, p. 343.
Note 25. Traditional Text, p. 12.
Note 26. Idem, p. 9.
Note 27. The New Testament in the Original Greek, vol. 2, London, 1881, p. 277.

CHAPTER TWO

Note 1. Works, edited by A. Dyce, London, 1838, vol. iii, p. 347-361.
Note 2. TS, vol. 2 (1891), p. 228.
Note 3. Alterations to the Text of the Synoptic Gospels and Acts, by C. S. C. Williams, Oxford, 1951 p. 16.
Note 4. TS, vol. 2 (1891), p. 228.
Note 5. Traditional Text, p. 261.
Note 6. Light on the Four Gospels from the Sinai Palimpsest, London, 1913, p. 13.
Note 7. The Four Gospels, London, 1924, p. 143.
Note 8. HTR, vol. 50 (1957), pp. 249-258.
Note 9. N. T. Graece, Leipzig, 1869, vol. 1, p. 75.
Note 10. N. T. in Greek, vol. 2, appendix, p. 12.
Note 11. Introduction to the New Testament (Eng. trans.), Edinburgh, 1909, vol. 2, p. 477.
Note 12. The Infallible Word, Philadelphia: Presbyterian Guardian Pub. Co., 1946, p. 162.
Note 13. The Westminster Assembly and Its Work, by B. B. Warfield, New York: Oxford University Press, 1931, p. 239.
Note 14. N. T. in Greek, vol. 2, p. 2.
Note 15. New Testament Manuscript Studies, Parvis & Wikgren, Chicago: University of Chicago Press, Copyright 1950 by the University of Chicago, p. 18.
Note 16. Side Lights on New Testament Research, by J. Rendel Harris, London: James Clarke & Co., 1908, p. 3.
Note 17. History of New Testament Criticism, by F. C. Conybeare, London: Watts & Co., 1910, p. 129.
Note 18. Family 13 (The Ferrar Group) by K. & S. Lake, Philadelphia: University of Pennsylvania Press, 1941, p. vii.
Note 19. The Text of the Greek Bible, by F. G. Kenyon, London: Duckworth, Studies in Theology, 1937, pp. 244-246.

Note 20. N. T. in Greek, vol. 2, p. 277.

CHAPTER THREE

Note 1. The Washington Manuscript of the Four Gospels, New York, 1912.
Note 2. Idem, p. 134.
Note 3. JBL, vol. 68 (1949), pp. 363-370.
Note 4. ZNW, vol. 48 (1957).
Note 5. Die Schriften des Neuen Testaments, Gottigen, 1911, 1. Teil, 2. Abt., pp. 1472-77, 3. Abt., pp. 16-72-74, 1949.
Note 6. The Chester Beatty Biblical Papyri, London, 1933-37.
Note 7. NTS, vol. 3 (1957), p. 283.
Note 8 Idem, p. 328.
Note 9. The Text of the Epistles, by G. Zuntz, London: Oxford University Press, 1953, p. 55.
Note 10. Papyrus Bodmer II, Evangile de Jean 1-14, Cologny-Geneve, 1956.
Note 11. NTS, vol. 3 (1957), p. 281.
Note 12. Idem, p. 279.
Note 13. Papyrus Bodmer II, pp. 141-152.
Note 14. NTS, vol. 3 (1957), p. 331.
Note 15. Idem, p. 283.
Note 16. The Biblical Archeologist, vol. 20 (1957), p. 61.
Note 17. NTS, vol. 3 (1957), pp. 280-281.
Note 18. Idem, pp. 333-334.
Note 19. Codex B and Its Allies, by H. C. Hoskier, London: Bernard Quaritch, 1914, Part I, p. vi.
Note 20. The Text and Canon of the New Testament, by A. Souter, London: Duckworth, Studies in Theology, 1912, p. 117.
Note 21. New Testament Manuscript Studies, p. 32.
Note 22. Studia Biblica et Ecclesiastica , vol. 5 (1903), pp. 187-237.
Note 23. The Text and Canon of the New Testament, 2nd edition revised by C. S. C. Williams, London: Duckworth, Studies in Theology, 1954, p. 56.
Note 24. Evangelion da-Mepharreshe, by F. C. Burkitt, Cambridge: Cambridge University Press, 1904, vol. 2, p. 161.
Note 25. Expository Times, vol. 26 (1914-15) pp. 379-381.
Note 26. The Acts of the Apostles, p. 297.
Note 27. Investigations into the Text of the New Testament used by Rabbula of Edessa, Pinneberg, 1947, p. 37.
Note 28. Researches on the Circulation of the Peshitta in the Middle of the Fifth Century, Pinneberg, 1948, pp. 13-55.

Note 29. Neue Angeben Ueber die Textgeschichtlichen Zustande in Edessa in den Jahren ca 326-340, Stockholm, 1951, pp. 12-55. See also, Voobus, Early Versions of the New Testament, Stockholm, 1954, pp. 94-95.

Note 30. Bulletin of the John Rylands Library, vol. 33 (1950-51) pp. 203-210.

Note 31. Revision Revised, p. 334.

Note 32. The Beginnings of Christianity, vol. 3, p. ccxliv.

Note 33. The Acts of the Apostles, 1933, p. viii.

Note 34. What is the Best New Testament, by E. C. Colwell, Chicago, University of Chicago Press, Copyright 1952 by the University of Chicago, p. 52.

Note 35. N. T. in Greek, vol. 2, pp. 137-139.

Note 36. Handbook to the Textual Criticism of the New Testament, by F. G. Kenyon, London: Macmillan, 1912, pp. 324-325.

Note 37. HTR, vol. 24 (1931), pp. 138-149.

Note 38. Die Schriften des Neuen Testaments, 1. Teil, 2. Abt., pp. 707-893.

Note 39. HTR, vol. 21 (1928), p. 339ff.

Note 40. Memorial Lagrange, Paris: J. Gabalda et Cie, 1940, p. 256.

Note 41. Die Schriften des Neuen Testaments, 1. Teil, 2. Abt., pp. 845-888, 1243-1259.

Note 42. E. C. Colwell & D. W. Riddle, Prolegomena to the Study of the Lectionary Text of the Gospels, Chicago, 1933.

J. R. Branton, The Common Text of the Gospel Lectionary, Chicago, 1934.

M. W. Redus, The Text of the Major Festivals of the Menologion, Chicago, 1936.

B. M. Metzger, The Saturday and Sunday lesson from Luke in the Greek Gospel Lectionary, Chicago, 1944.

Note 43. JTS, vol. 7 n.s. (1956), pp. 42, 198.

Note 44. Revision Revised, pp. 113-114.

TO

SIR ROUNDELL PALMER, Q.C., M.P.,

&c., &c., &c.

DEAR SIR ROUNDELL,

I do myself the honour of inscribing this volume to you. Permit me to explain the reason why.

It is not merely that I may give expression to a sentiment of private friendship which dates back from the pleasant time when I was Curate to your Father,—whose memory I never recal without love and veneration;—nor even in order to afford myself the opportunity of testifying how much I honour you for the noble example of conscientious uprightness and integrity which you set us on a recent public occasion. It is for no such reason that I dedicate to you this vindication of the last Twelve Verses of the Gospel according to S. Mark.

It is because I desire supremely to submit the argument contained in the ensuing pages to a practised judicial intellect of the loftiest stamp. Recent Editors of the New Testament insist that these "last Twelve Verses" are not genuine. The Critics, almost to a man, avow themselves of the same opinion. Popular Prejudice has been for a long time past warmly enlisted on the same side. I am as convinced as I am of my life, that the reverse is the truth. It is not even with me as it is with certain learned friends of mine, who, admitting the adversary's premisses, content themselves with denying the validity of his inference. However true it may be,—and it is true,—that from those premisses the proposed conclusion does not follow, I yet venture to deny the correctness of those premisses altogether. I insist, on the contrary, that the Evidence relied on is untrustworthy,—untrustworthy in every particular.

How, in the meantime, can such an one as *I* am hope to persuade the world that it is as *I* say, while the most illustrious Biblical Critics at home and abroad are agreed, and against me? Clearly, the first thing to be done is to secure for myself a full and patient hearing. With this view, *I* have written a book. But next, instead of waiting for the slow verdict of Public Opinion, (which yet, *I* know, must come after many days,) *I* desiderate for the Evidence *I* have collected, a competent and an impartial Judge. And that is why *I* dedicate my book to you. If *I* can but get this case fairly tried, *I* have no doubt whatever about the result.

Whether you are able to find time to read these pages, or not, it shall content me to have shewn in this manner the confidence with which *I* advocate my cause; the kind of test to which *I* propose to bring my reasonings. If *I* may be allowed to say so, —S. Mark's last Twelve Verses shall no longer remain a subject of dispute among men. *I* am able to prove that this portion of the Gospel has been declared to be spurious on wholly mistaken grounds: and this ought in fairness to close the discussion. But *I* claim to have done more. *I* claim to have shewn, from considerations which have been hitherto overlooked, that its genuineness must needs be reckoned among the things that are absolutely certain.

I am, with sincere regard and respect,

Dear Sir Roundell,

Very faithfully yours,

JOHN W. BURGON.

ORIEL,
July, 1871.

PREFACE.

THIS volume is my contribution towards the better understanding of a subject which is destined, when it shall have grown into a Science, to vindicate for itself a mighty province, and to enjoy paramount attention. I allude to the Textual Criticism of the New Testament Scriptures.

That this Study is still in its infancy, all may see. The very principles on which it is based are as yet only imperfectly understood. The reason is obvious. It is because the very foundations have not yet been laid, (except to a wholly inadequate extent,) on which the future superstructure is to rise. A careful collation of every extant Codex, (executed after the manner of the Rev. F. H. Scrivener's labours in this department,) is the first indispensable preliminary to any real progress. Another, is a revised Text, not to say a more exact knowledge, of the oldest Versions. Scarcely of inferior importance would be critically correct editions of the Fathers of the Church; and these must by all means be furnished with far completer Indices of Texts than have ever yet been attempted.—There is not a single Father to be named whose Works have been hitherto furnished with even a tolerably complete Index of the places in which he either quotes, or else clearly refers to, the Text of the New Testament : while scarcely a tithe of the known MSS. of the Gospels have as yet been satisfactorily collated. Strange to relate, we are to this hour without so much as a satisfactory Catalogue of the Copies which are known to be extant.

But when all this has been done,—(and the Science deserves, and requires, a little more public encouragement than has hitherto been bestowed on the arduous and—let me not be ashamed to add the word—*unremunerative* labour of Textual Criticism,)—it will be discovered that the popular and the prevailing Theory is a mistaken one. The plausible hypothesis on which recent recensions of the Text have been for the most part conducted, will be seen to be no longer tenable. The latest decisions will in consequence be generally reversed.

I am not of course losing sight of what has been already achieved in this department of Sacred Learning. While our knowledge of the uncial MSS. has been rendered tolerably exact and complete, an excellent beginning has been made, (chiefly by the Rev. F. H. Scrivener, the most judicious living Master of Textual Criticism,) in acquainting us with the contents of about seventy of the cursive MSS. of the New Testament. And though it is impossible to deny that the published Texts of Doctors Tischendorf and Tregelles as *Texts* are wholly inadmissible, yet is it equally certain that by the conscientious diligence with which those distinguished Scholars have respectively laboured, they have erected monuments of their learning and ability which will endure for ever. Their Editions of the New Testament will not be superseded by any new discoveries, by any future advances in the Science of Textual Criticism. The MSS. which they have edited will remain among the most precious materials for future study. All honour to them! If in the warmth of controversy I shall appear to have spoken of them sometimes without becoming deference, let me here once for all confess that I am to blame, and express my regret. When they have publicly begged S. Mark's pardon for the grievous wrong they have done *him*, I will very humbly beg their pardon also.

In conclusion, I desire to offer my thanks to the Rev. John Wordsworth, late Fellow of Brasenose College, for his patient perusal of these sheets as they have passed through the press, and for favouring me with several judicious suggestions. To him may be applied the saying of President Routh on receiving a visit from Bishop Wordsworth at his lodgings,— "I see the learned son of a learned Father, sir!"— Let me be permitted to add that my friend inherits the Bishop's fine taste and accurate judgment also.

And now I dismiss this Work, at which I have conscientiously laboured for many days and many nights; beginning it in joy and ending it in sorrow. The College in which I have for the most part written it is designated in the preamble of its Charter and in its Foundation Statutes, (which are already much more than half a thousand years old,) as *Collegium Scholarium in Sacrá Theologiá studentium,—perpetuis temporibus duraturum.* Indebted, under GOD, to the pious munificence of the Founder of Oriel for my opportunities of study, I venture, in what I must needs call evil days, to hope that I have to some extent "employed my advantages,"— (the expression occurs in a prayer used by this Society on its three solemn anniversaries,) — as our Founder and Benefactors "would approve if they were now upon earth to witness what we do."

J. W. B.

ORIEL,
July, 1871.

THE LAST TWELVE VERSES OF THE GOSPEL ACCORDING TO S. MARK.

CHAPTER I.

THE CASE OF THE LAST TWELVE VERSES OF S. MARK'S GOSPEL, STATED.

These Verses generally suspected at the present time. The popularity of this opinion accounted for.

IT has lately become the fashion to speak of the last Twelve Verses of the Gospel according to S. Mark, as if it were an ascertained fact that those verses constitute no integral part of the Gospel. It seems to be generally supposed, (1) That the evidence of MSS is altogether fatal to their claims; (2) That " the early Fathers" witness plainly against their genuineness; (3) That, from considerations of "internal evidence" they must certainly be given up. It shall be my endeavour in the ensuing pages to shew, on the contrary, That manuscript evidence is so overwhelmingly in their favour that no room is left for doubt or suspicion:—That there is not so much as *one* of the Fathers, early or late, who gives it as his opinion that these verses are spurious:— and, That the argument derived from internal considerations proves on inquiry to be baseless and unsubstantial as a dream.

But I hope that I shall succeed in doing more. It shall be my endeavour to shew not only that there really is no reason whatever for calling in question the genuineness of this portion of Holy Writ, but also that there exist sufficient reasons for feeling confident that it must needs be genuine. This is clearly as much as it is possible for me to achieve. But when this has been done, I venture to hope that the verses in dispute will for the future be allowed to retain their place in the second Gospel unmolested.

It will of course be asked,—And yet, if all this be so, how does it happen that both in very ancient, and also in very modern times, this proposal to suppress twelve verses of the Gospel has enjoyed a certain amount of popularity? At the two different periods, (I answer,) for widely different reasons.

(1.) In the ancient days, when it was the universal belief of Christendom that the Word of GOD must needs be consistent with itself in every part, and prove in every part (like its Divine Author) perfectly "faithful and true," the difficulty (which was deemed all but insuperable) of bringing certain statements in S. Mark's last Twelve Verses into harmony with certain statements of the other Evangelists, is discovered to have troubled Divines exceedingly. "In fact," (says Mr. Scrivener,) "it brought suspicion upon these verses, and caused their omission in some copies seen by Eusebius." That the maiming process is indeed attributable to this cause and came about in this particular way, I am unable to persuade myself; but, if the desire to provide an escape from a serious critical difficulty did not actually *occasion* that copies of S. Mark's Gospel were mutilated, it certainly was the reason why, in very early times, such mutilated copies were viewed without displeasure by some, and appealed to with complacency by others.

(2.) But times are changed. We have recently been assured on high authority that the Church has reversed her ancient convictions in this respect: that *now*, "most sound theologians have no dread whatever of acknowledging minute points of disagreement" (i.e. minute *errors*) "in the fourfold narrative even of the life of the Redeemer[a]." There has arisen in these last days a singular impatience of Dogmatic Truth, (especially Dogma of an unpalatable kind,) which has even rendered popular the pretext afforded by these same mutilated copies for the grave resuscitation of doubts, never as it would seem seriously entertained by any

---

[a] Abp. Tait's *Harmony of Revelation and the Sciences*, (1864,) p. 21.

of the ancients; and which, at all events for 1300 years and upwards, have deservedly sunk into oblivion.

Whilst I write, *that* "most-divine explication of the chiefest articles of our Christian belief," the Athanasian Creed [b], is made the object of incessant assaults [c]. But then it is remembered that statements quite as "uncharitable" as any which this Creed contains are found in the 16th verse of S. Mark's concluding chapter; are in fact the words of Him whose very Name is Love. The precious *warning clause*, I say, (miscalled "damnatory [d],") which an impertinent officiousness is for glossing with a rubric and weakening with an apology, proceeded from Divine lips,—at least if these concluding verses be genuine. How shall this inconvenient circumstance be more effectually dealt with than by accepting the suggestion of the most recent editors, that S. Mark's concluding verses are an unauthorised addition to his Gospel? "If it be acknowledged that the passage has a harsh sound," (remarks Dean Stanley,) "unlike the usual utterances of Him who came not to condemn but to save, the discoveries of later times have shewn, almost beyond doubt, that it is *not a part of S. Mark's Gospel, but an addition by another hand;* of which the weakness in the external evidence coincides with the internal evidence in proving its later origin [e]."

Modern prejudice, then,—added to a singularly exaggerated estimate of the critical importance of the testimony

---

[b] See by all means Hooker, E. P., v. xlii. 11—13.

[c] Abp. Tait is of opinion that it "should not retain its place in the public Service of the Church:" and Dean Stanley gives sixteen reasons for the same opinion,—the fifteenth of which is that "many excellent laymen, including King George III., have declined to take part in the recitation." (*Final*) *Report of the Ritual Commission*, 1870, p. viii. and p. xvii.

[d] In the words of **a** thoughtful friend, (Rev. C. P. Eden),—"*Condemnatory* is just what these clauses are *not*. I understand myself, in uttering these words, not to condemn a fellow creature, but to acknowledge a truth of Scripture, GOD'S judgment namely on the sin of unbelief. The further question,— In whom the sin of unbelief is found; *that* awful question I leave entirely in His hands who is the alone Judge of hearts; who made us, and knows our infirmities, and whose tender mercies are over all His works."

[e] "The Athanasian Creed," by the Dean of Westminster (*Contemporary Review*, Aug., 1870, pp. 158, 159).

of our two oldest Codices, (another of the "discoveries of later times," concerning which I shall have more to say by-and-by,)—must explain why the opinion is even popular that the last twelve verses of S. Mark are a spurious appendix to his Gospel.

Not that Biblical Critics would have us believe that the Evangelist left off at verse 8, intending that the words,— "neither said they anything to any man, for they were afraid," should be the conclusion of his Gospel. "No one can imagine," (writes Griesbach,) "that Mark cut short the thread of his narrative at that place [f]." It is on all hands eagerly admitted, that so abrupt a termination must be held to mark an incomplete or else an uncompleted work. How, then, in the original autograph of the Evangelist, is it supposed that the narrative proceeded? This is what no one has even ventured so much as to conjecture. It is assumed, however, that the original termination of the Gospel, whatever it may have been, has perished. We appeal, of course, to its actual termination: and,—Of what nature then, (we ask,) is the supposed necessity for regarding the last twelve verses of S. Mark's Gospel as a spurious substitute for what the Evangelist originally wrote? What, in other words, has been the history of these modern doubts; and by what steps have they established themselves in books, and won the public ear?

To explain this, shall be the object of the next ensuing chapters.

[f] *Commentarius Criticus*, ii. 197.

CHAPTER II.

THE HOSTILE VERDICT OF BIBLICAL CRITICS SHEWN TO BE QUITE OF RECENT DATE.

Griesbach the first to deny the genuineness of these Verses (84).—*Lachmann's fatal principle* (86) *the clue to the unfavourable verdict of Tischendorf* (87), *of Tregelles* (88), *of Alford* (90); *which has been generally adopted by subsequent Scholars and Divines* (91).—*The nature of the present inquiry explained* (93)

IT is only since the appearance of Griesbach's second edition [1796—1806] that Critics of the New Testament have permitted themselves to handle the last twelve verses of S. Mark's Gospel with disrespect. Previous critical editions of the New Testament are free from this reproach. "There is no reason for doubting the genuineness of this portion of Scripture," wrote Mill in 1707, after a review of the evidence (as far as he was acquainted with it) for and against. Twenty-seven years later, appeared Bengel's edition of the New Testament (1734); and Wetstein, at the end of another seventeen years (1751-2), followed in the same field. Both editors, after rehearsing the adverse testimony *in extenso,* left the passage in undisputed possession of its place. Alter in 1786-7, and Birch in 1788 [a], (suspicious as the latter evidently was of its genuineness,) followed their predecessors' example. But Matthaei, (who also brought his labours to a close in the year 1788,) was not content to give a silent suffrage. He had been for upwards of fourteen years a laborious collator of Greek MSS. of the New Testament, and was so convinced of the insufficiency of the arguments which had been brought against these twelve verses of S. Mark,

---

[a] *Quatuor Evangelia Graece cum variantibus a textu lectionibus Codd. MSS. Bibliothecae Vaticanae, etc. Jussu et sumtibus regiis edidit Andreas Birch, Havniae,* 1788. A copy of this very rare and sumptuous folio may be seen in the King's Library (Brit. Mus.).

that with no ordinary warmth, no common acuteness, he insisted on their genuineness.

"With Griesbach," (remarks Dr. Tregelles[b],) "Texts which may be called really critical begin;" and Griesbach is the first to insist that the concluding verses of S. Mark are spurious. That he did not suppose the second Gospel to have always ended at verse 8, we have seen already. He was of opinion, however, that "at some very remote period, the original ending of the Gospel perished,—disappeared perhaps *from the Evangelist's own copy*,—and that the present ending was by some one substituted in its place." Griesbach further invented the following elaborate and extraordinary hypothesis to account for the existence of S. Mark xvi. 9—20.

He invites his readers to believe that when, (before the end of the second century,) the four Evangelical narratives were collected into a volume and dignified with the title of "The Gospel,"—S. Mark's narrative was furnished by some unknown individual with its actual termination in order to remedy its manifest incompleteness; and that this volume became the standard of the Alexandrine recension of the text: in other words, became the fontal source of a mighty family of MSS. by Griesbach designated as "Alexandrine." But there will have been here and there in existence isolated copies of one or more of the Gospels; and in all of these, S. Mark's Gospel, (by the hypothesis,) will have ended abruptly at the eighth verse. These copies of single Gospels, when collected together, are presumed by Griesbach to have constituted "the Western recension." If, in codices of this family also, the self-same termination is now all but universally found, the fact is to be accounted for, (Griesbach says,) by the natural desire which possessors of the Gospels will have experienced to supplement their imperfect copies as best they might. "Let this conjecture be accepted," proceeds the learned veteran,—(unconscious apparently that he has been demanding acceptance for at least half-a-dozen wholly unsupported as well as entirely gratuitous conjectures,)—"and every difficulty disappears; and

---

[b] *Account of the Printed Text*, p. 83.

it becomes perfectly intelligible how there has crept into almost every codex which has been written, from the second century downwards, a section quite different from the original and genuine ending of S. Mark, which disappeared before the four Gospels were collected into a single volume."
—In other words, if men will but be so accommodating as to assume that the conclusion of S. Mark's Gospel disappeared before any one had the opportunity of transcribing the Evangelist's inspired autograph, they will have no difficulty in understanding that the present conclusion of S. Mark's Gospel was not really written by S. Mark.

It should perhaps be stated in passing, that Griesbach was driven into this curious maze of unsupported conjecture by the exigencies of his "Recension Theory;" which, inasmuch as it has been long since exploded, need not now occupy us. But it is worth observing that the argument already exhibited, (such as it is,) breaks down under the weight of the very first fact which its learned author is obliged to lay upon it. Codex B.,—the solitary manuscript witness for *omitting* the clause in question, (for Codex א had not yet been discovered,)—had been already claimed by Griesbach as a chief exponent of his so-called "Alexandrine Recension." But then, on the Critic's own hypothesis, (as we have seen already,) Codex B. ought, on the contrary, to have *contained* it. How was that inconvenient fact to be got over? Griesbach quietly remarks in a foot-note that Codex B. "*has affinity* with the Eastern family of MSS."—The misfortune of being saddled with a worthless theory was surely never more apparent. By the time we have reached this point in the investigation, we are reminded of nothing so much as of the weary traveller who, having patiently pursued an *ignis fatuus* through half the night, beholds it at last vanish; but not until it has conducted him up to his chin in the mire.

Neither Hug, nor Scholz his pupil,—who in 1808 and 1830 respectively followed Griesbach with modifications of his recension-theory,—concurred in the unfavourable sentence which their illustrious predecessor had passed on the concluding portion of S. Mark's Gospel. The latter even eagerly vindicated its genuineness [d]. But with Lachmann, —whose unsatisfactory text of the Gospels appeared in 1842, — originated a new principle of Textual Revision; the principle, namely, of paying exclusive and absolute deference to the testimony of a few arbitrarily selected ancient documents; no regard being paid to others of the same or of yet higher antiquity. This is not the right place for discussing this plausible and certainly most convenient scheme of textual revision. That it leads to conclusions little short of irrational, is certain. I notice it only because it supplies the clue to the result which, as far as S. Mark xvi. 9—20 is concerned, has been since arrived at by Dr. Tischendorf, Dr. Tregelles, and Dean Alford [e],— the three latest critics who have formally undertaken to reconstruct the sacred Text.

They agree in assuring their readers that the genuine Gospel of S. Mark extends no further than ch. xvi. ver. 8: in other words, that all that follows the words ἐφοβοῦντο γάρ is an unauthorized addition by some later hand; "a fragment,"—distinguishable from the rest of the Gospel not less by internal evidence than by external testimony. This verdict becomes the more important because it proceeds from men of undoubted earnestness and high ability; who cannot be suspected of being either unacquainted with the evidence on which the point in dispute rests, nor inexperienced in the art of weighing such evidence. Moreover, their verdict has been independently reached; is unanimous; is unhesitating; has been eagerly proclaimed by all three on many different occasions as well as in many different places [f]; and

[d] "Eam esse authenticam rationes internae et externae probant gravissimae."

[e] I find it difficult to say what distress the sudden removal of this amiable and accomplished Scholar occasions me, just as I am finishing my task. I consign these pages to the press with a sense of downright reluctance,—(constrained however by the importance of the subject,)—seeing that *he* is no longer among us either to accept or to dispute a single proposition. All I can do is to erase every word which might have occasioned him the least annoyance; and indeed, as seldom as possible to introduce his respected name. An open grave reminds one of the nothingness of earthly controversy; as nothing else does, or indeed can do.

[f] Tischendorf, besides eight editions of his laborious critical revision of the Greek Text, has edited our English "Authorized Version" (Tauchnitz, 1869,)

may be said to be at present in all but undisputed possession of the field g. The first-named Editor enjoys a vast reputation, and has been generously styled by Mr. Scrivener, "the first Biblical Critic in Europe." The other two have produced text-books which are deservedly held in high esteem, and are in the hands of every student. The views of such men will undoubtedly colour the convictions of the next generation of English Churchmen. It becomes absolutely necessary, therefore, to examine with the utmost care the grounds of their verdict, the direct result of which is to present us with a mutilated Gospel. If they are right, there is no help for it but that the convictions of eighteen centuries in this respect must be surrendered. But if Tischendorf and Tregelles are wrong in this particular, it follows of necessity that doubt is thrown over the whole of their critical method. The case is a crucial one. Every page of theirs incurs suspicion, if their deliberate verdict in *this* instance shall prove to be mistaken.

1. Tischendorf disposes of the whole question in a single sentence. "That these verses were not written by Mark,"

with an "Introduction" addressed to unlearned readers, and the various readings of Codd. ℵ, B and A, set down in English at the foot of every page.—Tregelles, besides his edition of the Text of the N. T., is very full on the subject of S. Mark xvi. 9—20, in his "Account of the Printed Text," and in his "Introduction to the Textual Criticism of the N. T." (vol. iv. of Horne's *Introd.*)—Dean Alford, besides six editions of his Greek Testament, and an abridgment "for the upper forms of Schools and for passmen at the Universities," put forth two editions of a "N. T. for English Readers," and three editions of "the Authorized Version newly compared with the original Greek and revised;"—in every one of which it is stated that these twelve verses are "probably an addition, placed here in very early times."

g The Rev. F. H. Scrivener, Bp. Ellicott, and Bp. Wordsworth, are honourable exceptions to this remark. The last-named excellent Divine reluctantly admitting that "this portion may not have been penned by S. Mark himself;" and Bishop Ellicott (*Historical Lectures*, pp. 26-7) asking "Why may not this portion have been written by S. Mark at a later period?;"—both alike resolutely insist on its genuineness and canonicity. To the honour of the best living master of Textual Criticism, the Rev. F. H. Scrivener, (of whom I desire to be understood to speak as a disciple of his master,) be it stated that he has never at any time given the least sanction to the popular outcry against this portion of the Gospel. "Without the slightest misgiving" he has uniformly maintained the genuineness of S. Mark xvi. 9—20. (*Introduction*, pp. 7 and 429—32.)

(he says,) "admits of satisfactory proof." He then recites in detail the adverse external testimony which his predecessors had accumulated; remarking, that it is abundantly confirmed by internal evidence. Of this he supplies a solitary sample; but declares that the whole passage is "abhorrent" to S. Mark's manner. "The facts of the case being such," (and with this he dismisses the subject,) "a healthy piety reclaims against the endeavours of those who are for palming off as Mark's what the Evangelist is so plainly shewn to have known nothing at all about [h]." A mass of laborious annotation which comes surging in at the close of verse 8, and fills two of Tischendorf's pages, has the effect of entirely divorcing the twelve verses in question from the inspired text of the Evangelist. On the other hand, the evidence *in favour* of the place is despatched in less than twelve lines. What can be the reason that an Editor of the New Testament parades elaborately every particular of the evidence, (such as it is,) *against* the genuineness of a considerable portion of the Gospel; and yet makes summary work with the evidence in its favour? That Tischendorf has at least entirely made up his mind on the matter in hand is plain. Elsewhere, he speaks of the Author of these verses as "*Pseudo Marcus* [i]."

2. Dr. Tregelles has expressed himself most fully on this subject in his "Account of the Printed Text of the Greek New Testament" (1854). The respected author undertakes to shew "that the early testimony that S. Mark did not write these verses is confirmed by existing monuments." Accordingly, he announces as the result of the propositions which he thinks he has established, "that the *book of Mark himself* extends no further than ἐφοβοῦντο γάρ." He is the

---

[h] "Hæc non a Marco scripta esse argumentis probatur idoneis," (p. 320.) "Quæ testimonia aliis corroborantur argumentis, ut quod conlatis prioribus versu 9. parum apte adduntur verba ἀφ' ἧς ἐκβεβ. item quod singula multifariam a Marci ratione abhorrent." (p. 322.)—I quote from the 7th Leipsic ed.; but in Tischendorf's 8th ed. (1866, pp. 403, 406,) the same verdict is repeated, with the following addition:—"Quæ quum ita sint, sanæ erga sacrum textum pietati adversari videntur qui pro apostolicis venditare pergunt quæ a Marco aliena esse tam luculenter docemur." (p. 407.)

[i] *Evangelia Apocrypha*, 1853, Proleg. p. lvi.

only critic I have met with to whom it does not seem incredible that S. Mark did actually conclude his Gospel in this abrupt way: observing that "perhaps we do not know enough of the circumstances of S. Mark when he wrote his Gospel to say whether he did or did not leave it with a complete termination." In this modest suggestion at least Dr. Tregelles is unassailable, since we know absolutely nothing whatever about "the circumstances of S. Mark," (or of any other Evangelist,) "when he wrote his Gospel:" neither indeed are we quite sure *who* S. Mark *was*. But when he goes on to declare, notwithstanding, "that the remaining twelve verses, by whomsoever written, have a full claim to be received as an authentic part of the second Gospel;" and complains that "there is in some minds a kind of timidity with regard to Holy Scripture, as if all our notions of its authority depended on our knowing who was the writer of each particular portion; instead of simply seeing and owning that it was given forth from GOD, and that it is as much His as were the Commandments of the Law written by His own finger on the tables of stone [k];"—the learned writer betrays a misapprehension of the question at issue, which we are least of all prepared to encounter in such a quarter. We admire his piety but it is at the expense of his critical sagacity. For the question is not at all one of *authorship*, but only one of *genuineness*. Have the codices been *mutilated* which do *not* contain these verses? If they have, then must these verses be held to be *genuine*. But on the contrary, Have the codices been *supplemented* which contain them? Then are these verses certainly *spurious*. There is no help for it but they must either be held to be an integral part of the Gospel, and therefore, in default of any proof to the contrary, as certainly by S. Mark as any other twelve verses which can be named; or else an unauthorized addition to it. If they belong to the post-apostolic age it is idle to insist on their Inspiration, and to claim that this "authentic anonymous addition to what Mark himself wrote down" is as much the work of GOD "as were the Ten Commandments written by His own

[k] pp. 253, 7—9.

finger on the tables of stone." On the other hand, if they "ought as much to be received as part of our second Gospel as the last chapter of Deuteronomy (unknown as the writer is) is received as the right and proper conclusion of the book of Moses,"—it is difficult to understand why the learned editor should think himself at liberty to sever them from their context, and introduce the subscription KATA MAPKON after ver. 8. In short, "How persons who believe that these verses did not form a part of the original Gospel of Mark, but were added afterwards, can say that they have a good claim to be received as an authentic or genuine part of the second Gospel, that is, a portion of canonical Scripture, passes comprehension." It passes even Dr. Davidson's comprehension; (for the foregoing words are his;) and Dr. Davidson, as some of us are aware, is not a man to stick at trifles [1].

3. Dean Alford went a little further than any of his predecessors. He says that this passage "was placed as a completion of the Gospel soon after the Apostolic period,—the Gospel itself having been, for some reason unknown to us, left incomplete. The most probable supposition" (he adds) "is, that *the last leaf of the original Gospel* was *torn away.*" The italics in this conjecture (which was originally Griesbach's) are not mine. The internal evidence (declares the same learned writer) "preponderates vastly against the authorship of Mark;" or (as he elsewhere expresses it) against "its genuineness as a work of the Evangelist." Accordingly, in his Prolegomena, (p. 38) he describes it as "*the remarkable fragment* at the end of the Gospel." After this, we are the less astonished to find that he *closes the second Gospel at ver.* 8; introduces the Subscription there; and encloses the twelve verses which follow within heavy brackets. Thus, whereas from the days of our illustrious countryman

---

[1] In his first edition (1848, vol. i. p. 163) Dr. Davidson pronounced it "manifestly untenable" that S. Mark's Gospel was the last written; and assigned A.D. 64 as "its most probable" date. In his second (1868, vol. ii. p. 117), he says:—"When we consider that *the Gospel was not written till the second century,* internal evidence loses much of its force against the authenticity of these verses."—*Introduction to N. T.*

Mill (1707), the editors of the N. T. have either been silent on the subject, or else have whispered only that this section of the Gospel is to be received with less of confidence than the rest,—it has been reserved for the present century to convert the ancient suspicions into actual charges. The latest to enter the field have been the first to execute Griesbach's adverse sentence pronounced fifty years ago, and to load the blessed Evangelist with bonds.

It might have been foreseen that when Critics so conspicuous permit themselves thus to handle the precious deposit, others would take courage to hurl their thunderbolts in the same direction with the less concern. "It is probable," (says Abp. Thomson in the *Bible Dictionary*,) "that this section is from a different hand, and was annexed to the Gospels soon after the times of the Apostles [m]."—The Rev. T. S. Green [n], (an able scholar, never to be mentioned without respect,) considers that "the hypothesis of very early interpolation satisfies the body of facts in evidence,"— which "point unmistakably in the direction of a spurious origin."—"In respect of Mark's Gospel," (writes Professor Norton in a recent work on the *Genuineness of the Gospels*,) "there is ground for believing that the last twelve verses were not written by the Evangelist, but were added by some other writer to supply a short conclusion to the work, which some cause had prevented the author from completing [o]."— Professor Westcott—who, jointly with the Rev. F. J. A. Hort, announces a revised Text—assures us that "the original text, from whatever cause it may have happened, terminated abruptly after the account of the Angelic vision." The rest "was added at another time, and probably by another hand." "It is in vain to speculate on the causes of this abrupt close." "The remaining verses cannot be regarded as part of the original narrative of S. Mark [p]."—Meyer insists that this is an "apocryphal fragment," and reproduces all the arguments, external and internal, which have ever been

---

[m] Vol. ii. p. 239.   [n] *Developed Criticism*, [1857], p. 53.
[o] Ed. 1847, i. p. 17. He recommends this view to his reader's acceptance in five pages,—pp. 216 to 221.
[p] *Introduction to the Study of the Gospels*, p. 311.

arrayed against it, without a particle of misgiving. The "note" with which he takes leave of the subject is even insolent[q]. A comparison (he says) of these "fragments" (ver. 9—18 and 19) with the parallel places in the other Gospels and in the Acts, shews how vacillating and various were the Apostolical traditions concerning the appearances of our LORD after His Resurrection, and concerning His Ascension. ("Hast thou killed, and also taken possession?")

Such, then, is the hostile verdict concerning these last twelve verses which I venture to dispute, and which I trust I shall live to see reversed. The writers above cited will be found to rely (1.) on the external evidence of certain ancient MSS.; and (2.) on Scholia which state "that the more ancient and accurate copies terminated the Gospel at ver. 8." (3.) They assure us that this is confirmed by a formidable array of Patristic authorities. (4.) Internal proof is declared not to be wanting. Certain incoherences and inaccuracies are pointed out. In fine, "the phraseology and style of the section" are declared to be "unfavourable to its authenticity;" not a few of the words and expressions being "foreign to the diction of Mark."—I propose to shew that all these confident and imposing statements are to a great extent either mistakes or exaggerations, and that the slender residuum of fact is about as powerless to achieve the purpose of the critics as were the seven green withs of the Philistines to bind Samson.

In order to exhibit successfully what I have to offer on this subject, I find it necessary to begin (in the next chapter) at the very beginning. I think it right, however, in this place to premise a few plain considerations which will be of use to us throughout all our subsequent inquiry; and which indeed we shall never be able to afford to lose sight of for long.

The question at issue being simply this,—Whether it is reasonable to suspect that the last twelve verses of S. Mark are a spurious accretion and unauthorized supplement to his Gospel, or not?—the whole of our business clearly resolves itself into an examination of what has been urged in proof

---

[q] *Critical and Exegetical Commentary*, 1855, 8vo. pp. 182, 186—92.

that the former alternative is the correct one. Our opponents maintain that these verses did not form part of the original autograph of the Evangelist. But it is a known rule in the Law of Evidence that *the burthen of proof lies on the party who asserts the affirmative of the issue* [r]. We have therefore to ascertain in the present instance what the supposed proof is exactly worth; remembering always that in this subject-matter a *high degree of probability* is the only kind of proof which is attainable. When, for example, it is contended that the famous words in S. John's first Epistle (1 S. John v. 7, 8,) are not to be regarded as genuine, the fact that they are away from almost every known Codex is accepted as a proof that they were also away from the autograph of the Evangelist. On far less weighty evidence, in fact, we are at all times prepared to yield the hearty assent of our understanding in this department of sacred science.

And yet, it will be found that evidence of overwhelming weight, if not of an entirely different kind, is required in the present instance: as I proceed to explain.

1. When it is contended that our LORD's reply to the young ruler (S. Matt. xix. 17) *was not* Τί με λέγεις ἀγαθόν; οὐδεὶς ἀγαθὸς, εἰ μὴ εἶς, ὁ Θεός,—it is at the same time insisted that *it was* Τί με ἐρωτᾷς περὶ τοῦ ἀγαθοῦ; εἶς ἐστὶν ὁ ἀγαθός. It is proposed to omit the former words *only* because an alternative clause is at hand, which it is proposed to substitute in its room.

2. Again. When it is claimed that some given passage of the Textus Receptus,—S. Mark xv. 28, for example, (καὶ ἐπληρώθη ἡ γραφὴ ἡ λέγουσα, Καὶ μετὰ ἀνόμων ἐλογίσθη,) or the Doxology in S. Matth. vi. 13,—is spurious, all that is pretended is that certain words are an unauthorized addition to the inspired text; and that by simply omitting them we are so far restoring the Gospel to its original integrity.—The same is to be said concerning *every other charge of interpolation which can be named.* If the celebrated "pericopa de adulterâ," for instance, be indeed

[r] In the Roman law this principle is thus expressed,—" Ei incumbit probatio qui dicit, non qui negat." Taylor *on the Law of Evidence*, 1868, i. p. 369.

not genuine, we have but to leave out those twelve verses of S. John's Gospel, and to read chap. vii. 52 in close sequence with chap. viii. 12; and we are assured that we are put in possession of the text as it came from the hands of its inspired Author. Nor, (it must be admitted), is any difficulty whatever occasioned thereby; for there is no reason assignable why the two last-named verses should *not* cohere; (there is no internal improbability, I mean, in the supposition;) neither does there exist any *à priori* reason why a considerable portion of narrative should be looked for in that particular part of the Gospel.

3. But the case is altogether different, as all must see, when it is proposed to get rid of the twelve verses which for 1700 years and upwards have formed the conclusion of S. Mark's Gospel; no alternative conclusion being proposed to our acceptance. For let it be only observed what this proposal practically amounts to and means.

(*a.*) And first, it does *not* mean that S. Mark himself, with design, brought his Gospel to a close at the words ἐφοβοῦντο γάρ. *That* supposition would in fact be irrational. It does not mean, I say, that by simply leaving out those last twelve verses we shall be restoring the second Gospel to its original integrity. And this it is which makes the present a different case from every other, and necessitates a fuller, if not a different kind of proof.

(*b.*) What then? It means that although an abrupt and impossible termination would confessedly be the result of omitting verses 9—20, no nearer approximation to the original autograph of the Evangelist is at present attainable. Whether S. Mark was *interrupted* before he could finish his Gospel,—(as Dr. Tregelles and Professor Norton suggest;)—in which case it will have been published by its Author in an unfinished state: or whether "*the last leaf was torn away*" before a single copy of the original could be procured,—(a view which is found to have recommended itself to Griesbach;)—in which case it will have once had a different termination from at present; which termination however, by the hypothesis, has since been irrecoverably lost;—(and to one of these two wild hypotheses the critics are logically reduced;)—*this* we are not certainly told. The critics are only agreed in assuming that S. Mark's Gospel *was at first without the verses which at present conclude it.*

But this assumption, (that a work which has been held to be a complete work for seventeen centuries and upwards was originally incomplete,) of course requires *proof.* The foregoing improbable theories, based on a gratuitous assumption, are confronted *in limine* with a formidable obstacle which must be absolutely got rid of before they can be thought entitled to a serious hearing. It is a familiar and a fatal circumstance that the Gospel of S. Mark has been furnished with its present termination ever since the second century of the Christian æra [s]. In default, therefore, of distinct historical evidence or definite documentary proof that *at some earlier period than that* it terminated abruptly, nothing short of the utter unfitness of the verses which at present conclude S. Mark's Gospel to be regarded as the work of the Evangelist, would warrant us in assuming that they are the spurious accretion of the post-apostolic age: and as such, at the end of eighteen centuries, to be deliberately rejected. We must absolutely be furnished, I say, with internal evidence of the most unequivocal character; or else with external testimony of a direct and definite kind, if we are to admit that the actual conclusion of S. Mark's Gospel is an unauthorized substitute for something quite different that has been lost. I can only imagine one other thing which could induce us to entertain such an opinion; and that would be the *general* consent of MSS., Fathers, and Versions in leaving these verses out. Else, it is evident that we are logically *forced* to adopt the far easier supposition that (*not* S. Mark, but) *some copyist of the third century* left a copy of S. Mark's Gospel unfinished; which unfinished copy became the fontal source of the mutilated copies which have come down to our own times [t].

---

[s] This is freely allowed by all. "Certiores facti sumus hanc pericopam jam in secundo sæculo lectam fuisse tanquam hujus evangelii partem." Tregelles *N. T.* p. 214.

[t] This in fact is how Bengel (N. T. p. 526) accounts for the phenomenon:—
"Fieri potuit ut librarius, scripto versu 8, reliquam partem scribere differret,

I have thought it right to explain the matter thus fully at the outset; not in order to prejudge the question, (for *that* could answer no good purpose,) but only in order that the reader may have clearly set before him the real nature of the issue. "Is it reasonable to suspect that the concluding verses of S. Mark are a spurious accretion and unauthorized supplement to his Gospel, or not?" *That* is the question which we have to consider,—the *one* question. And while I proceed to pass under careful review all the evidence on this subject with which I am acquainted, I shall be again and again obliged to direct the attention of my reader to its bearing on the real point at issue. In other words, we shall have again and again to ask ourselves, how far it is rendered probable by each fresh article of evidence that S. Mark's Gospel, when it left the hands of its inspired Author, was an unfinished work; the last chapter ending abruptly at ver. 8?

I will only point out, before passing on, that the course which has been adopted towards S. Mark xvi. 9—20, by the latest Editors of the New Testament, is simply illogical. Either they regard these verses as *possibly* genuine, or else as *certainly* spurious. If they entertain (as they say they do) a decided opinion that they are *not* genuine, they ought (if they would be consistent) *to banish them from the text*[u]. Conversely, *since they do not banish them from the text*, they have no right to pass a fatal sentence upon them; to designate their author as "pseudo-Marcus;" to handle them in contemptuous fashion. The plain truth is, these learned men are better than their theory; the worthlessness of which they are made to *feel* in the present most conspicuous instance. It reduces them to perplexity. It has landed them in inconsistency and error.—They will find it necessary in the end to reverse their convictions. They cannot too speedily reconsider their verdict, and retrace their steps.

et id exemplar, casu non perfectum, alii quasi perfectum sequerentur, praesertim quum ea pars cum reliquâ historiâ evangelicâ minus congruere videretur."

[u] It is thus that Tischendorf treats S. Luke xxiv. 12, and (in his latest edition) S. John xxi. 25.

CHAPTER III.

THE EARLY FATHERS APPEALED TO, AND OBSERVED TO BEAR FAVOURABLE WITNESS.

Patristic evidence sometimes the most important of any (98).—*The importance of such evidence explained* (99).—*Nineteen Patristic witnesses to these Verses, produced* (101).—*Summary* (108).

THE present inquiry must be conducted solely on grounds of Evidence, external and internal. For the full consideration of the former, seven Chapters will be necessary [a] : for a discussion of the latter, one seventh of that space will suffice [b]. We have first to ascertain whether the external testimony concerning S. Mark xvi. 9—20 is of such a nature as to constrain us to admit that it is highly probable that those twelve verses are a spurious appendix to S. Mark's Gospel.

1. It is well known that for determining the Text of the New Testament, we are dependent on three chief sources of information : viz. (1.) on MANUSCRIPTS,—(2.) on VERSIONS,—(3.) on FATHERS. And it is even self-evident that the *most ancient* MSS.,—the *earliest* Versions,—the *oldest* of the Fathers, will probably be in every instance the most trustworthy witnesses.

2. Further, it is obvious that a really ancient Codex of the Gospels must needs supply more valuable critical help in establishing the precise Text of Scripture than can possibly be rendered by any Translation, however faithful : while Patristic citations are on the whole a less decisive authority, even than Versions. The reasons are chiefly these : — (*a.*) Fathers often quote Scripture loosely, if not licentiously ; and sometimes *allude* only when they seem to *quote*. (*b.*) They appear to have too often depended on their memory, and sometimes are demonstrably loose and inac-

[a] Chap. III.—VIII., also Chap. X.   [b] Chap. IX.

curate in their citations; the same Father being observed to quote the same place in different ways. (*c.*) Copyists and Editors may not be altogether depended upon for the exact form of such supposed quotations. Thus the evidence of Fathers must always be to some extent precarious.

3. On the other hand, it cannot be too plainly pointed out that when,—instead of certifying ourselves of the *actual words employed* by an Evangelist, their precise *form* and exact *sequence*, — our object is only to ascertain whether a considerable passage of Scripture is genuine or not; is to be rejected or retained; was known or was not known in the earliest ages of the Church; then, instead of supplying the least important evidence, Fathers become by far the most valuable witnesses of all. This entire subject may be conveniently illustrated by an appeal to the problem before us.

4. Of course, if we possessed copies of the Gospels coeval with their authors, nothing could compete with such evidence. But then unhappily nothing of the kind is the case. The facts admit of being stated within the compass of a few lines. We have one Codex (the Vatican, B) which is thought to belong to the first half of the ivth century; and another, the newly discovered Codex Sinaiticus, (at St. Petersburg, א) which is certainly not quite so old,—perhaps by 50 years. Next come two famous codices; the Alexandrine (in the British Museum, A) and the Codex Ephraemi (in the Paris Library, C), which are probably from 50 to 100 years more recent still. The Codex Bezae (at Cambridge, D) is considered by competent judges to be the depository of a recension of the text as ancient as any of the others. Notwithstanding its strangely depraved condition therefore,— the many "monstra potius quam variae lectiones" which it contains, — it may be reckoned with the preceding four, though it must be 50 or 100 years later than the latest of them. After this, we drop down, (as far as S. Mark is concerned,) to 2 uncial MSS. of the viiith century,—7 of the ixth,—4 of the ixth or x$^{th\ c}$, while cursives of the xith and xiith

---

^{c} Viz. E, L, [viii]: K, M, V, Γ, Δ, Λ (quære), Π (Tisch. *ed.* 8va.) [ix]: G, X, S, U [ix, x]. The following uncials are defective here,—F (ver. 9—19), H (ver. 9—14), I, N, O, P, Q, R, T, W, Y, Z.

centuries are very numerous indeed,—the copies increasing in number in a rapid ratio as we descend the stream of Time. Our primitive manuscript witnesses, therefore, are but *five* in number at the utmost. And of these it has never been pretended that the oldest is to be referred to an earlier date than the beginning of the ivth century, while it is thought by competent judges that the last named may very possibly have been written quite late in the vith.

5. Are we then reduced to this fourfold, (or at most fivefold,) evidence concerning the text of the Gospels,—on evidence of not quite certain date, and yet (as we all believe) not reaching further back than to the ivth century of our æra? Certainly not. Here, FATHERS come to our aid. There are perhaps as many as an hundred Ecclesiastical Writers older than the oldest extant Codex of the N. T.: while between A.D. 300 and A.D. 600, (within which limits our five oldest MSS. may be considered certainly to fall,) there exist about two hundred Fathers more. True, that many of these have left wondrous little behind them; and that the quotations from Holy Scripture of the greater part may justly be described as rare and unsatisfactory. But what then? From the three hundred, make a liberal reduction; and an hundred writers will remain who *frequently* quote the New Testament, and who, when they do quote it, are probably as trustworthy witnesses to the Truth of Scripture as either Cod. ℵ or Cod. B. We have indeed heard a great deal too much of the precariousness of this class of evidence: not nearly enough of the gross inaccuracies which disfigure the text of those two Codices. Quite surprising is it to discover to what an extent Patristic quotations from the New Testament have evidently retained their exact original form. What we chiefly desiderate at this time is a more careful revision of the text of the Fathers, and more skilfully elaborated indices of the works of each: *not one* of them having been hitherto satisfactorily indexed. It would be easy to demonstrate the importance of bestowing far more attention on this subject than it seems to have hitherto enjoyed: but I shall content myself with citing a single instance; and for this, (in order not to distract the reader's

attention), I shall refer him to the Appendix [d]. What is at least beyond the limits of controversy, whenever *the genuineness of a considerable passage of Scripture* is the point in dispute, the testimony of Fathers who undoubtedly recognise that passage, is beyond comparison the most valuable testimony we can enjoy.

6. For let it be only considered what is implied by a Patristic appeal to the Gospel. It amounts to this:— that a conspicuous personage, probably a Bishop of the Church,—one, therefore, whose history, date, place, are all more or less matter of notoriety,—gives us his written assurance that the passage in question was found in that copy of the Gospels which he was accustomed himself to employ; *the uncial codex*, (it has long since perished) *which belonged to himself*, or to the Church which he served. It is evident, in short, that any objection to quotations from Scripture in the writings of the ancient Fathers can only apply to the *form* of those quotations; not to their *substance*. It is just as certain that a verse of Scripture was actually read by the Father who unmistakedly refers to it, as if we had read it with him; even though the gravest doubts may be entertained as to the 'ipsissima verba' which were found in his own particular copy. He may have trusted to his memory: or copyists may have taken liberties with his writings: or editors may have misrepresented what they found in the written copies. The *form* of the quoted verse, I repeat, may have suffered almost to any extent. The *substance*, on the contrary, inasmuch as it lay wholly beyond their province, may be looked upon as an indisputable *fact*.

7. Some such preliminary remarks, (never out of place when quotations from the Fathers are to be considered,) cannot well be withheld when the most venerable Ecclesiastical writings are appealed to. The earliest of the Fathers are observed to quote with singular licence,—to *allude* rather than to quote. Strange to relate, those ancient men seem scarcely to have been aware of the grave responsibility they incurred when they substituted expressions of their own for the utterances of the SPIRIT. It is evidently not so much

---

[d] See Appendix (A), on the true reading of S. Luke ii. 14.

that their *memory* is in fault, as their *judgment*,—in that they evidently hold themselves at liberty to paraphrase, to recast, to reconstruct [e].

I. Thus, it is impossible to resist the inference that PAPIAS refers to S. Mark xvi. 18 when he records a marvellous tradition concerning "Justus surnamed Barsabas," "how that after drinking noxious poison, through the LORD's grace he experienced no evil consequence [f]." He does not give *the words* of the Evangelist. It is even surprising how completely he passes them by; and yet the allusion to the place just cited is manifest. Now, Papias is a writer who lived so near the time of the Apostles that he made it his delight to collect their traditional sayings. His date (according to Clinton) is A.D. 100.

II. JUSTIN MARTYR, the date of whose first Apology is A.D. 151, is observed to say concerning the Apostles that, after our LORD's Ascension,—ἐξελθόντες πανταχοῦ ἐκήρυξαν [g]: which is nothing else but a quotation from the last verse of S. Mark's Gospel,—ἐκεῖνοι δὲ ἐξελθόντες ἐκήρυξαν πανταχοῦ. And thus it is found that the conclusion of S. Mark's Gospel was familiarly known within fifty years of the death of the last of the Evangelists.

III. When IRENÆUS, in his third Book against Heresies, deliberately quotes and remarks upon the 19th verse of the last chapter of S. Mark's Gospel [h], we are put in possession of

---

[e] Consider how Ignatius (*ad Smyrn.*, c. 3) quotes S. Luke xxiv. 39; and how he refers to S. John xii. 3 in his Ep. *ad Ephes.* c. 17.

[f] Ἱστορεῖ [sc. Παπίας] ἕτερον παράδοξον περὶ Ἰοῦστον τὸν ἐπικληθέντα Βαρσαβᾶν γεγονὸς,—evidently a slip of the pen for Βαρσαβᾶν τὸν ἐπικληθέντα Ἰοῦστον (see Acts i. 23, quoted by Eusebius immediately afterwards,)—ὡς δηλητήριον φάρμακον ἐμπιόντος καὶ μηδὲν ἀηδὲς διὰ τὴν τοῦ Κυρίου χάριν ὑπομείναντος. Euseb. *Hist. Eccl.* iii. 39.

[g] *Apol.* I. c. 45.—The supposed quotations in c. 9 from the Fragment *De Resurrectione* (Westcott and others) are clearly references to S. Luke xxiv.,— *not* to S. Mark xvi.

[h] lib. iii. c. x. *ad fin.* (ed. Stieren, i. p. 462). "In fine autem Evangelii ait Marcus, *et quidem Dominus Jesus, postquam locutus est eis, receptus est in caelos, et sedet ad dexteram Dei.*" Accordingly, against S. Mark xvi. 19 in Harl. MS. 5647 (= Evan. 72) occurs the following marginal scholium, which Cramer has already published:—Εἰρηναῖος ὁ τῶν Ἀποστόλων πλησίον, ἐν τῷ πρὸς τὰς αἱρέσεις γ΄ λόγῳ τοῦτο ἀνήνεγκεν τὸ ῥητὸν ὡς Μάρκῳ εἰρημένον.

the certain fact that the entire passage now under consideration was extant in a copy of the Gospels which was used by the Bishop of the Church of Lyons sometime about the year A.D. 180, and which therefore cannot possibly have been written much more than a hundred years after the date of the Evangelist himself: while it *may* have been written by a contemporary of S. Mark, and probably *was* written by one who lived immediately after his time.—Who sees not that this single piece of evidence is in itself sufficient to outweigh the testimony of any codex extant? It is in fact a mere trifling with words to distinguish between "Manuscript" and "Patristic" testimony in a case like this: for (as I have already explained) the passage quoted from S. Mark's Gospel by Irenæus is to all intents and purposes *a fragment from a dated manuscript;* and *that* MS., demonstrably older by at least one hundred and fifty years than the oldest copy of the Gospels which has come down to our times.

IV. Take another proof that these concluding verses of S. Mark were in the second century accounted an integral part of his Gospel. HIPPOLYTUS, Bishop of Portus near Rome (190—227), a contemporary of Irenæus, quotes the 17th and 18th verses in his fragment Περὶ Χαρισμάτων[1].

---

[1] First published as his by Fabricius (vol. i. 245.) Its authorship has never been disputed. In the enumeration of the works of Hippolytus (inscribed on the chair of his marble effigy in the Lateran Museum at Rome) is read,—ΠΕΡΙ ΧΑΡΙΣΜΑΤΩΝ; and by that name the fragment in question is actually designated in the third chapter of the (so called) "Apostolical Constitutions," (τὰ μὲν οὖν πρῶτα τοῦ λόγου ἐξεθέμεθα περὶ τῶν Χαρισμάτων, κ.τ.λ.),—in which singular monument of Antiquity the fragment itself is also found. It is in fact nothing else but the first two chapters of the "Apostolical Constitutions;" of which the ivth chapter is also claimed for Hippolytus, (though with evidently far less reason,) and as such appears in the last edition of the Father's collected works, (*Hippolyti Romani quæ feruntur omnia Græce*, ed. Lagarde, 1858,)—p. 74.

The work thus assigned to Hippolytus, (evidently on the strength of the heading,—Διατάξεις τῶν αὐτῶν ἁγίων 'Αποστόλων περὶ χειροτονιῶν, διὰ 'Ιππολύτου,) is part of the "Octateuchus Clementinus," concerning which Lagarde has several remarks in the preface to his *Reliquiæ Juris Ecclesiastici Antiquissimæ*, 1856. The composition in question extends from p. 5 to p. 18 of the last-named publication. The exact correspondence between the "Octateuchus Clementinus" and the Pseudo-Apostolical Constitutions will be found to ex-of Carthage,—Acta Pilati,—Ap. Constitutions.

Also in his Homily on the heresy of Noetus [k], Hippolytus has a plain reference to this section of S. Mark's Gospel. To an inattentive reader, the passage alluded to might seem to be only the fragment of a Creed; but this is not the case. In the Creeds, CHRIST is *invariably* spoken of as ἀνελθόντα: in the Scriptures, *invariably* as ἀναληφθέντα [l]. So that when Hippolytus says of Him, ἀναλαμβάνεται εἰς οὐρανοὺς καὶ ἐκ δεξιῶν Πατρὸς καθίζεται, the reference must needs be to S. Mark xvi. 19.

V. At the Seventh COUNCIL OF CARTHAGE held under Cyprian, A.D. 256, (on the baptizing of Heretics,) Vincentius, Bishop of Thibari, (a place not far from Carthage,) in the presence of the eighty-seven assembled African bishops, quoted two of the verses under consideration [m]; and Augustine, about a century and a half later, in his reply, recited the words afresh [n].

VI. The Apocryphal ACTA PILATI (sometimes called the "Gospel of Nicodemus") Tischendorf assigns without hesitation to the iii[rd] century; whether rightly or wrongly I have no means of ascertaining. It is at all events a very ancient forgery, and it contains the 15th, 16th, 17th and 18th verses of this chapter [o].

VII. This is probably the right place to mention that ver. 15 is clearly alluded to in two places of the (so-called) "APOSTOLICAL CONSTITUTIONS [p];" and that verse 16 is quoted (with

tend no further than the single chapter (the iv[th]) specified in the text. In the meantime the fragment περὶ χαρισμάτων (containing S. Mark xvi. 17, 18,) is identical throughout. It forms the first article in Lagarde's *Reliquiæ*, extending from p. 1 to p. 4, and is there headed Διδασκαλία τῶν ἁγίων Ἀποστόλων περὶ χαρισμάτων.

[k] *Ad fin.* See Routh's *Opuscula*, i. p. 80.

[l] For which reason I cordially subscribe to Tischendorf's remark (ed. 8va. p. 407), "Quod idem [Justinus] Christum ἀνεληλυθότα εἰς τοὺς οὐράνους dicit, [*Apol.* I. c. 50?] minus valet."

[m] "In nomine meo manum imponite, daemonia expellite," (Cyprian *Opp.* p. 237 [*Reliqq. Sacr.* iii. p. 124,] quoting S. Mark xvi. 17, 18,)—"*In nomine meo daemonia ejicient* . . . . super egrotos *manus imponent* et bene habebunt."

[n] *Responsa ad Episcopos*, c. 44, (*Reliqq.* v. 248.)

[o] *Evangelia Apocrypha*, ed. Tischendorf, 1853, pp. 243 and 351: also *Proleg.* p. lvi.

[p] In *l.* vii. c. 7 (*ad fin.*),—λαβόντες ἐντολὴν παρ' αὐτοῦ κηρύξαι τὸ εὐαγγέλιον

no variety of reading from the *Textus receptus* [q]) in an earlier part of the same ancient work. The "Constitutions" are assigned to the iii^rd^ or the iv^th^ century [r].

VIII and IX. It will be shewn in Chapter V. that EUSEBIUS, the Ecclesiastical Historian, was profoundly well acquainted with these verses. He discusses them largely, and (as I shall prove in the chapter referred to) was by no means disposed to question their genuineness. His Church History was published A.D. 325.

MARINUS also, (whoever that individual may have been,) a contemporary of Eusebius,—inasmuch as he is introduced to our notice by Eusebius himself as asking a question concerning the last twelve verses of S. Mark's Gospel without a trace of misgiving as to the genuineness of that about which he inquires,—is a competent witness in their favor who has hitherto been overlooked in this discussion.

X. Tischendorf and his followers state that Jacobus Nisibenus quotes these verses. For "Jacobus Nisibenus" read "APHRAATES the Persian Sage," and the statement will be correct. The history of the mistake is curious.

Jerome, in his Catalogue of Ecclesiastical writers, makes no mention of Jacob of Nisibis,—a famous Syrian Bishop who was present at the Council of Nicæa, A.D. 325. Gennadius of Marseille, (who carried on Jerome's list to the year 495) asserts that the reason of this omission was Jerome's ignorance of the Syriac language; and explains that Jacob was the author of twenty-two Syriac Homilies [s]. Of these, there exists a very ancient Armenian translation; which was accordingly edited as the work of Jacobus Nisibenus with a Latin version, at Rome, in 1756. Gallandius reprinted both the Armenian and the Latin; and to Gallandius (vol. v.) we are referred whenever "Jacobus Nisibenus" is quoted.

εἰς ὅλον τὸν κόσμον: and in *l.* viii. *c.* 1,—ἡμῖν τοῖς ἀποστόλοις μέλλουσι τὸ εὐαγγέλιον καταγγέλλειν πάσῃ τῇ κτίσει. Observe, this immediately follows the quotation of verses 17, 18.

[q] *Lib.* vi. *c.* 15.—The quotation (at the beginning of *lib.* viii.) of the 17th and 18th verses, has been already noticed in its proper place. *Supra*, p. 24.

[r] Scrivener's *Introduction*, p. 421.

[s] *Apud* Hieron. *Opp. ed.* Vallars., ii. 951-4.

But the proposed attribution of the Homilies in question, —though it has been acquiesced in for nearly 1400 years,— is incorrect. Quite lately the Syriac originals have come to light, and they prove to be the work of Aphraates, "the Persian Sage,"—a Bishop, and the earliest known Father of the Syrian Church. In the first Homily, (which bears date A.D. 337), verses 16, 17, 18 of S. Mark xvi. are quoted [t],— yet not from the version known as the Curetonian Syriac, nor yet from the Peshito exactly [u].—Here, then, is another wholly independent witness to the last twelve verses of S. Mark, coeval certainly with the two oldest copies of the Gospel extant,—B and ℵ.

XI. AMBROSE, Archbishop of Milan (A.D. 374—397) freely quotes this portion of the Gospel,—citing ver. 15 four times: verses 16, 17 and 18, each three times: ver. 20, once [x].

XII. The testimony of CHRYSOSTOM (A.D. 400) has been all but overlooked. In part of a Homily claimed for him by his Benedictine Editors, he points out that S. Luke alone of the Evangelists describes the Ascension : S. Matthew and S. John not speaking of it,—S. Mark recording the event only. Then he quotes verses 19, 20. "This" (he adds) "is the end of the Gospel. Mark makes no extended mention of the Ascension [y]." Elsewhere he has an unmistakable reference to S. Mark xvi. 9 [z].

XIII. JEROME, on a point like this, is entitled to more attention than any other Father of the Church. Living at a very early period, (for he was born in 331 and died in 420,) — endowed with extraordinary Biblical learning, — a man of excellent judgment,—and a professed Editor of

---

[t] See Dr. Wright's ed. of "Aphraates," (4[to]. 1869,) i. p. 21. I am entirely indebted to the learned Editor's *Preface* for the information in the text.

[u] From Dr. Wright, and my brother Archdeacon Rose.

[x] Vol. i. 796 E and vol. ii. 461 D quote ver. 15 : 1429 B quotes ver. 15 and 16 : vol. ii. 663 B, C quotes ver. 15 to 18. Vol. i. 127 A quotes ver. 16 to 18. Vol. i. 639 E and vol. ii. 400 A quote ver. 17, 18. Vol. i. 716 A quotes ver. 20.

[y] *Opp.* iii. 765 A, B.

[z] Καὶ μὴν τὸ εὐαγγέλιον τοὐναντίον λέγει, ὅτι τῇ Μαρίᾳ πρώτῃ [ὤφθη]. Chrys. *Opp.* x. 355 B.

the New Testament, for the execution of which task he enjoyed extraordinary facilities, — his testimony is most weighty. Not unaware am I that Jerome is commonly supposed to be a witness on the opposite side: concerning which mistake I shall have to speak largely in Chapter V. But it ought to be enough to point out that we should not have met with these last twelve verses in the Vulgate, had Jerome held them to be spurious [a]. He familiarly quotes the 9th verse in one place of his writings [b]; in another place he makes the extraordinary statement that in certain of the copies, (especially the Greek,) was found after ver. 14 *the reply of the eleven Apostles,* when our SAVIOUR "upbraided them with their unbelief and hardness of heart, because they believed not them which had seen Him after He was risen [c]." To discuss so weak and worthless a forgery,—no trace of which is found in any MS. in existence, and of which nothing whatever is known except what Jerome here tells us,—would be to waste our time indeed. The fact remains, however, that Jerome, besides giving these last twelve verses a place in the Vulgate, quotes S. Mark xvi. 14, as well as ver. 9, in the course of his writings.

XIV. It was to have been expected that AUGUSTINE would quote these verses: but he more than quotes them. He brings them forward again and again [d],—discusses them as the work of S. Mark,—remarks that "in diebus Paschalibus," S. Mark's narrative of the Resurrection was publicly

---

[a] " Cogis " (he says to Pope Damasus) " ut post exemplaria Scripturarum toto orbe dispersa quasi quidam arbiter sedeam; et quia inter se variant, quae sint illa quae cum Graecâ consentiant veritate decernam.—Haec praesens praefatiuncula pollicetur quatuor Evangelia .... codicum Graecorum emendata conlatione, sed et veterum."

[b] Vol. i. p. 327 C (*ed.* Vallars.)

[c] *Contra Pelagianos,* II. 15, (Opp. ii. 744-5) :—" In quibusdam exemplaribus et maxime in Graecis codicibus, juxta Marcum in fine Evangelii scribitur : *Postea quum accubuissent undecim, apparuit eis Jesus, et exprobravit incredulitatem et duritiam cordis eorum, quia his qui viderant eum resurgentem, non crediderunt. Et illi satisfaciebant dicentes : Sæculum istud iniquitatis et incredulitatis substantia est, quae non sinit per immundos spiritus veram Dei apprehendi virtutem : idcirco jam nunc revela justitiam tuam.*"

[d] e.g. ver. 12 in vol. ii. 515 C (Ep. 149); Vol. v. 988 C.—Verses 15, 16, in vol. v. 391 E, 985 A : vol. x. 22 F.

read in the Church [e]. All this is noteworthy. Augustine flourished A.D. 395—430.

XV. and XVI. Another very important testimony to the genuineness of the concluding part of S. Mark's Gospel is furnished by the unhesitating manner in which NESTORIUS, the heresiarch, quotes ver. 20; and CYRIL OF ALEXANDRIA accepts his quotation, adding a few words of his own [f]. Let it be borne in mind that this is tantamount to the discovery of *two* dated codices containing the last twelve verses of S. Mark,—and *that* date *anterior* (it is impossible to say by how many years) to A.D. 430.

XVII. VICTOR OF ANTIOCH, (concerning whom I shall have to speak very largely in Chapter V.,) flourished about A.D. 425. The critical testimony which he bears to the genuineness of these verses is more emphatic than is to be met with in the pages of any other ancient Father. It may be characterized as the most conclusive testimony which it was in his power to render.

XVIII. HESYCHIUS of Jerusalem, by a singular oversight, has been reckoned among the impugners of these verses. He is on the contrary their eager advocate and champion. It seems to have escaped observation that towards the close of his "Homily on the Resurrection," (published in the works of Gregory of Nyssa, and erroneously ascribed to that Father,) Hesychius appeals to the 19th verse, and quotes it as S. Mark's at length [g]. The date of Hesychius is uncertain; but he may, I suppose, be considered to belong to the vi[th] century. His evidence is discussed in Chapter V.

XIX. This list shall be brought to a close with a reference to the SYNOPSIS SCRIPTURAE SACRAE,—an ancient work

---

[e] Vol. v. 997 F, 998 B, C.

[f] ἐξελθόντες γάρ, φησι, διεκήρυσσον τὸν λόγον πανταχοῦ. τοῦ Κυρίου συνεργοῦντος, καὶ τὸν λόγον βεβαιοῦντος, διὰ τῶν ἐπακολουθησάντων σημείων. Nestorius c. *Orthodoxos* : (Cyril. Alexand. *adv. Nestorian*. Opp. vol. vi. 46 B.) To which, Cyril replies,— τῇ παρ' αὐτοῦ δυναστείᾳ χρώμενοι, διεκηρύττοντο καὶ εἰργάζοντο τὰς θεοσημείας οἱ θεσπέσιοι μαθηταί. (*Ibid*. D.) This quotation was first noticed by Matthaei (*Enthym. Zig.* i. 161.)

[g] ὁμοίως δὲ καὶ τὸ παρὰ τῷ Μάρκῳ γεγραμμένον· Ὁ μὲν οὖν Κύριος—ἐκ δεξιῶν τοῦ Θεοῦ. Greg. Nyss. *Opp*. iii. 415.

ascribed to Athanasius [h], but probably not the production of that Father. It is at all events of much older date than any of the later uncials; and it rehearses in detail the contents of S. Mark xvi. 9—20 [i].

It would be easy to prolong this enumeration of Patristic authorities; as, by appealing to Gregentius in the vi[th] century, and to Gregory the Great, and Modestus, patriarch of Constantinople in the vii[th];—to Ven. Bede and John Damascene in the viii[th];—to Theophylact in the xi[th];—to Euthymius in the xii[th k]: but I forbear. It would add no strength to my argument that I should by such evidence support it; as the reader will admit when he has read my X[th] chapter.

It will be observed then that *three* competent Patristic witnesses of the ii[nd] century,—*four* of the iii[rd],—*six* of the iv[th],—*four* of the vth,—and *two* (of uncertain date, but probably) of the vi[th],—have admitted their familiarity with these "last Twelve Verses." Yet do they not belong to one particular age, school, or country. They come, on the contrary, from every part of the ancient Church: Antioch and

[h] Athanasii *Opp.* vol. ii. p. 181 F, 182 A. See the *Præfat.*, pp. vii., viii.

[i] In dismissing this enumeration, let me be allowed to point out that there must exist many more Patristic citations which I have overlooked. The necessity one is under, on occasions like the present, of depending to a great extent on "Indices," is fatal; so scandalously inaccurate is almost every Index of Texts that can be named. To judge from the Index in Oehler's edition of Tertullian, that Father quotes these twelve verses not less than eight times. According to the Benedictine Index, Ambrose does not quote them so much as once. Ambrose, nevertheless, quotes five of these verses no less than fourteen times; while Tertullian, as far as I am able to discover, does not quote S. Mark xvi. 9—20 at all.

Again. One hoped that the Index of Texts in Dindorf's new Oxford ed. of Clemens Alex. was going to remedy the sadly defective Index in Potter's ed. But we are still exactly where we were. S. John i. 3 (or 4), so remarkably quoted in vol. iii. 433, l. 8: S. John i. 18, 50, memorably represented in vol. iii. 412, l. 26: S. Mark i. 13, interestingly referred to in vol. iii. 455, lines 5, 6, 7: —are nowhere noticed in the Index. The Voice from Heaven at our SAVIOUR'S Baptism,—a famous misquotation (vol. i. 145, l. 14),—does not appear in the Index of quotations from S. Matthew (iii. 17), S. Mark (i. 11), or S. Luke (iii. 22.)

[k] Gregentius *apud* Galland. xi. 653 E.—Greg. Mag. (Hom. xxix. in Evang.) —Modestus *apud* Photium *cod.* 275.—Johannis Damasceni *Opp.* (ed. 1712) vol. i. 608 E.—Bede, and Theophylact (who quotes *all* the verses) and Euthymius *in loc.*

Constantinople,—Hierapolis, Cæsarea and Edessa,—Carthage, Alexandria and Hippo,—Rome and Portus. And thus, upwards of nineteen early codexes have been to all intents and purposes inspected for us in various lands by unprejudiced witnesses,—*seven* of them at least of more ancient date than the oldest copy of the Gospels extant.

I propose to recur to this subject for an instant when the reader has been made acquainted with the decisive testimony which ancient Versions supply. But the Versions deserve a short Chapter to themselves.

CHAPTER IV.

THE EARLY VERSIONS EXAMINED, AND FOUND TO YIELD UNFALTERING TESTIMONY TO THE GENUINENESS OF THESE VERSES.

The Peshito,—the Curetonian Syriac,—and the Recension of Thomas of Hharkel (111.)—*The Vulgate* (112)—*and the Vetus Itala* (113)—*the Gothic* (113)—*and the Egyptian Versions* (113).— *Review of the Evidence up to this point,* (114).

IT was declared at the outset that when we are seeking to establish in detail *the Text* of the Gospels, the testimony of Manuscripts is incomparably the most important of all. To early Versions, the second place was assigned. To Patristic citations, the third. But it was explained that whenever (as here) the only question to be decided is whether a considerable portion of Scripture be genuine or not, then, Patristic references yield to no class of evidence in importance. To which statement it must now be added that second only to the testimony of Fathers on such occasions is to be reckoned the evidence of the oldest of the Versions. The reason is obvious. (*a.*) We know for the most part the approximate date of the principal ancient Versions of the New Testament :—(*b.*) Each Version is represented by at least one very ancient Codex :— and (*c.*) It may be safely assumed that Translators were never dependant on a single copy of the original Greek when they executed their several Translations. Proceed we now to ascertain what evidence the oldest of the Versions bear concerning the concluding verses of S. Mark's Gospel : and first of all for the Syriac.

I. "Literary history," (says Mr. Scrivener,) " can hardly afford a more powerful case than has been established for the identity of the Version of the Syriac now called the 'PESHITO' with that used by the Eastern Church long before the great schism had its beginning, in the native land of the blessed Gospel." The Peshito is referred by common consent to the ii[nd] century of our æra; and is found to contain the verses in question.

II. This, however, is not all. Within the last thirty years, fragments of *another* very ancient Syriac translation of the Gospels, (called from the name of its discoverer "THE CURETONIAN SYRIAC,") have come to light[a]: and in this translation also the verses in question are found[b]. This fragmentary codex is referred by Cureton to the middle of the vth century. At what earlier date the Translation may have been executed,—as well as how much older the original Greek copy may have been which this translator employed,—can of course only be conjectured. But it is clear that we are listening to another truly primitive witness to the genuineness of the text now under consideration;—a witness (like the last) vastly more ancient than either the Vatican Codex B, or the Sinaitic Codex א; more ancient, therefore, than any Greek copy of the Gospels in existence. We shall not be thought rash if we claim it for the iii[rd] century.

III. Even this, however, does not fully represent the sum of the testimony which the Syriac language bears on this subject. Philoxenus, Monophysite Bishop of Mabug (Hierapolis) in Eastern Syria, caused a revision of the Peshito Syriac to be executed by his Chorepiscopus Polycarp, A.D. 508; and by the aid of three[c] approved and accurate Greek manuscripts, this revised version of Polycarp was again revised by Thomas of Hharkel, in the monastery of Antonia at Alexandria, A.D. 616. The Hharklensian Revision, (commonly called the "PHILOXENIAN,") is therefore an extraordinary monument of ecclesiastical antiquity indeed: for, being the Revision of a revised Translation of the New Testament known to have been executed from MSS. which must have been at least as old as the vth century, it ex-

[a] Dr. Wright informs me (1871) that some more leaves of this Version have just been recovered.

[b] By a happy providence, one of the fragments contains the last four verses.

[c] In the margin, against S. Matth. xxviii. 5, Thomas writes,—"*In tribus codicibus Græcis*, et in uno Syriaco antiquæ versionis, non inventum est nomen, 'Nazarenus.'"—Cf. ad xxvii. 35.—Adler's *N. T. Verss. Syrr.*, p. 97.

hibits the result of what may be called a collation of copies made at a time when only four of our extant uncials were in existence. Here, then, is a singularly important accumulation of manuscript evidence on the subject of the verses which of late years it has become the fashion to treat as spurious. And yet, neither by Polycarp nor by Thomas of Hharkel, are the last twelve verses of S. Mark's Gospel omitted [d].

To these, if I do not add the "Jerusalem version,"—(as an independent Syriac translation of the Ecclesiastical Sections, perhaps of the Vth century, is called [e],)—it is because our fourfold Syriac evidence is already abundantly sufficient. In itself, it far outweighs in respect of antiquity anything that can be shewn on the other side. Turn we next to the Churches of the West.

IV. That Jerome, at the bidding of Pope Damasus (A.D. 382), was the author of that famous Latin version of the Scriptures called THE VULGATE, is known to all. It seems scarcely possible to overestimate the critical importance of such a work,—executed at such a time,—under such auspices, —and by a man of so much learning and sagacity as Jerome. When it is considered that we are here presented with the results of a careful examination of the best Greek Manuscripts to which a competent scholar had access in the middle of the fourth century,—(and Jerome assures us that

---

[d] That among the 437 various readings and marginal notes on the Gospels relegated to the Philoxenian margin, should occur the worthless supplement which is only found besides in Cod. L. (see ch. viii.)—is not at all surprising. Of these 437 readings and notes, 91 are not found in White's Edition; while 105 (the supplement in question being one of them) are found in White only. This creates a suspicion that in part at least the Philoxenian margin must exhibit traces of the assiduity of subsequent critics of the Syriac text. (So Adler on S. Matth. xxvi. 40.) To understand the character of some of those marginal notes and annotations, the reader has but to refer to Adler's learned work, (pp. 79—134) and examine the notes on the following places:—S. Matth. xv. 21: xx. 28 (= D): xxvi. 7. S. Mk. i. 16: xii. 42. S. Lu. x. 17 (= B D): 42 (= B א L): xi. 1: 53. S. Jo. ii. 1 [3] (= א): iii. 26: vii. 39 (partly = B): x. 8, &c. &c.

[e] This work has at last been published in 2 vols. 4to., Verona, 1861-4, under the following title:—*Evangeliarium Hierosolymitanum ex Codice Vaticano Palaestino demprompsit, edidit, Latine vertit, Prolegomenis et Glossario adornavit,* Comes FRANCISCUS MINISCALCHI ERIZZO.

IV.]   *The old Latin, the Gothic, and the Egyptian.*   113

he consulted several,)—we learn to survey with diminished complacency our own slender stores (if indeed any at all exist) of corresponding antiquity. It is needless to add that the Vulgate contains the disputed verses: that from no copy of this Version are they away. Now, in such a matter as this, Jerome's testimony is very weighty indeed.

V. The Vulgate, however, was but the revision of a much older translation, generally known as the VETUS ITALA. This Old Latin, which is of African origin and of almost Apostolic antiquity, (supposed of the iind century,) conspires with the Vulgate in the testimony which it bears to the genuineness of the end of S. Mark's Gospel[f]:—an emphatic witness that in the African province, from the earliest time, no doubt whatever was entertained concerning the genuineness of these last twelve verses.

VI. The next place may well be given to the venerable version of the Gothic Bishop Ulphilas,—A.D. 350. Himself a Cappadocian, Ulphilas probably derived his copies from Asia Minor. His version is said to have been exposed to certain corrupting influences; but the unequivocal evidence which it bears to the last verses of S. Mark is at least unimpeachable, and must be regarded as important in the highest degree[g]. The oldest extant copy of the GOTHIC of Ulphilas is assigned to the vth or early in the vith century: and the verses in question are there also met with.

VII. and VIII. The ancient Egyptian versions call next for notice: their testimony being so exceedingly ancient and respectable. The MEMPHITIC, or dialect of Lower Egypt, (less properly called the "Coptic" version), which is assigned to the ivth or vth century, contains S. Mark xvi. 9—20.—Fragments of the THEBAIC, or dialect of Upper Egypt, (a distinct version and of considerably earlier date,

---

[f] It does not sensibly detract from the value of this evidence that *one* ancient codex, the "Codex Bobbiensis" (k), which Tregelles describes as "a revised text, in which the influence of ancient MSS. is discernible," [*Printed text*, &c. p. 170.] and which therefore may not be cited in the present controversy,—exhibits after ver. 8 a Latin translation of the spurious words which are also found in Cod. L.

[g] "Quod Gothicum testimonium haud scio an critici satis agnoverint, vel pro dignitate aestimaverint." Mai, *Nova Patt. Bibl.* iv. 256.

less properly called the "Sahidic,") survive in MSS. of very nearly the same antiquity: and one of these fragments happily contains the last verse of the Gospel according to S. Mark. The Thebaic version is referred to the iii[rd] century.

After this mass of evidence, it will be enough to record concerning the Armenian version, that it yields inconstant testimony: some of the MSS. ending at ver. 8; others putting after these words the subscription, (εὐαγγέλιον κατὰ Μάρκον,) and then giving the additional verses with a new subscription: others going on without any break to the end. This version may be as old as the vth century; but like the Ethiopic [iv—vii?] and the Georgian [vi?] it comes to us in codices of comparatively recent date. All this makes it impossible for us to care much for its testimony. The two last-named versions, whatever their disadvantages may be, at least bear constant witness to the genuineness of the verses in dispute.

1. And thus we are presented with a mass of additional evidence, — so various, so weighty, so multitudinous, so venerable,—in support of this disputed portion of the Gospel, that it might well be deemed in itself decisive.

2. For these Versions do not so much shew what individuals held, as what Churches have believed and taught concerning the sacred Text,—mighty Churches in Syria and Mesopotamia, in Africa and Italy, in Palestine and Egypt.

3. We may here, in fact, conveniently review the progress which has been hitherto made in this investigation. And in order to bar the door against dispute and cavil, let us be content to waive the testimony of Papias as precarious, and that of Justin Martyr as too fragmentary to be decisive. Let us frankly admit that the citation of Vincentius à Thibari at the vii[th] Carthaginian Council is sufficiently inexact to make it unsafe to build upon it. The "Acta Pilati" and the "Apostolical Constitutions," since their date is somewhat doubtful, shall be claimed for the iv[th] century only, and not for the iii[rd]. And now, how will the evidence stand for the last Twelve Verses of S. Mark's Gospel?

(*a*) In the vth century, to which Codex A and Codex C are referred, (for Codex D is certainly later,) at least three famous Greeks and the most illustrious of the Latin Fathers, —(*four* authorities in all,)—are observed to recognise these verses.

(*b*) In the iv[th] century, (to which Codex B and Codex ℵ probably belong, five Greek writers, one Syriac, and two Latin Fathers,—besides the Vulgate, Gothic and Memphitic Versions,—(*eleven* authorities in all,)—testify to familiar acquaintance with this portion of S. Mark's Gospel.

(*c*) In the iii[rd] century, (and by this time MS. evidence has entirely forsaken us,) we find Hippolytus, the Curetonian Syriac, and the Thebaic Version, bearing plain testimony that at that early period, in at least *three* distinct provinces of primitive Christendom, no suspicion whatever attached to these verses. Lastly,—

(*d*) In the ii[nd] century, Irenæus, the Peshito, and the Italic Version as plainly attest that in Gaul, in Mesopotamia and in the African province, the same verses were unhesitatingly received within a century (more or less) of the date of the inspired autograph of the Evangelist himself.

4. Thus, we are in possession of the testimony of *at least six* independent witnesses, of a date considerably anterior to the earliest extant Codex of the Gospels. They are all of the best class. They deliver themselves in the most unequivocal way. And their testimony to the genuineness of these Verses is unfaltering.

5. It is clear that nothing short of direct adverse evidence of the weightiest kind can sensibly affect so formidable an array of independent authorities as this. What must the evidence be which shall set it entirely aside, and induce us to believe, with the most recent editors of the inspired Text, that the last chapter of S. Mark's Gospel, as it came from the hands of its inspired author, ended abruptly at ver. 8 ?

The grounds for assuming that his "last Twelve Verses" are spurious, shall be exhibited in the ensuing chapter.

CHAPTER V.

THE ALLEGED HOSTILE WITNESS OF CERTAIN OF THE EARLY FATHERS PROVED TO BE AN IMAGINATION OF THE CRITICS.

The mistake concerning Gregory of Nyssa (117).—*The misconception concerning Eusebius* (119).—*The oversight concerning Jerome* (129);—*also concerning Hesychius of Jerusalem, (or else Severus of Antioch)* (135);—*and concerning Victor of Antioch* (137¹).

It would naturally follow to shew that manuscript evidence confirms the evidence of the ancient Fathers and of the early Versions of Scripture. But it will be more satisfactory that I should proceed to examine without more delay the testimony, which, (as it is alleged,) is borne by a cloud of ancient Fathers against the last twelve verses of S. Mark. "The absence of this portion from some, from many, or from most copies of his Gospel, or that it was not written by S. Mark himself," (says Dr. Tregelles,) "is attested by Eusebius, Gregory of Nyssa, Victor of Antioch, Severus of Antioch, Jerome, and by later writers, especially Greeks[a]." The same Fathers are appealed to by Dr. Davidson, who adds to the list Euthymius; and by Tischendorf and Alford, who add the name of Hesychius of Jerusalem. They also refer to "many ancient Scholia." "These verses" (says Tischendorf) "are not recognised by the sections of Ammonius nor by the Canons of Eusebius: Epiphanius and Cæsarius bear witness to the fact[b]." "In the Catenæ on Mark" (proceeds Davidson) "the section is not explained. Nor is there any trace of acquaintance with it on the part of Clement of Rome or Clement of Alexandria;"—a remark which others have made also; as if it were a surprising circumstance that Clement of Alexandria, who appears to have no reference to the last chapter of *S. Matthew's* Gospel, should

---

[a] *Account of the Printed Text*, p. 247.   [b] *Gr. Test.* p. 322.

be also without any reference to the last chapter of S. Mark's: as if, too, it were an extraordinary thing that Clement of Rome should have omitted to quote from the last chapter of S. Mark, — seeing that the same Clement does not quote from S. Mark's Gospel *at all*. .... The alacrity displayed by learned writers in accumulating hostile evidence, is certainly worthy of a better cause. Strange, that their united industry should have been attended with such very unequal success when their object was to exhibit the evidence *in favour of* the present portion of Scripture.

(1) Eusebius then, and (2) Jerome; (3) Gregory of Nyssa and (4) Hesychius of Jerusalem; (5) Severus of Antioch, (6) Victor of Antioch, and (7) Euthymius:—Do the accomplished critics just quoted,—Doctors Tischendorf, Tregelles, and Davidson, really mean to tell us that "it is attested" by these seven Fathers that the concluding section of S. Mark's Gospel "was not written by S. Mark himself?" Why, there is *not one* of them who says so : while some of them say the direct reverse. But let us go on. It is, I suppose, because there are Twelve Verses to be demolished that the list is further eked out with the names of (8) Ammonius, (9) Epiphanius, and (10) Cæsarius,—to say nothing of (11) the anonymous authors of Catenæ, and (12) "later writers, especially Greeks."

I. I shall examine these witnesses one by one : but it will be convenient in the first instance to call attention to the evidence borne by,

GREGORY OF NYSSA.

This illustrious Father is represented as expressing himself as follows in his second "Homily on the Resurrection [c]:"—
" In the more accurate copies, the Gospel according to Mark has its end at 'for they were afraid.' In some copies, however, this also is added,—'Now when He was risen early the first day of the week, He appeared first to Mary Magdalene, out of whom He had cast seven devils.'"

[c] Ἐν μὲν τοῖς ἀκριβεστέροις ἀντιγράφοις τὸ κατὰ Μάρκον εὐαγγέλιον μέχρι τοῦ ἐφοβοῦντο γὰρ, ἔχει τὸ τέλος. ἐν δέ τισι πρόσκειται καὶ ταῦτα ἀναστὰς δὲ πρωῒ πρώτῃ σαββάτων (sic) ἐφάνη πρῶτον Μαρίᾳ τῇ Μαγδαληνῇ ἀφ' ἧς ἐκβεβλήκει ἑπτὰ δαιμόνια. *Opp.* (ed. 1638) iii. 411 B.

That this testimony should have been so often appealed to as proceeding from Gregory of Nyssa [d], is little to the credit of modern scholarship. One would have supposed that the gravity of the subject,—the importance of the issue,—the sacredness of Scripture, down to its minutest jot and tittle,—would have ensured extraordinary caution, and induced every fresh assailant of so considerable a portion of the Gospel to be very sure of his ground before reiterating what his predecessors had delivered. And yet it is evident that not one of the recent writers on the subject can have investigated this matter for himself. It is only due to their known ability to presume that had they taken ever so little pains with the foregoing quotation, they would have found out their mistake.

(1.) For, in the first place, the second "Homily on the Resurrection" printed in the iii[rd] volume of the works of Gregory of Nyssa, (and which supplies the critics with their quotation,) is, as every one may see who will take the trouble to compare them, *word for word the same Homily* which Combefis in his "Novum Auctarium," and Gallandius in his "Bibliotheca Patrum" printed as the work of Hesychius, and vindicated to that Father, respectively in 1648 and 1776 [*]. Now, if a critic chooses to risk his own reputation by maintaining that the Homily in question is indeed by Gregory of Nyssa, and is not by Hesychius,—well and good. But since the Homily can have had but one author, it is surely high time that one of these two claimants should be altogether dropped from this discussion.

(2.) Again. Inasmuch as page after page of the same Homily is observed to reappear, *word for word*, under the name of "Severus of Antioch," and to be unsuspiciously printed as his by Montfaucon in his "Bibliotheca Coisliniana" (1715), and by Cramer in his "Catena [e]" (1844),—although it may very reasonably become a question among critics whether Hesychius of Jerusalem or Severus of An-

---

[d] Tregelles, *Printed Text*, p. 248, also in Horne's *Introd.* iv. 434-6. So Norton, Alford, Davidson, and the rest, following Wetstein, Griesbach, Scholz, &c.

[*] *Nov. Auct.* i. 743-74.—*Bibl. Vett. PP.* xi. 221-6.

[e] *Bibl. Coisl.* pp. 68-75.—*Catena*, i. 243-51.

tioch was the actual author of the Homily in question [f], yet it is plain that critics must make their election between the two names; and not bring them *both* forward. No one, I say, has any right to go on quoting "Severus" *and* "Hesychius,"—as Tischendorf and Dr. Davidson are observed to do:—"Gregory of Nyssa" *and* "Severus of Antioch,"—as Dr. Tregelles is found to prefer.

(3.) In short, here are three claimants for the authorship of one and the same Homily. To whichever of the three we assign it,—(and competent judges have declared that there are sufficient reasons for giving it to Hesychius rather than to Severus,—while *no one* is found to suppose that Gregory of Nyssa was its author,)—*who* will not admit that no further mention must be made of the other two?

(4.) Let it be clearly understood, therefore, that henceforth the name of "Gregory of Nyssa" must be banished from this discussion. So must the name of "Severus of Antioch." The memorable passage which begins,—"In the more accurate copies, the Gospel according to Mark has its end at 'for they were afraid,'"—is found in *a Homily which was probably written by Hesychius, presbyter of Jerusalem,—a writer of the vi*[th] *century.* I shall have to recur to his work by-and-by. The next name is

EUSEBIUS,

II. With respect to whom the case is altogether different. What that learned Father has delivered concerning the conclusion of S. Mark's Gospel requires to be examined with attention, and must be set forth much more in detail. And yet, I will so far anticipate what is about to be offered, as to say at once that if any one supposes that Eusebius has anywhere plainly "stated that it is *wanted in many MSS.* [g]," —he is mistaken. Eusebius nowhere says so. The reader's attention is invited to a plain tale.

It was not until 1825 that the world was presented by

---

[f] Dionysius Syrus (i.e. the Monophysite Jacobus Bar-Salibi [see Dean Payne Smith's *Cat. of Syrr. MSS.* p. 411] who died A.D. 1171) in his *Exposition of S. Mark's Gospel* (published at Dublin by Dudley Loftus, 1672, 4to.) seems (at p. 59) to give this homily to Severus.—I have really no independent opinion on the subject.   [g] Alford, *Greek Test.* i. p. 433.

120   *The lost work by Eusebius of "Quæstiones*   [CHAP.

Cardinal Angelo Mai [h] with a few fragmentary specimens of a lost work of Eusebius on the (so-called) Inconsistencies in the Gospels, from a MS. in the Vatican [i]. These, the learned Cardinal republished more accurately in 1847, in his "Nova Patrum Bibliotheca [k];" and hither we are invariably referred by those who cite Eusebius as a witness against the genuineness of the concluding verses of the second Gospel.

It is much to be regretted that we are still as little as ever in possession of the lost work of Eusebius. It appears to have consisted of three Books or Parts; the former two (addressed "to Stephanus") being discussions of difficulties at the beginning of the Gospel,—the last ("to Marinus") relating to difficulties in its concluding chapters [l]. The Author's plan, (as usual in such works), was, first, to set forth a difficulty in the form of a Question; and straightway, to propose a Solution of it,—which commonly assumes the form of a considerable dissertation. But whether we are at present in possession of so much as a single entire specimen of these "Inquiries and Resolutions" exactly as it came from the pen of Eusebius, may reasonably be doubted. That

[h] *Scriptorum Vett. Nova Collectio*, 4to. vol. i. pp. 1—101.
[i] At p. 217, (ed. 1847), Mai designates it as "Codex Vat. Palat. cxx pulcherrimus, sæculi ferme x." At p. 268, he numbers it rightly,—ccxx. We are there informed that the work of Eusebius extends from fol. 61 to 96 of the Codex.
[k] Vol. iv. pp. 219—309.
[l] See *Nova P. P. Bibliotheca*, iv. 255.—That it was styled "Inquiries with their Resolutions" (Ζητήματα καὶ Λύσεις), Eusebius leads us to suppose by himself twice referring to it under that name, (*Demonstr. Evang. lib.* vii. 3: also in the Preface to Marinus, *Mai*, iv. 255:) which his abbreviator is also observed to employ (*Mai*, iv. 219, 255.) But I suspect that he and others so designate the work only from the nature of its contents; and that its actual title is correctly indicated by Jerome,—*De Evangeliorum Diaphoniâ*: "Edidit" (he says) "de Evangeliorum Diaphoniâ," (*De Scriptt. Illustt.* c. 81.) Again, Διαφωνία Εὐαγγελίων, (*Hieron. in Matth.* i. 16.) Consider also the testimony of Latinus Latinius, given below, p. 44, note (q). 'Indicated' by Jerome, I say: for the entire title was probably, Περὶ τῆς δοκούσης ἐν τοῖς εὐαγγελίοις κ.τ.λ. διαφωνίας. The Author of the Catena on S. Mark edited by Cramer (i. p. 266), quotes an opinion of Eusebius ἐν τῷ πρὸς Μαρῖνον περὶ τῆς δοκούσης ἐν τοῖς εὐι , γελίοις περὶ τῆς ἀναστάσεως διαφωνίας: words which are extracted from the same MS. by Simon, *Hist. Crit. N. T.* p. 89.

the work which Mai has brought to light is but a highly condensed exhibition of the original, (and scarcely that,) its very title shews; for it is headed,—" An abridged selection from the 'Inquiries and Resolutions [of difficulties] in the Gospels' by Eusebius[m]." Only *some* of the original Questions, therefore, are here noticed at all: and even these have been subjected to so severe a process of condensation and abridgment, that in some instances *amputation* would probably be a more fitting description of what has taken place. Accordingly, what were originally two Books or Parts, are at present represented by XVI. "Inquiries," &c., addressed " to Stephanus;" while the concluding Book or Part is represented by IV. more, "to Marinus,"—of which, *the first* relates to our LORD's appearing to Mary Magdalene after His Resurrection. Now, since the work which Eusebius addressed to Marinus is found to have contained " Inquiries, with their Resolutions, concerning our SAVIOUR's *Death* and Resurrection[n]," —while a quotation professing to be derived from "the *thirteenth* chapter" relates to Simon the Cyrenian bearing our SAVIOUR's Cross [o];—it is obvious that the original work must have been very considerable, and that what Mai has recovered gives an utterly inadequate idea of its extent and importance[p]. It is absolutely neces-

[m] Ἐκλογὴ ἐν συντόμῳ ἐκ τῶν συντεθέντων ὑπὸ Εὐσεβίου πρὸς Στέφανον [and πρὸς Μαρῖνον] περὶ τῶν ἐν τοῖς Εὐαγγελίοις ζητημάτων καὶ λύσεων. *Ibid.* pp. 219, 255.—(See the plate of fac-similes facing the title of vol. i. ed. 1825.)

[n] Εὐσέβιος .... ἐν ταῖς πρὸς Μαρῖνον ἐπὶ ταῖς περὶ τοῦ θείου πάθους καὶ τῆς ἀναστάσεως ζητήσεσι καὶ ἐκλύσεσι, κ.τ.λ. I quote the place from the less known Catena of Cramer, (ii. 389,) where it is assigned to Severus of Antioch: but it occurs also in *Corderii Cat. in Joan.* p. 436. (See Mai, iv. 299.)

[o] This passage is too grand to be withheld:—Οὐ γὰρ ἦν ἄξιός τις ἐν τῇ πόλει Ἰουδαίων, (ὥς φησιν Εὐσέβιος κεφαλαίῳ ιγ' πρὸς Μαρῖνον,) τὸ κατὰ τοῦ διαβόλου τρόπαιον τὸν σταυρὸν βαστάσαι· ἀλλ' ὁ ἐξ ἀγροῦ, ὃς μηδὲν ἐπικεκοινώνηκε τῇ κατὰ Χριστοῦ μιαιφονίᾳ. (*Possini Cat. in Marcum,* p. 343.)

[p] Mai, iv. p. 299.—The Catenæ, inasmuch as their compilers are observed to have been very curious in such questions, are evidently full of *disjecta membra* of the work. These are recognisable for the most part by their form; but sometimes they actually retain the name of their author. Accordingly, Catenæ have furnished Mai with a considerable body of additional materials; which (as far as a MS. Catena of Nicetas on S. Luke, [Cod. A. *seu* Vat. 1611,] enabled him,) he has edited with considerable industry; throwing them into a kind of Supplement. (Vol. iv. pp. 268—282, and pp. 283—298.) It is only surprising

sary that all this should be clearly apprehended by any one who desires to know exactly what the alleged evidence of Eusebius concerning the last chapter of S. Mark's Gospel is worth,—as I will explain more fully by-and-by. Let it, however, be candidly admitted that there seems to be no reason for supposing that whenever the lost work of Eusebius comes to light, (and it has been seen within about 300 years[q],) it will exhibit anything essentially different from what is contained in the famous passage which has given rise to so much debate, and which may be exhibited in English as follows. It is put in the form of a reply to one "Marinus," who is represented as asking, first, the following question :—

"How is it, that, according to Matthew [xxviii. 1], the SAVIOUR appears to have risen 'in the end of the Sabbath;' but, according to Mark [xvi. 9], 'early the first day of the week'?"—Eusebius answers,

"This difficulty admits of a twofold solution. He who is for

that with the stores at his command, Mai has not contrived to enlighten us a little more on this curious subject. It would not be difficult to indicate sundry passages which he has overlooked. Neither indeed can it be denied that the learned Cardinal has executed his task in a somewhat slovenly manner. He does not seem to have noticed that what he quotes at pp. 357-8—262—283 —295, is to be found in the *Catena* of Corderius at pp. 448-9—449—450—457. —He quotes (p. 300) from an unedited Homily of John Xiphilinus, (*Cod. Vat.* p. 160,) what he might have found in Possinus ; and in Cramer too, (p. 446.) He was evidently unacquainted with Cramer's work, though it had been published 3 (if not 7) years before his own,—else, at p. 299, instead of quoting Simon, he would have quoted Cramer's *Catenæ*, i. 266.—It was in his power to solve his own shrewd doubt, (at p. 299,—concerning the text of a passage in Possinus, p. 343,) seeing that the Catena which Possinus published was transcribed by Corderius from a MS. in the Vatican. (Possini *Præfat.* p. ii.) In the Vatican, too, he might have found the fragment he quotes (p. 300) from p. 364 of the *Catena* of Possinus. In countless places he might, by such references, have improved his often manifestly faulty text.

[q] Mai quotes the following from Latinus Latinius (*Opp.* ii. 116.) to Andreas Masius. Sirletus (Cardinalis) "scire te vult in Siciliâ inventos esse ... libros tres Eusebii Cæsariensis *de Evangeliorum Diaphoniá*, qui ut ipse sperat brevi in lucem prodibunt." The letter is dated 1563.

I suspect that when the original of this work is recovered, it will be found that Eusebius digested his "Questions" *under heads* : e.g. περὶ τοῦ τάφου, καὶ τῆς δοκούσης διαφωνίας (p. 264) : περὶ τῆς δοκούσης περὶ τῆς ἀναστάσεως διαφωνίας. (p. 299.)

getting rid of the entire passage[r], will say that it is not met with in *all* the copies of Mark's Gospel : the accurate copies, at all events, making the end of Mark's narrative come after the words of the young man who appeared to the women and said, 'Fear not ye! Ye seek JESUS of Nazareth,' &c. : to which the Evangelist adds,—' And when they heard it, they fled, and said nothing to any man, for they were afraid.' For at those words, in almost all copies of the Gospel according to Mark, comes the end. What follows, (which is met with seldom, [and only] in some copies, certainly not in all,) might be dispensed with ; especially if it should prove to contradict the record of the other Evangelists. This, then, is what a person will say who is for evading and entirely getting rid of a gratuitous problem.

"But another, on no account daring to reject anything whatever which is, under whatever circumstances, met with in the text of the Gospels, will say that here are two readings, (as is so often the case elsewhere ;) and that *both* are to be received,—inasmuch as by the faithful and pious, *this* reading is not held to be genuine rather than *that* ; nor *that* than *this*."

It will be best to exhibit the whole of what Eusebius has written on this subject,—as far as we are permitted to know it,—continuously. He proceeds :—

" Well then, allowing this piece to be really genuine, our business is to interpret the sense of the passage [s]. And certainly, if I divide the meaning into two, we shall find that it is not opposed to what Matthew says of our SAVIOUR's having risen 'in the end of the Sabbath.' For Mark's ex-

---

[r] I translate according to the sense,—the text being manifestly corrupt. Τὴν τοῦτο φάσκουσαν περικοπήν is probably a gloss, explanatory of τὸ κεφάλαιον αὐτό. In strictness, the κεφάλαιον begins at ch. xv. 42, and extends to the end of the Gospel. There are 48 such κεφάλαια in S. Mark. But this term was often loosely employed by the Greek Fathers, (as "capitulum" by the Latins,) to denote *a passage* of Scripture, and it is evidently so used here. Περικοπή, on the contrary, in this place seems to have its true technical meaning, and to denote the liturgical *section*, or "lesson."

[s] Ἀνάγνωσμα (like περικοπή, spoken of in the foregoing note,) seems to be here used in its technical sense, and to designate the liturgical *section*, or "lectio." See Suicer, *in voce.*

pression, ('Now when He was risen early the first day of the week,') we shall read with a pause, putting a comma after 'Now when He was risen,'—the sense of the words which follow being kept separate. Thereby, we shall refer [Mark's] 'when He was risen' to Matthew's 'in the end of the Sabbath,' (for it was *then* that He *rose*); and all that comes after, expressive as it is of a distinct notion, we shall connect with what follows; (for it was '*early*, the first day of the week,' that 'He *appeared to Mary Magdalene*.') This is in fact what John also declares; for he too has recorded that 'early,' 'the first day of the week,' [JESUS] appeared to the Magdalene. Thus then Mark also says that He appeared to her early: not that He *rose* early, but long before, (according to that of Matthew, 'in the end of the Sabbath:' for though He *rose* then, He did not *appear to Mary* then, but 'early.') In a word, two distinct seasons are set before us by these words: first, the season of the Resurrection,—which was 'in the end of the Sabbath;' secondly, the season of our SAVIOUR's Appearing,—which was 'early.' The former[t], Mark writes of when he says, (it requires to be read with a pause,)—' Now, when He was risen.' Then, after a comma, what follows is to be spoken,—'Early, the first day of the week, He appeared to Mary Magdalene, out of whom He had cast seven devils[u].'"— Such is the entire passage. Little did the learned writer anticipate what bitter fruit his words were destined to bear!

1. Let it be freely admitted that what precedes is calculated at first sight to occasion nothing but surprise and perplexity. For, in the first place, there really is *no problem to solve*. The discrepancy suggested by "Marinus" at the outset, is plainly imaginary, the result (chiefly) of a strange misconception of the meaning of the Evangelist's Greek, —as in fact no one was ever better aware than Eusebius himself. "These places of the Gospels would never have occasioned any difficulty," he writes in the very next page,

---

[t] The text of Eusebius seems to have experienced some disarrangement and depravation here.

[u] Mai, *Bibl. P.P. Nova*, iv. 255-7. For purposes of reference, the original of this passage is given in the Appendix (B).

(but it is the commencement of his reply to the *second* question of Marinus,)—"if people would but abstain from assuming that Matthew's phrase (ὀψὲ σαββάτων) refers to *the evening of the Sabbath-day* : whereas, (in conformity with the established idiom of the language,) it obviously refers to an advanced period of the ensuing night [v]." He proceeds:—"The self-same moment therefore, or very nearly the self-same, is intended by the Evangelists, only under different names : and there is no discrepancy whatever between Matthew's,—'in the end of the Sabbath, as it began to dawn toward the first day of the week,' and John's— 'The first day of the week cometh Mary Magdalen early, when it was yet dark.' The Evangelists indicate by different expressions one and the same moment of time, but in a broad and general way." And yet, if Eusebius knew all this so well, why did he not say so at once, and close the discussion? I really cannot tell; except on one hypothesis, —which, although at first it may sound somewhat extraordinary, the more I think of the matter, recommends itself to my acceptance the more. I suspect, then, that the discussion we have just been listening to, is, essentially, *not an original production* : but that Eusebius, having met with the suggestion in some older writer, (in Origen probably,) reproduced it in language of his own,—doubtless because he thought it ingenious and interesting, but not by any means because he regarded it as true. Except on some such theory, I am utterly unable to understand how Eusebius can have written so inconsistently. His admirable remarks just quoted, are obviously a full and sufficient answer,—the proper answer in fact,—to the proposed difficulty : and it is a memorable circumstance that the ancients generally were so sensible of this, that they are found to have *invariably* [x] substituted

---

[v] Mai, iv. 257. So far, I have given the substance only of what Eusebius delivers with wearisome prolixity. It follows,—ὥστε τὸν αὐτὸν σχεδὸν νοεῖσθαι καιρὸν, ἢ τὸν σφόδρα ἐγγὺς, παρὰ τοῖς εὐαγγελισταῖς διαφόροις ὀνόμασι τετηρημένον. μηδέν τε διαφέρειν Ματθαῖον ἰρηκότα " ὀψὲ—τάφον" [xxviii. 1.] Ἰωάννου φήσαντος "τῇ δὲ μιᾷ—ἔτι οὔσης σκοτίας." [xx. 1.] πλατυκῶς γὰρ ἕνα καὶ τὸν αὐτὸν δηλοῦσι χρόνον διαφόροις ῥήμασι.—For the principal words in the text, see the Appendix (B) *ad fin.*

[x] I allude to the following places :—Combefis, *Novum Auctarium*, col. 780.

what Eusebius wrote in reply to the *second* question of Marinus for what he wrote in reply to *the first;* in other words, for the dissertation which is occasioning us all this difficulty.

2. But next, even had the discrepancy been real, the remedy for it which is here proposed, and which is advocated with such tedious emphasis, would probably prove satisfactory to no one. In fact, the entire method advocated in the foregoing passage is hopelessly vicious. The writer begins by advancing statements which, if he believed them to be true, he must have known are absolutely fatal to the verses in question. This done, he sets about discussing the possibility of reconciling an isolated expression in S. Mark's Gospel with another in S. Matthew's: just as if on *that* depended the genuineness or spuriousness of the entire context: as if, in short, the major premiss in the discussion were some such postulate as the following:—" Whatever in one Gospel cannot be proved to be entirely consistent with something in another Gospel, is not to be regarded as genuine." Did then the learned Archbishop of Cæsarea really suppose that a comma judiciously thrown into the empty scale might at any time suffice to restore the equilibrium, and even counterbalance the adverse testimony of almost every MS. of the Gospels extant? Why does he not at least deny the truth of the alleged facts to which he began by giving currency, if not approval; and which, so long as they are allowed to stand uncontradicted, render all further argumentation on the subject simply nugatory? As before, I really cannot tell,—except on the hypothesis which has been already hazarded.

3. Note also, (for this is not the least extraordinary feature of the case,) what vague and random statements those are which we have been listening to. The entire section

—Cod. Mosq. 138, (printed by Matthaei, *Anectt. Græc.* ii. 62.)—also Cod. Mosq. 139, (see N. T. ix. 223-4.)—Cod. Coislin. 195 *fol.* 165.—Cod. Coislin. 23, (published by Cramer, *Catt.* i. 251.)—Cod. Bodl. ol. Meerman Auct. T. i. 4, *fol.* 169.—Cod. Bodl. Laud. Gr. 33, *fol.* 79.—Any one desirous of knowing more on this subject will do well to begin by reading Simon *Hist. Crit. du N. T.* p. 89. See Mai's foot-note, iv. p. 257.

(S. Mark xvi. 9—20,) "*is not met with in all* the copies:" at all events *not "in the accurate"* ones. Nay, it is "*met with seldom.*" In fact, it is *absent from " almost all "* copies. But, —Which of these four statements is to stand? The first is comparatively unimportant. Not so the second. The last two, on the contrary, would be absolutely fatal,—if trustworthy? But *are* they trustworthy?

To this question only one answer can be returned. The exaggeration is so gross that it refutes itself. Had it been merely asserted that the verses in question were wanting in *many* of the copies,—even had it been insisted that *the best copies* were without them,—well and good: but to assert that, in the beginning of the fourth century, from "*almost all*" copies of the Gospels they were away,—is palpably untrue. What had become then of the MSS. from which the Syriac, the Latin, *all* the ancient Versions were made? How is the contradictory evidence of *every copy of the Gospels in existence but two* to be accounted for? With Irenæus and Hippolytus, with the old Latin and the Vulgate, with the Syriac, and the Gothic, and the Egyptian versions to refer to, we are able to assert that the author of such a statement was guilty of monstrous exaggeration. We are reminded of the loose and random way in which the Fathers,—(giants in Interpretation, but very children in the Science of Textual Criticism,)—are sometimes observed to speak about the state of the Text in their days. We are reminded, for instance, of the confident assertion of an ancient Critic that the true reading in S. Luke xxiv. 13 is not "three-score" but "*an hundred* and three-score;" for that so "the accurate copies" used to read the place, besides Origen and Eusebius. And yet (as I have elsewhere explained) the reading ἑκατὸν καὶ ἑξήκοντα is altogether impossible. "Apud nos mixta sunt omnia," is Jerome's way of adverting to an evil which, serious as it was, was yet not nearly so great as he represents; viz. the unauthorized introduction into one Gospel of what belongs of right to another. And so in a multitude of other instances. The Fathers are, in fact, constantly observed to make critical remarks about the ancient copies which simply *cannot* be correct.

And yet the author of the exaggeration under review, be it observed, is clearly *not Eusebius*. It is evident that *he* has nothing to say against the genuineness of the conclusion of S. Mark's Gospel. Those random statements about the copies with which he began, do not even purport to express his own sentiments. Nay, Eusebius in a manner repudiates them; for he introduces them with a phrase which separates them from himself: and, "This then is what a person will say,"—is the remark with which he finally dismisses them. It would, in fact, be to make this learned Father stultify himself to suppose that he proceeds gravely to discuss a portion of Scripture which he had already deliberately rejected as spurious. But, indeed, the evidence before us effectually precludes any such supposition. "Here are two readings," he says, "(as is so often the case elsewhere;) *both* of which are to be received,—inasmuch as by the faithful and pious, *this* reading is not held to be genuine rather than *that*; nor *that* than *this*." And thus we seem to be presented with the actual opinion of Eusebius, as far as it can be ascertained from the present passage,—if indeed he is to be thought here to offer any personal opinion on the subject at all; which, for my own part, I entirely doubt. But whether we are at liberty to infer the actual sentiments of this Father from anything here delivered or not, quite certain at least is it that to print only the first half of the passage, (as Tischendorf and Tregelles have done,) and then to give the reader to understand that he is reading the adverse testimony of Eusebius as to the genuineness of the end of S. Mark's Gospel, is nothing else but to misrepresent the facts of the case; and, however unintentionally, to deceive those who are unable to verify the quotation for themselves.

It has been urged indeed that Eusebius cannot have recognised the verses in question as genuine, because a scholium purporting to be his has been cited by Matthaei from a Catena at Moscow, in which he appears to assert that "according to Mark," our SAVIOUR "is not recorded to have appeared to His Disciples after His Resurrection:" whereas in S. Mark xvi. 14 it is plainly recorded that "Afterwards

He appeared unto the Eleven as they sat at meat." May I be permitted to declare that I am distrustful of the proposed inference, and shall continue to feel so, until I know something more about the scholium in question? Up to the time when this page is printed I have not succeeded in obtaining from Moscow the details I wish for: but they must be already on the way, and I propose to embody the result in a "Postscript" which shall form the last page of the Appendix to the present volume.

Are we then to suppose that there was no substratum of truth in the allegations to which Eusebius gives such prominence in the passage under discussion? By no means. The mutilated state of S. Mark's Gospel in the Vatican Codex (B) and especially in the Sinaitic Codex (א) sufficiently establishes the contrary. Let it be freely conceded, (but in fact it has been freely conceded already,) that there must have existed in the time of Eusebius *many* copies of S. Mark's Gospel which were without the twelve concluding verses. I do but insist that there is nothing whatever in that circumstance to lead us to entertain one serious doubt as to the genuineness of these verses. I am but concerned to maintain that there is nothing whatever in the evidence which has hitherto come before us,—certainly not *in the evidence of Eusebius*,—to induce us to believe that they are a spurious addition to S. Mark's Gospel.

III. We have next to consider what

JEROME

has delivered on this subject. So great a name must needs command attention in any question of Textual Criticism: and it is commonly pretended that Jerome pronounces emphatically against the genuineness of the last twelve verses of the Gospel according to S. Mark. A little attention to the actual testimony borne by this Father will, it is thought, suffice to exhibit it in a wholly unexpected light; and induce us to form an entirely different estimate of its practical bearing upon the present discussion.

It will be convenient that I should premise that it is in one of his many exegetical Epistles that Jerome discusses this matter. A lady named Hedibia, inhabiting the furthest extremity of Gaul, and known to Jerome only by the ardour of her piety, had sent to prove him with hard questions. He resolves her difficulties from Bethlehem [y]: and I may be allowed to remind the reader of what is found to have been Jerome's practice on similar occasions,—which, to judge from his writings, were of constant occurrence. In fact, Apodemius, who brought Jerome the Twelve problems from Hedibia, brought him Eleven more from a noble neighbour of hers, Algasia [z]. Once, when a single messenger had conveyed to him out of the African province a quantity of similar interrogatories, Jerome sent two Egyptian monks the following account of how he had proceeded in respect of the inquiry,—(it concerned 1 Cor. xv. 51,)—which they had addressed to him:—" Being pressed for time, I have presented you with the opinions of all the Commentators; for the most part, translating their very words; in order both to get rid of your question, and to put you in possession of ancient authorities on the subject." This learned Father does not even profess to have been in the habit of delivering his own opinions, or speaking his own sentiments on such occasions. " This has been hastily dictated," he says in conclusion,—(alluding to his constant practice, which was to dictate, rather than to write,)— "in order that I might lay before you what have been the opinions of learned men on this subject, as well as the arguments by which they have recommended their opinions. My own authority, (who am but nothing,) is vastly inferior to that of our predecessors in the LORD." Then, after special commendation of the learning of Origen and Eusebius, and the valuable Scriptural expositions of many more,— " My plan," (he says,) " is to read the ancients; to prove all things, to hold fast that which is good; and to abide stedfast in the faith of the Catholic Church.—I must now dictate replies, either original or at second-hand, to other Questions which lie before me [a]." We are not surprised, after this straightforward avowal of what was the method

---

[y] Ep. cxx. *Opera*, (ed. Vallars.) vol. i. pp. 811–43.

[z] *Ibid.* p. 844.

[a] *Ibid.* p. 793–810. See especially pp. 794, 809, 810.

v.] *He is shewn to be here a Copyist of Eusebius.* 131

on such occasions with this learned Father, to discover that, instead of hearing Jerome addressing *Hedibia*,—(who had interrogated him concerning the very problem which is at present engaging our attention,)—we find ourselves only listening to *Eusebius* over again, addressing *Marinus*.

"This difficulty admits of a two-fold solution," Jerome begins; as if determined that no doubt shall be entertained as to the source of his inspiration. Then, (making short work of the tedious disquisition of Eusebius,)—" Either we shall reject the testimony of Mark, which is met with in scarcely any copies of the Gospel,—almost all the Greek codices being without this passage:—(especially since it seems to narrate what contradicts the other Gospels:)—or else, we shall reply that both Evangelists state what is true: Matthew, when he says that our LORD rose 'late in the week:' Mark,—when he says that Mary Magdalene saw Him 'early, the first day of the week.' For the passage must be thus pointed,—' When He was risen:' and presently, after a pause, must be added,—' Early, the first day of the week, He appeared to Mary Magdalene.' He therefore who had risen late in the week, according to Matthew,—Himself, early the first day of the week, according to Mark, appeared to Mary Magdalene. And this is what John also means, shewing that it was early on the next day that He appeared."—To understand how faithfully in what precedes Jerome treads in the footsteps of Eusebius, it is absolutely necessary to set the Latin of the one over against the Greek of the other, and to compare them. In order to facilitate this operation, I have subjoined both originals at foot of the page: from which it will be apparent that Jerome is here not so much adopting the sentiments of Eusebius as simply *translating his words*[b].

[b] "Hujus quæstionis duplex solutio est. [Τούτου διττὴ ἂν εἴη ἡ λύσις.] Aut enim non recipimus Marci testimonium, quod in raris fertur [σπανίως ἔν τισι φερόμενα] Evangeliis, omnibus Græciæ libris pene hoc capitulum [τὸ κεφάλαιον αὐτὸ] in fine non habentibus; [ἐν τουτῷ γὰρ σχεδὸν ἐν ἅπασι τοῖς ἀντιγράφοις τοῦ κατὰ Μάρκον εὐαγγελίου περιγέγραπται τὸ τέλος]; præsertim cum diversa atque contraria Evangelistis ceteris narrare videntur [μάλιστα εἴπερ ἔχοιεν ἀντιλογίαν τῇ τῶν λοιπῶν εὐαγγελιστῶν μαρτυρίᾳ.] Aut hoc respondendum, quod uterque verum dixerit [ἑκατέραν παραδεκτέαν ὑπάρχειν...συγχωρουμένου

This, however, is not by any means the strangest feature of the case. That Jerome should have availed himself ever so freely of the materials which he found ready to his hand in the pages of Eusebius cannot be regarded as at all extraordinary, after what we have just heard from himself of his customary method of proceeding. It would of course have suggested the gravest doubts as to whether we were here listening to the personal sentiment of this Father, or not; but that would have been all. What are we to think, however, of the fact that *Hedibia's question to Jerome* proves on inspection to be nothing more than a translation of *the very question which Marinus had long before addressed to Eusebius?* We read on, perplexed at the coincidence; and speedily make the notable discovery that her next question, and her next, are *also* translations *word for word* of the next two of Marinus. For the proof of this statement the reader is again referred to the foot of the page[c]. It is at least decisive:

εἶναι ἀληθοῦς.] Matthæus, quando Dominus surrexerit vespere sabbati: Marcus autem, quando tum viderit Maria Magdalena, id est, mane prima sabbati. Ita enim distinguendum est, Cum autem resurrexisset: [μετὰ διαστολῆς ἀναγνωστέον 'Αναστὰς δέ:] et, parumper, spiritu coarctato inferendum, Prima sabbati mane apparuit Mariæ Magdalenæ: [εἶτα ὑποστίξαντες ῥητέον, Πρωῒ τῇ μιᾷ τῶν σαββάτων ἐφάνη Μαρίᾳ τῇ Μαγδαληνῇ.] Ut qui vespere sabbati, juxta Matthæum surrexerat, [παρὰ τῷ Ματθαίῳ, ὀψὲ σαββάτων· τοτε γὰρ ἐγήγερτο.] ipse mane prima sabbati, juxta Marcum, apparuerit Mariæ Magdalenæ. [πρωῒ γὰρ τῇ μιᾷ τοῦ σαββάτου ἐφάνη Μαρίᾳ τῇ Μαγδαληνῇ.] Quod quidem et Joannes Evangelista significat, mane Eum alterius diei visum esse demonstrans." [τοῦτο γοῦν ἐδήλωσε καὶ ὁ 'Ιωάννης πρωῒ καὶ αὐτὸς τῇ μιᾷ τοῦ σαββάτου ὦφθαι αὐτὸν μαρτυρήσας.]

For the Latin of the above, see *Hieronymi Opera*, (ed. Vallars.) vol. i. p. 819: for the Greek, with its context, see Appendix (B).

[c] ἠρώτας τὸ πρῶτον,—Πῶς παρὰ μὲν τῷ Ματθαίῳ ὀψὲ σαββάτων φαίνεται ἐγεγερμένος ὁ Σωτήρ, παρὰ δὲ τῷ Μάρκῳ πρωῒ τῇ μιᾷ τῶν σαββάτων; [Eusebius *ad Marinum*, (Mai, iv. 255.)]

Primum quæris,—Cur Matthæus dixerit, vespere autem Sabbati illucescente in una Sabbate Dominum resurrexisse; et Marcus mane resurrectionem ejus factam esse commemorat. [Hieronymus *ad Hedibiam*, (Opp. i. 818-9.)]

Πῶς, κατὰ τὸν Ματθαῖον, ὀψὲ σαββάτων ἡ Μαγδαληνὴ τεθεαμένη τὴν ἀνάστασιν, κατὰ τὸν 'Ιωάννην ἡ αὐτὴ ἑστῶσα κλαίει παρὰ τῷ μνημείῳ τῇ μιᾷ τοῦ σαββάτου. [*Ut supra*, p. 257.]

Quomodo, juxta Matthæum, vespere Sabbati, Maria Magdalene vidit Dominum resurgentem; et Joannes Evangelista refert eam mane una sabbati juxta sepulcrum flere? [*Ut supra*, p. 819.]

and the fact, which admits of only one explanation, can be attended by only one practical result. It of course shelves the whole question as far as the evidence of Jerome is concerned. Whether Hedibia was an actual personage or not, let those decide who have considered more attentively than it has ever fallen in my way to do that curious problem,— What was the ancient notion of the allowable in Fiction? That different ideas have prevailed in different ages of the world as to where fiction ends and fabrication begins;—that widely discrepant views are entertained on the subject even in our own age;—all must be aware. I decline to investigate the problem on the present occasion. I do but claim to have established beyond the possibility of doubt or cavil that what we are here presented with *is not the testimony of Jerome at all.* It is evident that this learned Father amused himself with translating for the benefit of his Latin readers a part of the (lost) work of Eusebius; (which, by the way, he is found to have possessed in the same abridged form in which it has come down to ourselves:)—and he seems to have regarded it as allowable to attribute to "Hedibia" the problems which he there met with. (He may perhaps have known that Eusebius before him had attributed them, with just as little reason, to "Marinus.") In that age, for aught that appears to the contrary, it may have been regarded as a graceful compliment to address solutions of Scripture difficulties to persons of distinction, who possibly had never heard of those difficulties before; and even to represent the Interrogatories which suggested them as originating with themselves. I offer this only in the way of suggestion, and am not concerned to defend it. The only point I am concerned to establish is that Jerome is here a *translator*, not an original author: in other words, that it is *Eusebius* who here speaks, and not Jerome. For a critic to pretend that it

Πῶς, κατὰ τὸν Ματθαῖον, ὀψὲ σαββάτων ἡ Μαγδαληνὴ μετὰ τῆς ἄλλης Μαρίας ἀψαμένη τῶν ποδῶν τοῦ Σωτῆρος, ἡ αὐτὴ πρωῒ τῇ μιᾷ τοῦ σαββάτου ἀκούει μή μου ἅπτου, κατὰ τὸν Ἰωάννην. [*Ut suprà*, p. 262.]

Quomodo, juxta Matthæum, Maria Magdalene vespere Sabbati cum alterâ Mariâ advoluta sit pedibus Salvatoris; cum, secundum Joannem, audierit à Domino, Noli me tangere. [*Ut suprà*, p. 821.]

is in *any* sense the testimony of Jerome which we are here presented with; that Jerome is one of those Fathers "who, even though they copied from their predecessors, were yet competent to transmit the record of a fact[d],"—is entirely to misunderstand the case. The man who translates,—not adopts, but *translates,—the problem* as well as its solution: who deliberately asserts that it emanated from a Lady inhabiting the furthest extremity of Gaul, who nevertheless was demonstrably not its author: who goes on to propose as hers question after question *verbatim as he found them written in the pages of Eusebius;* and then resolves them one by one *in the very language of the same Father:*—such a writer has clearly conducted us into a region where his individual responsibility quite disappears from sight. We must hear no more about Jerome, therefore, as a witness against the genuineness of the concluding verses of S. Mark's Gospel.

On the contrary. Proof is at hand that Jerome held these verses to be genuine. The proper evidence of this is supplied by the fact that he gave them a place in his revision of the old Latin version of the Scriptures. If he had been indeed persuaded of their absence from "*almost all the Greek codices,*" does any one imagine that he would have suffered them to stand in the Vulgate? If he had met with them in "*scarcely any copies of the Gospel,*"—do men really suppose that he would yet have retained them? To believe this would, again, be to forget what was the known practice of this Father; who, because he found the expression "without a cause" ($\epsilon i\kappa\acute{\eta}$,—S. Matth. v. 22,) only "in certain of his codices," but not "in the true ones," *omitted* it from the Vulgate. Because, however, he read "righteousness" (where we read "alms") in S. Matth. vi. 1, he exhibits "*justitiam*" in his revision of the old Latin version. On the other hand, though he knew of MSS. (as he expressly relates) which read "works" for "children" ($\H{\epsilon}\rho\gamma\omega\nu$ for $\tau\acute{\epsilon}\kappa\nu\omega\nu$) in S. Matth. xi. 19, he does not admit that (manifestly corrupt) reading,—which, however, is found both in the Codex Vaticanus and the Codex Sinaiticus. Let this suffice. I forbear to press the matter further. It is an additional proof that Jerome accepted the

---

[d] Tregelles, *Printed Text*, p. 247.

conclusion of S. Mark's Gospel that he actually quotes it, and on more than one occasion: but to prove this, is to prove more than is here required [e]. I am concerned only to demolish the assertion of Tischendorf, and Tregelles, and Alford, and Davidson, and so many more, concerning the testimony of Jerome; and I have demolished it. I pass on, claiming to have shewn that the name of Jerome as an adverse witness must never again appear in this discussion.

IV. and V. But now, while the remarks of Eusebius are yet fresh in the memory, the reader is invited to recal for a moment what the author of the "Homily on the Resurrection," contained in the works of Gregory of Nyssa (above, p. 39), has delivered on the same subject. It will be remembered that we saw reason for suspecting that not

SEVERUS OF ANTIOCH, but

HESYCHIUS OF JERUSALEM,

(both of them writers of the vi[th] century,) has the better claim to the authorship of the Homily in question [f],—which, however, cannot at all events be assigned to the illustrious Bishop of Nyssa, the brother of Basil the Great. "In the more accurate copies," (says this writer,) "the Gospel according to Mark has its end at 'for they were afraid.' In some copies, however, this also is added,—'Now when He was risen early the first day of the week, He appeared first to Mary Magdalene, out of whom He had cast seven devils.' This, however, seems to contradict to some extent what we before delivered; for since it happens that the hour of the night when our SAVIOUR rose is not known, how does it come to be here written that He rose 'early?' But the saying will prove to be no ways contradictory, if we read with skill. We must be careful intelligently to introduce a comma after, 'Now when He was risen:' and then to proceed,—'Early in the Sabbath He appeared first to Mary Magdalene:' in order that 'when He was risen' may refer (in conformity with what Matthew says) to the foregoing season; while 'early' is connected with the appearance to Mary."*—I presume it would be to abuse a reader's patience to offer any remarks on all this. If a careful perusal of the foregoing passage

[e] See above, p. 28.   [f] See above, p. 40-1.   * See the Appendix (C) § 2.

does not convince him that Hesychius is here only reproducing what he had read in Eusebius, nothing that I can say will persuade him of the fact. The *words* indeed are by no means the same; but the sense is altogether identical. He seems to have also known the work of Victor of Antioch. However, to remove all doubt from the reader's mind that the work of Eusebius was in the hands of Hesychius while he wrote, I have printed in two parallel columns and transferred to the Appendix what must needs be conclusive [g]; for it will be seen that the terms are only not identical in which Eusebius and Hesychius discuss that favourite problem with the ancients,—the consistency of S. Matthew's ὀψὲ τῶν σαββάτων with the πρωὶ of S. Mark.

It is, however, only needful to read through the Homily in question to see that it is an attempt to weave into one piece a quantity of foreign and incongruous materials. It is in fact not a Homily at all, (though it has been thrown into that form;) but a Dissertation,—into which, Hesychius, (who is known to have been very curious in questions of that kind [h],) is observed to introduce solutions of most of those famous difficulties which cluster round the sepulchre of the world's Redeemer on the morning of the first Easter Day [i]; and which the ancients seem to have delighted in discussing,—as, the number of the Marys who visited the sepulchre; the angelic appearances on the morning of the Resurrection; and above all the seeming discrepancy, already adverted to, in the Evangelical notices of the time at which our LORD rose from the dead. I need not enter more particularly into an examination of this (so-called) 'Homily': but I must not dismiss it without pointing out that its author

---

[g] See the Appendix (C) § 1.—For the statement in line 5, see § 2.

[h] In the *Eccl. Græc. Monumenta* of Cotelerius, (iii. 1—53,) may be seen the discussion of 60 problems, headed,—Συναγωγή ἀποριῶν καὶ ἐπιλύσεων, ἐκλεγεῖσα ἐν ἐπιτομῇ ἐκ τῆς εὐαγγελικῆς συμφωνίας τοῦ ἁγίου Ἡσυχίου πρεσβυτέρου Ἱεροσολύμων. From this it appears that Hesychius, following the example of Eusebius, wrote a work on "Gospel Harmony,"—of which nothing but an abridgment has come down to us.

[i] He says that he writes,—Πρὸς τὴν τοῦ ὑποκειμένου προβλήματος λύσιν, καὶ τῶν ἄλλων τῶν κατὰ τὴν ἐξέτασιν τῶν ῥητῶν ἀναφυομένων ζητήσεων, κ.τ.λ. Greg. Nyss. *Opp.* iii. 400 c.

at all events cannot be thought to have repudiated the concluding verses of S. Mark: for at the end of his discourse, he quotes the 19th verse entire, without hesitation, in confirmation of one of his statements, and declares that the words are written by S. Mark [k].

I shall not be thought unreasonable, therefore, if I contend that Hesychius is no longer to be cited as a witness in this behalf: if I point out that it is entirely to misunderstand and misrepresent the case to quote *a passing allusion of his to what Eusebius had long before delivered on the same subject*, as if it exhibited his own individual teaching. It is demonstrable[1] that he is not bearing testimony to the condition of the MSS. of S. Mark's Gospel in his own age: neither, indeed, is he bearing testimony *at all*. He is simply amusing himself, (in what is found to have been his favourite way,) with reconciling an apparent discrepancy in the Gospels; and he does it by adopting certain remarks of Eusebius. Living so late as the vi[th] century; conspicuous neither for his judgment nor his learning; a copyist only, so far as his remarks on the last verses of S. Mark's Gospel are concerned;—this writer does not really deserve the space and attention we have been compelled to bestow upon him.

VI. We may conclude, by inquiring for the evidence borne by

VICTOR OF ANTIOCH.

And from the familiar style in which this Father's name is always introduced into the present discussion, no less than from the invariable practice of assigning to him the date "A.D. 401," it might be supposed that "Victor of Antioch" is a well-known personage. Yet is there scarcely a Commentator of antiquity about whom less is certainly known. Clinton (who enumerates cccxxii "Ecclesiastical Authors" from A.D. 70 to A.D. 685[m]) does not even record his name. The recent "Dictionary of Greek and Roman Biography" is just as silent concerning him. Cramer (his latest editor)

---

[k] ὁμοίως δὲ καὶ τὸ παρὰ τῷ Μάρκῳ γεγραμμένον· Ὁ μὲν οὖν Κύριος, κ.τ.λ. Greg. Nyss. *Opp.* iii. 415 D.—See above, p. 29, note (g).

[1] See below, chap. X.

[m] *Fasti Romani*, vol. ii. Appendix viii. pp. 395—495.

calls his very existence in question; proposing to attribute his Commentary on S. Mark to Cyril of Alexandria[n]. Not to delay the reader needlessly,—Victor of Antioch is an interesting and unjustly neglected Father of the Church; whose date,—(inasmuch as he apparently quotes sometimes from Cyril of Alexandria who died A.D. 444, and yet seems to have written soon after the death of Chrysostom, which took place A.D. 407), may be assigned to the first half of the vth century,—suppose A.D. 425—450. And in citing him I shall always refer to the best (and most easily accessible) edition of his work,—that of Cramer (1840) in the first volume of his "Catenae."

But a far graver charge is behind. From the confident air in which Victor's authority is appealed to by those who deem the last twelve verses of S. Mark's Gospel spurious, it would of course be inferred that his evidence is hostile to the verses in question; whereas his evidence to their genuineness is the most emphatic and extraordinary on record. Dr. Tregelles asserts that "his *testimony* to the absence of these twelve verses from some or many copies, stands in contrast to his own *opinion* on the subject." But Victor delivers *no* "opinion:" and his "testimony" is the direct reverse of what Dr. Tregelles asserts it to be. This learned and respected critic has strangely misapprehended the evidence[o].

I must needs be brief in this place. I shall therefore confine myself to those facts concerning "Victor of Antioch," or rather concerning his work, which are necessary for the purpose in hand [p].

Now, his Commentary on S. Mark's Gospel,—as all must see who will be at the pains to examine it,—is to a great extent a compilation. The same thing may be said, no doubt, to some extent, of almost every ancient Commentary in existence. But I mean, concerning this particular work,

---

[n] Vol. i. *Præfat.* p. xxviii. See below, note (p).

[o] "Victor Antiochenus" (writes Dr. Tregelles in his N. T. vol. i. p. 214,) "dicit ὅτι νενόθευται τὸ παρὰ Μάρκῳ τελευταῖον ἔν τισι φερόμενον."

[p] For additional details concerning Victor of Antioch, and his work, the studious in such matters are referred to the Appendix (D).

that it proves to have been the author's plan not so much
to give the general results of his acquaintance with the
writings of Origen, Apollinarius, Theodorus of Mopsuestia,
Eusebius, and Chrysostom; as, with or without acknowledgment, to transcribe largely (but with great license)
from one or other of these writers. Thus, the whole of his
note on S. Mark xv. 38, 39, is taken, without any hint that
it is not original, (much of it, *word for word*,) from Chrysostom's 88th Homily on S. Matthew's Gospel[q]. The
same is to be said of the first twelve lines of his note on
S. Mark xvi. 9. On the other hand, the latter half of the
note last mentioned professes to give the substance of what
Eusebius had written on the same subject. It is in fact an
extract from those very "Quaestiones ad Marinum" concerning which so much has been offered already. All this,
though it does not sensibly detract from the interest or the
value of Victor's work, must be admitted entirely to change
the character of his supposed evidence. He comes before
us rather in the light of a Compiler than of an Author: his
work is rather a "Catena" than a Commentary; and as
such in fact it is generally described. Quite plain is it, at
all events, that the sentiments contained in the sections last
referred to, are *not Victor's at all*. For one half of them,
no one but Chrysostom is responsible: for the other half, no
one but Eusebius.

But it is Victor's familiar use of the writings of Eusebius,
—especially of those Resolutions of hard Questions "concerning the seeming Inconsistencies in the Evangelical accounts
of the Resurrection," which Eusebius addressed to Marinus,
—on which the reader's attention is now to be concentrated.
Victor cites that work of Eusebius *by name* in the very *first*
page of his Commentary. That his *last* page also contains
a quotation from it, (also *by name*), has been already pointed
out[r]. Attention is now invited to what is found concerning
S. Mark xvi. 9—20 in the *last page but one* (p. 444) of

---

[q] *Opp.* vol. vii. p. 825 E—826 B: or, in Field's edition, p. 527, line 3 to 20.

[r] Cramer, i. p. 266, lines 10, 11,—ὥς φησιν Εὐσέβιος ὁ Καισαρείας ἐν τῷ πρὸς Μαρῖνον κ.τ.λ. And at p. 446, line 19,—Εὐσεβιός φησιν ὁ Καισαρείας κ.τ.λ.

140   *Victor of Antioch also shewn*   [CHAP.

Victor's work. It shall be given in English; because I will convince unlearned as well as learned readers. Victor, (after quoting four lines from the 89th Homily of Chrysostom [s]), reconciles (exactly as Eusebius is observed to do [t]) the notes of time contained severally in S. Matth. xxviii. 1, S. Mark xvi. 2, S. Luke xxiv. 1, and S. John xx. 1. After which, he proceeds as follows:—

"In certain copies of Mark's Gospel, next comes,—'Now when [JESUS] was risen early the first day of the week, He appeared to Mary Magdalene;'—a statement which seems inconsistent with Matthew's narrative. This might be met by asserting, that the conclusion of Mark's Gospel, though found in certain copies, is spurious, However, that we may not seem to betake ourselves to an off-hand answer, we propose to read the place thus:—'Now when [JESUS] was risen:' then, after a comma, to go on,—'early the first day of the week He appeared to Mary Magdalene.' In this way we refer [Mark's] 'Now when [JESUS] was risen' to Matthew's 'in the end of the sabbath,' (for *then* we believe Him to have *risen;*) and all that comes after, expressive as it is of a different notion, we connect with what follows. Mark relates that He who '*arose* (according to Matthew) *in the end of the Sabbath,*' *was seen* by Mary Magdalene '*early.*' This is in fact what John also declares; for he too has recorded that 'early,' 'the first day of the week,' [JESUS] appeared to the Magdalene. In a word, two distinct seasons are set before us by these words: first, the season of the Resurrection,—which was 'in the end of the Sabbath;' secondly, the season of our SAVIOUR's Appearing,—which was 'early [u].'"

No one, I presume, can read this passage and yet hesitate to admit that he is here listening to Eusebius "ad Marinum" over again. But if any one really retains a particle of doubt on the subject, he is requested to cast his eye to the foot of the present page; and even an unlearned reader,

---

[s] Compare Cramer's *Vict. Ant.* i. p. 444, line 6—9, with Field's *Chrys.* iii. p. 539, line 7—21.

[t] Mai, iv. p. 257-8.

[u] Cramer, vol. i. p. 444, line 19 to p. 445, line 4.

surveying the originals with attention, may easily convince himself that *Victor is here nothing else but a copyist* [x]. That the work in which Eusebius reconciles " seeming discrepancies in the Evangelical narratives," was actually lying open before Victor while he wrote, is ascertained beyond dispute. He is observed in his next ensuing Comment to quote from it, and to mention Eusebius as its author. At the end of the present note he has a significant allusion to Eusebius:—

[x] The following is the original of what is given above:—'Επειδὴ δέ ἔν τισι τῶν ἀντιγράφων πρόσκειται τῷ παρόντι εὐαγγελίῳ, "ἀναστὰς δὲ τῇ μιᾷ τοῦ σαββάτου πρωΐ, ἐφάνη (see below *) Μαρίᾳ τῇ Μαγδαληνῇ," δοκεῖ δὲ τοῦτο διαφωνεῖν τῷ ὑπὸ Ματθαίου εἰρημένῳ, ἐροῦμεν ὡς δυνατὸν μὲν εἰπεῖν ὅτι νενόθευται τὸ παρὰ Μάρκῳ τελευταῖον ἔν τισι φερόμενον. πλὴν ἵνα μὴ δόξωμεν ἐπὶ τὸ ἕτοιμον καταφεύγειν, οὕτως ἀναγνωσόμεθα· "ἀναστὰς δὲ," καὶ ὑποστίξαντες ἐπάγωμεν, "πρωΐ τῇ μιᾷ τοῦ σαββάτου ἐφάνη Μαρίᾳ τῇ Μαγδαληνῇ." ἵνα [*The extract from* VICTOR *is continued below in the right hand column: the left exhibiting the text of* EUSEBIUS *'ad Marinum.'*]

(EUSEBIUS.)
τὸ μὲν "ἀναστὰς," ἀν[απέμψωμεν?] ἐπὶ τὴν παρὰ τῷ Ματθαίῳ "ὀψὲ σαββάτων." (τότε γὰρ ἐγήγερτο.) τὸ δὲ ἑξῆς, ἑτέρας ὃν διανοίας ὑποστατικὸν, συνάψωμεν τοῖς ἐπιλεγομένοις.

("πρωΐ" γὰρ "τῇ μιᾷ τοῦ σαββάτου ἐφάνη Μαρίᾳ τῇ Μαγδαληνῇ.")

τοῦτο γοῦν ἐδήλωσε καὶ ὁ Ἰωάννης "πρωΐ" καὶ αὐτὸς "τῇ μιᾷ τοῦ σαββάτου" ὦφθαι αὐτὸν τῇ Μαγδαληνῇ μαρτυρήσας.
[31 words are here omitted.]
ὡς παρίστασθαι ἐν τούτοις καιροὺς δύο· τὸν μὲν γὰρ τῆς ἀναστάσεως τὸν "ὀψὲ τοῦ σαββάτου." τὸν δὲ τῆς τοῦ Σωτῆρος ἐπιφανείας, τὸν "πρωΐ."
[EUSEBIUS, *apud Mai,* iv. p. 256.]

(VICTOR.)
τὸ μὲν "ἀναστὰς," ἀναπέμψωμεν ἐπὶ τὴν παρὰ τῷ Ματθαίῳ "ὀψὲ σαββάτων." (τότε γὰρ ἐγηγέρθαι αὐτὸν πιστεύομεν.) τὸ δὲ ἑξῆς, ἑτέρας ὃν διανοίας παραστατικὸν, συνάψωμεν τοῖς ἐπιλεγομένοις·

(τὸν γὰρ "ὀψὲ σαββάτων" κατὰ Ματθαῖον ἐγηγερμένον ἱστορεῖ "πρωΐ" ἑωρακέναι Μαρίαν τὴν Μαγδαληνήν.)

τοῦτο γοῦν ἐδήλωσε καὶ ὁ Ἰωάννης, "πρωΐ" καὶ αὐτὸς "τῇ μιᾷ τῶν σαββάτων" ὦφθαι αὐτὸν τῇ Μαγδαληνῇ μαρτυρήσας.

ὡς παρίστασθαι ἐν τούτοις καιροὺς δύο· τὸν μὲν τῆς ἀναστάσεως, τὸν "ὀψὲ τοῦ σαββάτου·" τὸν δὲ τῆς τοῦ Σωτῆρος ἐπιφανείας, τὸ "πρωΐ."
[VICTOR ANTIOCH., ed. *Cramer,* i. p. 444-5: (*with a few slight emendations of the text from* Evan. Cod. Reg. 178.)]

* Note, that Victor *twice* omits the word πρῶτον, and *twice* reads τῇ μιᾷ τοῦ σαββάτου, (instead of πρώτῃ σαββάτου), *only because Eusebius had inadvertently* (three times) *done the same thing* in the place from which Victor is copying. See Mai *Nova P.P. Bibl.* iv. p. 256, line 19 and 26: p. 257 line 4 and 5.

"I know very well," he says, "what has been suggested *by those who are at the pains to remove the apparent inconsistencies in this place*ʸ." But when writing on S. Mark xvi. 9—20, he does more. After abridging, (as his manner is,) what Eusebius explains with such tedious emphasis, (giving the substance of five columns in about three times as many lines,) he adopts the exact expressions of Eusebius,—follows him in his very mistakes,—and finally transcribes his words. The reader is therefore requested to bear in mind that what he has been listening to is *not the testimony of Victor at all:* but *the testimony of Eusebius*. This is but one more echo therefore of a passage of which we are all beginning by this time to be weary; so exceedingly rash are the statements with which it is introduced, so utterly preposterous the proposed method of remedying a difficulty which proves after all to be purely imaginary.

What then *is* the testimony of Victor? Does he offer any independent statement on the question in dispute, from which his own private opinion (though nowhere stated) may be lawfully inferred? Yes indeed. Victor, though frequently a Transcriber only, is observed every now and then to come forward in his own person, and deliver his individual sentimentᶻ. But nowhere throughout his work does he deliver such remarkable testimony as in this place. Hear him!

"*Notwithstanding that in very many copies of the present Gospel, the passage beginning, 'Now when* [JESUS] *was risen early the first day of the week, He appeared first to Mary Magdalene,' be not found,—(certain individuals having supposed it to be spurious,)—yet* WE, AT ALL EVENTS, INASMUCH AS IN VERY MANY WE HAVE DISCOVERED IT TO EXIST, HAVE, OUT OF ACCURATE COPIES, SUBJOINED ALSO THE ACCOUNT OF OUR LORD'S ASCENSION, (FOLLOWING THE WORDS 'FOR THEY WERE AFRAID,') IN CONFORMITY WITH THE PALESTINIAN EXEMPLAR OF MARK

ʸ οὐκ ἀγνοῶ δὲ ὡς διαφόρους ὀπτασίας γεγενῆσθαί φασιν οἱ τὴν δοκοῦσαν διαφωνίαν διαλῦσαι σπουδάζοντες. Vict. Ant. ed. *Cramer*, vol. i. p. 445, l. 23-5: referring to what Eusebius says *apud Mai*, iv. 264 and 265 (§ iiii): 287—290 (§§ v, vi, vii).

ᶻ e.g. in the passage last quoted.

WHICH EXHIBITS THE GOSPEL VERITY: THAT IS TO SAY, FROM THE WORDS, 'NOW WHEN [JESUS] WAS RISEN EARLY THE FIRST DAY OF THE WEEK,' &c., DOWN TO 'WITH SIGNS FOLLOWING. AMEN [a]."—And with these words Victor of Antioch brings his Commentary on S. Mark to an end.

Here then we find it roundly stated by a highly intelligent Father, writing in the first half of the vth century,—

(1.) That the reason why the last Twelve Verses of S. Mark are absent from some ancient copies of his Gospel is *because they have been deliberately omitted by Copyists:*

(2.) That the ground for such omission was the *subjective judgment* of individuals,—*not* the result of any appeal to documentary evidence. Victor, therefore, clearly held that the Verses in question had been *expunged* in consequence of their (seeming) inconsistency with what is met with in the other Gospels:

(3.) That he, on the other hand, had convinced himself by reference to "very many" and "accurate" copies, that the verses in question are genuine:

(4.) That in particular the Palestinian Copy, which enjoyed the reputation of "exhibiting the genuine text of S. Mark," contained the Verses in dispute.—To *Opinion*, therefore, Victor opposes *Authority*. He makes his appeal to the most trustworthy documentary evidence with which he is acquainted; and the deliberate testimony which he delivers is a complete counterpoise and antidote to the loose phrases of Eusebius on the same subject:

(5.) That in consequence of all this, following the Palestinian Exemplar, he had from accurate copies *furnished his own work with the Twelve Verses in dispute;*—which is a categorical refutation of the statement frequently met with that the work of Victor of Antioch is *without* them.

We are now at liberty to sum up; and to review the progress which has been hitherto made in this Inquiry.

Six Fathers of the Church have been examined who are commonly represented as bearing hostile testimony to the last Twelve Verses of S. Mark's Gospel; and they have been

[a] For the original of this remarkable passage the reader is referred to the Appendix (E).

easily reduced to *one*. Three of them, (Hesychius, Jerome, Victor,) prove to be echoes, not voices. The remaining two, (Gregory of Nyssa and Severus,) are neither voices nor echoes, but merely *names*: GREGORY OF NYSSA having really no more to do with this discussion than Philip of Macedon; and "Severus" and "Hesychius" representing one and the same individual. Only by a Critic seeking to mislead his reader will any one of these five Fathers be in future cited as witnessing against the genuineness of S. Mark xvi. 9—20. Eusebius is the solitary witness who survives the ordeal of exact inquiry [b]. But,

I. EUSEBIUS, (as we have seen), instead of proclaiming his distrust of this portion of the Gospel, enters upon an elaborate proof that its contents are not inconsistent with what is found in the Gospels of S. Matthew and S. John. His testimony is reducible to two innocuous and wholly unconnected propositions: the first,—That there existed in his day a vast number of copies in which the last chapter of S. Mark's Gospel ended abruptly at ver. 8; (the correlative of which of course would be that there also existed a vast number which were furnished with the present ending.) The second,—That by putting a comma after the word ʼΑναστάς, S. Mark xvi. 9, is capable of being reconciled with S. Matth. xxviii. 1 [c]. . . . . I profess myself unable to understand how it can be pretended that Eusebius would have subscribed to the opinion of Tischendorf, Tregelles, and the rest, that the Gospel of S. Mark was never finished by its inspired Author, or was mutilated before it came abroad; at all events, that the last Twelve Verses are spurious.

---

[b] How shrewdly was it remarked by Matthaei, eighty years ago,—"Scholia certe, in quibus de integritate hujus loci dubitatur, omnia *ex uno fonte promanarunt*. Ex eodem fonte Hieronymum etiam hausisse intelligitur ex ejus loco quem laudavit Wetst. ad ver. 9.—Similiter Scholiastæ omnes in principio hujus Evangelii in disputatione de lectione ἐν ἡσαΐᾳ τῷ προφήτῃ ex uno pendent. *Fortasse Origenes auctor est hujus dubitationis.*" (N. T. vol. ii. p. 270.) —The reader is invited to remember what was offered above in p. 47 (line 23.)

[c] It is not often, I think, that one finds in MSS. a point actually inserted after ʼΑναστὰς δέ. Such a point is found, however, in Cod. 34 (= Coisl. 195,) and Cod. 22 (= Reg. 72,) and doubtless in many other copies.

II. The observations of Eusebius are found to have been adopted, and in part transcribed, by an unknown writer of the vi[th] century,—whether HESYCHIUS or SEVERUS is not certainly known: but if it were Hesychius, then it was not Severus; if Severus, then not Hesychius. This writer, however, (whoever he may have been,) is careful to convince us that individually he entertained *no doubt whatever* about the genuineness of this part of Scripture, for he says that he writes in order to remove the (hypothetical) objections of others, and to silence their (imaginary) doubts. Nay, he freely *quotes the verses as genuine*, and declares that they were read in his day on a certain Sunday night in the public Service of the Church. . . . To represent such an one,—(it matters nothing, I repeat, whether we call him "Hesychius of Jerusalem" or "Severus of Antioch,")—as a hostile witness, is simply to misrepresent the facts of the case. He is, on the contrary, the strenuous champion of the verses which he is commonly represented as impugning.

III. As for JEROME, since that illustrious Father comes before us in this place as a *translator* of Eusebius only, he is no more responsible for what Eusebius says concerning S. Mark xvi. 9—20, than Hobbes of Malmesbury is responsible for anything that Thucydides has related concerning the Peloponnesian war. Individually, however, it is certain that Jerome was convinced of the genuineness of S. Mark xvi. 9—20: for in two different places of his writings he not only quotes the 9th and 14th verses, but he exhibits all the twelve in the Vulgate.

IV. Lastly, VICTOR OF ANTIOCH, who wrote in an age when Eusebius was held to be an infallible oracle on points of Biblical Criticism, — having dutifully rehearsed, (like the rest,) the feeble expedient of that illustrious Father for harmonizing S. Mark xvi. 9 with the narrative of S. Matthew, —is observed to cite the statements of Eusebius concerning *the last Twelve Verses* of S. Mark, only in order to refute them. Not that he opposes opinion to opinion,—(for the opinions of Eusebius and of Victor of Antioch on this behalf were probably identical;) but statement he meets with counter-statement,—fact he confronts with fact. Scarcely can anything be imagined more emphatic than his testimony, or more conclusive.

For the reader is requested to observe that here is an Ecclesiastic, writing in the first half of the vth century, who *expressly witnesses to the genuineness* of the Verses in dispute. He had made reference, he says, and ascertained their existence in very many MSS. (ὡς ἐν πλείστοις). He had derived his text from "accurate" ones: (ἐξ ἀκριβῶν ἀντιγράφων.) More than that: he leads his reader to infer that he had personally resorted to the famous Palestinian Copy, the text of which was held to exhibit the inspired verity, and had satisfied himself that the concluding section of S. Mark's Gospel *was there*. He had, therefore, been either to Jerusalem, or else to Cæsarea; had inquired for those venerable records which had once belonged to Origen and Pamphilus[d]; and had inspected them. Testimony more express, more weighty,—I was going to say, more decisive,—can scarcely be imagined. It may with truth be said to close the present discussion.

With this, in fact, Victor lays down his pen. So also may I. I submit that nothing whatever which has hitherto come before us lends the slightest countenance to the modern dream that S. Mark's Gospel, as it left the hands of its inspired Author, ended abruptly at ver. 8. Neither Eusebius nor Jerome; neither Severus of Antioch nor Hesychius of Jerusalem; certainly not Victor of Antioch; least of all Gregory of Nyssa,—yield a particle of support to that monstrous fancy. The notion is an invention, a pure imagination of the Critics ever since the days of Griesbach.

It remains to be seen whether the MSS. will prove somewhat less unaccommodating.

VII. For it can be of no possible avail, at this stage of the discussion, to appeal to

EUTHYMIUS ZIGABENUS,

the Author of an interesting Commentary, or rather Compilation on the Gospels, assigned to A.D. 1116. Euthymius lived, in fact, full five hundred years too late for his testimony to be of the slightest importance. Such as it is, however, it is

---

[d] Scrivener's *Introduction*, pp. 47, 125, 431.

v.]   *a reference to Euthymius Zigabenus.*   147

not unfavourable. He says,—" Some of the Commentators state that here," (viz. at ver. 8,) "the Gospel according to Mark finishes; and that what follows is a spurious addition." (Which clearly is his version of the statements of one or more of the four Fathers whose testimony has already occupied so large a share of our attention.) "This portion we must also interpret, however," (Euthymius proceeds,) "since there is nothing in it prejudicial to the truth e."—But it is idle to linger over such a writer. One might almost as well quote " Poli *Synopsis*," and then proceed to discuss it. The cause must indeed be desperate which seeks support from a quarter like this. What possible sanction can an Ecclesiastic of the xii[th] century be supposed to yield to the hypothesis that S. Mark's Gospel, as it left the hands of its inspired Author, was an unfinished work?

It remains to ascertain what is the evidence of the MSS. on this subject. And the MSS. require to be the more attentively studied, because it is to *them* that our opponents are accustomed most confidently to appeal. On them in fact they rely. The nature and the value of the most ancient Manuscript testimony available, shall be scrupulously investigated in the next two Chapters.

---

e Φασὶ δέ τινες τῶν ἐξηγητῶν ἐνταῦθα συμπληροῦσθαι τὸ κατὰ Μάρκον εὐαγγέλιον· τὰ δὲ ἐφεξῆς προσθήκην εἶναι μεταγενεστέραν. Χρὴ δὲ καὶ ταύτην ἑρμηνεῦσαι μηδὲν τῇ ἀληθείᾳ λυμαινομένην.—Euthym. Zig. (*ed.* Matthaei, 1792), *in loc.*

CHAPTER VI.

MANUSCRIPT TESTIMONY SHEWN TO BE OVERWHELM-
INGLY IN FAVOUR OF THESE VERSES.—PART I.

S. *Mark* xvi. 9—20, *contained in every MS. in the world except two.—
Irrational Claim to Infallibility set up on behalf of Cod.* B (151)
and Cod. ℵ (153).—*These two Codices shewn to be full of gross
Omissions* (156), —*Interpolations* (158), —*Corruptions of the
Text* (159), —*and Perversions of the Truth* (161). —*The testimony of Cod.* B *to S. Mark* xvi. 9—20, *shewn to be favorable,
notwithstanding* (164).

THE two oldest Copies of the Gospels in existence are the famous Codex in the Vatican Library at Rome, known as "Codex B;" and the Codex which Tischendorf brought from Mount Sinai in 1859, and which he designates by the first letter of the Hebrew alphabet (ℵ). These two manuscripts are probably not of equal antiquity[a]. An interval of fifty years at least seems to be required to account for the marked difference between them. If the first belongs to the beginning, the second may be referred to the middle or latter part of the iv[th] century. But the two Manuscripts agree in this,—that *they are without the last twelve verses of S. Mark's Gospel.* In both, after ἐφοβοῦντο γάρ (ver. 8), comes the subscription: in Cod. B,—ΚΑΤΑ ΜΑΡΚΟΝ; in Cod. ℵ,—ΕΥΑΓΓΕΛΙΟΝ ΚΑΤΑ ΜΑΡΚΟΝ.

Let it not be supposed that we have any *more* facts of this class to produce. All has been stated. It is not that the evidence of Manuscripts is one,—the evidence of Fathers and Versions another. The very reverse is the case. Manuscripts, Fathers, and Versions alike, are *only not unanimous* in bearing consistent testimony. But the consentient witness

---

[a] For some remarks on this subject the reader is referred to the Appendix (F).

CH. VI.] *MSS. only not unanimous concerning these Verses.* 149

of the MSS. is even extraordinary. With the exception of the two uncial MSS. which have just been named, there is *not one* Codex in existence, uncial or cursive,—(and we are acquainted with, at least, eighteen other uncials [b], and about six hundred cursive Copies of this Gospel,)—which leaves out the last twelve verses of S. Mark.

The inference which an unscientific observer would draw from this fact, is no doubt in this instance the correct one. He demands to be shewn the Alexandrine (A) and the Parisian Codex (C),—neither of them probably removed by much more than fifty years from the date of the Codex Sinaiticus, and both unquestionably *derived from different originals;*—and he ascertains that no countenance is lent by either of those venerable monuments to the proposed omission of this part of the sacred text. He discovers that the Codex Bezae (D), the only remaining very ancient MS. authority,—notwithstanding that it is observed on most occasions to exhibit an extraordinary sympathy with the Vatican (B),—here sides with A and C against B and ℵ. He inquires after all the other uncials and all the cursive MSS. in existence, (some of them dating from the xth century,) and requests to have it explained to him *why* it is to be supposed that all these many witnesses,—belonging to so many different patriarchates, provinces, ages of the Church,—have entered into a grand conspiracy to bear false witness on a point of this magnitude and importance? But he obtains no intelligible answer to this question. How, then, is an unprejudiced student to draw any inference but one from the premisses? *That* single peculiarity (he tells himself) of bringing the second Gospel abruptly to a close at the 8th verse of the xvi[th] chapter, is absolutely fatal to the two Codices in question. It is useless to din into his ears that those Codices are probably both of the iv[th] century,—unless men are prepared to add the assurance that a Codex of the iv[th] century is *of necessity* a more trustworthy witness to the text of the Gospels than a Codex of the vth. The omission of these twelve verses, I repeat, in itself, destroys his confidence in

[b] Viz. A, C [v]; D [vi]; E, L [viii]; F, K, M, V, Γ, Δ, Λ (quære), Π [ix]; G, H, X, S, U [ix, x].

Cod. B and Cod. ℵ: for it is obvious that a copy of the Gospels which has been so seriously mutilated in one place may have been slightly tampered with in another. He is willing to suspend his judgment, of course. The two oldest copies of the Gospels in existence are entitled to great reverence *because* of their high antiquity. They must be allowed a most patient, most unprejudiced, most respectful, nay, a most indulgent hearing. But when all this has been freely accorded, on no intelligible principle can more be claimed for any two MSS. in the world.

The rejoinder to all this is sufficiently obvious. Mistrust will no doubt have been thrown over the evidence borne to the text of Scripture in a thousand other places by Cod. B and Cod. ℵ, *after demonstration that those two Codices exhibit a mutilated text* in the present place. But what else is this but the very point requiring demonstration? Why may not these two be right, and all the other MSS. wrong?

I propose, therefore, that we reverse the process. Proceed we to examine the evidence borne by these two witnesses on certain *other* occasions which admit of *no* difference of opinion; or next to none. Let us endeavour, I say, to ascertain *the character of the Witnesses* by a patient and unprejudiced examination of their Evidence,—not in one place, or in two, or in three; but on several important occasions, and throughout. If we find it invariably consentient and invariably truthful, then of course a mighty presumption will have been established, the very strongest possible, that their adverse testimony in respect of the conclusion of S. Mark's Gospel must needs be worthy of all acceptation. But if, on the contrary, our inquiries shall conduct us to the very opposite result,—what else can happen but that our confidence in these two MSS. will be hopelessly shaken? We must in such case be prepared to admit that it is just as likely as not that this is only *one more occasion* on which these "two false witnesses" have conspired to witness falsely. If, at this juncture, extraneous evidence of an entirely trustworthy kind can be procured to confront them: above all, if some one ancient witness of unimpeachable veracity can be found who shall bear contradictory evidence: what other

VI.]   *General Character of Codex B.*   151

alternative will be left us but to reject their testimony in respect of S. Mark xvi. 9—20 with something like indignation; and to acquiesce in the belief of universal Christendom for eighteen hundred years that these twelve verses are just as much entitled to our unhesitating acceptance as any other twelve verses in the Gospel which can be named?

I. It is undeniable, in the meantime, that for the last quarter of a century, it has become the fashion to demand for the readings of Codex B something very like absolute deference. The grounds for this superstitious sentiment, (for really I can describe it in no apter way,) I profess myself unable to discover. Codex B comes to us without a history: without recommendation of any kind, except that of its antiquity. It bears traces of careless transcription in every page. The mistakes which the original transcriber made are of perpetual recurrence. "They are chiefly omissions, of one, two, or three words; but sometimes of half a verse, a whole verse, or even of several verses.... I hesitate not to assert that it would be easier to find a folio containing three or four such omissions than to light on one which should be without any[c]." In the Gospels alone, Codex B leaves out words or whole clauses no less than 1,491 times[d]: of which by far the largest proportion is found in S. Mark's Gospel. Many of these, no doubt, are to be accounted for by the proximity of a "like ending[e]." The Vatican MS. (like the Sinaitic[f]) was originally de-

[c] Vercellone, — *Del antichissimo Codice Vaticano della Bibbia Greca*, Roma, 1860. (pp. 21.)

[d] *Dublin Univ. Mag.* (Nov. 1859,) p. 620, quoted by Scrivener, p. 93.

[e] ὁμοιοτέλευτον.

[f] See Scrivener's *Introduction* to his ed. of the Codex Bezæ, p. xxiii. The passage referred to reappears at the end of his Preface to the 2nd ed. of his *Collation of the Cod. Sinaiticus.*—Add to his instances, this from S. Matth. xxviii. 2, 3 :—

   ΚΑΙ ΕΚΑΘΗΤΟ Ε
   ΠΑΝΩ ΑΥΤΟΥ [ΗΝ ΔΕ
   Η ΕΙΔΕΑ ΑΥΤΟΥ] ΩΟ
   ΑΟΤΡΑΠΗ

It is plain why the scribe of ℵ wrote ἐπανω αυτου ως αστραπη.—The next is from S. Luke xxiv. 31 :—

   ΔΙΗΝΥΓΗ
   ΟΑΝ ΟΙ ΟΦΘΑΛΜΟΙ

rived from an older Codex which contained about twelve or thirteen letters in a line [g]. And it will be found that some of its omissions which have given rise to prolonged

ΚΑΙ [ЄΠЄΓΝѠCAN ΑΥΤὸ
ΚΑΙ] ΑΥΤΟC ΑΦΑΝ
ΤΟC ЄΓЄΝЄΤΟ

Hence the omission of και επεγνωσαν αυτον in א.—The following explains the omission from א (and D) of the Ascension at S. Luke xxiv. 52:—

ΑΠ ΑΥΤѠΝ ΚΑΙ [ΑΝ
ЄΦЄΡЄΤΟ ЄΙC ΤΟΝ
ΟΥΡΑΝΟΝ ΚΑΙ] ΑΥ
ΤΟΙ ΠΡΟCΚΥΝΗCΆ

The next explains why א reads περικαλυψαντες επηρωτων αυτον in S. Luke xxii. 64:—

ΔЄΡΟΝΤЄC ΚΑΙ ΠЄ
ΡΙΚΑΛΥΨΑΝΤЄC Є
[ΤΥΠΤΟΝ ΑΥΤΟΥ ΤΟ
ΠΡΟCѠΠΟΝ ΚΑΙ Є]
ΠΗΡѠΤѠΝ ΑΥΤὸ

The next explains why the words και πας εις αυτην βιαζεται are absent in א (and G) at S. Luke xvi. 16:—

ЄΥΑΓΓЄ
ΛΙΖЄΤΑΙ [ΚΑΙ ΠΑC
ЄΙC ΑΥΤΗΝ ΒΙ
ΑΖЄΤΑΙ] ЄΥΚΟΠѠ
ΤЄΡΟΝ ΔЄ ЄCΤΙΝ Τὸ

[g] In this way, (at S. John xvii. 15, 16), the obviously corrupt reading of Cod. B (ινα τηρησης αυτους εκ του κοσμου)—which, however, was the reading of the copy used by Athanasius (*Opp.* p. 1035 : *al. ed.* p. 825)—is explained:—

ЄΚ ΤΟΥ [ΠΟΝΗΡΟΥ.
ЄΚ ΤΟΥ] ΚΟCΜΟΥ
ΟΥΚ ЄΙCΙΝ ΚΑΘѠC

Thus also is explained why B (with א, A, D, L) omits a precious clause in S. Luke xxiv. 42:—

ΟΠΤΟΥ ΜЄΡΟC ΚΑΙ
[ΑΠΟ ΜЄΛΙCCΙ
ΟΥ ΚΗΡΙΟΥ ΚΑΙ]
ΛΑΒѠΝ ЄΝѠΠΙΟΝ

And why the same MSS. (all but A) omit an important clause in S. Luke xxiv. 53:—

ЄΝ ΤѠ ΙЄΡѠ [ΑΙΝ
ΟΥΝΤЄC ΚΑΙ] ЄΥΛΟ
ΓΟΥΝΤЄC ΤΟΝ Θ̄Ν̄

And why B (with א, L) omits an important clause in the history of the Temptation (S. Luke iv. 5):—

ΚΑΙ ΑΝΑΓΑΓѠΝ ΑΥ
ΤΟΝ [ЄΙC ΟΡΟC ΥΨΗ
ΛΟΝ] ЄΔΙΞЄΝ ΑΥΤѠ

discussion are probably to be referred to nothing else but the oscitancy of a transcriber with such a codex before him [h]: without having recourse to any more abstruse hypothesis; without any imputation of bad faith;—*certainly without supposing that the words omitted did not exist in the inspired autograph of the Evangelist.* But then it is undeniable that some of the omissions in Cod. B are not to be so explained. On the other hand, I can testify to the fact that the codex is disfigured throughout with *repetitions*. The original scribe is often found to have not only written the same words twice over, but to have failed whenever he did so to take any notice with his pen of what he had done.

What then, (I must again inquire,) are the grounds for the superstitious reverence which is entertained in certain quarters for the readings of Codex B? If it be a secret known to the recent Editors of the New Testament, they have certainly contrived to keep it wondrous close.

II. More recently, a claim to co-ordinate primacy has been set up on behalf of the Codex Sinaiticus. Tischendorf is actually engaged in remodelling his seventh Leipsic edition, chiefly in conformity with the readings of his lately discovered MS.[i] And yet the Codex in question abounds with "errors of the eye and pen, to an extent not unparalleled, but happily rather unusual in documents of first-rate importance." On many occasions, 10, 20, 30, 40 words are dropped through very carelessness [k]. "Letters and words, even whole sentences, are frequently written twice

[h] In this way the famous omission (ℵ, B, L) of the word δευτεροπρώτῳ, in S. Luke vi. 1, is (to say the least) capable of being explained:—

ΕΓΕΝΕΤΟ Δ Ε ΕΝ CAB
ΒΑΤΩ Δ[ΕΥΤΕΡΟ
ΠΡΩΤΩ Δ]ΙΑΠΟΡΕΥΕ
CΘΑΙ

and of υιου Βαραχιου (ℵ) in S. Matth. xxvii. 35:—

ΑΙΜΑΤΟC ΖΑΧΑΡΙΟΥ
[ΥΙΟΥ ΒΑΡΑΧΙΟΥ]
ΟΝ ΕΦΟΝΕΥCΑΤΕ

[i] He has reached the 480th page of vol. ii. (1 Cor. v. 7.)

[k] In this way 14 words have been omitted from Cod. ℵ in S. Mark xv. 47—xvi. 1:—19 words in S. Mark i. 32-4:—20 words in S. John xx. 5, 6:—39 words in S. John xix. 20, 21.

over, or begun and immediately cancelled: while that gross blunder... whereby a clause is omitted because it happens to end in the same words as the clause preceding, occurs no less than 115 times in the New Testament. Tregelles has freely pronounced that 'the state of the text, as proceeding from the first scribe, may be regarded as *very rough*[1].'" But when "the first scribe" and his "very rough" performance have been thus unceremoniously disposed of, one would like to be informed what remains to command respect in Codex ℵ? Is, then, *manuscript authority* to be confounded with *editorial caprice*,—exercising itself upon the corrections of "at least ten different revisers," who, from the vi[th] to the xii[th] century, have been endeavouring to lick into shape a text which its original author left "*very rough?*"

The co-ordinate primacy, (as I must needs call it,) which, within the last few years, has been claimed for Codex B and Codex ℵ, threatens to grow into a species of tyranny,— from which I venture to predict there will come in the end an unreasonable and unsalutary recoil. It behoves us, therefore, to look closely into this matter, and to require a reason for what is being done. The text of the sacred deposit is far too precious a thing to be sacrificed to an irrational, or at least a superstitious devotion to two MSS.,—simply because they may possibly be older by a hundred years than any other which we possess. "Id verius quod prius," is an axiom which holds every bit as true in Textual Criticism as in Dogmatic Truth. But on that principle, (as I have already shewn,) the last twelve verses of S. Mark's Gospel are fully established[m]; and by consequence, the credit of Codd. B and ℵ sustains a severe shock. Again, "Id verius quod prius;" but it does not of course follow that a Codex of the iv[th] century shall exhibit a more correct text of Scripture than one written in the vth, or even than one written in the xth. For the proof of this statement, (if it can be supposed to require proof,) it is enough to appeal to Codex D. That venerable copy of the Gospels is of the vi[th] century.

---

[1] Scrivener's *Full Collation*, &c., p. xv.; quoting Tregelles' N. T. Part II. page ii.

[m] See Chap. IV. p. 37.

It is, in fact, one of our five great uncials. No older MS. of the Greek Text is known to exist,—excepting always A, B, C and ℵ. And yet *no* text is more thoroughly disfigured by corruptions and interpolations than that of Codex D. In the Acts, (to use the language of its learned and accurate Editor,) "it is hardly an exaggeration to assert that it reproduces the *textus receptus* much in the same way that one of the best Chaldee Targums does the Hebrew of the Old Testament: so wide are the variations in the diction, so constant and inveterate the practice of expanding the narrative by means of interpolations which seldom recommend themselves as genuine by even a semblance of internal probability[n]." Where, then, is the *à priori* probability that two MSS. of the iv[th] century shall have not only a superior claim to be heard, but almost an exclusive right to dictate which readings are to be rejected, which retained?

How ready the most recent editors of the New Testament have shewn themselves to hammer the sacred text on the anvil of Codd. B and ℵ,—not unfrequently in defiance of the evidence of all other MSS., and sometimes to the serious detriment of the deposit,—would admit of striking illustration were this place for such details. Tischendorf's English "*New Testament*,"—"with various readings from the three most celebrated manuscripts of the Greek Text" translated at the foot of every page,—is a recent attempt (1869) to popularize the doctrine that we have to look exclusively to two or three of the oldest copies, if we would possess the Word of GOD in its integrity. Dean Alford's constant appeal in his revision of the Authorized Version (1870) to "the oldest MSS.," (meaning thereby generally Codd. ℵ and B with one or two others [o]), is an abler endeavour to familiarize the public mind with the same belief. I am bent on shewing that there is nothing whatever in the character of either of the Codices in question to warrant this servile deference.

(*a*) And first,—Ought it not sensibly to detract from our

---

[n] Scrivener's *Introduction to Con. Bezae*, p. liv.

[o] *e.g.* in S. John i. 42 (meaning only ℵ, B, L): iv. 42 (ℵ, B, C): v. 12 (ℵ, B, C, L): vi. 22 (A, B, L), &c.

opinion of the value of their evidence to discover that *it is easier to find two consecutive verses in which the two MSS. differ, the one from the other, than two consecutive verses in which they entirely agree?* Now this is a plain matter of fact, of which any one who pleases may easily convince himself. But the character of two witnesses who habitually contradict one another has been accounted, in every age, precarious. On every such occasion, only one of them can possibly be speaking the truth. Shall I be thought unreasonable if I confess that these *perpetual* inconsistencies between Codd. B and ℵ,—grave inconsistencies, and occasionally even gross ones,—altogether destroy my confidence in either?

(*b*) On the other hand, discrepant as the testimony of these two MSS. is throughout, they yet, strange to say, conspire every here and there in exhibiting minute corruptions of such an unique and peculiar kind as to betray a (probably not very remote) common corrupt original. These coincidences in fact are so numerous and so extraordinary as to establish a real connexion between those two codices; and that connexion is fatal to any claim which might be set up on their behalf as wholly independent witnesses [p].

(*c*) Further, it is evident that both alike have been subjected, probably during the process of transcription, to the same depraving influences. But because such statements require to be established by an induction of instances, the reader's attention must now be invited to a few samples of the grave blemishes which disfigure our two oldest copies of the Gospel.

1. And first, since it is the omission of the end of S. Mark's Gospel which has given rise to the present discussion, it becomes a highly significant circumstance that the original

[p] e.g. S. Matth. x. 25; xii. 24, 27: S. Luke xi. 15, 18, 19 (βεεζεβουλ).—
1 Cor. xiii. 3 (καυχησωμαι).—S. James i. 17 (αποσκιασματος).—Acts i. 5 (εν πν. βαπ. αγ.).—S. Mark vi. 20 (ηπορει).—S. Matth. xiv. 30 (ισχυρον).—S. Luke iii. 32 (Ιωβηλ).—Acts i. 19 (ιδίᾳ omitted).—S. Matth. xxv. 27 (τα αργυρια).— S. Matth. xvii. 22 (συστρεφομενων).—S. Luke vi. 1 (δευτεροπρώτῳ omitted).— See more in Tischendorf's *Prolegomena* to his 4to. reprint of the *Cod. Sin.* p. xxxvi. On this head the reader is also referred to Scrivener's very interesting *Collation of the Cod. Sinaiticus*, Introduction, p. xliii. *seq.*

scribe of Cod. ℵ had *also* omitted the *end of the Gospel according to S. John*[q]. In this suppression of ver. 25, Cod. ℵ stands *alone* among MSS. A cloud of primitive witnesses vouch for the genuineness of the verse. Surely, it is nothing else but the *reductio ad absurdum* of a theory of recension, (with Tischendorf in his last edition,) to accommodate our printed text to the vicious standard of the original penman of Cod. ℵ, and bring the last chapter of S. John's Gospel to a close at ver. 24!

Cod. B, on the other hand, omits the whole of those two solemn verses wherein S. Luke describes our LORD's "Agony and bloody Sweat," together with the act of the ministering Angel[r]. As to the genuineness of those verses, recognised as they are by Justin Martyr, Irenæus, Hippolytus, Epiphanius, Didymus, Gregory of Nazianzus, Chrysostom, Theodoret, by all the oldest versions, and by almost every MS. in existence, including Cod. ℵ,—it admits of *no* doubt. Here then is proof positive that in order to account for omissions from the Gospel in the oldest of the uncials, there is no need whatever to resort to the hypothesis that such portions of the Gospel are not the genuine work of the Evangelist. "The admitted error of Cod. B in this place," (to quote the words of Scrivener,) "ought to make some of its advocates more chary of their confidence in cases where it is less countenanced by other witnesses than in the instance before us."

Cod. B (not Cod. ℵ) is further guilty of the "grave error" (as Dean Alford justly styles it,) of omitting that solemn record of the Evangelist:—"Then said JESUS, Father, forgive them; for they know not what they do." It also withholds the statement that the inscription on the Cross was "in letters of Greek, and Latin, and Hebrew[s]." Cod ℵ, on the other hand, omits the confession of the man born blind (*ὁ δὲ ἔφη, πιστεύω κύριε· καὶ προσεκύνησεν αὐτῷ*) in S. John ix. 38.—Both Cod. ℵ and Cod. B retain nothing but the

[q] See Tischendorf's note in his reprint of the Cod. Sin., *Prolegg.* p. lix.

[r] Ὤφθη δὲ αὐτῷ ἄγγελος—καταβαίνοντα ἐπὶ τὴν γῆν. S. Luke xxii. 43, 44.

[s] ὁ δὲ Ἰησοῦς—τί ποιοῦσι, (xxiii. 34).—γράμμασιν Ἑλληνικοῖς καὶ Ῥωμαϊκοῖς καὶ Ἑβραϊκοῖς, (xxiii. 38.)

word υἱόν of the expression τὸν υἱὸν αὐτῆς τὸν πρωτότοκον, in S. Matth. i. 25; and suppress altogether the important doctrinal statement ὁ ὢν ἐν τῷ οὐρανῷ, in S. John iii. 13: as well as the clause διελθὼν διὰ μέσου αὐτῶν· καὶ παρῆγεν οὕτως, in S. John viii. 59. Concerning all of which, let it be observed that I am neither imputing motives nor pretending to explain *the design* with which these several serious omissions were made. All that is asserted is, that they cannot be imputed to the carelessness of a copyist, but were intentional: and I insist that they effectually dispose of the presumption that when an important passage is observed to be wanting from Cod. B or Cod. ℵ, its absence is to be accounted for by assuming that it was also absent *from the inspired autograph of the Evangelist.*

2. To the foregoing must be added the many places where the text of B or of ℵ, or of both, has clearly been *interpolated*. There does not exist in the whole compass of the New Testament a more monstrous instance of this than is furnished by the transfer of the incident of the piercing of our Redeemer's side from S. John xix. 24 to S. Matth. xxvii., in Cod. B and Cod. ℵ, where it is introduced at the end of ver. 49,—in defiance of reason as well as of authority [t]. "This interpolation" (remarks Mr. Scrivener) "which would represent the SAVIOUR as pierced while yet living, is a good example of the fact that some of our highest authorities may combine in attesting a reading unquestionably false [u]." Another singularly gross specimen of interpolation, in my judgment, is supplied by the purely apocryphal statement which is met with in Cod. ℵ, at the end of S. Matthew's account of the healing of the Centurion's servant,—και υποστρεψας ο εκατονταρχος εις τον οικον αυτου εν αυτη τη ωρα, ευρεν τον παιδα υγιαινοντα (viii. 13.)—Nor can anything well be weaker than the substitution (for ὑστερήσαντος οἴνου, in S. John ii. 3) of the following [v], which is found *only* in Cod. ℵ :—οινον ουκ ειχον, οτι συνετελεσθη ο οινος του γαμου.

---

[t] αλλος δε λαβων λογχην ενυξεν αυτου την πλευραν, και εξηλθεν υδωρ και αιμα. Yet B, C, L and ℵ contain this!   [u] *Coll. of the Cod. Sin.*, p. xlvii.

[v] So, in the margin of the Hharklensian revision.

But the inspired text has been depraved in the same licentious way throughout, by the responsible authors of Cod. B and Cod. ℵ, although such corruptions have attracted little notice from their comparative unimportance. Thus, the reading (in ℵ) ημας δει εργαζεσθαι τα εργα του πεμψαντος ημας (S. John ix. 4) carries with it its own sufficient condemnation; being scarcely rendered more tolerable by B's substitution of με for the second ημας.—Instead of τεθεμελίωτο γὰρ ἐπὶ τὴν πέτραν (S. Luke vi. 48), B and ℵ present us with the insipid gloss, δια το καλως οικοδομεισθαι αυτην.— In the last-named codex, we find the name of "Isaiah" (ησαιου) thrust into S. Matth. xiii. 35, in defiance of authority and of *fact*.—Can I be wrong in asserting that the reading ο μονογενης θεος (for υἱός) in S. John i. 18, (a reading found in Cod. B and Cod. ℵ alike,) is undeserving of serious attention?—May it not also be confidently declared that, in the face of all MS. evidence[x], no future Editors of the New Testament will be found to accept the highly improbable reading ο ανθρωπος ο λεγομενος Ιησους, in S. John ix. 11, although the same two Codices conspire in exhibiting it?—or, on the authority of *one* of them (ℵ), to read εν αυτω ζωη εστιν[y] (for ἐν αὐτῷ ζωὴ ἦν) in S. John i. 4?—Certain at least it is that no one will *ever* be found to read (with B) εβδομηκοντα δυο in S. Luke x. 1,—or (with ℵ) ο εκλεκτος του θεου (instead of ὁ υἱὸς τοῦ θεοῦ) in S. John i. 34.—But let me ask, With what show of reason can the pretence of *Infallibility*, (as well as the plea of Primacy), be set up on behalf of a pair of MSS. licentiously corrupt as these have already been *proved* to be? For the readings above enumerated, be it observed, are either critical depravations of the inspired Text, or else unwarrantable interpolations. They *cannot* have resulted from careless transcription.

3. Not a few of the foregoing instances are in fact of a kind

---

[x] Note, that it is a mistake for the advocates of this reading to claim the *Latin* versions as allies. Ἀπεκρίθη ἐκεῖνος, Ἄνθρωπος λεγόμενος Ἰησοῦς κ.τ.λ. is not "Respondit, Ille homo qui dicitur Jesus," (as both Tischendorf and Tregelles assume;) but "*Respondit ille*, Homo," &c.,—as in verses 25 and 36.

[y] This reading will be found discussed in a footnote (p) at the end of Chap. VII.,—p. 110.

to convince me that the text with which Cod. B and Cod. ℵ were chiefly acquainted, must have been once and again subjected to a clumsy process of *revision*. Not unfrequently, as may be imagined, the result (however tasteless and infelicitous) is not of serious importance; as when, (to give examples from Cod. ℵ,) for τὸν ὄχλον ἐπικεῖσθαι αὐτῷ (in S. Luke v. 1) we are presented with συναχθῆναι τον οχλον:— when for ζῶν ἀσώτως (in S. Luke xv. 13) we read εις χωραν μακραν; and for οἱ ἐξουσιάζοντες αὐτῶν (in S. Luke xxii. 25), we find οι αρχοντες των [εθνων] εξουσιαζουσιν αυτων, και, (which is only a weak reproduction of S. Matth. xx. 25):— when again, for σκοτία ἤδη ἐγεγόνει (in S. John vi. 17), we are shewn κατελαβεν δε αυτους η σκοτια: and when, for καὶ τίς ἐστιν ὁ παραδώσων αὐτόν (in S. John vi. 64) we are invited to accept και τις ην ο μελλων αυτον παραδιδοναι[z].

But it requires very little acquaintance with the subject to foresee that this kind of license may easily assume serious dimensions, and grow into an intolerable evil. Thus, when the man born blind is asked by the HOLY ONE if he believes ἐπὶ τὸν υἱὸν τοῦ Θεοῦ (S. John. ix. 35), we are by no means willing to acquiesce in the proposed substitute, τον υιον του ανθρωπου: neither, when the SAVIOUR says, γινώσκομαι ὑπὸ τῶν ἐμῶν (S. John x. 14) are we at all willing to put up with the weak equivalent γινωσκουσι με τα εμα. Still less is και εμοι αυτους εδωκας any equivalent at all for καὶ τὰ ἐμὰ πάντα σά ἐστι, καὶ τὰ σὰ ἐμά, in S. John xvii. 10: or, αλλοι

---

[z] The following may be added from Cod. ℵ:—μεγάλοι αὐτῶν (in S. Mark x. 42) changed into βασιλεις: ειπεν (in S. Mark xiv. 58) substituted for ἡμεῖς ἠκούσαμεν αὐτοῦ λέγοντος: εβδομηκοντα τεσσαρων (in S. Lu. ii. 37) for ὀγδοηκ: and εωρακεν σε (in S. Jo. viii. 57) for ἑώρακα:—in all which four readings Cod. ℵ is without support. [Scrivener, *Coll. Cod. Sin.* p. li.] The epithet μεγαν, introduced (in the same codex) before λίθον in S. Mark xv. 46; and και πατριας inserted into the phrase ἐξ οἴκου Δαβίδ in S. Lu. i. 27,—are two more specimens of mistaken officiousness. In the same infelicitous spirit, Cod. B and Cod. ℵ concur in omitting ἰσχυρόν (S. Matt. xiv. 30), and in substituting πυκνα for πυγμῇ, and ραντισωνται for βαπτίσωνται in S. Mark vii. 3 and 4:— while the interpolation of τασσομενος after ἐξουσίαν in S. Matth. viii. 9, because of the parallel place in S. Luke's Gospel; and the substitution of ανθρωπος αυστηρος ει (from S. Luke xix. 21) for σκληρὸς εἶ ἄνθρωπος in S. Matth. xxv. 24, are proofs that yet another kind of corrupting influence has been here at work besides those which have been already specified.

ζωσουσιν σε, και ποιησουσιν σοι οσα ου θελεις, for ἄλλος σε ζώσει, καὶ οἴσει ὅπου οὐ θέλεις, in S. John xxi. 18. Indeed, even when our LORD is not the speaker, such licentious depravation of the text is not to be endured. Thus, in S. Luke xxiii. 15, Cod. B and Cod. ℵ conspire in substituting for ἀνέπεμψα γὰρ ὑμᾶς πρὸς αὐτόν,—ανεπεμψεν γαρ αυτον προς ημας; which leads one to suspect the copyist was misled by the narrative in ver. 7. Similar instances might be multiplied to an indefinite extent.

Two yet graver corruptions of the truth of the Gospel, (but they belong to the same category,) remain to be specified. Mindful, I suppose, of S. James' explanation "how that *by works* a man is justified," the author of the text of Codices B and ℵ has ventured to alter our LORD'S assertion (in S. Matth. xi. 19,) "Wisdom is justified of *her children,*" into "Wisdom is justified by *her works;*" and, in the case of Cod. ℵ, his zeal is observed to have so entirely carried him away, that he has actually substituted εργων for τέκνων in the parallel place of S. Luke's Gospel.—The other example of error (S. Matth. xxi. 31) is calculated to provoke a smile. Finding that our SAVIOUR, in describing the conduct of the two sons in the parable, says of the one,—ὕστερον δὲ μεταμεληθεὶς ἀπῆλθεν, and of the other,—καὶ οὐκ ἀπῆλθεν; some ancient scribe, (who can have been but slenderly acquainted with the Greek language,) seems to have conceived the notion that a more precise way of identifying the son who "*afterwards* repented and went," would be to designate him as ὁ ὕστερος. Accordingly, in reply to the question,—τίς ἐκ τῶν δύο ἐποίησεν τὸ θέλημα τοῦ πατρός; we are presented (but *only in Cod.* B) with the astonishing information,—λεγουσιν ο υστερος. And yet, seeing clearly that this made nonsense of the parable, some subsequent critic is found to have *transposed the order of the two sons:* and in that queer condition the parable comes down to us in the famous Vatican Codex B.

4. Some of the foregoing instances of infelicitous tampering with the text of the Gospels are, it must be confessed, very serious. But it is a yet more fatal circumstance in connexion with Cod. B and Cod. ℵ that they are convicted

of certain perversions of the truth of Scripture which *must* have been made with deliberation and purpose. Thus, in S. Mark xiv, they exhibit a set of passages—(verses 30, 68, 72)—"which bear clear marks of wilful and critical correction, thoroughly carried out in Cod. ℵ, only partially in Cod. B; the object being so far to assimilate the narrative of Peter's denial with those of the other Evangelists, as to suppress the fact, vouched for by S. Mark only, that the cock crowed *twice*. (In Cod. ℵ, δίς is omitted in ver. 30,"—ἐκ δευτέρου and δίς in ver. 72,—"and καὶ ἀλέκτωρ ἐφώνησε in ver. 68: the last change being countenanced by B [a].") One such discovery, I take leave to point out, is enough to destroy all confidence in the text of these two manuscripts: for it proves that another kind of corrupting influence,—besides carelessness, and accident, and tasteless presumption, and unskilful assiduity,—has been at work on Codices B and ℵ. We are constrained to approach these two manuscripts with suspicion in all cases where a supposed critical difficulty in harmonizing the statements of the several Evangelists will account for any of the peculiar readings which they exhibit.

Accordingly, it does not at all surprise me to discover that in both Codices the important word ἐξελθοῦσαι (in S. Matth. xxviii. 8) has been altered into απελθουσαι. I recognise in that substitution of απο for ἐξ the hand of one who was not aware that the women, when addressed by the Angel, were *inside the sepulchre;* but who accepted the belief (it is found to have been as common in ancient as in modern times) that they beheld him " sitting on the stone [b]."
—In consequence of a similar misconception, both Codices are observed to present us with the word "*wine*" instead of "*vinegar*" in S. Matthew's phrase ὄξος μετὰ χολῆς μεμιγμένον: which results from a mistaken endeavour on the part of some ancient critic to bring S. Matth. xxvii. 34 into

[a] Scrivener, *Coll. Cod. Sin.* p. xlvii.
[b] Add to the authorities commonly appealed to for ἐξελθ. Chrys. [834] (twice,) (also quoted in Cramer's *Cat.* [241]). The mistake adverted to in the text is at least as old as the time of Eusebius, (Mai, iv. p. 264 = 287), who asks,—Πῶς παρά τῷ Ματθαίῳ ἡ Μαγδαληνὴ Μαρία μετὰ τῆς ἄλλης Μαρίας ἔξω τοῦ μνήματος ἑώρακεν τὸν ἕνα ἄγγελον ἐπικαθήμενον τῷ λίθῳ τοῦ μνήματος, κ.τ.λ.

VI.]   *of deliberate depravation.*   163

harmony with S. Mark xv. 23. The man did not perceive that the cruel insult of the "vinegar and gall" (which the Saviour tasted but would not drink) was quite a distinct thing from the proffered mercy of the "myrrhed wine" which the Saviour put away from Himself altogether.

So again, it was in order to bring S. Luke xxiv. 13 into harmony with a supposed fact of geography that Cod. ℵ states that Emmaus, (which Josephus also places at sixty stadia from Jerusalem), was "*an hundred* and sixty" stadia distant. The history of this interpolation of the text is known. It is because some ancient critic (Origen probably) erroneously assumed that *Nicopolis* was the place intended. The conjecture met with favour, and there are not wanting scholia to declare that this was the reading of "the accurate" copies,—notwithstanding the physical impossibility which is involved by the statement [c].—Another geographical misconception under which the scribe of Cod. ℵ is found to have laboured was that Nazareth (S. Luke i. 26) and Capernaum (S. Mark i. 28) were *in Judæa.* Accordingly he has altered the text in both the places referred to, to suit his private notion [d].—A yet more striking specimen of the preposterous method of the same scribe is supplied by his substitution of Καισαριας for Σαμαρείας in Acts viii. 5,—evidently misled by what he found in viii. 40 and xxi. 8.

—Again, it must have been with a view of bringing Revelation into harmony with the (supposed) facts of physical Science that for the highly significant Theological record καὶ ἐσκοτίσθη ὁ ἥλιος at the Crucifixion [e], has been substituted both in B and ℵ, του ηλιου εκλιποντος,—a state-

[c] Tischendorf accordingly *is forced*, for once, to reject the reading of his oracle ℵ.—witnessed to though it be by Origen and Eusebius. His discussion of the text in this place is instructive and even diverting. How is it that such an instance as the present does not open the eyes of Prejudice itself to the danger of pinning its faith to the consentient testimony even of Origen, of Eusebius, and of Cod. ℵ? .... The reader is reminded of what was offered above, in the lower part of p. 49.

[d] A similar perversion of the truth of Scripture is found at S. Luke iv. 44, (cf. the parallel place, S. Matth. iv. 23 : S. Mark i. 39). It does not mend the matter to find ℵ supported this time by Codd. B, C, L, Q, R.

[e] S. Lu. xxiii. 45 :—ὅπερ οὐδέποτε πρότερον συνέβη, ἀλλ' ἢ ἐν Αἰγύπτῳ μόνον, ὅτε τὸ πάσχα τελεῖσθαι ἔμελλε· καὶ γὰρ ἐκεῖνα τούτων τύπος ἦν. (Chrys. vii. 824 c.)

ment which (as the ancients were perfectly well aware [f]) introduces into the narrative an astronomical contradiction. —It may be worth adding, that Tischendorf with singular inconsistency admits into his text the astronomical contradiction, while he rejects the geographical impossibility.— And this may suffice concerning the text of Codices B and ℵ.

III. We are by this time in a condition to form a truer estimate of the value of the testimony borne by these two manuscripts in respect of the last twelve verses of S. Mark's Gospel. If we were disposed before to regard their omission of an important passage as a serious matter, we certainly cannot any longer so regard it. We have by this time seen enough to disabuse our minds of every prejudice. Codd. B and ℵ are the very reverse of infallible guides. Their deflections from the Truth of Scripture are more constant, as well as more licentious by far, than those of their younger brethren: their unauthorized omissions from the sacred text are not only far more frequent but far more flagrant also. And yet the main matter before us,—*their omission of the last twelve verses of S. Mark's Gospel*,—when rightly understood, proves to be an entirely different phenomenon from what an ordinary reader might have been led to suppose. Attention is specially requested for the remarks which follow.

IV. To say that in the Vatican Codex (B), which is unquestionably the oldest we possess, S. Mark's Gospel ends abruptly at the 8th verse of the xvi[th] chapter, and that the

---

[f] ὅπως δὲ μὴ εἴπωσί τινες ἔκλειψιν εἶναι τὸ γεγενημένον, ἐν τῇ τεσσαρεσκαιδεκάτῃ ἡμέρᾳ τῆς σελήνης γέγονε τὸ σκότος :—ὅτε ἔκλειψιν συμβῆναι ἀμήχανον. So Victor of Antioch, in his Catena on S. Mark (ed. Possin.) He makes the remark twice: first (p. 351) in the midst of an abridgment of the beginning of Chrysostom's 88th Homily on S. Matthew: next (p. 352) more fully, after quoting "the great Dionysius" of Alexandria. See also an interesting passage on the same subject in Cramer's *Catena in Matth.* i. p. 237,—from whom derived, I know not; but professing to be from Chrysostom. (Note, that the 10 lines ἐξ ἀνεπιγράφου, beginning p. 236, line 33 = Chrys. vii. 824, D, E.) The very next words in Chrysostom's published Homily (p. 825 A.) are as follows :—Ὅτε γὰρ οὐκ ἦν ἔκλειψις, ἀλλ' ὀργή τε καὶ ἀγανάκτησις, οὐκ ἐντεῦθεν μόνον δῆλον ἦν, ἀλλὰ καὶ ἀπὸ τοῦ καιροῦ· τρεῖς γὰρ ὥρας παρέμεινεν, ἡ δὲ ἔκλειψις ἐν μιᾷ γίνεται καιροῦ ῥοπῇ.—Anyone who would investigate this matter further should by all means read Matthaei's long note on S. Luke xxiii. 45.

customary subscription (κατα μαρκον) follows,—is true; but it is far from being *the whole* truth. It requires to be stated in addition that the scribe, whose plan is found to have been to begin every fresh book of the Bible at the top of *the next ensuing column* to that which contained the concluding words of the preceding book, has at the close of S. Mark's Gospel deviated from his else invariable practice. He has left in this place one column entirely vacant. It is *the only vacant column* in the whole manuscript;—a blank space *abundantly sufficient to contain the twelve verses which he nevertheless withheld.* Why did he leave that column vacant? What can have induced the scribe on this solitary occasion to depart from his established rule? The phenomenon,—(I believe I was the first to call distinct attention to it,)—is in the highest degree significant, and admits of only one interpretation. *The older MS.* from which Cod. B was copied must have infallibly *contained* the twelve verses in dispute. The copyist was instructed to leave them out,—and he obeyed: but he prudently left a blank space *in memoriam rei*. Never was blank more intelligible! Never was silence more eloquent! By this simple expedient, strange to relate, the Vatican Codex is made to *refute itself* even while it seems to be bearing testimony against the concluding verses of S. Mark's Gospel, by withholding them: for it forbids the inference which, under ordinary circumstances, must have been drawn from that omission. It does more. By *leaving room* for the verses it omits, it brings into prominent notice at the end of fifteen centuries and a half, *a more ancient witness than itself.* The venerable Author of the original Codex from which Codex B was copied, is thereby brought to view. And thus, our supposed adversary (Codex B) proves our most useful ally: for it procures us the testimony of an hitherto unsuspected witness. The earlier scribe, I repeat, unmistakably comes forward at this stage of the inquiry, to explain that *he* at least is prepared to answer for the genuineness of these Twelve concluding Verses with which the later scribe, his copyist, from his omission of them, might unhappily be thought to have been unacquainted.

It will be perceived that nothing is gained by suggesting

that the scribe of Cod. B. *may* have copied from a MS. which exhibited the same phenomenon which he has himself reproduced. This, by shifting the question a little further back, does but make the case against Cod. ℵ the stronger.

But in truth, after the revelation which has been already elicited from Cod. B, the evidence of Cod. ℵ may be very summarily disposed of. I have already, on independent grounds, ventured to assign to that Codex a somewhat later date than is claimed for the Codex Vaticanus [g]. My opinion is confirmed by observing that the Sinaitic contains no such blank space at the end of S. Mark's Gospel as is conspicuous in the Vatican Codex. I infer that the Sinaitic was copied from a Codex which had been already mutilated, and reduced to the condition of Cod. B; and that the scribe, only because he knew not what it meant, exhibited S. Mark's Gospel in consequence as if it really had no claim to those twelve concluding verses which, nevertheless, *every* authority we have hitherto met with has affirmed to belong to it of right.

Whatever may be thought of the foregoing suggestion, it is at least undeniable that Cod. B and Cod. ℵ are at variance on the main point. They *contradict* one another concerning the twelve concluding verses of S. Mark's Gospel. For while Cod. ℵ refuses to know anything at all about those verses, Cod. B admits that it remembers them well, by volunteering the statement that they were found in the older codex, of which it is in every other respect a faithful representative. The older and the better manuscript (B), therefore, refutes its junior (ℵ). And it will be seen that logically this brings the inquiry to a close, as far as the evidence of the manuscripts is concerned. We have referred to the oldest extant copy of the Gospels in order to obtain its testimony: and,—"Though without the Twelve Verses concerning which you are so solicitous," (it seems to say,) "I yet hesitate not to confess to you that an older copy than myself, —the ancient Codex from which I was copied,—actually did contain them."

The problem may, in fact, be briefly stated as follows. Of

---

[g] See above, p. 70, and the Appendix (F).

the four oldest Codices of the Gospels extant,—B, ℵ, A, C,— two (B and ℵ) are *without* these twelve verses: two (A and C) are *with* them. Are these twelve verses then an unauthorized *addition* to A and C? or are they an unwarrantable *omission* from B and ℵ? B itself declares plainly that from itself they are an omission. And B is the oldest Codex of the Gospel in existence. What candid mind will persist in clinging to the solitary fact that from the single Codex ℵ these verses are away, in proof that " S. Mark's Gospel was at first without the verses which at present conclude it?"

Let others decide, therefore, whether the present discussion has not already reached a stage at which an unprejudiced Arbiter might be expected to address the prosecuting parties somewhat to the following effect:—

"This case must now be dismissed. The charge brought by yourselves against these Verses was, that they are an unauthorized addition to the second Gospel; a spurious appendix, of which the Evangelist S. Mark can have known nothing. But so far from substantiating this charge, you have not adduced a single particle of evidence which renders it even probable.

"The appeal was made by yourselves to Fathers and to MSS. It has been accepted. And with what result?

(*a*) "Those many Fathers whom you represented as hostile, prove on investigation to be reducible to *one*, viz. Eusebius: and Eusebius, as we have seen, *does not say* that the verses are spurious, but on the contrary labours hard to prove that they may very well be genuine. On the other hand, there are earlier Fathers than Eusebius who quote them without any signs of misgiving. In this way, the positive evidence in their favour is carried back to the ii[nd] century.

(*b*) "Declining the testimony of the Versions, you insisted on an appeal to MSS. On the MSS., in fact, you still make your stand,—or rather you rely on *the oldest* of them; for, (as you are aware,) *every MS. in the world except the two oldest* are against you.

"I have therefore questioned the elder of those two MSS.; and it has volunteered the avowal that an older MS. than itself—*the Codex from which it was copied*—was furnished with those very Verses which you wish me to believe that some older MS. still must needs have been without. What else can be said, then, of your method but that it is frivolous? and of your charge, but that it is contradicted by the evidence to which you yourselves appeal?

"But it is illogical; that is, it is unreasonable, besides.

"For it is high time to point out that even if it so happened that the oldest known MS. was observed to be without these twelve concluding verses, it would still remain a thing unproved (not to say highly improbable) that from the autograph of the Evangelist himself they were also away. Supposing, further, that no Ecclesiastical writer of the iind or iiird century could be found who quoted them: even so, it would not follow that there existed no such verses for a primitive Father to quote. The earliest of the Versions might in addition yield faltering testimony; but even so, *who* would be so rash as to raise on such a slender basis the monstrous hypothesis, that S. Mark's Gospel when it left the hands of its inspired Author was without the verses which at present conclude it? How, then, would you have proposed to account for the consistent testimony of an opposite kind yielded by every other known document in the world?

"But, on the other hand, what are the facts of the case? (1) The earliest of the Fathers,—(2) the most venerable of the Versions,—(3) the oldest MS. of which we can obtain any tidings,—*all* are observed to *recognize these Verses*. 'Cadit quaestio' therefore. The last shadow of pretext has vanished for maintaining with Tischendorf that 'Mark the Evangelist knew nothing of' these verses:—with Tregelles that 'The book of Mark himself extends no further than ἐφοβοῦντο γάρ:'—with Griesbach that 'the *last leaf of the original Gospel was probably torn away.*' ... It is high time, I say, that this case were dismissed. But there are also costs to be paid. Cod. B and Cod. ℵ are convicted of being 'two false witnesses,' and must be held to go forth from this inquiry with an injured reputation."

This entire subject is of so much importance that I must needs yet awhile crave the reader's patience and attention.

CHAPTER VII.

MANUSCRIPT TESTIMONY SHEWN TO BE OVERWHELM-
INGLY IN FAVOUR OF THESE VERSES.—Part II.

The other chief peculiarity of Codices B and ℵ (viz. the omission of the words ἐν Ἐφέσῳ from Ephes. i. 1) considered. — Antiquity unfavourable to the omission of those words (171).—*The Moderns infelicitous in their attempts to account for their omission* (178).—*Marcion probably the author of this corruption of the Text of Scripture* (184).—*Other peculiarities of Codex ℵ disposed of* (187).

THE subject which exclusively occupied our attention throughout the foregoing chapter admits of apt and powerful illustration. Its vast importance will be a sufficient apology for the particular disquisition which follows, and might have been spared, but for the plain challenge of the famous Critic to be named immediately.

"There are two remarkable readings," (says Tischendorf, addressing English readers on this subject in 1868,) " which are very instructive towards determining the age of the manuscripts [ℵ and B], and *their authority*." He proceeds to adduce,—

1. The absence from both, of the last Twelve Verses of S. Mark's Gospel,—concerning which, the reader probably thinks that by this time he has heard enough. Next,—

2. He appeals to their omission of the words ἐν Ἐφέσῳ from the first verse of S. Paul's Epistle to the Ephesians,—*another peculiarity, in which Codd. ℵ and B stand quite alone among MSS.*

I. Here is an extraordinary note of sympathy between two copies of the New Testament indeed. Altogether unique is it: and that it powerfully corroborates the general opinion of their high antiquity, no one will deny. But how about "their *authority*"? Does the coincidence also raise our opinion of *the trustworthiness of the Text*, which these two MSS. concur in exhibiting? for *that* is the question which has to be considered,—the *only* question. The ancientness of a reading is one thing: its genuineness, (as I have explained elsewhere,) quite another. The questions are entirely distinct. It may even be added that while the one is really of little moment, the latter is of all the importance in the world. I am saying that it matters very little whether Codd. ℵ and B were written in the beginning of the iv[th] century, or in the beginning of the vth: whereas it matters much, or rather it matters *everything*, whether they exhibit the Word of GOD faithfully, or occasionally with scandalous license. How far the reading which results from the suppression of the last two words in the phrase τοῖς ἁγίοις τοῖς οὖσιν ἐν 'Εφέσῳ, is *critically allowable* or not, I forbear to inquire. That is not the point which we have to determine. The one question to be considered is,—May it *possibly* be the true reading of the text after all? Is it any way *credible* that S. Paul began his Epistle to the Ephesians as follows:—Παῦλος ἀπόστολος 'Ιησοῦ Χριστοῦ διὰ θελήματος Θεοῦ, τοῖς ἁγίοις τοῖς οὖσι καὶ πιστοῖς ἐν Χριστῷ 'Ιησοῦ? ... If it be eagerly declared in reply that the thing is simply incredible: that the words ἐν 'Εφέσῳ are required for the sense; and that the commonly received reading is no doubt the correct one: then,—there is an end of the discussion. Two extraordinary notes of sympathy between two Manuscripts will have been appealed to as crucial proofs of the *trustworthiness of the Text* of those Manuscripts: (for of their high *Antiquity*, let me say it once more, there can be no question whatever:) and it will have been proved in one case,—admitted in the other,—that *the omission is unwarrantable.*—If, however, on the contrary, it be maintained that the words ἐν 'Εφέσῳ probably had no place in the original copy of this Epistle, but are to be regarded as an unauthorized addition to it,—then, (as in the case of the Twelve Verses omitted from the end of S. Mark's Gospel, and which it was *also* pretended are an unauthorized supplement,) we demand to be shewn the evidence on the strength of which this opinion is maintained, in order that we may ascertain what it is precisely worth.

Tischendorf,—the illustrious discoverer and champion of Codex ℵ, and who is accustomed to appeal triumphantly to its omission of the words ἐν Ἐφέσῳ as *the other* conclusive proof of the trustworthiness of its text,—may be presumed to be the most able advocate it is likely to meet with, as well as the man best acquainted with what is to be urged in its support. From him, we learn that the evidence for the omission of the words in question is as follows:—"In the beginning of the Epistle to the Ephesians we read, 'to the saints which are at Ephesus;' but Marcion (A.D. 130—140), did not find the words 'at Ephesus' in his copy. The same is true of Origen (A.D. 185—254); and Basil the Great (who died A.D. 379), affirmed that those words were wanting in *old* copies. And this omission accords very well with the encyclical or general character of the Epistle. At the present day, our ancient Greek MSS., and all ancient Versions, contain the words 'at Ephesus;' yea (*sic*), even Jerome knew no copy with a different reading. Now, only the Sinaitic and the Vatican correspond with the *old* copies of Basil, and those of Origen and Marcion [a]."—This then is the sum of the evidence. Proceed we to examine it somewhat in detail.

(1) And first, I take leave to point out that the learned writer is absolutely without authority for his assertion that "Marcion *did not find* the words ἐν Ἐφέσῳ in his copy" of S. Paul's Epistle to the Ephesians. Tischendorf's one pretence for saying so is Tertullian's statement that certain heretics, (Marcion he specifies by name,) had given to S. Paul's "Epistle to the Ephesians" the unauthorized title of "Epistle *to the Laodiceans* [b]." This, (argues Tischendorf,) Marcion could not have done had he found ἐν Ἐφέσῳ in the first verse [c]. But the proposed inference is clearly invalid.

---

[a] Tischendorf's "*Introduction*" to his (Tauchnitz) edition of the English N. T., 1869,—p. xiii.

[b] "Epistola quam nos 'ad Ephesios' præscriptam habemus, hæretici vero. 'ad Laodicenos.'" *Adv. Marcion.* lib. v. c. xi, p. 309 (ed. Oehler).

[c] "'Titulum' enim '*ad Laodicenos*' ut addidisse accusatur a Tertulliano,

For, with what show of reason can Marcion,—whom Tertullian taxes with having dared "*titulum interpolare*" in the case of S. Paul's "Epistle to the Ephesians,"—be *therefore*, assumed to have read the first verse differently from ourselves? Rather is the directly opposite inference suggested by the very language in which Tertullian (who was all but the contemporary of Marcion) alludes to the circumstance [d].

Those, however, who would really understand the work of the heretic, should turn from the African Father,—(who after all does but say that Marcion and his crew feigned concerning S. Paul's Epistle to the *Ephesians*, that it was addressed to the *Laodiceans*,)—and betake themselves to the pages of Epiphanius, who lived about a century and a half later. This Father had for many years made Marcion's work his special study [e], and has elaborately described it, as well as presented us with copious extracts from it [f]. And

ita in salutatione verba ἐν Ἐφέσῳ omnino non legisse censendus est." (N. T. *in loc.*)

[d] "Ecclesiæ quidem veritate Epistolam istam 'ad Ephesios' habemus emissam, non 'ad Laodicenos;' sed Marcion ei titulum aliquando interpolare gestiit, quasi et in isto diligentissimus explorator." *Adv. Marcion.* lib. v. c. xvii, pp. 322-3 (ed. Oehler.)

[e] ἀπὸ ἐτῶν ἱκανῶν. (Epiphan. *Opp.* i. 310 c.)

[f] He describes its structure minutely at vol. i. pp. 309—310, and from pp. 312-7; 318—321. [Note, by the way, the gross blunder which has crept into the printed text of Epiphanius at p. 321 D: pointed out long since by Jones, *On the Canon*, ii. 38.] His plan is excellent. Marcion had rejected every Gospel except S. Luke's, and of S. Paul's Epistles had retained only ten,—viz. (1st) Galatians, (2nd and 3rd) I and II Corinthians, (4th) Romans, (5th and 6th) I and II Thessalonians, (7th) *Ephesians*, (8th) Colossians, (9th) Philemon, (10th) Philippians. Even these he had mutilated and depraved. And yet out of that one mutilated Gospel, Epiphanius selects 78 passages, (pp. 312-7), and out of those ten mutilated Epistles, 40 passages more (pp. 318 —21); by means of which 118 texts he undertakes to refute the heresy of Marcion. (pp. 322—50: 350—74.) [It will be perceived that Tertullian goes over Marcion's work in much the same way.] .. Very beautiful, and well worthy of the student's attention, (though it comes before us in a somewhat incorrect form,) is the remark of Epiphanius concerning the living energy of GOD's Word, even when dismembered and exhibited in a fragmentary shape. Ὅλου γὰρ τοῦ σώματος ζῶντος, ὡς εἰπεῖν, τῆς θείας γραφῆς, ποῖον ηὕρισκε (sc. Marcion) μέλος νεκρὸν κατὰ τὴν αὐτοῦ γνώμην, ἵνα παρεισαγάγῃ ψεῦδος κατὰ τῆς ἀληθείας; .... παρέκοψε πολλὰ τῶν μελῶν, κατέσχε δὲ ἔνιά τινα παρ' ἑαυτῷ· καὶ αὐτὰ δὲ τὰ κατασχεθέντα ἔτι ζῶντα οὐ δύναται νεκροῦσθαι, ἀλλ' ἐκεῖ μὲν τὸ ζωτικὸν τῆς ἐμφάσεως, κἄν τε μυρίως παρ' αὐτῷ κατὰ λεπτὸν ἀποτμηθείη. (p. 375 B.)

the account in Epiphanius proves that Tischendorf is mistaken in the statement which he addresses to the English reader, (quoted above;) and that he would have better consulted for his reputation if he had kept to the "ut videtur" with which (in his edition of 1859) he originally broached his opinion. It proves in fact to be no matter of opinion at all. Epiphanius states distinctly that *the Epistle to the Ephesians* was one of the ten Epistles of S. Paul which Marcion *retained*. In his "Apostolicon," or collection of the (mutilated) Apostolical Epistles, the "Epistle to the Ephesians," (identified by the considerable quotations which Epiphanius makes from it [g],) stood (he says) *seventh* in order; while the (so called) "Epistle to the Laodiceans,"— a distinct composition therefore,—had the *eleventh*, that is, the last place assigned to it [h]. That this latter Epistle contained a corrupt exhibition of Ephes. iv. 5 is true enough. Epiphanius records the fact in two places [i]. But then it is to be borne in mind that he charges Marcion with having derived that quotation *from the Apocryphal Epistle to the Laodiceans* [k]; instead of taking it, as he ought to have done, from the genuine Epistle to the Ephesians. The passage, when faithfully exhibited, (as Epiphanius points out,) by its very form refutes the heretical tenet which the context of Marcion's spurious epistle to the Laodiceans was intended to establish; and which the verse in question, in its interpolated form, might seem to favour [l].—I have entered into

He seems to say of Marcion,—
  Fool! to suppose thy shallow wits
  Could quench a life like that. Go, learn
  That cut into ten thousand bits
  Yet every bit would breathe and burn!

[g] He quotes Ephes. ii. 11, 12, 13, 14: v. 14: v. 31. (See Epiphanius, *Opp.* i. p. 318 and 371-2.)

[h] *Ibid.* p. 318 c (= 371 B), and 319 A (= 374 A.)

[i] *Ibid.* p. 319 and 374. But note, that through error in the copies, or else through inadvertence in the Editor, the depravation commented on at p. 374 B, C, is lost sight of at p. 319 B.

[k] See below, at the end of the next note.

[l] Προσέθετο δὲ ἐν τῷ ἰδίῳ Ἀποστολικῷ καλουμένῳ καὶ τῆς καλουμένης πρὸς Λαοδικέας:—"Εἷς Κύριος, μία πίστις, ἓν βάπτισμα, εἷς Χριστὸς, εἷς Θεὸς, καὶ Πατὴρ πάντων, ὁ ἐπὶ πάντων καὶ διὰ πάντων καὶ ἐν πᾶσιν." (Epiphan. *Opp.* vol. i. p. 374.) Here is obviously a hint of τριῶν ἀνάρχων ἀρχῶν διαφορὰς πρὸς

174   *The Evidence of Origen considered.*   [CHAP.

this whole question more in detail perhaps than was necessary: but I was determined to prove that Tischendorf's statement that "Marcion (A.D. 130—140) did not find the words 'at Ephesus' in his copy,"—is absolutely without foundation. It is even *contradicted* by the known facts of the case. I shall have something more to say about Marcion by-and-by; who, it is quite certain, read the text of Ephes. i. 1 exactly as we do.

(2.) The *only* Father who so expresses himself as to warrant the inference that the words ἐν Ἐφέσῳ were absent from his copy, is Origen, in the beginning of the third century. "Only in the case of the Ephesians," (he writes), "do we meet with the expression 'the Saints which are :' and we inquire,—Unless that additional phrase be simply redundant, what can it possibly signify? Consider, then, whether those who have been partakers of *His* nature who revealed Himself to Moses by the Name of I AM, may not, in consequence of such union with Him, be designated as 'those *which are :*' persons, called out, of a state of *not-being*, so to speak, into a state of *being*[m]."—If Origen had read τοῖς ἁγίοις τοῖς οὖσιν ἐν Ἐφέσῳ in his copy, it is to me incredible that he would have gone so very far out of his way to miss the sense of such a plain, and in fact,

ἀλλήλας ἐχουσῶν: [Μαρκίωνος γὰρ τοῦ ματαιόφρονος δίδαγμα, εἰς τρεῖς ἀρχὰς τῆς μοναρχίας τομὴν καὶ διαίρεσιν. Athanas. i. 231 E.] but, (says Epiphanius), οὐχ οὕτως ἔχει ἡ τοῦ ἁγίου Ἀποστόλου ὑπόθεσις καὶ ἠσφαλισμένον κήρυγμα. ἀλλὰ ἄλλως παρὰ τὸ σὸν ποιήτευμα. Then he contrasts with the 'fabrication' of Marcion, the inspired verity,—Eph. iv. 5: declaring ἕνα Θεὸν, τὸν αὐτὸν πατέρα πάντων,—τὸν αὐτὸν ἐπὶ πάντων, καὶ ἐν πᾶσι, κ.τ.λ.—p. 374 C.

Epiphanius reproaches Marcion with having obtained materials ἐκτὸς τοῦ Εὐαγγελίου καὶ τοῦ Ἀποστόλου· οὐ γὰρ ἔδοξε τῷ ἐλεεινοτάτῳ Μαρκίωνι ἀπὸ τῆς πρὸς Ἐφεσίους ταύτην τὴν μαρτυρίαν λέγειν, (sc. the words quoted above,) ἀλλὰ τῆς πρὸς Λαοδικέας, τῆς μὴ οὔσης ἐν τῷ Ἀποστόλῳ. (p. 375 A.) (Epiphanius here uses Ἀπόστολος in its technical sense,—viz. as synonymous with S. Paul's Epistles.)

[m] Ὠριγένης δέ φησι,—Ἐπὶ μόνων Ἐφεσίων εὕρομεν κείμενον τὸ "τοῖς ἁγίοις τοῖς οὖσι·" καὶ ζητοῦμεν, εἰ μὴ παρέλκει προσκείμενον τὸ "τοῖς ἁγίοις τοῖς οὖσι," τί δύναται σημαίνειν; ὅρα οὖν εἰ μὴ ὥσπερ ἐν τῇ Ἐξόδῳ ὄνομά φησιν ἑαυτοῦ ὁ χρηματίζων Μωσεῖ τὸ ὪΝ οὕτως οἱ μετέχοντες τοῦ ὄντος γίνονται "ὄντες," καλούμενοι οἱονεὶ ἐκ τοῦ μὴ εἶναι εἰς τὸ εἶναι. "ἐξελέξατο γὰρ ὁ Θεὸς τὰ μὴ ὄντα," φησὶν ὁ αὐτὸς Παῦλος, "ἵνα τὰ ὄντα καταργήσῃ."—Cramer's *Catena in Ephes.* i. 1,—vol. vi. p. 102.

unmistakable an expression. Bishop Middleton, and Michaelis before him,—*reasoning however only from the place in Basil,* (to be quoted immediately,)—are unwilling to allow that the words ἐν Ἐφέσῳ were ever away from the text. It must be admitted as the obvious inference from what Jerome has delivered on this subject (*infrà,* p. 98 *note* (s)) that he, too, seems to know nothing of the reading (if reading it can be called) of Codd. B and ℵ.

(3) The influence which Origen's writings exercised over his own and the immediately succeeding ages of the Church, was prodigious. Basil, bishop of Cæsarea in Cappadocia, writing against the heresy of Eunomius about 150 years later,—although he read ἐν Ἐφέσῳ in his own copy of S. Paul's Epistles,—thought fit to avail himself of Origen's suggestion. It suited his purpose. He was proving the eternal existence of the SON of GOD. Even *not to know* GOD (he remarks) is *not to be:* in proof of which, he quotes S. Paul's words in 1 Cor. i. 28 :—" Things *which are not,* hath GOD chosen." "Nay," (he proceeds,) the same S. Paul, " in his Epistle to the Ephesians, inasmuch as he is addressing persons who by intimate knowledge were truly joined to Him who 'IS,' designates them specially as ' those *which are:*' saying,—' To the Saints *which are,* and faithful in CHRIST JESUS.' " That this fancy was not original, Basil makes no secret. He derived it, (he says,) from "those who were before us;" a plain allusion to the writings of Origen. But neither was *the reading* his own, either. This is evident. He had *found* it, he says,—(an asseveration indispensable to the validity of his argument,)—but only after he had made *search* [n],—" *in the old copies* [o]." No doubt, Origen's strange fancy must have been even *unintelligible* to Basil when first he met with it. In plain terms, it sounds to this day incredibly foolish,—when read apart from the mutilated text which alone suggested it to Origen's fervid ima-

[n] Consider S. John i. 42, 44, 46 : v. 14 : ix. 35 : xii. 14, &c.

[o] Ἀλλὰ καὶ τοῖς Ἐφεσίοις ἐπιστέλλων ὡς γνησίως ἡνωμένοις τῷ Ὄντι δι' ἐπιγνώσεως, " ὄντας " αὐτοὺς ἰδιαζόντως ὠνόμασεν, εἰπών· " τοῖς ἁγίοις τοῖς οὖσι, καὶ πιστοῖς ἐν Χριστῷ Ἰησοῦ." οὕτω γὰρ καὶ οἱ πρὸ ἡμῶν παραδεδώκασι, καὶ ἡμεῖς ἐν τοῖς παλαιοῖς τῶν ἀντιγράφων εὑρήκαμεν. Note also what immediately follows. (Basil *Opp.* i. p. 254 E, 255 A.)

gination.—But what there is in all this to induce us to suspect that Origen's reading was after all the *right* one, and *ours* the *wrong*, I profess myself wholly at a loss to discover. Origen himself complains bitterly of the depraved state of the copies in his time; and attributes it (1) to the carelessness of the scribes: (2) to the rashness of correctors of the text: (3) to the licentiousness of individuals, adopting some of these corrections and rejecting others, according to their own private caprice [q].

(4) Jerome, a man of severer judgment in such matters than either Origen or Basil, after rehearsing the preceding gloss, (but only to reject it,) remarks that "certain persons" had been "over-fanciful" in putting it forth. He alludes probably to Origen, whose Commentary on the Ephesians, in three books, he expressly relates that he employed [r]: but he does not seem to have apprehended that Origen's text *was without the words ἐν Ἐφέσῳ*. If he *was* acquainted with Origen's *text*, (of which, however, his writings afford no indication,) it is plain that he disapproved of it. Others, he says, understand S. Paul to say not "the Saints *which are:*" but, —"the Saints and faithful *which are at Ephesus* [s]."

(5) The witnesses have now all been heard: and I submit that there has been elicited from their united evidence nothing at all calculated to shake our confidence in the universally received reading of Ephesians i. 1. The facts of the case are so scanty that they admit of being faithfully stated in a single sentence. Two MSS. of the iv[th] century, (exhibiting in other respects several striking notes of vicious sympathy,) are found to conspire in omitting a clause in Ephesians i. 1, which, (necessary as it is to the sense,) may be inferred to have been absent from Origen's copy: and

[q] See the places quoted by Scrivener, *Introd.* pp. 381—91; particularly p. 385.   [r] Hieron. *Opp.* vol. vii. p. 543:—"Illud quoque in Præfatione commoneo, ut sciatis Origenem tria volumina in hanc Epistolam conscripsisse, quem et nos ex parte sequuti sumus."

[s] "Quidam curiosius quam necesse est putant ex eo quod Moysi dictum est 'Haec dices filiis Israel, QUI EST misit me,' etiam eos qui Ephesi sunt [Note this. Cf. "qui sunt Ephesi," *Vulg.*] sancti et fideles, essentiae vocabulo nuncupatos: ut . . . ab Eo 'qui est,' hi 'qui sunt' appellentur . . . . Alii vero simpliciter, non ad eos 'qui sint,' sed 'qui Ephesi sancti et fideles sint' scriptum arbitrantur." Hieron. *Opp.* vii. p. 545 A, B.

Basil testifies that it was absent from "the old copies" to which he himself obtained access. This is really the whole of the matter: in which it is much to be noted that Origen does not say that he *approved* of this reading. Still less does Basil. They both witness to *the fact* that the words ἐν Ἐφέσῳ were omitted from *some* copies of the iiird century, just as Codd. B and ℵ witness to the same fact in the ivth. But what then? Origen is known occasionally to go out of his way to notice readings confessedly worthless; and, why not here? For not only is the text all but *unintelligible* if the words ἐν Ἐφέσῳ be omitted: but (what is far more to the purpose) the direct evidence of *all* the copies, whether uncial or cursive [t],—and of *all* the Versions,—is *against* the omission. In the face of this overwhelming mass of unfaltering evidence to insist that Codd. B and ℵ must yet be accounted right, and all the rest of Antiquity wrong, is simply irrational. To uphold the authority, in respect of this nonsensical reading, of *two* MSS. confessedly untrustworthy in countless other places,—against *all* the MSS.—*all* the Versions,—is nothing else but an act of vulgar prejudice. I venture to declare,—(and with this I shall close the discussion and dismiss the subject,)—*that there does not exist one single instance in the whole of the New Testament* of a reading even probably correct in which the four following notes of spurious origin concur,—which nevertheless are observed to attach to the two readings which have been chiefly discussed in the foregoing pages: viz.

1. The adverse testimony of *all the uncial MSS. except two.*

2. The adverse testimony of all, or *very nearly all*, the cursive MSS.

---

[t] The cursive "Cod. N°. 67 **" (or "67²") is improperly quoted as "omitting" (Tisch.) these words. The reference is to a MS. in the Imperial Library at Vienna, (Nessel 302: Lambec. 34, which = our Paul 67), collated by Alter (N. T. 1786, vol. ii. pp. 415—558), who says of it (p. 496),—"*cod. ἐν ἐφέσῳ punctis notat.*" ..... The MS. must have a curious history. H. Treschow describes it in his *Tentamen Descriptionis Codd. aliquot Graece,* &c. Havn. 1773, pp. 62—73.—Also, A. C. Hwiid in his *Libellus Criticus de indole Cod. MS. Graeci N. T. Lambec. xxxiv.* &c. Havn. 1785.—It appears to have been corrected by some Critic,—perhaps from Cod. B itself.

3. The adverse testimony of *all the Versions,* without exception.

4. The adverse testimony of *the oldest Ecclesiastical Writers.*
To which if I do not add, as I reasonably might,—

5. *The highest inherent improbability,—*
it is only because I desire to treat this question purely as one *of Evidence.*

II. Learned men have tasked their ingenuity *to account for* the phenomenon on which we have been bestowing so many words. The endeavour is commendable; but I take leave to remark in passing that if we are to set about discovering reasons at the end of fifteen hundred years for every corrupt reading which found its way into the sacred text during the first three centuries subsequent to the death of S. John, we shall have enough to do. Let any one take up the Codex Bezae, (with which, by the way, Cod. B shews marvellous sympathy [u],) and explain if he can why there is a grave omission, or else a gross interpolation, in almost every page; and how it comes to pass that Cod. D " reproduces the ' textus receptus' of the Acts much in the same way that one of the best Chaldee Targums does the Hebrew of the Old Testament; so wide are the variations in the diction, so constant and inveterate the practice of expounding the narrative by means of interpolations which seldom recommend themselves as genuine by even a semblance of internal probability [x]." Our business as Critics is not *to invent theories* to account for the errors of Copyists; but rather to ascertain where they have erred, where not. What with the inexcusable depravations of early Heretics,—the preposterous emendations of ancient Critics,—the injudicious assiduity of Harmonizers,—the licentious caprice of individuals;—what with errors resulting from the inopportune recollection of similar or parallel places, — or from the familiar phraseology of the Ecclesiastical Lections,—or from the inattention of Scribes, — or from marginal glosses ;— however arising, endless are the corrupt readings of the oldest MSS. in existence; and it is by no means safe to

---

[u] So indeed does Cod. ℵ occasionally. See Scrivener's *Collation,* p. xlix.

[x] Scrivener's *Introduction to Codex Bezae,* p. liv.

follow up the detection of a depravation of the text with a theory to account for its existence. Let me be allowed to say that such theories are seldom satisfactory. *Guesses* only they are at best.

Thus, I profess myself wholly unable to accept the suggestion of Ussher,—(which, however, found favour with Garnier (Basil's editor), Bengel, Benson, and Michaelis; and has since been not only eagerly advocated by Conybeare and Howson following a host of German Critics, but has even enjoyed Mr. Scrivener's distinct approval;)—that the Epistle to the Ephesians "was *a Circular* addressed to other Asiatic Cities besides the capital Ephesus,—to Laodicea perhaps among the rest (Col. iv. 16); and that while some Codices may have contained the name of Ephesus in the first verse, *others may have had another city substituted, or the space after* τοῖς οὖσιν *left utterly void*[y]." At first sight, this conjecture has a kind of interesting plausibility which recommends it to our favour. On closer inspection,—(i) It is found to be not only gratuitous; but (ii) altogether unsupported and unsanctioned by the known facts of the case; and (what is most to the purpose) (iii) it is, as I humbly think, demonstrably erroneous. I demur to it,—

(1) Because of its exceeding Improbability: for (*a*) when S. Paul sent his Epistle to the Ephesians we know that Tychicus, the bearer of it[z], was charged with *a distinct Epistle* to the Colossians[a]: an Epistle nevertheless so singularly like the Epistle to the Ephesians that it is scarcely credible S. Paul would have written those two several Epistles to two of the Churches of Asia, and yet have sent only a duplicate of one of them, (*that* to the Ephesians,) furnished with a different address, to so large and important a place as Laodicea, for example. (*b*) Then further, the provision which S. Paul made at this very time for communicating with the Churches of Asia which he did not separately address is found to have been different. The Laodiceans were to read in their public assembly S. Paul's "*Epistle to the Colossians*," which the Colossians were ordered to send them. The Colos-

---

[y] Scrivener, *Coll. of Cod. Sin.* p. xlv.
[z] Eph. vi. 21, 22.   [a] Coloss. iv. 7, 16.

sians in like manner were to read the Epistle,—(to whom addressed, we know not),—which S. Paul describes as τὴν ἐκ Λαοδικείας [b]. If then it had been S. Paul's desire that the Laodiceans (suppose) should read publicly in their Churches his Epistle to the Ephesians, surely, he would have charged the Ephesians to procure that *his Epistle to them should be read in the Church of the Laodiceans*. Why should the Apostle be gratuitously assumed to have simultaneously adopted one method with the Churches of *Colosse* and Laodicea,—another with the Churches of *Ephesus* and Laodicea, —in respect of his epistolary communications?

(2) (*a*) But even supposing, for argument's sake, that S. Paul *did* send duplicate copies of his Epistle to the Ephesians to certain of the principal Churches of Asia Minor,— why should he have left the salutation *blank*, ("carta bianca," as Bengel phrases it [c],) for Tychicus to fill up when he got into Asia Minor? And yet, by the hypothesis, nothing short of *this* would account for the reading of Codd. B and ℵ.

(*b*) Let the full extent of the demand which is made on our good nature be clearly appreciated. We are required to believe that there was (1) A copy of what we call S. Paul's "Epistle to the Ephesians" sent into Asia Minor by S. Paul with a blank address; i.e. "with the space after τοῖς οὖσιν left utterly void:" (2) That Tychicus neglected to fill up that blank: and, (what is remarkable) (3) That no one was found to fill it up for him. Next, (4) That the same copy became the fontal source of the copy seen by Origen, and (5) Of the "old copies" seen by Basil; as well as (6) Of Codd. B and ℵ. And even this is not all. The same hypothesis constrains us to suppose that, on the contrary, (7) *One other* copy of this same "Encyclical Epistle," filled up with the Ephesian address, became the archetype of *every other copy of this Epistle in the world*..... But of what nature, (I would ask,) is the supposed necessity for building up such a marvellous structure of hypothesis,—of which the top story overhangs and overbalances all the rest of the edifice? The thing which puzzles us in Codd. B and ℵ is not that we find the name of *another City* in the salutation of S. Paul's "Epis-

[b] *Ubi supra*.   [c] *Gnomon*, in Ephes. i. 1, *ad init*.

tle to the Ephesians," but that we find the name of *no* city at all; nor meet with any vacant space there.

(c) On the other hand, supposing that S. Paul actually did address to different Churches copies of the present Epistle, and was scrupulous (as of course he was) to fill in the addresses himself before the precious documents left his hands, —then, doubtless, each several Church would have received, cherished, and jealously guarded its own copy. But if *this* had been the case, (or indeed if Tychicus had filled up the blanks for the Apostle,) is it not simply incredible that we should never have heard a word about the matter until now? unaccountable, above all, that there should nowhere exist traces of *conflicting testimony* as to the Church to which S. Paul's Epistle to the Ephesians was addressed? whereas *all* the most ancient writers, without exception,—(Marcion himself [A.D. 140 d], the "Muratorian" fragment [A.D. 170 or earlier], Irenæus [A.D. 175], Clemens Alexandrinus, Tertullian, Origen, Dionysius Alexandrinus, Cyprian, Eusebius,)—and all copies wheresoever found, give one unvarying, unfaltering witness. Even in Cod. B. and Cod. ℵ, (and this is much to be noted,) *the superscription of the Epistle* attests that it was addressed "to the Ephesians." Can we be warranted (I would respectfully inquire) in inventing facts in the history of an Apostle's practice, in order to account for what seems to be after all only an ordinary depravation of his text e?

 d See above, pp. 93—6. As for the supposed testimony of Ignatius (*ad Ephes.* c. xii.), see the notes, ed. Jacobson. See also Lardnei, vol. ii.

 e Let it be clearly understood by the advocates of this expedient for accounting for the state of the text of Codd. B. and ℵ, that nothing whatever is gained for the credit of those two MSS. by their ingenuity. Even if we grant them all they ask, the Codices in question remain, by their own admission, *defective*.

Quite plain is it, by the very hypothesis, that one of two courses alone remains open to them in editing the text: either (1) To leave *a blank space* after τοῖς οὖσιν: or else, (2) To let the words ἐν Ἐφέσῳ stand,—which I respectfully suggest is the wisest thing they can do. [For with Conybeare and Howson (*Life and Letters of S. Paul*, ii. 491), to eject the words "at Ephesus" from the text of Ephes. i. 1, and actually to substitute in their room the words "in Laodicea,"—is plainly abhorrent to every principle of rational criticism. The remarks of C. and H. on this subject (pp. 486 ff) have been faithfully met and sufficiently disposed of by Dean Alford (vol. iii. *Prolegg.* pp. 13-8); who infers, "in accordance with the prevalent belief of the Church in all ages, that this Epistle was *veritably addressed to the Saints in Ephesus*, and *to no other*

(3) But, in fact, it is high time to point out that such "*a Circular*" as was described above, (each copy furnished with a blank, to be filled up with the name of a different City,) would be a document without parallel in the annals of the primitive Church. It is, as far as I am aware, essentially a modern notion. I suspect, in short, that the suggestion before us is only another instance of the fatal misapprehension which results from the incautious transfer of the notions suggested by some familiar word in a living language to its supposed equivalent in an ancient tongue. Thus, because κύκλιος or ἐγκύκλιος confessedly signifies "circularis," it seems to be imagined that ἐγκύκλιος ἐπιστολή may mean "a Circular Letter." Whereas it really means nothing of the sort; but—"*a Catholic Epistle* [f]."

An "*Encyclical*," (and *that* is the word which has been imported into the present discussion), was quite a different document from what *we* call "a Circular." Addressed to no one Church or person in particular, it was Catholic or General,—the common property of all to whom it came. The General (or Catholic) Epistles of S. James, S. Peter, S. John are "Encyclical [g]." So is the well-known Canonical Epistle which Gregory, Bp. of Neocæsaræa in Pontus, in the middle of the third century, sent to the Bishops of his province [h]. As for "*a blank circular*," to be filled up with

Church."] In the former case, they will be exhibiting a curiosity; viz. they will be shewing us how (they think) a duplicate ("carta bianca") copy of the Epistle looked with "the space after τοῖς οὖσι left utterly void:" in the latter, they will be representing the archetypal copy which was sent to the Metropolitan see of Ephesus. But by printing the text thus,—τοῖς ἁγίοις τοῖς οὖσιν [ἐν Ἐφέσῳ] καὶ πιστοῖς κ.τ.λ., they are acting on an entirely different theory. They are merely testifying their mistrust of the text of every MS. in the world except Codd. B and א. This is clearly to forsake the "Encyclical" hypothesis altogether, and to put Ephes. i. 1 on the same footing as any other disputed text of Scripture which can be named.

[f] Ἐγκύκλιον ἐπιστολήν, vel ἐγκύκλια γράμματα Christophorsonus et alii interpretantur *literas circulares*: ego cum viris doctis malim *Epistolas* vel *literas publicas*, ad omnes fideles pertinentes, quas Græci aliàs vocant ἐπιστολὰς καθολικάς.—Suicer *in voce*.

[g] Καθολικαὶ λέγονται αὗται, οἱονεὶ ἐγκύκλιοι.—See Suicer *in voce*, Ἐγκύκλιος.

[h] Routh's *Reliquiæ*, vol. iii. p. 266.—"Tum ex Conciliis, tum ex aliis Patrum scriptis notum est, consuevisse primos Ecclesiae Patres acta et decreta Conciliorum passim ad omnes Dei Ecclesias mittere per epistolas, quas non uni

the words "in Ephesus," "in Laodicea," &c.,—its like (I repeat) is wholly unknown in the annals of Ecclesiastical Antiquity. The two notions are at all events inconsistent and incompatible. If S. Paul's Epistle to the Ephesians was "a Circular," then it was not "Encyclical:" if it was "Encyclical" then it was not "a Circular."

Are we then deliberately to believe, (for to this necessity we are logically reduced,) that the Epistle which occupies the fifth place among S. Paul's writings, and which from the beginning of the second century,—that is, from the very dawn of Historical evidence,—has been known as "the Epistle to the Ephesians," was an "Encyclical," "Catholic" or "General Epistle,"—addressed τοῖς ἁγίοις τοῖς οὖσι, καὶ πιστοῖς ἐν Χριστῷ Ἰησοῦ? There does not live the man who will accept so irrational a supposition. The suggestion therefore by which it has been proposed to account for the absence of the words ἐν Ἐφέσῳ in Ephes. i. 1 is not only in itself in the highest degree improbable, and contradicted by all the evidence to which we have access; but it is even inadmissible on critical grounds, and must be unconditionally surrendered[i]. It is observed to collapse before every test which can be applied to it.

privatim dicârunt, sed publice describi ab omnibus, dividi passim et pervulgari, atque cum omnibus populis communicari voluerunt. Hac igitur epistolae ἐγκύκλιοι vocatae sunt, quia κυκλόσε, quoquò versum et in omnem partem mittebantur."—Suicer *in voc.*

[i] "On the whole," says Bishop Middleton, (*Doctrine of the Greek Art.* p. 355) " I see nothing so probable as the opinion of Macknight (on Col. iv. 16,) —'that the Apostle sent the Ephesians word by Tychicus, who carried their letter, to send a copy of it to the Laodiceans; with an order to them to communicate it to the Colossians.'"—This suggestion is intended to meet *another* difficulty, and leaves the question of the reading of Ephes. i. 1 untouched. It proposes only to explain what S. Paul means by the enigmatical expression which is found in Col. iv. 16.

Macknight's suggestion, though it has found favour with many subsequent Divines, appears to me improbable in a high degree. S. Paul is found not to have sent *the Colossians* "word by Tychicus, who carried their letter, to send a copy of it to the Laodiceans." He charged them, himself, to do so. Why, at the same instant, is the Apostle to be thought to have adopted two such different methods of achieving one and the same important end? And why, instead of this roundabout method of communication, were not *the Ephesians* ordered,—if not by S. Paul himself, at least by Tychicus,—to send a copy of

III. Altogether marvellous in the meantime it is to me,—if men must needs account for the omission of the words ἐν Ἐφέσῳ from this place,—that they should have recourse to wild, improbable, and wholly unsupported theories, like those which go before; while an easy,—I was going to say the obvious,—solution of the problem is close at hand, and even solicits acceptance.

Marcion the heretic, (A.D. 140) is distinctly charged by Tertullian (A.D. 200), and by Jerome a century and a half later, with having abundantly mutilated the text of Scripture, and of S. Paul's Epistles in particular. Epiphanius compares the writing which Marcion tampered with to a moth-eaten coat[k]. "Instead of a stylus," (says Tertullian,) "Marcion employed a knife." "What wonder if he omits syllables, since often he omits whole pages[l]?" S. Paul's Epistle to the Ephesians, Tertullian even singles out by name; accusing Marcion of having furnished it with a new title. All this has been fully explained above, from page 93 to page 96.

Now, that Marcion recognised as S. Paul's Epistle "*to the Ephesians*" that Apostolical writing which stands fifth in our Canon, (but which stood seventh in his,) is just as certain as that he recognised as such S. Paul's Epistles to the Galatians, Corinthians, Romans, Thessalonians, Colos-

their Epistle to Colosse direct? And why do we find the Colossians charged to read publicly τὴν ἐκ Λαοδικείας, which (by the hypothesis) would have been only a copy,—instead of τὴν ἐξ Ἐφέσου, which, (by the same hypothesis,) would have been the original? Nay, why is it not designated by S. Paul, τὴν πρὸς Ἐφεσίους,—(if indeed it was his Epistle to the Ephesians which is alluded to,) instead of τὴν ἐκ Λαοδικείας; which would hardly be an intelligible way of indicating the document? Lastly, why are not the Colossians ordered to communicate a copy of their Epistle to the illustrious Church of the *Ephesians* also, which had been originally addressed by S. Paul? If the Colossians must needs read the Epistle (so like their own) which the Apostle had just written to the Ephesians, surely the Ephesians must also be supposed to have required a sight of the Epistle which S. Paul had at the same time written to the Colossians!

[k] Epiphan. *Opp.* i. 311 D.

[l] "Marcion exerte et palam machæra non stilo usus est, quoniam ad materiam suam cædem Scripturarum confeci*t*" (Tertullian *Præscript. Hær.* c. 38, p. 50.) "Non miror si syllabas subtrahit, cum paginas totas plerumque subducat." (*Adv. Marcion.* lib. v, c. xvii, p. 455.)

sians, Philippians. All this has been fully explained in a preceding page [m].

But it is also evident that Marcion put forth as S. Paul's *another* Epistle,—of which all we know for certain is, that it contained portions of the Epistle to the Ephesians, and purported to be addressed by S. Paul "to the Laodiceans." To ascertain with greater precision the truth of this matter at the end of upwards of seventeen centuries is perhaps impossible. Nor is it necessary. Obvious is it to suspect that not only did this heretical teacher at some period of his career prefix a new heading to certain copies of the Epistle to the Ephesians, but also that some of his followers industriously erased from certain other copies the words ἐν Ἐφέσῳ in ver. 1,—as being *the only two words in the entire Epistle* which effectually refuted their Master. It was not needful, (be it observed,) to multiply copies of the Epistle for the propagation of Marcion's deceit. Only two words had to be erased,—*the very two words whose omission we are trying to account for,*— in order to give some colour to his proposed attribution of the Epistle, ("quasi in isto diligentissimus explorator,")—to the Laodiceans. One of these mutilated copies will have fallen into the hands of Origen,—who often complains of the corrupt state of his text: while the critical personages for whom Cod. B and Cod. ℵ were transcribed will probably have been acquainted with other such mutilated copies. Are we not led, as it were by the hand, to take some such view of the case? In this way we account satisfactorily, and on grounds of historic evidence, for the omission which has exercised the Critics so severely.

I do not lose sight of the fact that the Epistle to the Ephesians ends without salutations, without personal notices of any kind. But in this respect it is not peculiar [n]. *That,* —joined to a singular absence of identifying allusion,—sufficiently explains why Marcion selected this particular Epistle for the subject of his fraud. But, to infer from this circumstance, in defiance of the Tradition of the Church Universal, and in defiance of its very Title, that the Epistle is

---

[m] See above p. 95, and see note (f) p. 94.

[n] See, by all means, Alford on this subject, vol. iii. *Prolegg.* pp. 13—15.

'Encyclical,' in the technical sense of that word; and to go on to urge this characteristic as an argument in support of the omission of the words ἐν Ἐφέσῳ,—is clearly the device of an eager Advocate; not the method of a calm and unprejudiced Judge. True it is that S. Paul,—who, writing to the Corinthians from Ephesus, says "*the Churches of Asia salute you*," (1 Cor. xvi. 19,)—may have known very well that an Epistle of his "to the Ephesians," would, as a matter of course, be instantly communicated to others besides the members of that particular Church: and in fact this may explain why there is nothing specially "Ephesian" in the contents of the Epistle. The Apostle,—(as when he addressed " the Churches of Galatia,")—may have had certain of the other neighbouring Churches in his mind while he wrote. But all this is wholly foreign to the question before us: the one *only* question being *this*,—Which of the three following addresses represents what S. Paul must be considered to have actually written in the first verse of his " Epistle to the Ephesians "?—

(1) τοῖς ἁγίοις τοῖς οὖσιν ἐν Ἐφέσῳ καὶ πιστοῖς ἐν Χ. Ἰ.
(2) τοῖς ἁγίοις τοῖς οὖσιν ἐν . . . . . . καὶ πιστοῖς ἐν Χ. Ἰ.
(3) τοῖς ἁγίοις τοῖς οὖσι, καὶ πιστοῖς ἐν Χ. Ἰ.

What I have been saying amounts to this: that it is absolutely unreasonable for men to go out of their way to invent a theory wanting every element of probability in order to account for the omission of the words ἐν Ἐφέσῳ from S. Paul's Epistle to the Ephesians; while they have under their eyes the express testimony of a competent witness of the ii[nd] century that a certain heretic, named Marcion, "presumed to prefix an unauthorized title to that very Epistle," ("Marcion ei titulum aliquando interpolare gestiit,")—which title obviously *could not stand unless those two words were first erased from the text*. To interpolate that new title, and to erase the two words which were plainly inconsistent with it, were obviously correlative acts which must always have been performed together.

But however all this may be, (as already pointed out,) the only question to be determined by us is,—whether it be credible that the words ἐν Ἐφέσῳ are an unauthorized addition; foisted into the text of Ephes. i. 1 as far back as the Apostolic age: an interpolation which, instead of dying out, and at last all but disappearing, has spread and established itself, until the words are found in every copy,—are represented in every translation,—have been recognised in every country,—witnessed to by every Father,—received in every age of the Church? I repeat that the one question which has to be decided is, not *how* the words ἐν Ἐφέσῳ came to be put in, or came to be left out; but simply whether, on an impartial review of the evidence, it be reasonable (with Tischendorf, Tregelles, Conybeare and Howson, and so many more,) to suspect their genuineness and enclose them in brackets? Is it *credible* that the words ἐν Ἐφέσῳ are a spurious and unauthorized addition to the inspired autograph of the Apostle?... We have already, as I think, obtained a satisfactory answer to this question. It has been shewn, as conclusively as in inquiries of this nature is possible, that in respect of the reading of Ephesians i. 1, Codd. B and ℵ are even *most* conspicuously at fault.

IV. But if these two Codices are thus convicted of error in respect of the one remaining text which their chief upholders have selected, and to which they still make their most confident appeal,—what remains, but to point out that it is high time that men should be invited to disabuse their minds of the extravagant opinion which they have been so industriously taught to entertain of the value of the two Codices in question? It has already degenerated into an unreasoning prejudice, and threatens at last to add one more to the already overgrown catalogue of "vulgar errors."

V. I cannot, I suppose, act more fairly by Tischendorf than by transcribing in conclusion his remarks on the four remaining readings of Codex ℵ to which he triumphantly appeals: promising to dismiss them all with a single remark. He says, (addressing unlearned readers,) in his "Introduction" to the Tauchnitz (English) New Testament [o]:—

"To these examples, others might be added. Thus, Origen says on John i. 4, that in some copies it was written, 'in Him *is* life,' for 'in Him *was* life.' This is a reading which

---

[o] p. xiv.—See above, pp. 8, 9, note (f).

we find in sundry quotations before the time of Origen[p]; but now, among all known Greek MSS. it is *only in the Sinaitic, and the famous old Codex Bezae*, a copy of the Gospels at Cambridge; yet it is also found in most of the early Latin versions, in the most ancient Syriac, and in the oldest Coptic.—Again, in Matth. xiii. 35, Jerome ob-

[p] One is rather surprised to find the facts of the case so unfairly represented in addressing unlearned readers; who are entitled to the largest amount of ingenuousness, and to entire sincerity of statement. The facts are these :—
(1) Valentt. (*apud* Irenæum), (2) Clemens Alex., and (3) Theodotus (*apud* Clem.) read ἔστι: but then (1) Irenæus himself, (2) Clemens Alex., and (3) Theodotus (*apud* Clem.) *also* read ἦν. These testimonies, therefore, clearly neutralize each other. Cyprian also has *both* readings.—Hippolytus, on the other hand, reads ἔστι; but Origen, (though he remarks that ἔστι is "perhaps not an improbable reading,") reads ἦν *ten or eleven times.* ἯHν is also the reading of Eusebius, of Chrysostom, of Cyril, of Nonnus, of Theodoret,—of the Vulgate, of the Memphitic, of the Peshito, and of the Philoxenian Versions; as well as of B, A, C,—in fact of *all the MSS. in the world*, except of ℵ and D.
All that remains to be set on the other side are the Thebaic and Cureton's Syriac, together with most copies of the early Latin.
And now, with the evidence thus all before us, will any one say that it is lawfully a question for discussion which of these two readings must exhibit the genuine text of S. John i. 4 ? (For I treat it as a question of authority, and reason from *the evidence*,—declining to import into the argument what may be called *logical* considerations; though I conceive them to be all on my side.) I suspect, in fact, that the inveterate practice of the primitive age of reading the place after the following strange fashion,—ὃ γέγονεν ἐν αὐτῷ ζωὴ ἦν, was what led to this depravation of the text. Cyril in his Commentary [heading of lib. i, c. vi.] so reads S. John i. 3, 4. And to substitute ἐστί (for ἦν) in such a sentence as *that*, was obvious. . . . Chrysostom's opinion is well known, "Let us beware of putting the full stop" (he says) "at the words οὐδὲ ἕν,—as do the heretics." [He alludes to Valentinus, Heracleon (Orig. *Opp*. i. 130), and to Theodotus (*apud* Clem. Alex.). But it must be confessed that Irenæus, Hippolytus (*Routh, Opusc.* i. 68), Clemens Alex., Origen, Concil. Antioch. (A.D. 269, *Routh* iii. 293), Theophilus Antioch., Athanasius, Cyril of Jer.,—besides of the Latins, Tertullian, Lactantius, Victorinus (*Routh* iii. 459), and Augustine,—point the place in the same way. "It is worth our observation," (says Pearson,) "that Eusebius citing the place of S. John to prove that the HOLY GHOST was made by the SON, leaves out those words twice together by which the Catholics used to refute that heresy of the Arians, viz. ὃ γέγονεν."]
Chrysostom proceeds,—"In order to make out that THE SPIRIT is a creature, they read Ὃ γέγονε, ἐν αὐτῷ ζωὴ ἦν; by which means, the Evangelist's language is made unintelligible." (*Opp.* viii. 40.)—This punctuation is nevertheless adopted by Tregelles,—but not by Tischendorf. The Peshito, Epiphanius (quoted in Pearson's note, referred to *infrà*), Cyprian, Jerome and the Vulgate divide the sentence as we do.—See by all means on this subject Pearson's *note* (*z*), ART. viii, (ii. p. 262 ed. Burton). Also Routh's *Opusc.* i. 88-9.

serves that in the third century Porphyry, the antagonist of Christianity, had found fault with the Evangelist Matthew for having said, 'which was spoken by the prophet Esaias.' A writing of the second century had already witnessed to the same reading; but Jerome adds further that well-informed men had long ago removed the name of Esaias. Among all our MSS. of a thousand years old and upwards, there *is not a solitary example containing the name of Esaias in the text referred to,—except the Sinaitic*, to which a few of less than a thousand years old may be added.—Once more, Origen quotes John xiii. 10 six times; but *only the Sinaitic and several ancient Latin MSS.* read it the same as Origen: 'He that is washed needeth not to wash, but is clean every whit.'—In John vi. 51, also, where the reading is very difficult to settle, the *Sinaitic is alone among all Greek copies* indubitably correct; and Tertullian, at the end of the second century, confirms the Sinaitic reading: 'If any man eat of my bread, he shall live for ever. The bread that I will give for the life of the world is my flesh.' We omit to indicate further illustrations of this kind, although there are many others like them q."

Let it be declared without offence, that there appears to

   q It may not be altogether useless that I should follow this famous Critic of the text of the N. T. over the ground which he has himself chosen. He challenges attention for the four following readings of the Codex Sinaiticus:—
   (1.) S. JOHN i. 4: εν αυτω ζωη εστιν.—(2.) S. MATTH. xiii. 35: το ρηθεν δια ησαιου του προφητου.—(3.) S. JOHN xiii. 10: ο λελουμενος ουχ εχι χρειαν νιψασθαι.—(4.) S. JOHN vi. 51: αν τις φαγη εκ του εμου αρτου, ζησει εις τον αιωνα·—ο αρτος ον εγω δωσω υπερ της του κοσμου ζωης η σαρξ μου εστιν. (And this, Dr. Tischendorf asserts to be "indubitably correct.")

On inspection, these four readings prove to be exactly what might have been anticipated from the announcement that they are almost the private property of the single Codex א. The last three are absolutely worthless. They stand self-condemned. To examine is to reject them: the second (of which Jerome says something *very* different from what Tisch. pretends) and fourth being only two more of those unskilful attempts at critical emendation of the inspired Text, of which this Codex contains so many sorry specimens: the third being clearly nothing else but the result of the carelessness of the transcriber. Misled by the like ending (ὁμοιοτέλευτον) he has *dropped a line:* thus:—

OYX EXI XPEIAN [EI
MH TOYC ΠΟΔΑC] NI
ΨΑCΘΑΙ ΑΛΛΑ ECTIN

The first, I have discussed briefly in the foregoing footnote (p) p. 110.

exist in the mind of this illustrious Critic a hopeless confusion between the *antiquity* of a Codex and the *value* of its readings. I venture to assert that a reading is valuable or the contrary, exactly in proportion to the probability of its being true or false. Interesting it is sure to be, be it what it may, if it be found in a very ancient codex,—interesting and often instructive: but the editor of Scripture must needs bring every reading, wherever found, to this test at last:—Is it to be thought that what I am here presented with is what the Evangelist or the Apostle actually wrote? If an answer in the negative be obtained to this question, then, the fact that one, or two, or three of the early Fathers appear to have so read the place, will not avail to impart to the rejected reading one particle of *value*. And yet Tischendorf thinks it enough in *all* the preceding passages to assure his reader that a given reading in Cod. א was recognised by Origen, by Tertullian, by Jerome. To have established this one point he evidently thinks sufficient. There is implied in all this an utterly false major premiss: viz. That Scriptural quotations found in the writings of Origen, of Tertullian, of Jerome, must needs be the *ipsissima verba* of the SPIRIT. Whereas it is notorious "that the worst corruptions to which the New Testament has ever been subjected originated within a hundred years after it was composed: that Irenæus and the whole Western, with a portion of the Syrian Church, used far inferior manuscripts to those employed by Stunica, or Erasmus, or Stephens, thirteen centuries later, when moulding the Textus Receptus[r]." And one is astonished that a Critic of so much sagacity, (who of course knows better,) should deliberately put forth so gross a fallacy,— not only without a word of explanation, a word of caution, but in such a manner as inevitably to mislead an unsuspecting reader. Without offence to Dr. Tischendorf, I must be allowed to declare that, in the remarks we have been considering, he shews himself far more bent on glorifying the "Codex Sinaiticus" than in establishing the Truth of the pure Word of GOD. He convinces me that to have found

---

[r] Scrivener's *Introduction*, p. 386. The whole Chapter deserves careful study.

an early uncial Codex, is every bit as fatal as to have "taken a gift." Verily, "*it doth blind the eyes of the wise*[s]."

And with this, I shall conclude my remarks on these two famous Codices. I humbly record my deliberate conviction that when the Science of Textual Criticism, which is at present only in its infancy, comes to be better understood; (and a careful collation of every existing Codex of the New Testament is one indispensable preliminary to its being ever placed on a trustworthy basis;) a very different estimate will be formed of the importance of not a few of those readings which at present are received with unquestioning submission, chiefly on the authority of Codex B and Codex ℵ. On the other hand, it is perfectly certain that no future collations, no future discoveries, will ever make it credible that the last Twelve Verses of S. Mark's Gospel are a spurious supplement to the Evangelical Narrative; or that the words ἐν Ἐφέσῳ are an unauthorized interpolation of the inspired Text.

And thus much concerning Codex B and Codex ℵ.

I would gladly have proceeded at once to the discussion of the "Internal Evidence," but that the external testimony commonly appealed to is not yet fully disposed of. There remain to be considered certain ancient "Scholia" and "Notes," and indeed whatever else results from the critical inspection of ancient MSS., whether uncial or cursive: and all this may reasonably claim one entire Chapter to itself.

[s] Deut. xvi. 19.

μη εκθαμβεισθαι
ιν̅ ζητειτε τον
ναζωραιον τὸ
ἐσταυρωμενον
ηγερθη ουκ εστ[ιν]
ὡδε· ιδε ὁ τοπος
ὁπου εθηκαν αυ
τον· αλλα υπαγε
τε ειπατε τοις μα
θηταις αυτου και
τω πετρω· ὁτι
προαγει ϋμας εις
την γαλιλαιαν·
ἐκει αυτον ὀψες
θε· καθως ειπε
ϋμιν

Καὶ ἐξελθουσαι ἐ
φυγον απο του
μνημειου· ει
χεν δε αυτας τρο
μος και ἐκστασις
και ουδενι ουδεν
ειπον· ἐφοβουν
το γαρ·

Θερετε του
και ταυτα·

Παντα δε τα παρη
γγελμενα τοις
περι τον πετρον
συντομως ἐξη
γγιλαν· μετα
δε ταυτα και αυτος
ὁ ι̅ς̅ απο ανατολης
και αχρι δυσεως
ἐξαπεστειλεν δι
αυτων το ιερον
και αφθαρτον κη
ρυγμα· της αιω
νιου σωτηριας·

ἐστιν δε και
ταυτα φερο
μενα μετα το
ἐφοβουντο
γαρ·

Αναστας δε πρωϊ
πρωτη σαββατο[υ]

THE opposite page exhibits an *exact Fac-simile*, obtained by Photography, of fol. 113 of EVAN. COD. L, ("Codex Regius," No. 62,) at Paris; containing S. Mark xvi. 6 to 9;—as explained at pp. 203-4. The Text of that MS. has been published by Dr. Tischendorf in his "Monumenta Sacra Inedita," (1846, pp. 57—399.) See p. 206.

The original Photograph was executed (Oct. 1869) by the obliging permission of M. de Wailly, who presides over the Manuscript Department of the "Bibliothèque." He has my best thanks for the kindness with which he promoted my wishes and facilitated my researches.

It should perhaps be stated that *the margin* of "Codex L" is somewhat ampler than can be represented in an octavo volume; each folio measuring very nearly nine inches, by very nearly six inches and a half.

CHAPTER VIII.

THE PURPORT OF ANCIENT SCHOLIA, AND NOTES IN MSS. ON THE SUBJECT OF THESE VERSES, SHEWN TO BE THE REVERSE OF WHAT IS COMMONLY SUPPOSED.

Later Editors of the New Testament the victims of their predecessors' inaccuracies.—Birch's unfortunate mistake (196).—Scholz' serious blunders (195 and 197-8).—Griesbach's sweeping misstatement (pp. 121-2).—*The grave misapprehension which has resulted from all this inaccuracy of detail* (200-3).
Codex L (203).—*Ammonius not the author of the so-called "Ammonian" Sections* (205).—*Epiphanius* (212).—*" Caesarius," a misnomer.*—*" The Catenae," misrepresented* (213).

IN the present Chapter, I propose to pass under review whatever manuscript testimony still remains unconsidered; our attention having been hitherto exclusively devoted to Codices B and ℵ. True, that the rest of the evidence may be disposed of in a single short sentence :—*The Twelve Verses under discussion are found in every copy of the Gospels in existence with the exception of Codices B and* ℵ. But then,

I. We are assured,—(by Dr. Tregelles for example,)—that "a Note or a Scholion stating the absence of these verses from *many*, from *most*, or from the *most correct* copies (often from Victor or Severus) is found in twenty-five other cursive Codices[a]." Tischendorf has nearly the same words: "Scholia" (he says) "in very many MSS. state that the Gospel of Mark in the most ancient (and most accurate) copies ended at the ninth verse." That distinguished Critic supports his assertion by appealing to seven MSS. in particular,—and referring generally to "about twenty-five others." Dr. Davidson adopts every word of this blindfold.

1. Now of course if all that precedes were true, this department of the Evidence would become deserving of serious

[a] *Printed Text*, p. 254.

CHAP. VIII.] *Later Editors the victims of their predecessors.* 195

attention. But I simply *deny the fact.* I entirely deny that the "Note or Scholion" which these learned persons affirm to be of such frequent occurrence has any existence whatever, —except in their own imaginations. On the other hand, I assert that notes or scholia which state the exact reverse, (viz. that "in the older" or "the more accurate copies" the last twelve verses of S. Mark's Gospel *are contained,*) recur even perpetually. The plain truth is this :—These eminent persons have taken their information at second-hand,— partly from Griesbach, partly from Scholz,—without suspicion and without inquiry. But then they have slightly misrepresented Scholz; and Scholz (1830) slightly misunderstood Griesbach; and Griesbach (1796) took liberties with Wetstein; and Wetstein (1751) made a few serious mistakes. The consequence might have been anticipated. The Truth, once thrust out of sight, certain erroneous statements have usurped its place,—which every succeeding Critic now reproduces, evidently to his own entire satisfaction; though not, it must be declared, altogether to his own credit. Let me be allowed to explain in detail what has occurred.

2. Griesbach is found to have pursued the truly German plan of setting down *all* the twenty-five MSS.[b] and *all* the five Patristic authorities which up to his time had been cited as bearing on the genuineness of S. Mark xvi. 9—20 : giving the former *in numerical order*, and stating generally concerning them that in one or other of those authorities it would be found recorded "that the verses in question were anciently *wanting* in some, or in most, or in almost all the Greek copies, or in the most accurate ones :—or else that they were *found* in a few, or in the more accurate copies, or in many, or in most of them, specially in the Palestinian Gospel." The learned writer (who had made up his mind long before that the verses in question are to be rejected) no doubt perceived that this would be the most convenient way of disposing of the evidence for and against: but one is at a loss to understand how English scholars can have acquiesced in such a slipshod statement for well nigh

---

[b] Viz. Codd. L, 1, 22, 24, 34, 36, 37, 38, 39, 40, 41,—108, 129, 137, 138, 143, 181, 186, 195, 199, 206, 209, 210, 221, 222.

a hundred years. A very little study of the subject would have shewn them that Griesbach derived the first eleven of his references from Wetstein [c], the last fourteen from Birch [d]. As for Scholz, he unsuspiciously adopted Griesbach's fatal enumeration of Codices; adding five to the number; and only interrupting the series here and there, in order to insert the quotations which Wetstein had already supplied from certain of them. With Scholz, therefore, rests the blame of everything which has been written since 1830 concerning the MS. evidence for this part of S. Mark's Gospel; subsequent critics having been content to adopt his statements without acknowledgment and without examination. Unfortunately Scholz did his work (as usual) in such a slovenly style, that besides perpetuating old mistakes he invented new ones; which, of course, have been reproduced by those who have simply translated or transcribed him. And now I shall examine his note "(z) [e]", with which practically all that has since been delivered on this subject by Tischendorf, Tregelles, Davidson, and the rest, is identical.

(1.) Scholz (copying Griesbach) first states that in two MSS. in the Vatican Library [f] the verses in question "are marked with an asterisk." The original author of this statement was Birch, who followed it up by explaining the fatal signification of this mark [g]. From that day to this, the asterisks in Codd. Vatt. 756 and 757 have been religiously reproduced by every Critic in turn; and it is universally taken for granted that they represent two ancient

[c] Wetstein quoted 14 Codices in all: but Griesbach makes no use of his reference to Reg. 2868, 1880, and 2282 (leg. 2242?) which = Evan. 15, 19, 299 (?) respectively.

[d] *Variae Lectiones*, &c. (1801, p. 225-6.)—He cites Codd. Vatt. 358, 756, 757, 1229 (= our 129, 137, 138, 143): Cod. Zelada (= 181): Laur. vi. 18, 34 (= 186, 195): Ven. 27 (= 210): Vind. Lamb. 38, 39, Kol. 4 (= 221, 222, 108): Cod. iv. (*leg.* 5?) S. Mariæ Bened. Flor. (= 199): Codd. Ven. 6, 10 (= 206, 209).

[e] *Nov. Test.* vol. i. p. 199.

[f] Vat. 756, 757 = our Evan. 137, 138.

[g] Quo signo tamquam censoria virgula usi sunt librarii, qua Evangelistarum narrationes, in omnibus Codicibus non obvias, tamquam dubias notarent.— *Variae Lectiones,* &c. p. 225.

witnesses against the genuineness of the last twelve verses of the Gospel according to S. Mark.

And yet, (let me say it without offence,) a very little attention ought to be enough to convince any one familiar with this subject that the proposed inference is absolutely inadmissible. For, in the first place, a *solitary* asterisk (not at all a rare phenomenon in ancient MSS.[h]) has of necessity no such signification. And even if it does sometimes indicate that all the verses which follow are suspicious, (of which, however, I have never seen an example,) it clearly *could* not have that signification here,—for a reason which I should have thought an intelligent boy might discover.

Well aware, however, that I should never be listened to, with Birch and Griesbach, Scholz and Tischendorf, and indeed every one else against me,—I got a learned friend at Rome to visit the Vatican Library for me, and inspect the two Codices in question[*]. That he would find Birch right *in his facts,* I had no reason to doubt; but I much more than doubted the correctness of his proposed inference from them. I even felt convinced that the meaning and purpose of the asterisks in question would be demonstrably different from what Birch had imagined.

Altogether unprepared was I for the result. It is found that the learned Dane has here made one of those (venial, but) unfortunate blunders to which every one is liable who registers phenomena of this class in haste, and does not methodize his memoranda until he gets home. To be brief, —*there proves to be no asterisk at all,—either in Cod.* 756, *or in Cod.* 757.

On the contrary. After ἐφοβοῦντο γάρ, the former Codex has, in the text of S. Mark xvi. 9 (*fol.* 150 *b*), a plain cross, —(*not* an asterisk, thus ⁜ or ※ or ⁕ or ⁑, but a cross, thus +),—the intention of which is to refer the reader to an annotation on *fol.* 151 *b*, (marked, of course, with a cross also,) *to the effect that S. Mark xvi.* 9—20 *is undoubtedly*

---

[h] In Cod. 264 (= Paris 65) for instance, besides at S. Mk. xvi. 9, ※ occurs at xi. 12, xii. 38, and xiv. 12. On the other hand, no such sign occurs at the *pericope de adulterá*.   [*] Further obligations to the same friend are acknowledged in the Appendix (D).

genuine[i]. The evidence, therefore, not only breaks hopelessly down; but it is discovered that this witness has been by accident put into the wrong box. This is, in fact, a witness not for the plaintiff, but *for the defendant!*—As for the other Codex, it exhibits neither asterisk nor cross; but contains the same note or scholion attesting the genuineness of the last twelve verses of S. Mark.

I suppose I may now pass on: but I venture to point out that unless the Witnesses which remain to be examined are able to produce very different testimony from that borne by the last two, the present inquiry cannot be brought to a close too soon. ("I took thee to curse mine enemies, and, behold, thou hast blessed them altogether.")

(2.) In Codd. 20 and 300 (Scholz proceeds) we read as follows:—" From here to the end forms no part of the text in some of the copies. *In the ancient copies, however, it all forms part of the text*[k]." Scholz (who was the first to adduce this important testimony to the genuineness of the verses now under consideration) takes no notice of the singular circumstance that the two MSS. he mentions have been *exactly* assimilated in ancient times to a common model; and that they correspond one with the other so entirely[1] that the foregoing rubrical annotation appears *in the wrong place* in both of them, viz. *at the close of ver.* 15, where it interrupts the text. This was, therefore, once a scholion written in the margin of some very ancient Codex, which has lost its way in the process of transcription; (for there can be no doubt that it was originally written against ver. 8.) And let it be noted that its testimony is express; and that it avouches for the fact that "*in the ancient copies,*" S. Mark xvi. 9—20 "*formed part of the text.*"

[1] Similarly, in Cod. Coisl. 20, in the Paris Library, (which = our 36,) against S. Mark xvi. 9, is this sign ※. It is intended (like an asterisk in a modern book) to refer the reader to the self-same annotation which is spoken of in the text as occurring in Cod. Vat. 756, and which is observed to occur in the margin of the Paris MS. also.

[k] ἐντεῦθεν ἕως τοῦ τέλους ἔν τισι τῶν ἀντιγράφων οὐ κεῖται· ἐν δε τοῖς ἀρχαίοις, πάντα ἀπαράλειπτα κεῖται.
—(Codd. 20 and 300 = Paris 188, 186.)

[l] See more concerning this matter in the Appendix (D), *ad fin.*

(3.) Yet more important is the record contained in the same two MSS., (of which also Scholz says nothing,) viz. that they exhibit a text which had been "collated with the ancient and approved copies at Jerusalem[m]." What need to point out that so remarkable a statement, taken in conjunction with the express voucher that "although some copies of the Gospels are without the verses under discussion, yet that *in the ancient copies* all the verses are found," is a *critical attestation to the genuineness* of S. Mark xvi. 9 to 20, far outweighing the bare statement (next to be noticed) of the undeniable historical fact that, "*in some copies,*" *S. Mark ends at ver.* 8,—but "in many *does not*"?

(4.) Scholz proceeds:—" In Cod. 22, after εφοβοῦντο ράρ + τέλοс is read the following rubric :"—

ἔν τισι τῶν ἀντιγράφων ἕως ὧδε πληροῦται ὁ εὐαγγελιστής· ἐν πολλοῖς δὲ καὶ ταῦτα φέρεται[n].

And the whole of this statement is complacently copied by *all* subsequent Critics and Editors,—cross, and "τέλοс," and all,—as an additional ancient attestation to the fact that "*The End*" (τέλοс) *of S. Mark's Gospel* is indeed at ch. xvi. 8. Strange,—incredible rather,—that among so many learned persons, not one should have perceived that "τέλοс" in this place merely denotes that here *a well-known Ecclesiastical section comes to an end !* ... As far, therefore, as the present discussion is concerned, the circumstance is purely irrelevant[o];

[m] At the end of S. Matthew's Gospel in Cod. 300 (at fol. 89) is found,—

εὐαγγέλιον κατὰ Ματθαῖον ἐγράφη καὶ ἀντεβλήθη ἐκ τῶν Ἱεροσολύμοις παλαιῶν ἀντιγράφων, ἐν στίχοις βφιδ

and at the end of S. Mark's, (at fol. 147 *b*)—

εὐαγγέλιον κατὰ Μάρκον ἐγράφη καὶ ἀντεβλήθη ὁμοίως ἐκ τῶν ἐσπουδασμένων στίχοις αφς κεφαλαίοις сλξ

This second colophon (though not the first) is found in Cod. 20. *Both* reappear in Cod. 262 (= Paris 53), and (with an interesting variety in the former of the two) in [what I suppose is the first half of] the uncial Codex Λ. See Scrivener's *Introduction*, p. 125.

[n] = Paris 72, *fol.* 107 *b*. He might have added, (for Wetstein had pointed it out 79 years before,) that *the same note precisely* is found between verses 8 and 9 in Cod. 15 (= Paris 64,) *fol.* 98 *b*.

[o] See more at the very end of Chap. XI.

and, (as I propose to shew in Chapter XI,) the less said about it by the opposite party, the better.

(5.) Scholz further states that in four, (he means three,) other Codices very nearly the same colophon as the preceding recurs, with an important additional clause. In Codd. 1, 199, 206, 209, (he says) is read,—

"In certain of the copies, the Evangelist finishes here; *up to which place Eusebius the friend of Pamphilus canonized.* In other copies, however, is found as follows [p]." And then comes the rest of S. Mark's Gospel.

I shall have more to say about this reference to Eusebius, and what he "canonized," by-and-by. But what is there in all this, (let me in the meantime ask), to recommend the opinion that the Gospel of S. Mark was published by its Author in an incomplete state; or that the last twelve verses of it are of spurious origin?

(6.) The reader's attention is specially invited to the imposing statement which follows. Codd. 23, 34, 39, 41, (says Scholz,) "contain these words of Severus of Antioch:—

"In the more accurate copies, the Gospel according to Mark has its end at 'for they were afraid.' In some copies, however, this also is added,—'Now when He was risen,' &c. This, however, seems to contradict to some extent what was before delivered," &c.

It may sound fabulous, but it is strictly true, that every word of this, (unsuspiciously adopted as it has been by *every* Critic who has since gone over the same ground,) is a mere tissue of mistakes. For first, — Cod. 23 contains *nothing whatever pertinent to the present inquiry.* (Scholz, evidently through haste and inadvertence, has confounded *his own*

---

[p] Cod. 1. (at Basle), and Codd. 206, 209 (which = Venet. 6 and 10) contain as follows :—

ἔν τισι μὲν τῶν ἀντιγράφων ἕως ὧδε πληροῦται ὁ Εὐαγγελιστής, ἕως οὗ καὶ ʼΕυσέβιος ὁ Παμφίλου ἐκανόνισεν· ἐν ἄλλοις δὲ ταῦτα φέρεται· ἀναστάς, κ.τ.λ.

But Cod. 199 (which = S. Mariae Benedict. Flor. Cod. IV. [*lege* 5], according to Birch (p. 226) who supplies the quotation, has only this :—

ἔν τισι τῶν ἀντιγράφων οὐ κεῖνται [?] ταῦτα.

"23" with "*Coisl.* 23," but "Coisl. 23" is his "39,"—of which by-and-by. This reference therefore has to be cancelled.)—Cod. 41 contains a scholion of *precisely the opposite tendency:* I mean, a scholion which avers that *the accurate copies of S. Mark's Gospel contain these last twelve verses.* (Scholz borrowed this wrong reference from Wetstein,—who, by an oversight, quotes Cod. 41 three times instead of twice.) —There remain but Codd. 34 and 39 ; and in neither of those two manuscripts, from the first page of S. Mark's Gospel to the last, does there exist *any "scholion of Severus of Antioch" whatever.* Scholz, in a word, has inadvertently made a gross misstatement [q]; and every Critic who has since written on this subject has adopted his words,—without acknowledgment and without examination..... Such is the evidence on which it is proposed to prove that S. Mark did not write the last twelve verses of his Gospel!

(7.) Scholz proceeds to enumerate the following twenty-two Codices:—24, 34, 36, 37, 38, 39, 40, 41, 108, 129, 137, 138, 143, 181, 186, 195, 199, 206, 209, 210, 221, 222. And this imposing catalogue is what has misled Tischendorf, Tregelles and the rest. They have not perceived that it is *a mere transcript of Griesbach's list;* which Scholz interrupts only to give from Cod. 24, (imperfectly and at second-hand,) the weighty scholion, (Wetstein had given it from Cod. 41,) which relates, on the authority of an eye-witness, that S. Mark xvi. 9—20 existed in the ancient Palestinian Copy. (About that Scholion enough has been offered already [r].) Scholz adds that very nearly the same words are found in 374.—What he says concerning 206 and 209 (and he might have added 199,) has been explained above.

But when the twenty MSS. which remain [s] undisposed of have been scrutinized, their testimony is found to be quite

---

[q] It originated in this way. At the end of S. Matthew's Gospel, in both Codices, are found those large extracts from the "2nd Hom. on the Resurrection" which Montfaucon published in the *Bibl. Coisl.* (pp. 68—75), and which Cramer has since reprinted at the end of his *Catena in S. Matth.* (i. 243—251.) In Codd. 34 and 39 they are ascribed to "Severus of Antioch." See above (p. 40.) See also pp. 39 and 57.

[r] See above, pp. 64, 65.   [s] 22—3 (199, 206, 209) = 19 + 1 (374) = 20.

different from what is commonly supposed. One of them (N°. 38) has been cited in error: while the remaining nineteen are nothing else but copies of *Victor of Antioch's commentary on S. Mark*,—no less than *sixteen* of which contain the famous attestation that in *most of the accurate copies, and in particular the authentic Palestinian Codex, the last twelve verses of S. Mark's Gospel* WERE FOUND. (See above, pp. 64 and 65.) . . . . And this exhausts the evidence.

(8.) So far, therefore, as "Notes" and "Scholia" in MSS. are concerned, the sum of the matter proves to be simply this:—(*a*) Nine Codices [t] are observed to contain a note to the effect that the end of S. Mark's Gospel, though wanting "in some," was yet found "in others,"—"in many,"—"*in the ancient copies.*"

(*b*) Next, four Codices [*] contain subscriptions vouching for the genuineness of this portion of the Gospel by declaring that those four Codices had been *collated with approved copies preserved at Jerusalem.*

(*c*) Lastly, sixteen Codices, — (to which, besides that already mentioned by Scholz [u], I am able to add at least five others, making twenty-two in all [x],)—contain a weighty critical scholion asserting categorically that in "very many" and "accurate copies," specially in the "true Palestinian exemplar," *these verses had been found by one who seems to have verified the fact of their existence there for himself.*

(9.) And now, shall I be thought unfair if, on a review of the premises, I assert that I do not see a shadow of reason for the imposing statement which has been adopted by Tischendorf, Tregelles, and the rest, that "there exist about thirty Codices which state that from the more ancient and more accurate copies of the Gospel, the last twelve verses of S. Mark were absent?" I repeat, there is not so much as *one single Codex* which contains such a scholion;

[t] viz. Codd. L, 1, 199, 206, 209 :—20, 300 :—15, 22.

[*] Cod. Λ, 20, 262, 300.

[u] Evan. 374.

[x] viz. Evan. 24, 36, 37, 40, 41 (Wetstein.) Add Evan. 108, 129, 137, 138, 143, 181, 186, 195, 210, 221, 222. (Birch *Varr. Lectt.* p. 225.) Add Evan. 374 (Scholz.) Add Evan. 12, 129, 299, 329, and the Moscow Codex (qu. Evan. 253?) employed by Matthaei.

while twenty-four[y] of those commonly enumerated state *the exact reverse.*—We may now advance a step: but the candid reader is invited to admit that hitherto the supposed hostile evidence is on the contrary entirely *in favour* of the verses under discussion. ("I called thee to curse mine enemies, and, behold, thou hast altogether blessed them these three times.")

II. Nothing has been hitherto said about Cod. L.* This is the designation of an uncial MS. of the viii[th] or ix[th] century, in the Library at Paris, chiefly remarkable for the correspondence of its readings with those of Cod. B and with certain of the citations in Origen; a peculiarity which recommends Cod. L, (as it recommends three cursive Codices of the Gospels, 1, 33, 69,) to the especial favour of a school with which whatever is found in Cod. B is necessarily right. It is described as the work of an ignorant foreign copyist, who probably wrote with several MSS. before him; but who is found to have been wholly incompetent to determine which reading to adopt and which to reject. Certain it is that he interrupts himself, at the end of ver. 8, to write as follows:—

"SOMETHING TO THIS EFFECT
IS ALSO MET WITH:

"All that was commanded them they immediately rehearsed unto Peter and the rest. And after these things, from East even unto West, did JESUS Himself send forth by their means the holy and incorruptible message of eternal Salvation.

"BUT THIS ALSO IS MET WITH AFTER
THE WORDS, 'FOR THEY WERE AFRAID:'

"Now, when He was risen early, the first day of the week[z]," &c.

[y] 2 (viz. Evan. 20, 200) + 16 + 1 + 5 (enumerated in the preceding note) = 24.   * Paris 62, *olim*, 2861 and 1558.

[z] See the facsimile.—The original, (which knows nothing of Tischendorf's crosses,) reads as follows :—

ΦΕΡΕΤΕ ΠΟΥ
ΚΑΙ ΤΑῦΤΑ -

ΠΆΝΤΑ ΔΕ ΤΑ ΠΑΡΗ
ΓΓΕΛΜΕΝΑ ΤΟΙ͂C
ΠΕΡΙ ΤΟΝ ΠΕΤΡΟΝ

It cannot be needful that I should delay the reader with any remarks on such a termination of the Gospel as the foregoing. It was evidently the production of some one who desired to remedy the conspicuous incompleteness of his own copy of S. Mark's Gospel, but who had imbibed so little of the spirit of the Evangelical narrative that he could not in the least imitate the Evangelist's manner. As for the scribe who executed Codex L, he was evidently incapable of distinguishing the grossest fabrication from the genuine text. The same worthless supplement is found in the margin of the Hharklensian Syriac (A.D. 616), and in a few other quarters of less importance [a].—I pass on, with the single remark that I am utterly at a loss to understand on what principle Cod. L,—a solitary MS. of the viii[th] or ix[th] century which exhibits an exceedingly vicious text,—is to

CΥΝΤΟΜѠC ΕΞΗ
ΓΓΙΛΑΝ · ΜΕΤΑ
ΔΕ ΤΑῦΤΑ ΚΑῚ ΑΥ̓ΤΟC
Ὁ ΙC, ἈΠΟ ἈΝΑΤΟΛΗC
ΚΑῚ ἌΧΡΙ ΔΥCΕѠC
ἘΞΑΠΕCΤΙΛΕΝ ΔΙ
ΑΥ̓ΤѠΝ ΤΟ ἸΕΡΟΝ
ΚΑῚ ἌΦΘΑΡΤΟΝ ΚΗ
ΡΥΓΜΑ · ΤΗC ΑἸѠ
ΝΙΟΥ CѠΤΗΡΙΑC ·

ΕCΤΗΝ ΔΕ ΚΑΙ
ΤΑῦΤΑ ΦΕΡΟ
ΜΕΝΑ ΜΕΤΑ ΤΟ
ἘΦΟΒΟΥΝΤΟ
ΓΑΡ ·

Αʹ ΝΑCΤᾺC ΔῈ ΠΡѠῚ
ΠΡѠΤΗ CΑΒΒΑΤΟΥ̓ ·

i.e :—φέρεταί που καὶ ταῦτα.
Πάντα δὲ τὰ παρηγγελμένα τοῖς περὶ τὸν Πέτρον συντόμως ἐξήγγειλαν· μετὰ δὲ ταῦτα καὶ αὐτὸς ὁ Ἰησοῦς ἀπὸ ἀνατολῆς καὶ ἄχρι δύσεως ἐξαπέστειλεν δι' αὐτῶν τὸ ἱερὸν καὶ ἄφθαρτον κήρυγμα τῆς αἰωνίου σωτηρίας.
Ἔστιν δὲ καὶ ταῦτα φερόμενα μετὰ τὸ ἐφοβοῦντο γάρ.
Ἀναστὰς δὲ πρωῒ πρώτῃ σαββάτου.

[a] As, the Codex Bobbiensis (k) of the old Latin, and the margin of two Æthiopic MSS.—I am unable to understand what Scholz and his copyists have said concerning Cod. 274. I was assured again and again at Paris that they knew of no such codex as "Reg, 79ᵃ," which is Scholz' designation (*Prolegg.* p. lxxx.) of the Cod. Evan. which, after him, we number "274."

be thought entitled to so much respectful attention on the present occasion, rebuked as it is for the fallacious evidence it bears concerning the last twelve verses of the second Gospel by all the seventeen remaining Uncials, (three of which are from 300 to 400 years more ancient than itself;) and by *every cursive copy of the Gospels in existence.* Quite certain at least is it that not the faintest additional probability is established by Cod. L that S. Mark's Gospel when it left the hands of its inspired Author was in a mutilated condition. The copyist shews that he was as well acquainted as his neighbours with our actual concluding Verses: while he betrays his own incapacity, by seeming to view with equal favour the worthless alternative which he deliberately transcribes as well, and to which he gives the foremost place. *Not* S. Mark's Gospel, *but Codex L* is the sufferer by this appeal.

III. I go back now to the statements found in certain Codices of the xth century, (derived probably from one of older date,) to the effect that "the marginal references to the Eusebian Canons extend no further than ver. 8:"—for so, I presume, may be paraphrased the words, (see p. 120,) ἕως οὗ Εὐσέβιος ὁ Παμφίλου ἐκανόνισεν, which are found at the end of ver. 8 in Codd. 1, 206, 209.

(1.) Now this statement need not have delayed us for many minutes. But then, therewith, recent Critics have seen fit to connect another and an entirely distinct proposition: viz. that

AMMONIUS

also, a contemporary of Origen, conspires with Eusebius in disallowing the genuineness of the conclusion of S. Mark's Gospel. This is in fact a piece of evidence to which recently special prominence has been given: every Editor of the Gospels in turn, since Wetstein, having reproduced it; but no one more emphatically than Tischendorf. "Neither by *the sections of Ammonius* nor yet by the canons of Eusebius are these last verses recognised[b]." "Thus it is seen,"

---

[b] Nec AMMONII Sectionibus, nec EUSEBII Canonibus, agnoscuntur ultimi versus.—Tisch. *Nov. Test.* (*ed. 8vo*), p. 406.

proceeds Dr. Tregelles, "that just as Eusebius found these verses absent in his day from the best and most numerous copies (sic), so was also the case with Ammonius when he formed his Harmony in the preceding century [c]."

A new and independent authority therefore is appealed to,—one of high antiquity and evidently very great importance,—Ammonius of Alexandria, A.D. 220. But Ammonius has left behind him *no known writings whatsoever*. What then do these men mean when they appeal in this confident way to the testimony of "Ammonius?"

To make this matter intelligible to the ordinary English reader, I must needs introduce in this place some account of what are popularly called the "Ammonian Sections" and the "Eusebian Canons:" concerning both of which, however, it cannot be too plainly laid down that nothing whatever is known beyond what is discoverable from a careful study of the "Sections" and "Canons" themselves; added to what Eusebius has told us in that short Epistle of his "to Carpianus,"—which I suppose has been transcribed and reprinted more often than any other uninspired Epistle in the world.

Eusebius there explains that Ammonius of Alexandria constructed with great industry and labour a kind of Evangelical Harmony; the peculiarity of which was, that, retaining S. Matthew's Gospel in its integrity, it exhibited the corresponding sections of the other three Evangelists by the side of S. Matthew's text. There resulted this inevitable inconvenience; that the sequence of the narrative, in the case of the three last Gospels, was interrupted throughout; and their context hopelessly destroyed [d].

The "Diatessaron" of Ammonius, (so Eusebius styles it), has long since disappeared; but it is plain from the foregoing account of it by a competent witness that it must

[c] *Printed Text*, p. 248.

[d] The reader is invited to test the accuracy of what precedes for himself:—
'Αμμώνιος μὲν ὁ 'Αλεξανδρεὺς, πολλὴν, ὡς εἰκὸς, φιλοπονίαν καὶ σπουδὴν εἰσαγηοχὼς, τὸ διὰ τεσσάρων ἡμῖν καταλέλοιπεν εὐαγγέλιον, τῷ κατὰ Ματθαῖον τὰς ὁμοφώνους τῶν λοιπῶν εὐαγγελιστῶν περικοπὰς παραθεὶς, ὡς ἐξ ἀνάγκης συμβῆναι τὸν τῆς ἀκολουθίας εἱρμὸν τῶν τριῶν διαφθαρῆναι, ὅσον ἐπὶ τῷ ὕφει τῆς ἀναγνώσεως.

have been a most unsatisfactory performance. It is not easy to see how room can have been found in such a scheme for entire chapters of S. Luke's Gospel; as well as for the larger part of the Gospel according to S. John: in short, for anything which was not capable of being brought into some kind of agreement, harmony, or correspondence with something in S. Matthew's Gospel. How it may have fared with the other Gospels in the work of Ammonius is not in fact known, and it is profitless to conjecture. What we know for certain is that Eusebius, availing himself of the hint supplied by the very imperfect labours of his predecessor, devised an entirely different expedient, whereby he extended to the Gospels of S. Mark, S. Luke and S. John all the advantages, (and more than all,) which Ammonius had made the distinctive property of the first Gospel[e]. His plan was to retain the Four Gospels in their integrity; and, besides enabling a reader to ascertain at a glance the places which S. Matthew has in common with the other three Evangelists, or with any two, or with any one of them, (which, I suppose, was the sum of what had been exhibited by the work of Ammonius,)—to shew which places S. Luke has in common with S. Mark,—which with S. John only; as well as which places are peculiar to each of the four Evangelists in turn. It is abundantly clear therefore what Eusebius means by saying that the labours of Ammonius had "*suggested to him*" his own[*]. The sight of that Harmony of the other three Evangelists with S. Matthew's Gospel had suggested to him the advantage of establishing a series of parallels throughout *all the Four Gospels*. But then, whereas Ammonius had placed alongside of S. Matthew *the dislocated sections themselves* of the

---

[e] "Ἵνα δὲ σωζομένου καὶ τοῦ τῶν λοιπῶν δι᾿ ὅλου σώματός τε καὶ εἱρμοῦ, εἰδέναι ἔχοις τοὺς οἰκείους ἑκάστου εὐαγγελιστοῦ τό πους, ἐν οἷς κατὰ τῶν αὐτῶν ἠνέχθησαν φιλαληθῶς εἰπεῖν, ἐκ τοῦ πονήματος τοῦ προειρημένου ἀνδρὸς εἰληφὼς ἀφορμὰς, καθ᾿ ἑτέραν μέθοδον κανόνας δέκα τὸν ἀριθμὸν διεχάραξά σοι τοὺς ὑποτεταγμένους.

[*] This seems to represent *exactly* what Eusebius means in this place. The nearest English equivalent to ἀφορμή is "a hint." Consider Euseb. *Hist. Eccl.* v. 27. Also the following :—πολλὰς λαβόντες ἀφορμάς. (Andreas, *Proleg. in Apocalyps.*).—λαβόντες τὰς ἀφορμάς. (Anastasius Sin., *Routh's Rell.* i. 15.)

other three Evangelists which are of corresponding purport, Eusebius conceived the idea of accomplishing the same object by means of a system of double numerical *references*. He invented X Canons, or Tables : he subdivided each of the Four Gospels into a multitude of short Sections. These he numbered ; (a fresh series of numbers appearing in each Gospel, and extending from the beginning right on to the end ;) and immediately under every number, he inserted, in vermillion, another numeral (I to X); whose office it was to indicate in which of his X Canons, or Tables, the reader would find the corresponding places in any of the other Gospels [f]. (If the section was unique, it belonged to his last or X[th] Canon.) Thus, against S. Matthew's account of the Title on the Cross, is written $\frac{335}{I}$: but in the I[st] Canon (which contains the places common to all four Evangelists) parallel with 335, is found,—214, 324, 199: and the Sections of S. Mark, S. Luke, and S. John thereby designated, (which are discoverable by merely casting one's eye down the margin of each of those several Gospels in turn, until the required number has been reached,) will be found to contain the parallel record in the other three Gospels.

All this is so purely elementary, that its very introduction in this place calls for apology. The extraordinary method of the opposite party constrains me however to establish thus clearly the true relation in which the familiar labours of Eusebius stand to the unknown work of Ammonius.

[f] κανόνας .... διεχάραξά σοι τοὺς ὑποτεταγμένους. This at least is decisive as to the authorship of the Canons. When therefore Jerome says of Ammonius,—"*Evangelicos canones excogitavit* quos postea secutus est Eusebius Cæsariensis," (*De Viris Illust.* c. lv. vol. ii. p. 881,) we learn the amount of attention to which such off-hand gain statements of this Father are entitled.

What else can be inferred from the account which Eusebius gives of the present sectional division of the Gospels but that it was also his own ?—Αὕτη μὲν οὖν ἡ τῶν ὑποτεταγμένων κανόνων ὑπόθεσις· ἡ δὲ σαφὴς αὐτῶν διήγησις, ἔστιν ἥδε. Ἐφ᾽ ἑκάστῳ τῶν τεσσάρων εὐαγγελίων ἀριθμός τις πρόκειται κατὰ μέρος, ἀρχόμενος ἀπὸ τοῦ πρώτου, εἶτα δευτέρου, καὶ τρίτου, καὶ καθεξῆς προϊὼν δι᾽ ὅλου μέχρι τοῦ τέλους τοῦ βιβλίου. He proceeds to explain how the sections thus numbered are to be referred to his X Canons :—καθ᾽ ἕκαστον δὲ ἀριθμὸν ὑποσημείωσις διὰ κινναβάρεως πρόκειται, δηλοῦσα ἐν ποίῳ τῶν δέκα κανόνων κείμενος ὁ ἀριθμὸς τυγχάνει.

For if that earlier production be lost indeed [g],—if its precise contents, if the very details of its construction, can at this distance of time be only conjecturally ascertained,—what right has any one to appeal to "*the Sections of Ammonius*," as to a known document? Why above all do Tischendorf, Tregelles, and the rest deliberately claim "Ammonius" for their ally on an occasion like the present; seeing that they must needs be perfectly well aware that they have no means whatever of knowing (except from the precarious evidence of Catenæ) what Ammonius thought about any single verse in any of the four Gospels? At every stage of this discussion, I am constrained to ask myself,—Do then the recent Editors of the Text of the New Testament really suppose that their statements will *never* be examined? their references *never* verified? or is it thought that they enjoy a monopoly of the learning (such as it is) which enables a man to form an opinion in this department of sacred Science? For,

(1st.) *Where* then and *what* are those "Sections of Ammonius" to which Tischendorf and Tregelles so confidently appeal? It is even notorious that when they *say* the "Sections of Ammonius," what they *mean* are the "Sections of *Eusebius*."—But, (2dly.) Where is the proof,—where is even the probability,—that these two are identical? The Critics cannot require to be reminded by me that we are absolutely

[g] "Frustra ad Ammonium aut Tatianum in Harmoniis provocant. Quæ supersunt vix quicquam cum Ammonio aut Tatiano commune habent." (Tischendorf *on S. Mark* xvi. 8).—Dr. Mill (1707),—because he assumed that the anonymous work which Victor of Capua brought to light in the vi[th] century, and conjecturally assigned to Tatian, was the lost work of Ammonius, (*Proleg.* p. 63, § 660,)—was of course warranted in appealing to the authority of Ammonius *in support* of the last twelve verses of S. Mark's Gospel. But in truth Mill's assumption cannot be maintained for a moment, as Wetstein has convincingly shewn. (*Proleg.* p. 68.) Any one may easily satisfy himself of the fact who will be at the pains to examine a few of the chapters with attention, bearing in mind what Eusebius has said concerning the work of Ammonius. Cap. lxxiv, for instance, contains as follows:—Mtt. xiii. 33, 34. Mk. iv. 33. Mtt. xiii. 34, 35: 10, 11. Mk. iv. 34. Mtt. xiii. 13 to 17. But here it is *S. Matthew's* Gospel which is dislocated,—for verses 10, 11, and 13 to 17 of ch. xiii. come *after* verses 33—35; while ver. 12 has altogether disappeared.

The most convenient edition for reference is Schmeller's,—*Ammonii Alexandrini quæ et Tatiani dicitur Harmonia Evangeliorum.* (Vienna, 1841.)

without proof that so much as *one* of the Sections of Ammonius corresponded with *one* of those of Eusebius; and yet, (3dly.) Who sees not that unless the Sections of Ammonius and those of Eusebius can be proved to have corresponded throughout, the name of Ammonius has no business whatever to be introduced into such a discussion as the present? They must at least be told that in the entire absence of proof of any kind,—(and certainly nothing that Eusebius says warrants any such inference [h],)—to reason from the one to the other as if they were identical, is what no sincere inquirer after Truth is permitted to do.

It is time, however, that I should plainly declare that it happens to be no matter of opinion at all whether the lost Sections of Ammonius were identical with those of Eusebius or not. It is demonstrable that they *cannot* have been so; and the proof is supplied by the Sections themselves. It is discovered, by a careful inspection of them, that they *imply* and *presuppose the Ten Canons;* being in many places even meaningless,—nugatory, in fact, (I do not of course say that they are *practically* without *use*,)—except on the theory that those Canons were already in existence [i]. Now the Canons are confessedly the invention of Eusebius. He distinctly claims them [j]. Thus much then concerning the supposed testimony of Ammonius. It is *nil.*—And now for what is alleged concerning the evidence of Eusebius.

The starting-point of this discussion, (as I began by remarking), is the following memorandum found in certain ancient MSS.:—" Thus far did Eusebius canonize [k];" which

---

[h] Only by the merest license of interpretation can εἰληφὼς ἀφορμάς be assumed to mean that Eusebius had found the four Gospels ready divided to his hand by Ammonius into exactly 1165 sections,—every one of which he had simply adopted for his own. Mill, (who nevertheless held this strange opinion,) was obliged to invent the wild hypothesis that Eusebius, *besides* the work of Ammonius which he describes, must have found in the library at Cæsarea the private copy of the Gospels which belonged to Ammonius,—an unique volume, in which the last-named Father (as he assumes) will have numbered the Sections and made them exactly 1165. It is not necessary to discuss such a notion. We are dealing with facts,—not with fictions.

[i] For proofs of what is stated above, as well as for several remarks on the (so-called) " Ammonian" Sections, the reader is referred to the Appendix (G).

[j] See above, p. 128, note (f). [k] See above, p. 125.

means either: (1) That his Canons recognise no section of S. Mark's Gospel subsequent to § 233, (which number is commonly set over against ver. 8 :) or else, (which comes to the same thing,)—(2) That no sections of the same Gospel, after § 233, are referred to any of his X Canons.

On this slender foundation has been raised the following precarious superstructure. It is assumed,

(1st.) That the Section of S. Mark's Gospel which Eusebius numbers "233," and which begins at our ver. 8, *cannot have extended beyond* ver. 8;—whereas it may have extended, and probably did extend, down to the end of ver. 11.

(2dly.) That because no notice is taken in the Eusebian Canons of any sectional *number* in S. Mark's Gospel subsequent to § 233, no *Section* (with, or without, such a subsequent number) can have existed:—whereas there may have existed one or more subsequent Sections all duly numbered[1]. This notwithstanding, Eusebius, (according to the memorandum found in certain ancient MSS.), may have *canonized* no further than § 233.

I am not disposed, however, to contest the point as far as Eusebius is concerned. I have only said so much in order to shew how unsatisfactory is the argumentation on the other side. Let it be assumed, for argument sake, that the statement "Eusebius canonized no farther than ver. 8" is equivalent to this,—"*Eusebius numbered no Sections after ver. 8:*" (and more it cannot mean :)—What *then?* I am at a loss to see what it is that the Critics propose to themselves by insisting on the circumstance. For we knew before,—it was in fact Eusebius himself who told us,—that Copies of the Gospel ending abruptly at ver. 8, were anciently of frequent occurrence. Nay, we heard the same Eusebius remark that one way of shelving a certain awkward problem would be, to plead that the subsequent portion of S. Mark's Gospel is frequently wanting. What *more* have we learned when we have ascertained that the same Eusebius allowed no place to that subsequent portion in his Canons? The new fact, (supposing it to be a fact,) is but the correla-

---

[1] As a matter of fact, Codices abound in which the Sections are noted *without* the Canons, throughout. See more on this subject in the Appendix (G).

tive of the old one; and since it was Eusebius who was the voucher for *that*, what additional probability do we establish that the inspired autograph of S. Mark ended abruptly at ver. 8, by discovering that Eusebius is consistent with himself, and omits to "canonize" (or even to "sectionize") what he had already hypothetically hinted might as well be left out altogether? (See above, pp. 44-6.)

So that really I am at a loss to see that one atom of progress is made in this discussion by the further discovery that, (in a work written about A.D. 373,)

EPIPHANIUS

states casually that "the four Gospels contain 1162 sections [m]." From this it is argued [n] that since 355 of these are commonly assigned to S. Matthew, 342 to S. Luke, and 232 to S. John, there do but remain for S. Mark 233; and the 233rd section of S. Mark's Gospel confessedly begins at ch. xvi. 8.—The probability may be thought to be thereby slightly increased that the sectional numbers of Eusebius extended no further than ver. 8: but—Has it been rendered one atom more probable that the inspired Evangelist himself ended his Gospel abruptly at the 8th verse? *That* fact —(the *only* thing which our opponents have to establish)— remains exactly where it was; entirely unproved, and in the highest degree improbable.

To conclude, therefore. When I read as follows in the pages of Tischendorf:—"These verses are not recognised by the Sections of Ammonius, nor by the Canons of Eusebius: Epiphanius and Cæsarius bear witness to the fact;"— I am constrained to remark that the illustrious Critic has drawn upon his imagination for three of his statements, and that the fourth is of no manner of importance.

(1.) About the "Sections of Ammonius," he really knows no more than about the lost Books of Livy. He is, therefore, without excuse for adducing them in the way of evidence.

---

[m] τέσσαρά εἰσιν εὐαγγέλια κεφαλαίων χιλίων ἑκατὸν ἑξηκονταδύο. The words are most unexpectedly, (may I not say *suspiciously*?), found in Epiphanius, *Ancor.* 50, (*Opp.* ii. 54 B.)

[n] By Tischendorf, copying Mill's *Proleg.* p. 63, § 662:—the fontal source, by the way, of the twin references to "Epiphanius and Cæsarius."

(2.) That Epiphanius bears no witness whatever either as to the "Sections of Ammonius" or to "Canons of Eusebius," Tischendorf is perfectly well aware. So is my reader.

(3.) His appeal to

CÆSARIUS

is worse than infelicitous. He intends thereby to designate the younger brother of Gregory of Nazianzus; an eminent physician of Constantinople, who died A.D. 368; and who, (as far as is known,) *never wrote anything.* A work called Πεύσεις, (which in the xth century was attributed to Cæsarius, but concerning which nothing is certainly known except that Cæsarius was certainly *not* its author,) is the composition to which Tischendorf refers. Even the approximate date of this performance, however, has never been ascertained. And yet, if Tischendorf had condescended to refer to it, (instead of taking his reference at second-hand,) he would have seen at a glance that the entire context in which the supposed testimony is found, is *nothing else but a condensed paraphrase of that part of Epiphanius*, in which the original statement occurs [o].

Thus much, then, for the supposed evidence of AMMONIUS, of EPIPHANIUS, and of CÆSARIUS on the subject of the last Twelve Verses of S. Mark's Gospel. It is exactly *nil.* In fact Pseudo-Cæsarius, so far from "bearing witness to the fact" that the concluding verses of S. Mark's Gospel are spurious, *actually quotes the* 16*th verse as genuine* [p].

(4.) As for Eusebius, nothing whatever has been added to what we knew before concerning his probable estimate of these verses.

IV. We are now at liberty to proceed to the only head of external testimony which remains undiscussed. I allude to the evidence of

THE CATENÆ.

"In the Catenæ on Mark," (crisply declares Dr. Davidson,) "there is no explanation of this section [q]."

---

[o] Comp. Epiph. (*Ancor.* 50,) *Opp.* ii. 53 c to 55 A, with Galland. *Bibl.* vi. 26 c to 27 A.   [p] Galland. *Bibl.* vi. 147 A.

[q] Vol. i. 165 (ii. 112).—It is only fair to add that Davidson is not alone in this statement. In substance, it has become one of the common-places of those who undertake to prove that the end of S. Mark's Gospel is spurious.

"The Catenæ on Mark :" as if they were quite common things,—" plenty, as blackberries!" But,—*Which* of "the Catenæ" may the learned Critic be supposed to have examined?

1. Not the Catena which Possinus found in the library of Charles de Montchal, Abp. of Toulouse, and which forms the basis of his Catena published at Rome in 1673 ; because *that* Codex is expressly declared by the learned Editor to be defective from ver. 8 to the end [r].

2. Not the Catena which Corderius transcribed from the Vatican Library and communicated to Possinus; because in *that* Catena the 9th and 12th verses are distinctly commented on [s].

3. Still less can Dr. Davidson be thought to have inspected the Catena commonly ascribed to Victor of Antioch,—which Peltanus published in Latin in 1580, but which Possinus was the first to publish in Greek (1673). Dr. Davidson, I say, cannot certainly have examined *that* Catena; inasmuch as it contains, (as I have already largely shewn, and, in fact, as every one may see,) a long and elaborate dissertation on the best way of reconciling the language of S. Mark in ver. 9 with the language of the other Evangelists [t].

4. Least of all is it to be supposed that the learned Critic has inspected either of the last two editions of the same

[r] See Possini *Cat.* p. 363.

[s] Ἐφάνη πρῶτον Μαρίᾳ τῇ Μαγδαληνῇ. [= ver. 9.] ταύτην Εὐσέβιος ἐν τοῖς πρὸς Μαρῖνον ἑτέραν λέγει Μαρίαν παρὰ τὴν θεασαμένην τὸν νεανίσκον. ἢ καὶ ἀμφότεραι ἐκ τῆς Μαγδαληνῆς ἦσαν. μετὰ δὲ ταῦτα δυσὶν ἐξ αὐτῶν περιπατοῦσι. καὶ τὰ ἑξῆς [= ver. 12.] τοὺς ἀμφὶ τὸν Κλεόπαν, καθὼς ὁ Λουκᾶς ἱστορεῖ, (Possini *Cat.* p. 364) :—Where it will be seen that *Text* (κείμενον) and *Interpretation* (ἑρμηνεία) are confusedly thrown together. "Anonymus [Vaticanus]" also quotes S. Mark xvi. 9 at p. 109, *ad fin.*—Matthaei (N. T. ii. 269),—overlooking the fact that "*Anonymus Vaticanus*" (or simply "*Anonymus*") and "*Anonymus Tolosanus*" (or simply "*Tolosanus*") denote two distinct Codices, —falls into a mistake himself while contradicting our learned countryman Mill, who says,—" Certe Victor Antioch. ac Anonymus Tolosanus huc usque [sc. ver. 8] nec ultra commentantur."—Scholz' dictum is,—" Commentatorum qui in catenis SS. Patrum ad Marcum laudantur, nulla explicatio hujus pericopæ exhibetur."

[t] See above pp. 62-3. The Latin of Peltanus may be seen in such Collections as the *Magna Bibliotheca Vett. PP.* (1618,) vol. iv. p. 330, col. 2 E, F.—For the Greek, see Possini *Catena*, pp. 359 - 61.

Catena: viz. that of Matthaei, (Moscow 1775,) or that of Cramer, (Oxford 1844,) from MSS. in the Royal Library at Paris and in the Bodleian. This is simply impossible, because (as we have seen), in *these* is contained the famous passage which categorically asserts the genuineness of the last Twelve Verses of S. Mark's Gospel[u].

Now this exhausts the subject.

To *which*, then, of "the Catenæ on Mark," I must again inquire, does this learned writer allude?—I will venture to answer the question myself; and to assert that this is only one more instance of the careless, second-hand (and third-rate) criticism which is to be met with in every part of Dr. Davidson's book: one proof more of the alacrity with which worn-out objections and worthless arguments are furbished up afresh, and paraded before an impatient generation and an unlearned age, whenever (*tanquam vile corpus*) the writings of Apostles or Evangelists are to be assailed, or the Faith of the Church of CHRIST is to be unsettled and undermined.

V. If the Reader will have the goodness to refer back to p. 39, he will perceive that I have now disposed of every witness whom I originally undertook to examine. He will also, in fairness, admit that there has not been elicited one particle of evidence, from first to last, which renders it in the slightest degree probable that the Gospel of S. Mark, as it originally came from the hands of its inspired Author, was either an imperfect or an unfinished work. Whether there have not emerged certain considerations which render such a supposition in the highest degree *un*likely,—I am quite content that my Reader shall decide.

Dismissing the external testimony, therefore, proceed we now to review those internal evidences, which are confidently appealed to as proving that the concluding Verses of S. Mark's Gospel cannot be regarded as really the work of the Evangelist.

---

[u] See above, pp. 64-5, and Appendix (E).

CHAPTER IX.

INTERNAL EVIDENCE DEMONSTRATED TO BE THE VERY REVERSE OF UNFAVOURABLE TO THESE VERSES.

The " Style" and " Phraseology" of these Verses declared by Critics to be not S. Mark's.—Insecurity of such Criticism (220).—*The " Style" of chap.* xvi. 9—20 *shewn to be the same as the style of chap.* i. 9—20 (222).—*The " Phraseology" examined in twenty-seven particulars, and shewn to be suspicious in none* (225),— *but in twenty-seven particulars shewn to be the reverse* (250).— *Such Remarks fallacious* (253).—*Judged of by a truer, a more delicate and philosophical Test, these Verses proved to be most probably genuine* (255).

A DISTINCT class of objections remains to be considered. An argument much relied on by those who deny or doubt the genuineness of this portion of S. Mark's Gospel, is derived from considerations of internal evidence. In the judgment of a recent Editor of the New Testament,—These twelve verses "bear traces of *another hand* from that which has shaped the *diction* and *construction* of the rest of the Gospel [a]." They are therefore "an addition to the narrative,"—of which "the internal evidence will be found to preponderate vastly against the authorship of Mark."—" A difference," (says Dr. Tregelles,) "has been remarked, and truly remarked, between *the phraseology* of this section and the rest of this Gospel."—According to Dr. Davidson,— " The *phraseology and style* of the section are unfavourable to its authenticity." "The characteristic peculiarities which pervade Mark's Gospel do not appear in it; but, on the contrary, terms and expressions," " phrases and words, are introduced which Mark never uses; or terms for which he employs others [b]."—So Meyer,—" With ver. 9, we suddenly come upon an excerpting process totally different from the previous mode of narration. The passage contains none of Mark's peculiarities (no εὐθέως, no πάλιν, &c., but the bald-

---

[a] Alford on S. Mark xvi. 9—20. [b] *Introduction*, &c. ii. p. 113.

ness and lack of clearness which mark a compiler;) while in single expressions, it is altogether contrary to Mark's manner."—" There is" (says Professor Norton) " a difference so great between the use of language in this passage, and its use in the undisputed portion of Mark's Gospel, as to furnish strong reasons for believing the passage not genuine."—No one, however, has expressed himself more strongly on this subject than Tischendorf." "Singula" (he says) "multifariam a Marci ratione abhorrent[c]." ... Here, then, is something very like a consensus of hostile opinion: although the terms of the indictment are somewhat vague. Difference of "Diction and Construction,"—difference of "Phraseology and Style,"—difference of "Terms and Expressions,"—difference of "Words and Phrases;"—the absence of S. Mark's "characteristic peculiarities." I suppose, however, that all may be brought under two heads,—(I.) STYLE, and (II.) PHRASEOLOGY: meaning by "Style" whatever belongs to the Evangelist's manner; and by "Phraseology" whatever relates to the words and expressions he has employed. It remains, therefore, that we now examine the proofs by which it is proposed to substantiate these confident assertions, and ascertain exactly what they are worth by constant appeals to the Gospel. Throughout this inquiry, we have to do not with Opinion but with Fact. The unsupported dicta of Critics, however distinguished, are entitled to no manner of attention.

1. In the meantime, as might have been expected, these confident and often-repeated asseverations have been by no means unproductive of mischievous results:

> Like ceaseless droppings, which at last are known
> To leave their dint upon the solid stone.

I observe that Scholars and Divines of the best type (as the Rev. T. S. Green[d]) at last put up with them. The wisest however reproduce them under protest, and with apology. The names of Tischendorf and Tregelles, Meyer and Davidson, command attention. It seems to be thought incredible that they can *all* be *entirely* in the wrong. They impose upon learned and unlearned readers alike. "Even Barnabas

[c] *Nov. Test.* Ed. 8[va] i. p. 406.   [d] *Developed Crit.* pp. 51-2.

has been carried away with their dissimulation." He has (to my surprise and regret) two suggestions:—

(*a*) The one,—That this entire section of the second Gospel may possibly have been written long after the rest; and that therefore its verbal peculiarities need not perplex or trouble us. It was, I suppose, (according to this learned and pious writer,) a kind of after-thought, or supplement, or Appendix to S. Mark's Gospel. In this way I have seen the last Chapter of S. John once and again accounted for.— To which, it ought to be a sufficient answer to point out that there is *no appearance whatever* of any such interval having been interposed between S. Mark xvi. 8 and 9 : that it is highly improbable that any such interval occurred : and that until the "verbal peculiarities" have been ascertained to exist, it is, to say the least, a gratuitous exercise of the inventive faculty to discover reasons for their existence. Whether there be not something radically unsound and wrong in all such conjectures about "after-thoughts," "supplements," "appendices," and "second editions" when the everlasting Gospel of JESUS CHRIST is the thing spoken of,— a confusing of things heavenly with things earthly which must make the Angels weep,—I forbear to press on the present occasion. It had better perhaps be discussed at another opportunity. But φίλοι ἄνδρες [e] will forgive my freedom in having already made my personal sentiment on the subject sufficiently plain.

(*b*) His other suggestion is,—That this portion may not have been penned by S. Mark himself after all. By which he clearly means no more than this,—that as we are content not to know *who* wrote the conclusion of the Books of Deuteronomy and Joshua, so, if needful, we may well be content not to know who wrote the end of the Gospel of S. Mark.—In reply to which, I have but to say, that after cause has been shewn why we should indeed believe that not S. Mark but some one else wrote the end of S. Mark's Gospel, we shall be perfectly willing to acquiesce in the new fact:—but *not till then.*

[e] ἀμφοῖν γὰρ ὄντων φίλοιν, ὅσιον προτιμᾶν τὴν ἀλήθειαν.—Arist. *Eth. Nic.* I. iii.

2. True indeed it is that here and there a voice has been lifted up in the way of protest[f] against the proposed inference from the familiar premises; (for the self-same statements have now been so often reproduced, that the eye grows weary at last of the ever-recurring string of offending vocables:)—but, with *one* honorable exception[g], men do not seem to have ever thought of calling the premises themselves in question: examining the statements one by one: contesting the ground inch by inch: refusing absolutely to submit to any dictation whatever in this behalf: insisting on bringing the whole matter to the test of severe inquiry, and making every detail the subject of strict judicial investigation. This is what I propose to do in the course of the present Chapter. I altogether deny the validity of the inference which has been drawn from "the style," "the phraseology," "the diction" of the present section of the Gospel. But I do more. I entirely deny the accuracy of almost *every individual statement* from which the unfavourable induction is made, and the hostile inference drawn. Even *this* will not nearly satisfy

[f] To the honour of the Rev. F. H. Scrivener be it said, that *he* at least absolutely refuses to pay any attention at all "to the argument against these twelve verses arising from their alleged difference in style from the rest of the Gospel." See by all means his remarks on this subject. (*Introduction*, pp. 431-2.)—One would have thought that a recent controversy concerning a short English Poem,—which some able men were confident *might* have been written by Milton, while others were just as confident that it could not possibly be his,—ought to have opened the eyes of all to the precarious nature of such Criticism.

[g] Allusion is made to the Rev. John A. Broadus, D.D.,—"Professor of Interpretation of the New Testament in the Southern Baptist Theological Seminary, Greenville, S.C.,"—the author of an able and convincing paper entitled "Exegetical Studies" in "*The Baptist Quarterly*" for July, 1869 (Philadelphia), pp. 355—62: in which "the words and phrases" contained in S. Mark xvi. 9—20 are exclusively examined.

If the present volume should ever reach the learned Professor's hands, he will perceive that I must have written the present Chapter *before* I knew of his labours: (an advantage which I owe to Mr. Scrivener's kindness:) my treatment of the subject and his own being so entirely different. But it is only due to Professor Broadus to acknowledge the interest and advantage with which I have compared my lucubrations with his, and the sincere satisfaction with which I have discovered that we have everywhere independently arrived at precisely the same result.

me. I insist that one only result can attend the exact analysis of this portion of the Gospel into its elements; namely, a profound conviction that S. Mark is most certainly its Author.

3. Let me however distinctly declare beforehand that remarks on "the style" of an Evangelist are singularly apt to be fallacious, especially when (as here) it is proposed to apply them to a very limited portion of the sacred narrative. Altogether to be mistrusted moreover are they, when (as on the present occasion) it is proposed to make them the ground for possibly rejecting such a portion of Scripture as spurious. It becomes a fatal objection to such reasoning that *the style* may indeed be exceedingly diverse, and yet *the Author* be confessedly one and the same. How exceedingly dissimilar in style are the Revelation of S. John and the Gospel of S. John! Moreover, practically, the promised remarks on "style," when the Authorship of some portion of Scripture is to be discussed, are commonly observed to degenerate at once into what is really quite a different thing. Single words, perhaps some short phrase, is appealed to, which (it is said) does not recur in any part of the same book; and thence it is argued that the Author can no longer be the same. "According to this argument, *the recurrence of the same words* constitutes identity of style; the want of such recurrence implies difference of style;—difference of style in such a sense as compels us to infer diversity of authorship. Each writer is supposed to have at his disposal a limited number of 'formulæ' within the range of which he must work. He must in each chapter employ these formulæ, and these only. He must be content with one small portion of his mother-tongue, and not dare to venture across the limits of that portion,—on pain of losing his identity [h]."

4. How utterly insecure must be every approximation to

---

[h] Dr. Kay's *Crisis Hupfeldiana*, p. 34,—the most masterly and instructive exposure of Bp. Colenso's incompetence and presumption which has ever appeared. Intended specially of *his* handling of the writings of Moses, the remarks in the text are equaly applicable to much which has been put forth concerning the authorship of the end of S. Mark's Gospel.

such a method of judging about the Authorship of any twelve verses of Scripture which can be named, scarcely requires illustration. The attentive reader of S. Matthew's Gospel is aware that a mode of expression which is *six times repeated* in his viii[th] and ix[th] chapters is perhaps only once met with besides in his Gospel,—viz. in his xxi[st] chapter[i]. The "style" of the 17th verse of his i[st] chapter may be thought unlike anything else in S. Matthew. S. Luke's five opening verses are unique, both in respect of manner and of matter. S. John also in his five opening verses seems to me to have adopted a method which is not recognisable anywhere else in his writings; "rising strangely by degrees," (as Bp. Pearson expresses it[k],) "making the last word of the former sentence the first of that which followeth."—"*He* knoweth that he saith true," is the language of the same Evangelist concerning himself in chap. xix. 35. But, "*we* know that his testimony is true," is his phrase in chap. xxi. 24. Twice, and twice only throughout his Gospel, (viz. in chap. xix. 35: xx. 31), is he observed to address his readers, and on both occasions in the same words: ("that *ye* may believe.") But what of all this? Is it to be supposed that S. Matthew, S. Luke, S. John are not the authors of those several places? From facts like these no inference whatever is to be drawn as to the genuineness or the spuriousness of a writing. It is quite to mistake the Critic's vocation to imagine that he is qualified, or called upon, to pass any judgment of the sort.

5. I have not said all this, of course, as declining the proposed investigation. I approach it on the contrary right willingly, being confident that it can be attended by only one result. With what is true, endless are the harmonies which evolve themselves: from what is false, the true is equally certain to stand out divergent[1]. And we all desire nothing but the Truth.

[i] S. Matth. viii. 1 (καταβάντι αὐτῷ):—5 (εἰσελθόντι τῷ 'Ι.):—23 (ἐμβάντι αὐτῷ):—28 (ἐλθόντι αὐτῷ):—ix. 27 (παράγοντι τῷ 'Ι.):—28 (ἐλθόντι):—xxi. 23 (ἐλθόντι αὐτῷ).

[k] *On the Creed*, Art. ii. (vol. i. p. 155.)

[1] τῷ μὲν γὰρ ἀληθεῖ πάντα συνᾴδει τὰ ὑπάρχοντα, τῷ δὲ ψευδεῖ ταχὺ διαφωνεῖ τἀληθές. Aristot. *Eth. Nic.* I. c. vi.

I. To begin then with the "STYLE AND MANNER" of S. Mark in this place.

1. We are assured that "instead of the *graphic, detailed* description by which this Evangelist is distinguished, we meet with an abrupt, sententious manner, resembling that of brief notices extracted from larger accounts and loosely linked together [m]." Surely if this be so, the only lawful inference would be that S. Mark, in this place, *has* "extracted brief notices from larger accounts, and loosely linked them together:" and unless such a proceeding on the part of the Evangelist be judged incredible, it is hard to see what is the force of the adverse criticism, as directed against the *genuineness* of the passage now under consideration.

2. But in truth, (when divested of what is merely a gratuitous assumption,) the preceding account of the matter is probably not far from the correct one. Of S. Mark's practice of making "*extracts*," I know nothing: nor Dr. Davidson either. That there existed *any* "larger accounts" which would have been available for such a purpose, (except the Gospel according to S. Matthew,) there is neither a particle of evidence, nor a shadow of probability. On the other hand, that, notwithstanding the abundant oral information to which confessedly he had access, S. Mark has been divinely guided in this place to handle, in the briefest manner, some of the chiefest things which took place after our LORD's Resurrection,—is simply undeniable. And without at all admitting that the style of the Evangelist is in consequence either "abrupt" or "sententious [n]," I yet recognise the

---

[m] Davidson's *Introduction*, &c. i. 170.

[n] And yet, if it were ever so "sententious," ever so "abrupt;" and if his "brief notices" were ever so "loosely linked together;"—these, *according to Dr. Davidson*, would only be indications that S. Mark actually *was* their Author. Hear him discussing S. Mark's "characteristics," at p. 151:—"In the consecution of his narrations, Mark *puts them together very loosely.*" "Mark is also characterised by a *conciseness* and apparent incompleteness of delineation which are allied to the obscure." "The *abrupt* introduction" of many of his details is again and again appealed to by Dr. Davidson, and illustrated by references to the Gospel. What, in the name of common sense, is the value of such criticism as this? What is to be thought of a gentleman who blows hot and cold in the same breath: denying at p. 170 the genuineness

inevitable consequence of relating many dissimilar things within very narrow limits; namely, that the transition from one to the other forces itself on the attention. What wonder that the same phenomenon should *not* be discoverable in other parts of the Gospel where the Evangelist is *not* observed to be doing the same thing?

3. But wherever in his Gospel S. Mark *is* doing the same thing, he is observed to adopt the style and manner which Dr. Davidson is pleased to call "sententious" and "abrupt." Take twelve verses in his first chapter, as an example. Between S. Mark xvi. 9—20 and S. Mark i. 9—20, I profess myself unable to discern any real difference of style. I proceed to transcribe the passage which I deliberately propose for comparison; *the twelve corresponding verses*, namely, in S. Mark's *first* chapter, which are to be compared with the twelve verses already under discussion, from his *last;* and they may be just as conveniently exhibited in English as in Greek:—

(S. MARK i. 9—20.)

(ver. 9.) "And it came to pass in those days, that JESUS "came from Nazareth of Galilee, and was baptized of John "in Jordan. (10.) And straightway coming up out of the "water, He saw the heavens opened, and the SPIRIT like "a dove descending upon Him: (11.) and there came a "voice from heaven saying, Thou art My beloved SON, in "whom I am well pleased. (12.) And immediately the "SPIRIT driveth Him into the wilderness. (13.) And He "was there in the wilderness forty days, tempted of Satan; "and was with the wild beasts; and the Angels ministered "unto Him. (14.) Now after that John was put in prison, "JESUS came into Galilee, preaching the gospel of the "kingdom of GOD, (15.) and saying, The time is fulfilled, "and the Kingdom of GOD is at hand: repent ye, and be- "lieve the Gospel. (16.) Now, as He walked by the sea "of Galilee, He saw Simon and Andrew his brother casting "a net into the sea: for they were fishers. (17.) And JESUS

of a certain portion of Scripture *because* it exhibits the very peculiarities which at p. 151 he had volunteered the information are *characteristic* of its reputed Author?

"said unto them, Come ye after Me, and I will make you
"to become fishers of men. (18.) And straightway they
"forsook their nets, and followed Him. (19.) And when
"He had gone a little farther thence, He saw James the
"son of Zebedee, and John his brother, who also were in
"the ship mending their nets. (20.) And straightway He
"called them; and they left their father Zebedee in the
"ship with the hired servants, and went after Him."

4. The candid reader must needs admit that precisely the self-same manner is recognisable in this first chapter of S. Mark's Gospel which is asserted to be peculiar to the last. Note, that from our SAVIOUR'S Baptism (which occupies the first three verses) the Evangelist passes to His Temptation, which is dismissed in two. Six months elapse. The commencement of the Ministry is dismissed in the next two verses. The last five describe the call of four of the Apostles,—without any distinct allusion to the miracle which was the occasion of it.... How was it *possible* that when incidents considerable as these had to be condensed within the narrow compass of twelve verses, the same "graphic, detailed description" could reappear which renders S. Mark's description of the miracle performed in the country of the Gadarenes (for example) so very interesting; where a single incident is spread over twenty verses, although the action did not perhaps occupy an hour? I rejoice to observe that "the *abrupt transitions* of this section" (ver. 1—13) have also been noticed by Dean Alford: who very justly accounts for the phenomenon by pointing out that here "Mark appears as *an abridger of previously well-known facts*[o]." But then, I want to know what there is in this to induce us to suspect *the genuineness* of either the beginning or the end of S. Mark's Gospel?

5. For it is a mistake to speak as if "graphic, detailed description" *invariably* characterise the second Gospel. S. Mark is quite as remarkable for his practice of occasionally exhibiting a considerable transaction in a highly abridged form. The opening of his Gospel is singularly concise, and altogether *sudden*. His account of John's preach-

[o] N. T. vol. i. *Prolegg.* p. 38.

ing (i. 1—8) is the shortest of all. Very concise is his account of our SAVIOUR's Baptism (ver. 9—11). The brevity of his description of our LORD's Temptation is even extraordinary (ver. 12, 13.)—I pass on; premising that I shall have occasion to remind the reader ·by-and-by of certain peculiarities in these same Twelve Verses, which seem to have been hitherto generally overlooked.

II. Nothing more true, therefore, than Dr. Tregelles' admission "that arguments on *style* are often very fallacious, and that *by themselves* they prove very little. But" (he proceeds) "when there does exist external evidence; and when internal proofs as to style, manner, verbal expression, and connection, are in accordance with such independent grounds of forming a judgment; then, these internal considerations possess very great weight."

I have already shewn that there exists *no* such external evidence as Dr. Tregelles supposes. And in the absence of it, I am bold to assert that since nothing in the "Style" or the "Phraseology" of these verses ever aroused suspicion in times past, we have rather to be *on our guard* against suffering our judgment to be warped by arguments drawn from such precarious considerations now. As for determining from such data the authorship of an isolated passage; asserting or denying its genuineness for no other reason but because it contains certain words and expressions which do or do not occur elsewhere in the Gospel of which it forms part;—let me again declare plainly that the proceeding is in the highest degree uncritical. We are not competent judges of what words an Evangelist was likely on any given occasion to employ. We have no positive knowledge of the circumstances under which any part of any one of the four Gospels was written; nor the influences which determined an Evangelist's choice of certain expressions in preference to others. We are learners,—we *can* be only learners here. But having said all this, I proceed (as already declared) without reluctance or misgiving to investigate the several charges which have been brought against this section of the Gospel; charges derived from its PHRASEOLOGY; and which will be found to be nothing else but repeated assertions that a certain Word or Phrase,—(there are about twenty-four such words and phrases in all [p],)—"occurs nowhere in the Gospel of Mark;" with probably the alarming asseveration that it is "abhorrent to Mark's manner."....The result of the inquiry which follows will perhaps be not exactly what is commonly imagined.

The first difficulty of this class is very fairly stated by one whose name I cannot write without a pang,—the late Dean Alford :—

(I.) The expression πρώτη σαββάτου, for the "first day of the week" (in ver. 9) "is remarkable" (he says) "as occurring so soon after" μία σαββάτων (a precisely equivalent expression) in ver. 2.—Yes, it is remarkable.

Scarcely more remarkable, perhaps, than that S. Luke *in the course of one and the same chapter* should four times designate the Sabbath τὸ σάββατον, and twice τὰ σάββατα: again, twice, τὸ σάββατον,—twice, ἡ ἡμέρα τοῦ σαββάτου,—

---

[p] It may be convenient, in this place, to enumerate the several words and expressions about to be considered :—

(i.) πρώτη σαββάτου (ver. 9.)—See above.
(ii.) ἀφ' ἧς ἐκβεβλήκει ἑπτὰ δαιμόνια (ver. 9.)—See p. 152.
(iii.) ἐκβάλλειν ἀπό (ver. 9.)—See p. 153.
(iv.) πορεύεσθαι (vers. 10, 12, 15.)—*Ibid.*
(v.) οἱ μετ' αὐτοῦ γενόμενοι (ver. 10.)—See p. 155.
(vi.) θεᾶσθαι (ver. 11 and 14.)—See p. 156.
(vii.) θεαθῆναι ὑπό (ver. 11.)—See p. 158.
(viii.) ἀπιστεῖν (ver. 11 and 16.)—*Ibid.*
(ix.) μετὰ ταῦτα (ver. 12.)—See p. 159.
(x.) ἕτερος (ver. 12.)—See p. 160.
(xi.) ὕστερον (ver. 14.)—*Ibid.*
(xii.) βλάπτειν (ver. 18.)—*Ibid.*
(xiii.) πανταχοῦ (ver. 20.)—See p. 161.
(xiv. and xv.) συνεργεῖν—βεβαιοῦν (ver. 20.)—*Ibid.*
(xvi.) πᾶσα ἡ κτίσις (ver. 15.)—*Ibid.*
(xvii.) ἐν τῷ ὀνόματί μου (ver. 17.)—See p. 162.
(xviii. and xix.) παρακολουθεῖν—ἐπακολουθεῖν (ver. 17 and 19.)—See p. 163.
(xx.) χεῖρας ἐπιθεῖναι ἐπί τινα (ver. 18.)—See p. 164.
(xxi. and xxii.) μὲν οὖν—ὁ Κύριος (ver. 19 and 20.)—*Ibid.*
(xxiii.) ἀναληφθῆναι (ver. 19.)—See p. 166.
(xxiv.) ἐκεῖνος used in a peculiar way (*verses* 10, 11 [and 13 ?].)—*Ibid.*
(xxv.) "Verses without a copulative," (*verses* 10 and 14.)—*Ibid.*
(xxvi. and xxvii.) Absence of εὐθέως and πάλιν.—See p. 168.

and once, τὰ σάββατα [q]. Or again, that S. Matthew should in one and the same chapter five times call the Sabbath, τὰ σάββατα, and three times, τὸ σάββατον [r]. Attentive readers will have observed that the Evangelists seem to have been fond in this way of varying their phrase; suddenly introducing a new expression for something which they had designated differently just before. Often, I doubt not, this is done with the profoundest purpose, and sometimes even with manifest design; but the phenomenon, however we may explain it, still remains. Thus, S. Matthew, (in his account of our LORD's Temptation,—chap. iv.,) has ὁ διάβολος in ver. 1, and ὁ πειράζων in ver. 3, for him whom our SAVIOUR calls Σατανᾶς in ver. 10.—S. Mark, in chap. v. 2, has τὰ μνημεῖα,—but in ver. 5, τὰ μνήματα.—S. Luke, in xxiv. 1, has τὸ μνῆμα; but in the next verse, τὸ μνημεῖον.—'Επί with an accusative twice in S. Matth. xxv. 21, 23, is twice exchanged for ἐπί with a genitive in the same two verses: and ἔριφοι (in ver. 32) is exchanged for ἐρίφια in ver. 33.—Instead of ἄρχων τῆς συναγωγῆς (in S. Luke viii. 41) we read, in ver. 49, ἀρχισυνάγωγος: and for οἱ ἀπόστολοι (in ix. 10) we find οἱ δώδεκα in ver. 12.—Οὖς in S. Luke xxii. 50 is exchanged for ὠτίον in the next verse.—In like manner, those whom S. Luke calls οἱ νεώτεροι in Acts v. 6, he calls νεανίσκοι in ver. 10. . . . All such matters strike me as highly interesting, but not in the least as suspicious. It surprises me a little, of course, that S. Mark should present me with πρώτῃ σαββάτου (in ver. 9) instead of the phrase μία σαββάτων, which he had employed just above (in ver. 2.) But it does not surprise me much,—when I observe that μία σαββάτων *occurs only once in each of the Four Gospels* [s]. Whether surprised much or little, however,—Am I constrained in consequence, (with Tischendorf and the rest,) to regard this expression (πρώτῃ σαββάτου) as a note of *spuriousness?* That is the only thing

---

[q] S. Luke vi. 1, 2, 5, 6, 7, 9 : xiii. 10, 14, 15, 16.   S. Luke has, in fact, all the four different designations for the Sabbath which are found in the Septuagint version of the O. T. Scriptures: for, in the Acts (xiii. 14 : xvi. 13), he twice calls it ἡ ἡμέρα τῶν σαββάτων.

[r] S. Matth. xii. 1, 2, 5, 8, 10, 11, 12.

[s] It occurs in S. Matth. xxviii. 1. S. Mark xvi. 2. S. Luke xxiv. 1. S. John xx. i. 19. Besides, only in Acts xx. 7.

I have to consider. Am I, with Dr. Davidson, to reason as follows:—" πρώτη, Mark would scarcely have used. It should have been μία, &c. as is proved by Mark xvi. 2, &c. The expression could scarcely have proceeded from a Jew. It betrays a Gentile author[t]." Am I to reason thus? ... I propose to answer this question somewhat in detail.

(I.) That among the Greek-speaking Jews of Palestine, in the days of the Gospel, ἡ μία τῶν σαββάτων was the established method of indicating "the first day of the week," is plain, not only from the fact that the day of the Resurrection is so designated by each of the Four Evangelists in turn[u]; (S. John has the expression twice;) but also from S. Paul's use of the phrase in 1 Cor. xvi. 2. It proves, indeed, to have been the ordinary Hellenistic way of exhibiting the vernacular idiom of Palestine[x]. The cardinal (μία) for the ordinal (πρώτη) in this phrase was a known Talmudic expression, which obtained also in Syriac[y]. Σάββατον and σάββατα,—designations in strictness of the *Sabbath-day*,—had come to be *also* used as designations of the *week*. A reference to S. Mark xvi. 9 and S. Luke xviii. 12 establishes this concerning σάββατον: a reference to the six places cited just now in note ([s]) establishes it concerning σάββατα. To see how indifferently the two forms (σάββατον and σάββατα) were employed, one has but to notice that S. Matthew, *in the course of one and the same chapter*, five times designates the Sabbath as τὰ σάββατα, and three times as τὸ σάββατον[z]. The origin and history of both words will be found explained in a note at the foot of the page[a].

[t] *Introduction*, &c. i. 169.   [u] See the foregoing note (s).
[x] See Buxtorf's *Lexicon Talmudicum*, p. 2323.
[y] Lightfoot (on 1 Cor. xvi. 2) remarks concerning S. Paul's phrase κατὰ μίαν σαββάτων,— "בְּחַד בְּשַׁבַּת [*b'had b'shabbath*,] 'In the first [lit. one] *of the Sabbath*,' would the Talmudists say."—Professor Gandell writes,—"in Syriac, the days of the week are similarly named. See Bernstein s. v. ܚܕ ܒܫܒܐ . ܬܠܬܐ ܒܫܒܐ , ܬܪܝܢ ܒܫܒܐ , ܚܕ ܒܫܒܐ [lit. *one in the Sabbath, two in the Sabbath, three in the Sabbath.*]
[z] S. Mark xii. 1, 2, 5, 8, 10, 11, 12.
[a] The Sabbath-day, in the Old Testament, is invariably שַׁבָּת (*shabbath*): a word which the Greeks could not exhibit more nearly than by the word σάββατον. The Chaldee form of this word is שַׁבְּתָא (*shabbatha*:) the

(2.) Confessedly, then, a double Hebraism is before us, which must have been simply unintelligible to Gentile readers. Μία τῶν σαββάτων sounded as enigmatical to an ordinary Greek ear, as "*una sabbatorum*" to a Roman. A convincing proof, (if proof were needed,) how abhorrent to a Latin reader was the last-named expression, is afforded by the old Latin versions of S. Matthew xxviii. 1; where ὄψε σαββάτων, τῇ ἐπιφωσκούσῃ εἰς μίαν σαββάτων is invariably rendered, "Vespere *sabbati*, quæ lucescit in *prima sabbati*."

(3.) The reader will now be prepared for the suggestion, that when S. Mark, (who is traditionally related to have written his Gospel *at Rome*[b],) varies, in ver. 9, the phrase

final ן (*a*) being added for emphasis, as in Abb*a*, Aceldam*a*, Bethesd*a*, Ceph*a*, Pasch*a*, &c. : and this form,—(I owe the information to my friend Professor Gandell,)—because it was so familiar to the people of Palestine, (who spoke Aramaic,) *gave rise to another form of the Greek name for the Sabbath*, —viz. σάββατα : which, naturally enough, attracted the article (τό) into agreement with its own (apparently) plural form. By the Greek-speaking population of Judæa, the Sabbath day was therefore indifferently called τὸ σάββατον and τὰ σάββατα : sometimes again, ἡ ἡμέρα τοῦ σαββάτου, and sometimes ἡ ἡμέρα τῶν σαββάτων.

Σάββατα, although plural in sound, was strictly singular in sense. (Accordingly, it is *invariably* rendered "*Sabbatum*" in the Vulgate.) Thus, in Exod. xvi. 23,—σάββατα ἀνάπαυσις ἁγία τῷ Κυρίῳ : and 25,—ἔστι γὰρ σάββατα ἀνάπαυσις τῷ Κυρίῳ. Again,—τῇ δὲ ἡμέρᾳ τῇ ἑβδόμῃ σάββατα. (Exod. xvi. 26 : xxxi. 14. Levit. xxiii. 3.) And in the Gospel, what took place on *one definite Sabbath-day*, is said to have occurred ἐν τοῖς σάββασι (S. Luke xiii. 10. S. Mark xii. 1.)

It will, I believe, be invariably found that the form ἐν τοῖς σάββασι is strictly equivalent to ἐν τῷ σαββάτῳ ; and was adopted for convenience in contradistinction to ἐν τοῖς σαββάτοις (1 Chron. xxiii. 31 and 2 Chron. ii. 4) where Sabbath *days* are spoken of.

It is not correct to say that in Levit. xxiii. 15 שַׁבָּתוֹת is put for "*weeks* ;" though the Septuagint translators have (reasonably enough) there rendered the word ἑβδομάδας. In Levit. xxv. 8, (where the same word occurs twice,) it is once rendered ἀναπαύσεις ; once, ἑβδομάδες. Quite distinct is שָׁבוּעַ (shavooa) i.e. ἑβδομάς ; nor is there any substitution of the one word for the other. But inasmuch as the recurrence of the *Sabbath-day* was what constituted *a week ;* in other words, since the essential feature of a week, as a Jewish division of time, was the recurrence of the Jewish day of rest ;—τὸ σάββατον or τὰ σάββατα, the Hebrew name for *the day of rest*, became transferred to *the week*. The former designation, (as explained in the text,) is used once by S. Mark, once by S. Luke ; while the phrase μία τῶν σαββάτων occurs in the N.T., in all, six times.

[b] So Eusebius (*Eccl. Hist.* ii. 15), and Jerome (*De Viris Illust.* ii. 827), on

he had employed in ver. 2, he does so for an excellent and indeed for an obvious reason. In ver. 2, he had conformed to the prevailing usage of Palestine, and followed the example set him by S. Matthew (xxviii. 1) in adopting the enigmatical expression, ἡ μία σαββάτων. That this would be idiomatically represented *in Latin* by the phrase "prima sabbati," we have already seen. In ver. 9, therefore, he is solicitous to record the fact of the Resurrection afresh ; and *this* time, his phrase is observed to be *the Greek equivalent for the Latin "prima sabbati ;"* viz. πρώτη σαββάτου. How strictly equivalent the two modes of expression were felt to be by those who were best qualified to judge, is singularly illustrated by the fact that the *Syriac* rendering of both places is *identical*.

(4.) But I take leave to point out that this substituted phrase, instead of being a suspicious circumstance, is on the contrary a striking note of genuineness. For do we not recognise here, in the last chapter of the Gospel, the very same hand which, in the first chapter of it, was careful to inform us, just for once, that "Judæa," is "a *country*," (ἡ Ἰουδαία χώρα,)—and "Jordan," "a *river*," (ὁ Ἰορδάνης ποταμός)?—Is not this the very man who explained to his readers (in chap. xv. 42) that the familiar Jewish designation for "Friday," ἡ παρασκευή, denotes "*the day before the Sabbath*[c] ?"—and who was so minute in informing us (in chap. vii. 3, 4) about certain ceremonial practices of "the Pharisees and all the Jews?" Yet more,—Is not the self-same writer clearly recognisable in this xvi[th] chapter, who in chap. vi. 37 presented us with σπεκουλάτωρ (the Latin *spiculator*) for "an executioner?" and who, in chap. xv. 39, for "a *centurion*," wrote—not ἑκατόνταρχος, but—κεντυρίων?—and, in chap. xii. 42, explained that the two λεπτά

---

the authority of Clemens Alex. and of Papias. See also Euseb. *Hist. Eccl.* vi. 14.—The colophon in the Syriac Version shews that the same traditional belief prevailed in the Eastern Church. It also finds record in the *Synopsis Scripturæ* (wrongly) ascribed to Athanasius.

[c] παρασκευὴ, ὅ ἐστι προσάββατον.—Our E. V. "preparation" is from Augustine,—" Parasceve Latine præparatio est."—See Pearson's interesting note on the word.

which the poor widow cast into the Treasury were equivalent to κοδράντης, the Latin *quadrans*?—and in chap. vii. 4, 8, introduced the Roman measure *sextarius*, (ξέστης)? —and who volunteered the information (in chap. xv. 16) that αὐλή is only another designation of πραιτώριον (*Prætorium*)?—Yes. S. Mark,—who, alone of the four Evangelists, (in chap. xv. 21,) records the fact that Simon the Cyrenian was "*the father of Alexander and Rufus,*" evidently for the sake of his *Latin* readers* : S. Mark,—who alone ventures to write in Greek letters (οὐά,—chap. xv. 29,) the Latin interjection "*Vah!*"—obviously because he was writing where that exclamation was most familiar, and the force of it best understood [d] : S. Mark,—who attends to the Roman division of the day, in relating our LORD's prophecy to S. Peter [e] :— S. Mark, I say, no doubt it was who,—having conformed himself to the precedent set him by S. Matthew and the familiar usage of Palestine; and having written τῆς μιᾶς σαββάτων, (which he knew would sound like "*una sabbatorum* [f],") in ver. 2;—introduced, also for the benefit of his Latin readers, the Greek equivalent for "*prima sabbati,*" (viz. πρώτη σαββάτου,) in ver. 9.—This, therefore, I repeat, so far from being a circumstance "*unfavourable* to its authenticity," (by which, I presume, the learned writer means its *genuineness*), is rather corroborative of the Church's constant belief that the present section of S. Mark's Gospel is, equally with the rest of it, the production of S. Mark. "Not only was the document intended for Gentile converts :" (remarks Dr. Davidson, p. 149,) "but there are also appearances of its adaptation to the use of Roman Christians in particular." Just so. And I venture to say that in the whole of "the document" Dr. Davidson will not find a more striking "appearance of its adaptation to the use of Roman Christians,"—*and therefore of its genuineness*,—than this. I shall have to request my reader by-and-by to accept it as one of the most striking notes of Divine origin which these verses contain.—For the moment, I pass on.

---

* Consider Rom. xvi. 13.   [d] Townson's *Discourses*, i. 172.   [e] *Ibid.*
[f] See the Vulgate transl. of S. Mark xvi. 2 and of S. John xx. 19. In the same version, S. Luke xxiv. 1 and S. John xx. 1 are rendered "*una sabbati.*"

(II.) Less excusable is the coarseness of critical perception betrayed by the next remark. It has been pointed out as a suspicious circumstance that in ver. 9, "the phrase ἀφ' ἧς ἐκβεβλήκει ἑπτὰ δαιμόνια is attached to the name of Mary Magdalene, although she had been mentioned three times before without such appendix. It seems to have been taken from Luke viii. 2 [g]."—Strange perversity, and yet stranger blindness!

(1.) The phrase *cannot* have been taken from S. Luke; because S. Luke's Gospel was written after S. Mark's. It *was* not taken from S. Luke; because *there* ἀφ' ἧς δαιμόνια ἑπτὰ ἐξεληλύθει,—here, ἀφ' ἧς ἐκβεβλήκει ἑπτὰ δαιμόνια is read.

(2.) More important is it to expose the shallowness and futility of the entire objection. — Mary Magdalene "had been mentioned three times before, *without such appendix.*" Well but,—What *then?* After twice (ch. xiv. 54, 66) using the word αὐλή without any "appendix," in the very next chapter (xv. 16) S. Mark adds, ὅ ἐστι πραιτώριον.—The beloved Disciple having mentioned himself without any "appendix" in S. John xx. 7, mentions himself with a very elaborate "appendix" in ver. 20. But what of it?—The sister of the Blessed Virgin, having been designated in chap. xv. 40, as Μαρία ἡ Ἰακώβου τοῦ μικροῦ καὶ Ἰωσῆ μήτηρ; is mentioned with one half of that "appendix," (Μαρία ἡ Ἰωσῆ) in ver. 47, and *in the very next verse*, with the other half (Μαρία ἡ τοῦ Ἰακώβου.)—I see no reason why the Traitor, who, in S. Luke vi. 16, is called Ἰούδας Ἰσκαριώτης, should be designated as Ἰούδαν τὸν ἐπικαλούμενον Ἰσκαριώτην in S. Luke xxii. 3.—I am not saying that such "appendices" are either uninteresting or unimportant. That I attend to them habitually, these pages will best evince. I am only insisting that to infer from such varieties of expression that a different author is recognisable, is abhorrent to the spirit of intelligent Criticism.

(3.) But in the case before us, the hostile suggestion is peculiarly infelicitous. There is even inexpressible tenderness and beauty, the deepest Gospel significancy, in the reserva-

[g] Davidson's *Introduction*, &c. i. 169, *ed.* 1848 : (ii. 113, *ed.* 1868.)

tion of the clause "out of whom He had cast seven devils," for this place. The reason, I say, is even obvious why an "appendix," which would have been meaningless before, is introduced in connexion with Mary Magdalene's august privilege of being the first of the human race to behold the risen SAVIOUR. Jerome (I rejoice to find) has been beforehand with me in suggesting that it was done, in order to convey by an example the tacit assurance that "where Sin had abounded, there did Grace much more abound[h]." Are we to be cheated of our birthright by Critics[i] who, entirely overlooking a solution of the difficulty (*if* difficulty it be) Divine as this, can see in the circumstance grounds only for suspicion and cavil? Ἄπαγε.

(III.) Take the next example.—The very form of the "appendix" which we have been considering (ἀφ' ἧς ἐκβεβλήκει ἑπτὰ δαιμόνια) breeds offence. "Instead of ἐκβάλλειν ἀπό," (oracularly remarks Dr. Davidson,) "Mark has ἐκβάλλειν ἐκ[k]."

Nothing of the sort, I answer. S. Mark *once* has ἐκβάλλειν ἐκ[l], and *once* ἐκβάλλειν ἀπό. So has S. Matthew, (viz. in chap. vii. 4 and 5): and so has S. Luke, (viz. in chap. vi. 42, and in Acts xiii. 50.)—But what of all this? Who sees not that such Criticism is simply nugatory?

(IV.) We are next favoured with the notable piece of information that the word πορεύεσθαι, "never used by S. Mark, is three times contained in this passage;" (viz. in verses 10, 12 and 15.)

(1.) Yes. The uncompounded verb, never used *elsewhere* by S. Mark, is found here three times. But what then? The *compounds* of πορεύεσθαι are common enough in his Gospel. Thus, short as his Gospel is, he alone has εἰσπορεύεσθαι, ἐκ-πορεύεσθαι, συμ-πορεύεσθαι, παρα-πορεύεσθαι, *oftener than all the other three Evangelists put together*,—viz. twenty-four times against their nineteen: while the com-

---

[h] "Maria Magdalene ipsa est 'a quâ septem dæmonia expulerat': *ut ubi abundaverat peccatum, superabundaret gratiæ*." (Hieron. *Opp.* i. 327.)

[i] So Tischendorf,—"Collatis prioribus, parum apte adduntur verba ἀφ' ἧς ἐκβεβλήκει ἑ. δ." (p. 322.) I am astonished to find the same remark reiterated by most of the Critics : e.g. Rev. T. S. Green, p. 52.

[k] *Introduction, &c.* vol. i. p. 169.   [l] viz. in chap. vii. 26.

pound προσπορεύεσθαι is *peculiar to his Gospel.*—I am therefore inclined to suggest that the presence of the verb πορεύεσθαι in these Twelve suspected Verses, instead of being an additional element of suspicion, is rather a circumstance slightly corroborative of their genuineness.

(2.) But suppose that the facts had been different. The phenomenon appealed to is of even perpetual recurrence, and may on no account be represented as *suspicious.* Thus, παρουσία, a word used only by S. Matthew among the Evangelists, is by him used four times; yet are all those four instances found *in one and the same chapter.* S. Luke alone has χαρίζεσθαι, and he has it three times: but all three cases are met with *in one and the same chapter.* S. John alone has λύπη, and he has it four times: but all the four instances occur *in one and the same chapter.*

(3.) Such instances might be multiplied to almost any extent. Out of the fifteen occasions when S. Matthew uses the word τάλαντον, no less than fourteen occur in one chapter. The nine occasions when S. Luke uses the word μνᾶ all occur in one chapter. S. John uses the verb ἀνιστάναι transitively only four times: but all four instances of it are found in one chapter.—Now, these three words (be it observed) are *peculiar to the Gospels* in which they severally occur.

(4.) I shall of course be reminded that τάλαντον and μνᾶ are unusual words,—admitting of no substitute in the places where they respectively occur. But I reply,—Unless the Critics are able to shew me *which* of the ordinary compounds of πορεύομαι S. Mark could *possibly* have employed for the uncompounded verb, in the three places which have suggested the present inquiry, viz.:—

ver. 10:—ἐκείνη πορευθεῖσα ἀπήγγειλε τοῖς μετ' αὐτοῦ γενομένοις.

ver. 12:—δυσὶν ἐξ αὐτῶν ... πορευομένοις εἰς ἀγρόν.

ver. 13:—πορευθέντες εἰς τὸν κόσμον ἅπαντα, κηρύξατε τὸ εὐαγγέλιον;—

their objection is simply frivolous, and the proposed adverse reasoning, worthless. Such, in fact, it most certainly is; for it will be found that πορευθεῖσα in ver. 10,—πορευομένοις in ver. 12,—πορευθέντες in ver. 15,—*also* "admit of no substitute in the places where they severally occur;" and therefore, since the verb itself is one of S. Mark's favourite verbs, not only are these three places above suspicion, but they may be fairly adduced as indications that *the same* hand was at work here which wrote all the rest of his Gospel [m].

(V.) Then further,—the phrase τοῖς μετ' αὐτοῦ γενομένοις (in ver. 10) is noted as suspicious. "Though found in the Acts (xx. 18) it *never occurs in the Gospels:* nor does the word μαθηταί in this passage."

(1.) The phrase οἱ μετ' αὐτοῦ γενόμενοι occurs nowhere in the Acts or in the Gospels, *except here.* But,—Why *should* it appear elsewhere? or rather,—How *could* it? Now, if the expression be (as it is) an ordinary, easy, and obvious one,—*wanted* in this place, where it *is* met with; but *not* met with elsewhere, simply because elsewhere it is *not* wanted;—surely it is unworthy of any one calling himself a Critic to pretend that there attaches to it the faintest shadow of suspicion!

(2.) The essence of the phrase is clearly the expression οἱ μετ' αὐτοῦ. (The aorist participle of γίνομαι is added of necessity to mark the persons spoken of. In no other, (certainly in no simpler, more obvious, or more precise) way could the followers of the risen SAVIOUR have been designated at such a time. For had He not just now "overcome the sharpness of Death"?) But this expression, which occurs four times in S. Matthew and four times in S. Luke, occurs also four times in S. Mark: viz. in chap. i. 36; ii. 25; v. 40, *and here.* This, therefore, is a slightly corroborative circumstance,—not at all a ground of suspicion.

(3.) But it seems to be implied that S. Mark, because he mentions τοὺς μαθητάς often elsewhere in his Gospel, ought to have mentioned them here.

(*a*) I answer:—He does not mention τοὺς μαθητάς nearly so often as S. Matthew; while S. John notices them twice as often as he does.

(*b*) Suppose, however, that he elsewhere mentioned them five hundred times, because he had occasion five hundred

---

[m] Professor Broadus has some very good remarks on this subject.

times to speak of them;—what reason would *that* be for his mentioning them here, where he is *not* speaking of them?

(c) It must be evident to any one reading the Gospel with attention that besides οἱ μαθηταί,—(by which expression S. Mark always designates *the Twelve Apostles*,)—there was a considerable company of believers assembled together throughout the first Easter Day[n]. S. Luke notices this circumstance when he relates how the Women, on their return from the Sepulchre, "told all these things unto the Eleven, and *to all the rest*," (xxiv. 9): and again when he describes how Cleopas and his companion (δύο ἐξ αὐτῶν as S. Luke and S. Mark call them) on their return to Jerusalem, "found the Eleven gathered together, *and them that were with them*." (xxiv. 33.) But this was at least as well known to S. Mark as it was to S. Luke. Instead, therefore, of regarding the designation "*them that had been with Him*" with suspicion,—are we not rather to recognise in it one token more that the narrative in which it occurs is unmistakably genuine? What else is this but one of those delicate discriminating touches which indicate the hand of a great Master; one of those evidences of minute accuracy which stamp on a narrative the impress of unquestionable Truth?

(VI.) We are next assured by our Critic that θεᾶσθαι "is unknown to Mark;" but it occurs twice in this section, (viz. in ver. 11 and ver. 14.) *Another* suspicious circumstance!

(1.) A strange way (as before) of stating an ordinary fact, certainly! What else is it but to assume the thing which has to be proved? If the learned writer had said instead, that the verb θεᾶσθαι, here twice employed by S. Mark, occurs *nowhere else* in his Gospel,—he would have acted more loyally, not to say more fairly by the record: but then he would have been stating a strictly ordinary phenomenon,—of no significancy, or relevancy to the matter in hand. He is probably aware that παραβαίνειν in like manner is to be found in two consecutive verses of S. Matthew's Gospel; παρακούειν, twice in the course of one

---

[n] Consider the little society which was assembled on the occasion alluded to, in Acts i. 13, 14. Note also what is clearly implied by ver. 21—6, as to the persons who were *habitually* present at such gatherings.

verse: neither word being used on any other occasion *either by S. Matthew, or by any other Evangelist*. The same thing *precisely* is to be said of ἀναζητεῖν and ἀνταποδιδόναι, of ἀντιπαρέρχεσθαι and διατίθεσθαι, in S. Luke: of ἀνιστάναι and ζωννύναι in S. John. But who ever dreamed of insinuating that the circumstance is suspicious?

(2.) As for θεᾶσθαι, we should have reminded our Critic that this verb, which is used seven times by S. John, and four times by S. Matthew, is used only three times by S. Luke, and only twice by S. Mark. And we should have respectfully inquired,—What possible suspicion does θεᾶσθαι throw upon the last twelve verses of S. Mark's Gospel?

(3.) None whatever, would have been the reply. But in the meantime Dr. Davidson hints that the verb *ought* to have been employed by S. Mark in chap. ii. 14 º.—It is, I presume, sufficient to point out that S. Matthew, at all events, was not of Dr. Davidson's opinion P: and I respectfully submit that the Evangelist, inasmuch as he happens to be here *writing about himself*, must be allowed, just for once, to be the better judge.

(4.) In the meantime,—Is it not perceived that θεᾶσθαι is the very word specially required in these two places,—though *nowhere else in S. Mark's Gospel* ᵠ? The occasion is *one*,—viz. the 'beholding' of the person of the risen SAVIOUR. Does not even natural piety suggest that the uniqueness of such a 'spectacle' as *that* might well set an Evangelist on casting about for a word of somewhat less ordinary occurrence? The occasion cries aloud for this very verb θεᾶσθαι; and I can hardly conceive a more apt illustration of a darkened eye,—a spiritual faculty perverted from its lawful purpose,—than that which only discovers "a stumbling-block and occasion of falling" in expressions like the present which "should have been only for their wealth," being so manifestly designed for their edification.

º S. Luke (v. 27) has ἐθεάσατο τελώνην. S. Matthew (ix. 9) and S. Mark (ii. 14) have preferred εἶδεν ἄνθρωπον (Λευὶν τὸν τοῦ Ἀλφαίου) καθήμενον ἐπὶ τὸ τελώνιον. P See S. Matth. ix. 9.

ᵠ One is reminded that S. Matthew, in like manner, carefully *reserves* the verb θεωρεῖν (xxvii. 55: xxviii. 1) for the contemplation of the SAVIOUR's Cross and of the SAVIOUR's Sepulchre.

(VII.) But,—(it is urged by a Critic of a very different stamp,)—ἐθεάθη ὑπ' αὐτῆς (ver. 11) "is a construction only found here in the New Testament."

(1.) Very likely; but what then? The learned writer has evidently overlooked the fact that the passive θεᾶσθαι occurs but *three times* in the New Testament *in all*[q]. S. Matthew, on the *two* occasions when he employs the word, connects it with a dative[r]. What is there *suspicious* in the circumstance that θεᾶσθαι ὑπό should be the construction preferred by S. Mark? The phenomenon is not nearly so remarkable as that S. Luke, on one solitary occasion, exhibits the phrase μὴ φοβεῖσθε ἀπό[s],—instead of making the verb govern the accusative, as he does three times *in the very next verse;* and, indeed, eleven times in the course of his Gospel. To be sure, S. Luke in this instance is but copying S. Matthew, who *also* has μὴ φοβεῖσθε ἀπό once[t]; and seven times makes the verb govern an accusative. This, nevertheless, constitutes no reason whatever for suspecting the genuineness either of S. Matth. x. 28 or of S. Luke xii. 4.

(2.) In like manner, the phrase ἐφοβήθησαν φόβον μέγαν will be found to occur once, and once *only*, in S. Mark,— once, and once only, in S. Luke[u]; although S. Mark and S. Luke use the verb φοβεῖσθαι upwards of forty times. Such facts are interesting. They may prove important. But no one who is ever so little conversant with such inquiries will pretend that they are in the least degree *suspicious*.—I pass on.

(VIII.) It is next noted as a suspicious circumstance that ἀπιστεῖν occurs in ver. 11 and in ver. 16; but nowhere else in the Gospels,—except in S. Luke xxiv. 11, 14.

But really, such a remark is wholly without force, as an argument against the genuineness of the passage in which the word is found: for,

(1.) Where else in the course of this Gospel *could* ἀπιστεῖν have occurred? Now, unless some reason can be shewn why the word *should*, or at least *might* have been employed elsewhere, to remark upon its introduction in this place, *where it*

---

[q] S. Matth. vi. 1: xxiii. 5. S. Mark xvi. 11.
[r] Πρὸς τὸ θεαθῆναι αὐτοῖς, (vi. 1); and τοῖς ἀνθρώποις, xxiii. 5).
[s] S. Luke xii. 4. [t] S. Matth. x. 28. [u] S. Mark iv. 41. S. Luke ii. 9.

IX.]   *S. Mark's use of the verb* ἀπιστεῖν, *considered.*   239

could scarcely be dispensed with, as a ground of suspicion, is simply irrational. It might just as well be held to be a suspicious circumstance, in respect of verses 3 and 4, that the verb ἀποκυλίζειν occurs there, *and there only,* in this Gospel. Nothing whatever follows from the circumstance. It is, in fact, a point scarcely deserving of attention.

(2.) To be sure, if the case of a verb exclusively used by the two Evangelists, S. Mark and S. Luke, were an unique, or even an exceedingly rare phenomenon, it might have been held to be a somewhat suspicious circumstance that the phenomenon presented itself in the present section. But nothing of the sort is the fact. There are no fewer than forty-five verbs *exclusively used by S. Mark and S. Luke.* And why should not ἀπιστεῖν be, (as it is,) one of them?

(3.) Note, next, that this word *is used twice,* and in the course of his last chapter too, also *by S. Luke.* Nowhere else does it occur in the Gospels. It is at least as strange that the word ἀπιστεῖν should be found twice in the last chapter of the Gospel according to S. Luke, as in the last chapter of the Gospel according to S. Mark. And if no shadow of suspicion is supposed to result from this circumstance in the case of the third Evangelist, why should it in the case of the second?

(4.) But, lastly, *the noun* ἀπιστία (which occurs in S. Mark xvi. 14) occurs in two other places of the same Gospel. And this word (which S. Matthew uses twice,) is employed by none of the other Evangelists.—What need to add another word? Do not many of these supposed suspicious circumstances,—*this* one for example,—prove rather, on closer inspection, to be confirmatory facts?

(IX.) We are next assured that μετὰ ταῦτα (ver. 12) "*is not found in Mark,* though many opportunities occurred for using it."

(1.) I suppose that what this learned writer means, is this; that if S. Mark had coveted an opportunity for introducing the phrase μετὰ ταῦτα earlier in his Gospel, he might have found one. (More than this cannot be meant: for *nowhere* before does S. Mark employ *any other phrase* to express "after these things," or "after this," or "afterwards.")

But what is the obvious inference from the facts of the case, as stated by the learned Critic, except that the blessed Evangelist *must be presumed to have been unconscious of any desire to introduce the expression under consideration on any other occasion except the present?*

(2.) Then, further, it is worth observing that while the phrase μετὰ ταῦτα occurs five times in S. Luke's Gospel, it is found only twice in the Acts; while S. Matthew *never employs it at all.* Why, then,—I would respectfully inquire—*why* need S. Mark introduce the phrase *more than once?* Why, especially, is his solitary use of the expression to be represented as a suspicious circumstance ; and even perverted into an article of indictment against the genuineness of the last twelve verses of his Gospel? " Would any one argue that S. Luke was not the author of the Acts, because the author of the Acts has employed this phrase only twice,—' often as he *could* have used it?' (Meyer's phrase here[x].)"

(X.) Another objection awaits us.—Ἕτερος also "is unknown to Mark," says Dr. Davidson ;—which only means that the word occurs in chap. xvi. 12, but not elsewhere in his Gospel.

It so happens, however, that ἕτερος also occurs once only in the Gospel of S. John. Does it therefore throw suspicion on S. John xix. 37 ?

(XI.) The same thing is said of ὕστερον (in ver. 14) viz. that it "occurs nowhere" in the second Gospel.

But why not state the case thus ?—"Ὕστερον, a word which is twice employed by S. Luke, occurs only *once* in S. Mark and *once* in S. John.—*That* would be the true way of stating the facts of the case. But it would be attended with this inconvenient result,—that it would make it plain that the word in question has no kind of bearing on the matter in hand.

(XII.) The same thing he says of βλάπτειν (in ver. 18).

But what is the fact? The word occurs *only twice in the Gospels,*—viz. in S. Mark xvi. 18 and S. Luke iv. 35. It is one of the eighty-four words which are peculiar to S. Mark

---

[x] Professor Broadus, *ubi suprà.*

and S. Luke. What possible significancy would Dr. Davidson attach to the circumstance?

(XIII.) Once more.—"$\pi\alpha\nu\tau\alpha\chi o\hat{v}$" (proceeds Dr. Davidson) "is unknown to Mark;" which (as we begin to be aware) is the learned gentleman's way of stating that it is only found in chap. xvi. 20.

Tischendorf, Tregelles, and Alford insist that it *also* occurs in S. Mark i. 28. I respectfully differ from them in opinion: but when it has been pointed out that the word *is only used besides in S. Luke* ix. 6, what *can* be said of such Criticism but that it is simply frivolous?

(XIV. and XV.) Yet again:—$\sigma\nu\nu\epsilon\rho\gamma\epsilon\hat{\iota}\nu$ and $\beta\epsilon\beta\alpha\iota o\hat{v}\nu$ are also said by the same learned Critic to be "unknown to Mark."

S. Mark certainly uses these two words only once,—viz. in the last verse of the present Chapter: but what there is suspicious in this circumstance, I am at a loss even to divine. He *could* not have used them oftener; and since one hundred and fifty-six words are peculiar to his Gospel, why should not $\sigma\nu\nu\epsilon\rho\gamma\epsilon\hat{\iota}\nu$ and $\beta\epsilon\beta\alpha\iota o\hat{v}\nu$ be two of them?

(XVI.) "$\Pi\hat{\alpha}\sigma\alpha$ $\kappa\tau\iota\sigma\iota\varsigma$ is Pauline," proceeds Dr. Davidson, (referring to a famous expression which is found in ver. 15.)

(1.) All very oracular,—to be sure: but *why* $\pi\hat{\alpha}\sigma\alpha$ $\kappa\tau\iota\sigma\iota\varsigma$ should be thought "Pauline" rather than "Petrine," I really, once more, cannot discover; seeing that S. Peter has the expression as well as S. Paul[y].

(2.) In this place, however, the phrase is $\pi\hat{\alpha}\sigma\alpha$ $\dot{\eta}$ $\kappa\tau\iota\sigma\iota\varsigma$. But even this expression is no more to be called "Pauline" than "Marcine;" seeing that as S. Mark uses it once and once only, so does S. Paul use it once and once only, viz. in Rom. viii. 22.

(3.) In the meantime, how does it come to pass that the learned Critic has overlooked the significant fact that the word $\kappa\tau\iota\sigma\iota\varsigma$ occurs besides in S. Mark x. 6 and xiii. 19; and that it is a word which *S. Mark alone of the Evangelists uses?* Its occurrence, therefore, in this place is a circumstance the very reverse of suspicious.

(4.) But lastly, inasmuch as the opening words of our

[y] Col. i. 15, 23. 1 S. Pet. ii. 13.

242   *A Coincidence and a Conjecture.*   [CHAP.

LORD's Ministerial Commission to the Apostles are these,— κηρύξατε τὸ εὐαγγέλιον πάσῃ τῇ κτίσει (ver. 15): inasmuch, too, as S. Paul in his Epistle to the Colossians (i. 23) almost reproduces those very words; speaking of the Hope τοῦ εὐαγγελίου ... τοῦ κηρυχθέντος ἐν πάσῃ [τῇ] κτίσει τῇ ὑπὸ τὸν οὐρανόν:"—Is it not an allowable conjecture that *a direct reference* to *that* place in S. Mark's Gospel is contained in *this* place of S. Paul's Epistle? that the inspired Apostle "beholding the universal tendency of Christianity already realized," announces (and from imperial Rome!) the fulfilment of his LORD's commands in his LORD's own words as recorded by the Evangelist S. Mark?

I desire to be understood to deliver this only as a conjecture. But seeing that S. Mark's Gospel is commonly thought to have been written at Rome, and under the eye of S. Peter; and that S. Peter (and therefore S. Mark) must have been at Rome before S. Paul visited that city in A.D. 61;—seeing, too, that it was in A.D. 61-2 (as Wordsworth and Alford are agreed) that S. Paul wrote his Epistle to the Colossians, and wrote it from *Rome;*—I really can discover nothing unreasonable in the speculation. If, however, it be well founded, —(and it is impossible to deny that the coincidence of expression *may* be such as I have suggested,)—then, what an august corroboration would *this* be of "the last Twelve Verses of the Gospel according to S. Mark!" ... If, indeed, the great Apostle on reaching Rome inspected S. Mark's Gospel for the first time, with what awe will he have recognised in his own recent experience the fulfilment of his SAVIOUR's great announcement concerning the "signs which should follow them that believe!" Had he not himself "cast out devils?"—"spoken with tongues more than they all?"— and at Melita, not only "shaken off the serpent into the fire and felt no harm," but also "laid hands on the sick" father of Publius, "and he had recovered?" ... To return, however, to matters of fact; with an apology (if it be thought necessary) for what immediately goes before.

(XVII.) Next,—ἐν τῷ ὀνόματί μου (ver. 17) is noticed as another suspicious peculiarity. The phrase is supposed to occur only in this place of S. Mark's Gospel; the Evangelist else-

IX.] ἐν τῷ ὀνόματι—παρ- and ἐπ- ἀκολουθεῖν. 243

where employing the preposition ἐπί:—(viz. in ix. 37 : ix. 39 : xiii. 6.)

(1.) Now really, if it were so, the reasoning would be nugatory. *S. Luke* also once, and once only, has ἐν τῷ ὀνόματί σου: his usage elsewhere being, (like S. Mark's) to use ἐπί. Nay, in two consecutive verses of ch. ix, ἐπὶ τῷ ὀνόματί μου —σου is read: and yet, in the very next chapter, his Gospel exhibits an unique instance of the usage of ἐν. Was it ever thought that suspicion is thereby cast on S. Luke x. 17?

(2.) But, in fact, the objection is an oversight of the learned (and generally accurate) objector. The phrase recurs in S. Mark ix. 38,—as the text of that place has been revised by Tischendorf, by Tregelles and by himself. This is therefore a slightly *corroborative*, not a suspicious circumstance.

(XVIII. and XIX.) We are further assured that παρακολουθεῖν (in ver. 17) and ἐπακολουθεῖν (in ver. 20) " are both *foreign to the diction of Mark.*"

(1.) But what can the learned author of this statement possibly mean? He is not speaking of the uncompounded verb ἀκολουθεῖν, of course; for S. Mark employs it at least twenty times. He cannot be speaking of the compounded verb; for συνακολουθεῖν occurs in S. Mark v. 37. He cannot mean that παρακολουθεῖν, because the Evangelist uses it only once, is suspicious; for that would be to cast a slur on S. Luke i. 3. He cannot mean generally that verbs compounded with prepositions are " foreign to the diction of Mark;" for there are no less than *forty-two* such verbs which are even *peculiar to S. Mark's short Gospel,*—against thirty which are peculiar to S. Matthew, and seventeen which are peculiar to S. John. He cannot mean that verbs compounded with παρά and ἐπί have a suspicious look; for at least *thirty-three* such compounds, (besides the two before us,) occur in his sixteen chapters [z]. What, then, I must

---

[z] παραβάλλειν [I quote from the Textus Receptus of S. Mark iv. 30,—confirmed as it is by the Peshito and the Philoxenian, the Vetus and the Vulgate, the Gothic and the Armenian versions,—besides Codd. A and D, and all the other uncials (except B, L, Δ, ℵ,) and almost every cursive Codex. The evidence of Cod. C and of Origen is doubtful. *Who* would subscribe to the different reading adopted on countless similar occasions by the most recent Editors of the N. T.?] : παραγγέλλειν : παράγειν : παραγίνεσθαι : παραδιδόναι : παραλαμβάνειν :

really ask, can the learned Critic possibly mean?—I respectfully pause for an answer.

(2.) In the meantime, I claim that as far as such evidence goes,—(and it certainly goes a very little way, yet, *as far as it goes,*)—it is a note of S. Mark's authorship, that within the compass of the last twelve verses of his Gospel these two compounded verbs should be met with.

(XX.) Dr. Davidson points out, as another suspicious circumstance, that (in ver. 18) the phrase χεῖρας ἐπιτιθέναι ἐπί τινα occurs ; " instead of χεῖρας ἐπιτιθέναι τινι."

(1.) But on the contrary, the phrase "*is in Mark's manner,*" says Dean Alford: the plain fact being that it occurs no less than three times in his Gospel,—viz. in chap. viii. 25 : x. 16 : xvi. 18. (The other idiom, he has four times [a].) Behold, then, one and the same phrase is appealed to as a note of genuineness *and* as an indication of spurious origin. What *can* be the value of such Criticism as this?

(2.) Indeed, the phrase before us supplies no unapt illustration of the precariousness of the style of remark which is just now engaging our attention. Within the space of three verses, S. Mark has *both* expressions,—viz. ἐπιθεὶς τὰς χεῖρας αὐτῷ (viii. 23) and also ἐπέθηκε τὰς χεῖρας ἐπί (ver. 25.) S. Matthew has the latter phrase once ; the former, twice [b]. *Who* will not admit that all this (so-called) Criticism is the veriest trifling ; and that to pretend to argue about the genuineness of a passage of Scripture from such evidence as the present is an act of rashness bordering on folly ? . . . The reader is referred to what was offered above on Art. VII.

(XXI. and XXII.) Again: the words μὲν οὖν—ὁ Κύριος (ver. 19 and ver. 20) are also declared to be "*foreign to the diction of Mark.*" I ask leave to examine these two charges separately.

παρατηρεῖν : παρατιθέναι : παραφέρειν : παρέρχεσθαι : παρέχειν : παριστάναι.—
ἐπαγγέλλεσθαι : ἐπαισχύνεσθαι : ἐπανίστασθαι : ἐπερωτᾶν : ἐπιβάλλειν : ἐπιγινώσκειν : ἐπιγράφειν : ἐπιζητεῖν : ἐπιλαμβάνεσθαι : ἐπιλανθάνεσθαι : ἐπιλύειν : ἐπιπίπτειν : ἐπιρράπτειν : ἐπισκιάζειν : ἐπιστρέφειν : ἐπισυνάγειν : ἐπισυντρέχειν : ἐπιτάσσειν : ἐπιτιθέναι : ἐπιτιμᾶν : ἐπιτρέπειν.

[a] S. Mark v. 23 : vi. 5 : vii. 32 : viii. 23.
[b] S. Matth. ix. 18 :—xix. 13, 15.

(1.) μὲν οὖν occurs only once in S. Mark's Gospel, truly: but then *it occurs only once in S. Luke* (iii. 18) ;—only twice in S. John (xix. 24 : xx. 30) :—in S. Matthew, never at all. What imaginable plea can be made out of such evidence as this, for or against the genuineness of the last Twelve Verses of S. Mark's Gospel ?—Once more, I pause for an answer.

(2.) As for ὁ Κύριος being "*foreign to the diction of Mark in speaking of the* LORD,"—I really do not know what the learned Critic can possibly mean; except that he finds our LORD *nowhere called* ὁ Κύριος *by S. Mark, except in this place.*

But then, he is respectfully reminded that neither does he find our LORD anywhere called by S. Mark " JESUS CHRIST," except in chap. i. 1. Are we, therefore, to suspect the beginning of S. Mark's Gospel as well as the end of it? By no means, (I shall perhaps be told :) a reason is assignable for the use of *that* expression in chap. i. 1. And so, I venture to reply, there is a fully sufficient reason assignable for the use of *this* expression in chap. xvi. 19 [c].

(3.) By S. Matthew, by S. Mark, by S. John, our LORD is called Ἰησοῦς Χριστός,—but *only in the first Chapter* of their respective Gospels. By S. Luke nowhere. The appellation may,—or may not,—be thought " foreign to the diction" of those Evangelists. But surely it constitutes no reason whatever why we should suspect the genuineness of the beginning of the first, or the second, or the fourth Gospel.

(4.) S. John *three times in the first verse of his first Chapter* designates the Eternal SON by the extraordinary title ὁ Λόγος; but *nowhere else in his Gospel,* (except once in ver. 14,) does that Name recur. Would it be reasonable to represent *this* as a suspicious circumstance ? Is not the Divine fitness of that sublime appellation generally recognised and admitted [d] ?—Surely, we come to Scripture to be learners only : not to teach the blessed Writers how they ought to have spoken about GOD ! When will men learn that " the

---

[c] See below, pp. 184-6.
[d] See Pearson *on the Creed,* (ed. Burton), vol. i. p. 151.

Scripture-phrase, or *language of the Holy Ghost*[e]" is as much above them as Heaven is above Earth?

(XXIII.) Another complaint:—ἀναληφθῆναι, which is found in ver. 19, occurs nowhere else in the Gospels.

(1.) True. S. Mark has no fewer than seventy-four verbs which "occur nowhere else in the Gospels:" and this happens to be one of them? What possible inconvenience can be supposed to follow from that circumstance?

(2.) But the remark is unreasonable. 'Αναληφθῆναι and ἀνάληψις are words *proper to the Ascension of our* LORD *into Heaven*. The two Evangelists who do *not* describe that event, are *without* these words: the two Evangelists who *do* describe it, *have* them [f]. Surely, these are marks of genuineness, not grounds for suspicion!

It is high time to conclude this discussion.—Much has been said about two other minute points:—

(XXIV.) It is declared that ἐκεῖνος " is nowhere found absolutely used by S. Mark:" (the same thing may be said of S. Matthew and of S. Luke also:) "but always emphatically: whereas in verses 10 and 11, it is absolutely used [g]." Another writer says,—"The use of ἐκεῖνος in verses 10, 11, and 13 (twice) in a manner synonymous with ὁ δέ, is peculiar [h]."

(1.) Slightly peculiar it is, no doubt, but not very, that an Evangelist who employs an ordinary word in the ordinary way about thirty times in all, should use it "absolutely" in two consecutive verses.

(2.) But really, until the Critics can agree among themselves as to *which* are precisely the offending instances,—(for it is evidently a moot point whether ἐκεῖνος be emphatic in ver. 13, or not,)—we may be excused from a prolonged discussion of such a question. I shall recur to the subject in the consideration of the next Article (XXV.)

(XXV.) So again, it may be freely admitted that "in the 10th and 14th verses there are sentences without a copula-

---

[e] *Ibid.* p. 183,—at the beginning of the exposition of "*Our* LORD."
[f] S. Mark xvi. 19. S. Luke ix. 51. Acts i. 2.
[g] Alford. [h] Davidson.

tive: whereas Mark always has the copulative in such cases, particularly καί." But then,—

(1.) Unless we can be shewn at least two or three other sections of S. Mark's Gospel *resembling the present*,—(I mean, passages in which S. Mark summarizes many disconnected incidents, as he does here,)—is it not plain that such an objection is wholly without point?

(2.) Two instances are cited. In the latter, (ver. 14), Lachmann and Tregelles read ὕστερον δέ: and the reading is not impossible. So that the complaint is really reduced to this,—That in ver. 10 the Evangelist begins Ἐκείνη πορευθεῖσα, instead of saying Καὶ ἐκείνη πορευθεῖσα. And (it is implied) there is something so abhorrent to probability in this, as slightly to strengthen the suspicion that the entire context is not the work of the Evangelist.

(3.) Now, suppose we had S. Mark back among us: and suppose that he, on being shewn this objection, were to be heard delivering himself somewhat to the following effect:—"Aye. But men may not find fault with *that* turn of phrase. I derived it from Simon Peter's lips. I have always suspected that it was a kind of echo, so to say, of what he and 'the other Disciple' had many a time rehearsed in the hearing of the wondering Church concerning the Magdalene on the morning of the Resurrection." And then we should have remembered the familiar place in the fourth Gospel:—

γύναι τί κλαίεις; τίνα ζητεῖς; ἘΚΕΙΝΗ δοκοῦσα κ.τ.λ.

After which, the sentence would not have seemed at all strange, even though it *be* "without a copulative:"—

ἀφ' ἧς ἐκβεβλήκει ἑπτὰ δαιμόνια. ἘΚΕΙΝΗ πορευθεῖσα κ.τ.λ.

(4.) For after all, the *only* question to be asked is,—Will any one pretend that such a circumstance as this is *suspicious*? Unless *that* be asserted, I see not what is gained by raking together,—(*as one easily might do in any section of any of the Gospels,*)—every minute peculiarity of form or expression which can possibly be found within the space of these twelve verses. It is an evidence of nothing so much as an incorrigible coarseness of critical fibre, that every slight variety of manner or language should be thus pounced upon and represented as a note of spuriousness,—in the face of (*a*) the unfaltering tradition of the Church universal that the document has *never* been hitherto suspected: and (*b*) the known proclivity of all writers, as free moral and intellectual agents, sometimes to deviate from their else invariable practice.—May I not here close the discussion?

There will perhaps be some to remark, that however successfully the foregoing objections may seem to have been severally disposed of, yet that the combined force of such a multitude of slightly suspicious circumstances must be not only appreciable, but even remain an inconvenient, not to say a formidable fact. Let me point out that the supposed remark is nothing else but a fallacy; which is detected the instant it is steadily looked at.

For if there really had remained after the discussion of each of the foregoing XXV Articles, a slight residuum of suspiciousness, *then* of course the aggregate of so many fractions would have amounted to something in the end.

But since it has been proved that there is absolutely *nothing at all* suspicious in *any* of the alleged circumstances which have been hitherto examined, the case becomes altogether different. The sum of ten thousand nothings is still nothing[i]. This may be conveniently illustrated by an appeal to the only charge which remains to be examined.

(XXVI. and XXVII.) The absence from these twelve verses of the adverbs εὐθέως and πάλιν,—(both of them favourite words with the second Evangelist,)—has been pointed out as one more suspicious circumstance. Let us take the words singly:—

(*a*) The adverb εὐθέως (or εὐθύς) is indeed of *very* frequent occurrence in S. Mark's Gospel. And yet its absence from

---

[i] Exactly so Professor Broadus:—"Now it will not do to say that while no one of these peculiarities would itself prove the style to be foreign to Mark, the whole of them combined will do so. It is very true that the multiplication of *littles* may amount to much; but not so the multiplication of *nothings*. And how many of the expressions which are cited, appear, in the light of our examination, to retain the slightest real force as proving difference of authorship? Is it not true that most of them, and those the most important, are reduced to absolutely nothing, while the remainder possess scarcely any appreciable significance?"—p. 360, (see above, p. 139, note g.)

chap. xvi is *proved* to be in no degree a suspicious circumstance, from the discovery that though it occurs as many as

	12 times in	chap. i;
and	6 „	chap. v;
and	5 „	chap. iv, vi;
and	3 „	chap. ii, ix, xiv;
and	2 „	chap. vii, xi;
it yet occurs only	1 „	chap. iii, viii, x, xv;
while it occurs	0 „	chap. xii, xiii, xvi.

(b) In like manner, πάλιν, which occurs as often as

	6 times in	chap. xiv;
and	5 „	chap. x;
and	3 „	chap. viii, xv;
and	2 „	chap. ii, iii, vii, xi, xii;
and	1 „	chap. iv, v;
occurs	0 „	chap. i, vi, ix, xiii. xvi. [k]

(1.) Now,—How can it possibly be more suspicious that πάλιν should be absent from *the last twelve* verses of S. Mark, than that it should be away from *the first forty-five?*

(2.) Again. Since εὐθέως is not found in the xii[th] or the xiii[th] chapters of this same Gospel,—nor πάλιν in the i[st], vi[th], ix[th], or xiii[th] chapter,—(for the sufficient reason that *neither word is wanted in any of those places,*)—what possible "suspiciousness" can be supposed to result from the absence of both words from the xvi[th] chapter also, where *also* neither of them is wanted? *Why* is the xvi[th] chapter of S. Mark's Gospel,—or rather, why are "the last twelve verses" of it, —to labour under such special disfavor and discredit?

(3.) Dr. Tregelles makes answer,—"I am well aware that arguments on *style* are often very fallacious, and that *by themselves* they prove very little: but when there does exist external evidence, and when internal proofs as to style, manner, verbal expression, and connection, are in accordance with such independent grounds of forming a judgment; then these internal considerations possess very great weight[1]."—For all

---

[k] S. John has πάλιν (47 times) much oftener than S. Mark (29 times). And yet, πάλιν is not met with in the ii[nd], or the iii[rd], or the vth, or the vii[th], or the xv[th], or the xvii[th] chapter of S. John's Gospel.

[1] *Printed Text*, p. 256.

rejoinder, the respected writer is asked, — (*a*) But when there *does not* exist any such external evidence: what then? Next, he is reminded (*b*) That whether there does, or does not, it is at least certain that *not one* of those " proofs as to style," &c., of which he speaks, has been able to stand the test of strict examination. Not only is the precariousness of all such Criticism as has been brought to bear against the genuineness of S. Mark xvi. 9—20 excessive, but the supposed facts adduced in evidence have been found out to be every one of them *mistakes;*—being either, (1) demonstrably without argumentative cogency of any kind;—or else, (2) distinctly corroborative and confirmatory circumstances: indications that this part of the Gospel is indeed by S. Mark,—*not* that it is probably the work of another hand.

And thus the formidable enumeration of twenty-seven grounds of suspicion vanishes out of sight: fourteen of them proving to be frivolous and nugatory; and *thirteen*, more or less clearly witnessing *in favour* of the section [m].

III. Of these thirteen expressions, some are even eloquent in their witness. I am saying that it is impossible not to be exceedingly struck by the discovery that this portion of the Gospel contains (as I have explained already) so many indications of S. Mark's undoubted manner. Such is the reference to ἡ κτίσις (in ver. 15):—the mention of ἀπιστία (in ver. 14):—the occurrence of the verb πορεύεσθαι (in ver. 10 and 12),—of the phrase ἐν τῷ ὀνόματί μου (in ver. 17),—and of the phrase χεῖρας ἐπιτιθέναι ἐπί τινα (in ver. 18):—of the Evangelical term for our LORD's Ascension, viz. ἀνελήφθη (in ver. 19):—and lastly, of the compounds παρακολουθεῖν and ἐπακολουθεῖν (in verses 17 and 20.)

To these Thirteen, will have to be added all those other notes of identity of authorship,—such as they are,—which result from recurring identity of phrase, and of which the assailants of this portion of the Gospel have prudently said nothing. Such are the following:—

(xiv.) Ἀνίστανται, for rising *from the dead;* which is one

---

[m] It will be found that of the former class (1) are the following:—Article iii: vii: ix: x: xi: xii: xiii: xiv: xv: xxi: xxiv: xxv: xxvi: xxvii. Of the latter (2):—Art. i: ii: iv: v: vi: viii: xvi: xvii: xviii: xix: xx: xxii: xxiii.

of S. Mark's words. Taking into account the shortness of his Gospel, he has it thrice as often as S. Luke; *twelve times* as often as S. Matthew or S. John.

(xv.) The idiomatic expression πορευομένοις εἰς ἀγρόν, of which S. Matthew does not present a single specimen; but which occurs three times in the short Gospel of S. Mark[n], —of which ver. 12 is one.

(xvi.) The expression πρωΐ (in ver. 9,)—of which S. Mark avails himself six times: i.e. (if the length of the present Gospel be taken into account) almost five times as often as either S. Matthew or S. John,—S. Luke never using the word at all. In his first chapter (ver. 35), and here in his last (ver. 2), S. Mark uses λίαν in connexion with πρωΐ.

(xvii.) The *phrase* κηρύσσειν τὸ εὐαγγέλιον (in ver. 15) is another of S. Mark's phrases. Like S. Matthew, he employs it four times (i. 14: xiii. 10: xiv. 9: xvi. 15): but it occurs neither in S. Luke's nor in S. John's Gospel.

(xviii.) The same *words* singly are characteristic of his Gospel. Taking the length of their several narratives into account, S. Mark has the word κηρύσσειν more than twice as often as S. Matthew: three times as often as S. Luke.

(xix.) εὐαγγέλιον,—a word which occurs only in the first two Gospels,—is found twice as often in S. Mark's as in S. Matthew's Gospel: and if the respective length of their Gospels be considered, the proportion will be as three to one. It occurs, as above stated, in ver. 15.

(xx.) If such Critics as Dr. Davidson had been concerned to vindicate *the genuineness* of this section of the Gospel, we should have been assured that φανεροῦσθαι is another of S. Mark's words: by which they would have meant no more than this,—that though employed neither by S. Matthew nor by S. Luke it is used thrice by S. Mark,—being found twice in this section (verses 12, 14), as well as in ch. iv. 22.

(xxi.) They would have also pointed out that σκληροκαρδία is another of S. Mark's words: being employed neither by S. Luke nor by S. John,—by S. Matthew only once,—but by S. Mark on *two* occasions; of which ch. xvi. 14 is one.

---

[n] Ch. xiii. 16,—ὁ εἰς τὸν ἀγρὸν ὤν: and ch. xv. 21,—ἐρχόμενον ἀπ' ἀγροῦ,—an expression which S. Luke religiously reproduces in the corresponding place of his Gospel, viz. in ch. xxiii. 26.

(xxii.) In the same spirit, they would have bade us observe that πανταχοῦ (ver. 20)—unknown to S. Matthew and S. John, and employed only once by S. Luke,—is *twice* used by S. Mark; one instance occurring in the present section. Nor would it have been altogether unfair if they had added that the precisely similar word πανταχόθεν (or πάντοθεν) is only found in this same Gospel,—viz. in ch. i. 45.

(xxiii.) They would further have insisted (and this time with a greater show of reason) that the adverb καλῶς (which is found in ver. 18) is another favorite word with S. Mark: occurring as it does, (when the length of these several narratives is taken into account,) more than twice as often in S. Mark's as in S. John's Gospel,—just three times as often as in the Gospel of S. Matthew and S. Luke.

(xxiv.) A more interesting (because a more just) observation would have been that ἔχειν, in the sense of "to be," (as in the phrase καλῶς ἔχειν, ver. 18,) is characteristic of S. Mark. He has it oftener than any of the Evangelists, viz. six times in all (ch. i. 32; 34 : ii. 17 : v. 23 : vi. 55 : xvi. 18.) Taking the shortness of his Gospel into account, he employs this idiom twice as often as S. Matthew ;—three times as often as S. John ;—four times as often as S. Luke.

(xxv.) They would have told us further that ἄρρωστος is another of S. Mark's favorite words: for that he has it *three* times,—viz. in ch. vi. 5, 13, and here in ver. 18. S. Matthew has it only once. S. Luke and S. John not at all.

(xxvi.) And we should have been certainly reminded by them that the conjunction of πενθοῦσι καὶ κλαίουσι (in ver. 10) is characteristic of S. Mark,—who has κλαίοντας καὶ ἀλαλάζοντας in ch. v. 38 : θορυβεῖσθε καὶ κλαίετε in the very next verse. As for πενθεῖν, it is one of the 123 words common to S. Matthew and S. Mark, and peculiar to their two Gospels.

(xxvii.) Lastly, "κατακρίνω (in ver. 16), instead of κρίνω, is Mark's word, (comp. x. 33 : xiv. 64)." The simple verb which is used four times by S. Matthew, five times by S. Luke, nineteen times by S. John, is never at all employed by S. Mark : whereas the compound verb he has oftener in proportion than S. Matthew,—more than twice as often as either S. Luke or S. John.

Strange,—that there should be exactly "xxvii" notes of genuineness discoverable in these twelve verses, instead of "XXVII" grounds of suspicion!

But enough of all this. Here, we may with advantage review the progress hitherto made in this inquiry.

I claim to have demonstrated long since that all those imposing assertions respecting the "Style" and "Phraseology" of this section of the Gospel which were rehearsed at the outset ,—are destitute of foundation. But from this discovery alone there results a settled conviction which it will be found difficult henceforth to disturb. A page of Scripture which has been able to endure so severe an ordeal of hostile inquiry, has been *proved* to be above suspicion. *That* character is rightly accounted *blameless* which comes out unsullied after Calumny has done her worst; done it systematically; done it with a will; done it for a hundred years.

But this is not an adequate statement of the facts of the case in respect of the conclusion of S. Mark's Gospel. Something *more* is certain than that the charges which have been so industriously brought against this portion of the Gospel are without foundation. It has been also proved that instead of there being discovered twenty-seven suspicious words and phrases scattered up and down these twelve verses of the Gospel, there actually exist exactly as many words and phrases which attest with more or less certainty that those verses are nothing else but the work of the Evangelist.

IV. And now it is high time to explain that though I have hitherto condescended to adopt the method of my opponents, I have only done so in order to shew that it proves fatal to *themselves*. I am, to say the truth, ashamed of what has last been written,—so untrustworthy do I deem the method which, (following the example of those who have preceded me in this inquiry,) I have hitherto pursued. The " Concordance test,"—(for *that* is probably as apt and intelligible a designation as can be devised for the purely *mechanical* process whereby it is proposed by a certain school of Critics to judge of the authorship of Scripture,)—is about the coarsest as well as about the most delusive that could be devised. By means of this clumsy and vulgar instrument, especially when applied, (as in the case before us,) without skill and discrimination, it would be just as easy to prove that *the first* twelve verses of S. Mark's Gospel are of a suspicious character as *the last*[p]. In truth, except in very skilful hands, it is no test at all, and can only mislead.

Thus, (in ver. 1,) we should be informed (i.) that "Mark nowhere uses the appellation JESUS CHRIST:" and (ii.) that "εὐαγγέλιον Ἰησοῦ Χριστοῦ" is "*Pauline.*"—We should be reminded (iii.) that this Evangelist nowhere introduces any of the Prophets by name, and that therefore the mention of "Isaiah[*]" (in ver. 2) is a suspicious circumstance:—(iv.) that a quotation from the Old Testament is "foreign to his manner,"—(for writers of this class would not hesitate to assume that S. Mark xv. 28 is no part of the Gospel;)—and (v.) that the fact that here are quotations from *two* different prophets, betrays an unskilful hand.—(vi.) Because S. Mark three times calls Judæa by its usual name (Ἰουδαία, viz. in iii. 7: x. 1: xiii. 14), the *unique* designation, ἡ Ἰουδαία χώρα (in ver. 5) would be pronounced decisive against "the authorship of Mark."—(vii.) The same thing would be said of the *unique*

---

[p] The reader will be perhaps interested with the following passage in the pages of Professor Broadus already (p. 139 note g) alluded to:—"It occurred to me to examine the twelve just preceding verses, (xv. 44 to xvi. 8,) and by a curious coincidence, the words and expressions not elsewhere employed by Mark, footed up precisely the same number, seventeen. Those noticed are the following (text of Tregelles):—ver. 44, τέθνηκεν (elsewhere ἀποθνήσκω):— ver. 45, γνοὺς ἀπό, a construction found nowhere else in the New Testament: also ἐδωρήσατο and πτῶμα: ver. 46, ἐνείλησεν, λελατομημένον, πέτρας, προσεκύλισεν:—chap. xvi. ver. 1, διαγενομένου, and ἀρώματα: ver. 2, μιᾷ τῶν σαββάτων:—ver. 3, ἀποκυλίσει:—ver. 4, ἀνεκεκύλισται. Also, σφόδρα, (Mark's word is λίαν.) Ver. 5, ἐν τοῖς δεξιοῖς is a construction not found in Mark, or the other Gospels, though the word δεξιός occurs frequently:—ver. 8, εἶχεν, in this particular sense, not elsewhere in the New Testament: τρόμος.

"This list is perhaps not complete, for it was prepared in a few hours— about as much time, it may be said, without disrespect, as Fritsche and Meyer appear to have given to their collections of examples from the other passage. It is not proposed to discuss the list, though some of the instances are curious. It is not claimed that they are all important, but that they are all real. And as regards the single question of the *number* of peculiarities, they certainly form quite an offset to the number upon which Dean Alford has laid stress." —p. 361.   [*] Tischendorf, Tregelles, Alford.

expression, ἐν Ἰορδάνῃ ποταμῷ, which is found in ver. 5,—seeing that this Evangelist three times designates Jordan simply as Ἰορδάνης (i. 9 : iii. 8 : x. 1).—(viii.) *That* entire expression in ver. 7 (*unique*, it must be confessed, in the Gospel,) οὗ οὐκ εἰμὶ ἱκανός—ὑποδημάτων αὐτοῦ, would be pronounced "abhorrent to the style of Mark."—(ix.) τὸ Πνεῦμα *twice*, (viz. in ver. 10 and ver. 12) we should be told is never used by the Evangelist absolutely for the HOLY GHOST: but always τὸ Πνεῦμα τὸ Ἅγιον (as in ch. iii. 29 : xii. 36 : xiii. 11).—(x.) The same would be said of οἱ Ἱεροσολυμῖται (in ver. 5) for "the inhabitants of Jerusalem:" we should be assured that S. Mark's phrase would rather be οἱ ἀπὸ Ἱεροσολύμων,—as in ch. iii. 8 and 22.—And (xi.) the expression πιστεύειν ἐν τῷ εὐαγγελίῳ (ver. 15), we should be informed "cannot be Mark's;"—who either employs εἰς and the accusative (as in ch. ix. 92), or else makes the verb take a dative (as in ch. xi. 31 : xvi. 13, 14.)—We should also probably be told that the ten following words are all "unknown to Mark:"—(xii.) τρίχες,—(xiii.) δερματίνη,—(xiv.) ὀσφύς,—(xv.) ἀκρίδες,—(xvi.) μέλι,—(xvii.) ἄγριος, (six instances in a single verse (ver. 6) : a highly suspicious circumstance !),—(xviii.) κύπτειν,—(xix.) ἱμάς,—(xx.) ὑποδήματα, (all three instances in ver. 7 !) – (xxi.) εὐδοκεῖν,—(xxii.) καὶ ἐγένετο . . ἦλθεν (ver. 9),—unique in S. Mark !—(xxiii.) βαπτίζεσθαι εἰς (ver 9), another unique phrase !—(xxiv.) οἱ οὐρανοί *twice*, (viz. in verses 10, 11) yet elsewhere, when *S. Mark* speaks of Heaven, (ch. vi. 41 : vii. 34: viii. 11 : xvi. 19) he always uses the singular.—Lastly, (xxv.) the same sorry objection which was brought against the "last twelve verses," (that πάλιν, a favourite adverb with S. Mark, is not found there,) is here even more conspicuous.

Turning away from all this,—(not, however, without an apology for having lingered over such frivolous details so long,)—I desire to point out that we have reverently to look below the surface, if we would ascertain how far it is to be presumed from internal considerations whether S. Mark was indeed the author of this portion of his Gospel, or not.

V. We must devise, I say, some more delicate, more philosophical, more *real* test than the coarse, uncritical expedient which has been hitherto considered of ascertaining by reference to the pages of a Greek Concordance whether a certain word which is found in this section of the Gospel is, or is not, used elsewhere by S. Mark. And I suppose it will be generally allowed to be deserving of attention,—in fact, to be a singularly corroborative circumstance,—that within the narrow compass of these Twelve Verses we meet with *every principal characteristic of S. Mark's manner* :—Thus,

(i.) Though he is the Author of the shortest of the Gospels, and though to all appearance he often merely reproduces what S. Matthew has said before him, or else anticipates something, which is afterwards delivered by S. Luke,— it is surprising how often we are indebted to S. Mark for precious pieces of information which we look for in vain elsewhere. Now, this is a feature of the Evangelist's manner which is susceptible of memorable illustration from the section before us.

How many and how considerable are the *new circumstances* which S. Mark here delivers!—(1) That Mary Magdalene was *the first* to behold the risen SAVIOUR: (2) That it was *He* who had cast out from her the "seven devils :" (3) *How the men were engaged* to whom she brought her joyful message,—(4) who not only did not believe *her* story, but when Cleopas and his companion declared what had happened to themselves, "*neither believed they them.*" (5) The terms of the Ministerial Commission, as set down in verses 15 and 16, are unique. (6) The announcement of the "signs which should follow them that believe" is even extraordinary. Lastly, (7) this is the only place in the Gospel where *The Session at the right Hand of GOD* is recorded. . . . So many, and such precious incidents, showered into the Gospel Treasury at the last moment, and with such a lavish hand, must needs have proceeded if not from an Apostle at least from a companion of Apostles. O, if we had no other token to go by, there could not be a reasonable doubt that this entire section is by no other than S. Mark himself!

(ii.) A second striking characteristic of the second Evangelist is his love of picturesque, or at least of striking details, —his proneness to introduce exceedingly minute particulars, often of the profoundest significancy, and always of considerable interest. Not to look beyond the Twelve Verses (chap. i. 9—20) which were originally proposed for comparison,—We are reminded (*a*) that in describing our SAVIOUR's Baptism, it is only S. Mark who relates that "He came *from Nazareth*" to be baptized.—(*b*) In his highly elliptical account of our LORD's Temptation, it is only he who relates that "He was *with the wild beasts.*"—(*c*) In his description of the Call of the four Disciples, S. Mark alone it is who, (notwithstanding the close resemblance of his account to what is found in S. Matthew,) records that the father of S. James and S. John was left "in the ship *with the hired servants* q."—Now, of this characteristic, we have also within these twelve verses, at least four illustrations:—

(*a*) Note in ver. 10, that life-like touch which evidently proceeded from an eye-witness,—"πενθοῦσι καὶ κλαίουσι." S. Mark relates that when Mary conveyed to the Disciples the joyous tidings of the LORD's Resurrection, *she found them overwhelmed with sorrow,*—"mourning and weeping."

(*b*) Note also that the unbelief recorded in ver. 13 *is recorded only there.*

(*c*) Again. S. Mark not only says that as the two Disciples were "going into the country," (πορευόμενοι εἰς ἀγρόν r, ver. 12,) JESUS also "went with them"—(συν-επορεύετο, as S. Luke relates;)—but that it was *as they actually* "*walked*" *along* (περιπατοῦσιν) that this manifestation took place.

(*d*) Among the marvellous predictions made concerning "them that believe;" what can be imagined more striking than the promise that they should "*take up serpents;*" and suffer no harm even if they should "*drink any deadly thing*"?

(iii) Next,—all have been struck, I suppose, with S. Mark's proneness to substitute some expression of his own for what he found in the Gospel of his predecessor S. Matthew: or, when he anticipates something which is afterwards met with in the Gospel of S. Luke, his aptness to deliver it in language entirely independent of the later Evangelist. I allude, for instance, to his substitution of ἐπιβαλὼν ἔκλαιε (xiv. 72)

---

q S. Mark i. 9: 14: 20.   r The same word is found also in S. Luke's narrative of the same event, ch. xxiv. 13.

for S. Matthew's ἔκλαυσε πικρῶς (xxvi. 75) ;—and of ὁ τέκτων (vi. 3) for ὁ τοῦ τέκτονος υἱός (S. Matth. xiii. 55).—The "woman of Canaan" in S. Matthew's Gospel (γυνὴ Χαναναία, ch. xv. 22), is called "a Greek, a Syrophenician by nation" in S. Mark's (Ἑλληνὶς, Συροφοίνισσα τῷ γένει, ch. vii. 26).—At the Baptism, "instead of the "*opened*" heavens of S. Matthew (ἀνεῴχθησαν, ch. iii. 16) and S. Luke (ἀνεῳχθῆναι, ch. iii. 22), we are presented by S. Mark with the striking image of the heavens "*cleaving*" or "*being rent asunder*" (σχιζομένους*, ch. i. 10).—What S. Matthew calls τὰ ὅρια Μαγδαλά (ch. xv. 39), S. Mark designates as τὰ μέρη Δαλμανουθά (ch. viii. 10.)—In place of S. Matthew's ζύμη Σαδδουκαίων (ch. xvi. 6), S. Mark has ζύμη Ἡρῴδου (ch. viii. 15.)—In describing the visit to Jericho, for the δύο τυφλοί of S. Matthew (ch. xx. 29), S. Mark gives υἱὸς Τιμαίου Βαρτίμαιος ὁ τυφλὸς . . . . προσαιτῶν (ch. x. 46.)—For the κλάδους of S. Matth. xxi. 8, S. Mark (ch. xi. 8) has στοιβάδας; and for the other's πρὶν ἀλέκτορα φωνῆσαι (xxvi. 34), he has πρὶν ἢ δίς (xiv. 30.)—It is so throughout.

Accordingly,—(as we have already more than once had occasion to remark,)—whereas the rest say only ἡ μία τῶν σαββάτων, S. Mark says πρώτη σαββάτου (in ver. 9).—Whereas S. Luke (viii. 2) says ἀφ' ἧς δαιμόνια ἑπτὰ ἐξεληλύθει,— S. Mark records that from her ἐκβεβλήκει ἑπτὰ δαιμόνια.— Very different is the great ministerial Commission as set down by S. Mark in ver. 15, 16, from what is found in S. Matthew xxviii. 19, 20.—And whereas S. Luke says "*their eyes were holden* that they should not know Him," S. Mark says that "He appeared to them *in another form*." . . . Is it credible that any one fabricating a conclusion to S. Mark's narrative after S. Luke's Gospel had appeared, would have ventured so to paraphrase S. Luke's statement? And yet, let the consistent truthfulness of either expression be carefully noted. *Both* are historically accurate, but they proceed from opposite points of view. Viewed on the heavenly side, (GOD's side), the Disciples' "eyes" (of course) "*were*

---

* On which, Victor of Antioch (if inded it be he) finely remarks,—Σχίζονται δὲ οἱ οὐρανοί, ἢ κατὰ Ματθαῖον ἀνοίγονται, ἵνα τοῖς ἀνθρώποις ἀποδοθῇ ἐξ οὐρανοῦ ὁ ἁγιασμὸς, καὶ συναφθῇ τοῖς ἐπιγείοις τὰ οὐράνια.—(Cramer i. p. 271.)

holden :"—viewed on the earthly side, (Man's side), the risen SAVIOUR (no doubt) *" appeared in another form."*

(iv.) Then further, S. Mark is observed to introduce many expressions into his Gospel which confirm the prevalent tradition that it was *at Rome* he wrote it; and that it was with an immediate view to *Latin* readers that it was published. Twelve such expressions were enumerated above (at p. 150-1); and such, it was also there shewn, most unmistakably is the phrase πρώτη σαββάτου in ver. 9.—It is simply incredible that any one but an Evangelist writing under the peculiar conditions traditionally assigned to S. Mark, would have hit upon such an expression as this,—the strict equivalent, to Latin ears, for ἡ μία σαββάτων, which has occurred just above, in ver. 2. Now this, it will be remembered, is one of the hacknied objections to the genuineness of this entire portion of the Gospel;—quite proof enough, if proof were needed, of the exceeding *improbability* which attaches to the phrase, in the judgment of those who have considered this question the most.

(v.) The last peculiarity of S. Mark to which I propose to invite attention is supplied by those expressions which connect his Gospel with S. Peter, and remind us of the constant traditional belief of the ancient Church that S. Mark was the companion of the chief of the Apostles.

That the second Gospel contains many such hints has often been pointed out; never more interestingly or more convincingly than by Townson[s] in a work which deserves to be in the hands of every student of Sacred Science. Instead of reproducing any of the familiar cases in order to illustrate my meaning, I will mention one which has perhaps never been mentioned in this connexion before.

(a) Reference is made to our LORD's sayings in S. Mark vii, and specially to what is found in ver. 19. *That* expression, "purging all meats" (καθαρίζων[t] πάντα τὰ βρώματα), does really seem to be no part of the Divine discourse; but the Evangelist's inspired comment on the SAVIOUR's words[u].

---

[s] Disc. v. Sect. ii.   [t] This appears to be the true reading.
[u] So Chrysostom :—ὁ δὲ Μάρκος φησὶν, ὅτι "καθαρίζων τὰ βρώματα," ταῦτα ἔλεγεν. [vii. 526 A].—He seems to have derived that remark from Origen [*in*

Our SAVIOUR (he explains) by that discourse of His—ipso facto—"*made all meats clean.*" How doubly striking a statement, when it is remembered that probably Simon Peter himself was the actual author of it;—the same who, on the house-top at Joppa, had been shewn in a vision that "GOD had made clean" (ὁ Θεὸς ἐκαθάρισε [x]) all His creatures!

(b) Now, let a few words spoken by the same S. Peter on a memorable occasion be considered:—"Wherefore of these men which have companied with us all the time that the LORD JESUS went in and out among us, *beginning from the Baptism of John*, unto that same day that *He was taken up* (ἀνελήφθη) from us, must one be ordained to be a witness with us of His Resurrection [y]." Does not S. Peter thereby define the precise limits of our SAVIOUR'S Ministry,—shewing it to have "begun" (ἀρξάμενος) "from the Baptism of John,"—and closed with the Day of our LORD'S Ascension? And what else are those but the exact bounds of S. Mark's Gospel,—of which the ἀρχή (ch. i. 1) is signally declared to have been *the Baptism of John*,—and the utmost limit, the day when (as S. Mark says) "*He was taken up* (ἀνελήφθη) into Heaven,"—(ch. xvi. 19)?

(c) I will only further remind the reader, in connexion with the phrase, πάσῃ τῇ κτίσει, in ver. 15,—(concerning which, the reader is referred back to page 162-3,)—that both S. Peter and S. Mark (but no other of the sacred writers) conspire to use the expression ἀπ' ἀρχῆς κτίσεως [z]. S. Mark has besides κτίσεως ἧς ἔκτισε ὁ Θεός (ch. xiii. 19); while S. Peter alone styles the ALMIGHTY, from His work of Creation, ὁ κτίστης (1 S. Pet. iv. 19).

VI. But besides, and over and above such considerations

Matth. ed. Huet. i. 249 D] :—κατὰ τὸν Μάρκον ἔλεγε ταῦτα ὁ Σωτὴρ "καθαρίζων πάντα τὰ βρώματα."—From the same source, I suspect, Gregory Thaumaturgus (Origen's disciple), Bp. of Neocæsarea in Pontus, A.D. 261, [*Routh*, iii. 257] derived the following :—καὶ ὁ Σωτὴρ ὁ "πάντα καθαρίζων τὰ βρώματα" οὐ τὸ εἰσπορευόμενον, φησὶ, κοινοῖ τὸν ἄνθρωπον, ἀλλὰ τὸ ἐκπορευόμενον.—See, by all means, Field's most interesting *Adnotationes in Chrys.*, vol. iii. p. 112.....
'Εντεῦθεν (finely says Victor of Antioch) ὁ καινὸς ἄρχεται νόμος ὁ κατὰ τὸ πνεῦμα. (*Cramer* i. 335.)   [x] Acts x. 15.
[y] Acts i. 22, 23. Cf. ver. 2,—ἄχρι ἧς ἡμέρας ... ἀνελήφθη.
[z] S. Mark x. 6 : xiii. 19.—2 S. Pet. iii. 4 (Cf. 1 S. Pet. ii. 13).

as those which precede,—(some of which, I am aware, might be considerably evacuated of their cogency; while others, I am just as firmly convinced, will remain forcible witnesses of GOD's Truth to the end of Time,)—I hesitate not to avow my personal conviction that abundant and striking evidence is garnered up within the brief compass of these Twelve Verses that they are identical in respect of fabric with the rest of the Gospel; were clearly manufactured out of the same Divine materials,—wrought in the same heavenly loom.

It was even to have been expected, from what is found to have been universally the method in other parts of Scripture,—(for it was of course foreseen by ALMIGHTY GOD from the beginning that this portion of His Word would be, like its Divine Author, in these last days cavilled at, reviled, hated, rejected, denied,)—that the SPIRIT would not leave Himself without witness in this place. It was to have been anticipated, I say, that Eternal Wisdom would carefully—(I trust there is no irreverence in so speaking of GOD and His ways!)—would carefully make provision: meet the coming unbelief (as His Angel met Balaam) with a drawn sword: plant up and down throughout these Twelve Verses of the Gospel, sure indications of their Divine Original,—unmistakable notes of purpose and design,—mysterious traces and tokens of Himself; not visible indeed to the scornful and arrogant, the impatient and irreverent; yet clear as if written with a sunbeam to the patient and humble student, the man who "trembleth at GOD's Word[a]." Or, (if the Reader prefers the image,) the indications of a Divine Original to be met with in these verses shall be likened rather to those cryptic characters, invisible so long as they remain unsuspected, but which shine forth clear and strong when exposed to the Light or to the Heat; (Light and Heat, both emblems of Himself!) so that even he that gropeth in darkness must now see them, and admit that of a truth "the LORD is in this place" although he "knew it not!"

(i.) I propose then that in the first instance we compare the conclusion of S. Mark's Gospel with the beginning of it. We did this before, when our object was to ascertain whether

[a] Is. lxvi. 2.

262 *Verbal coincidences between* i. 9-20 & xvi. 9-20, [CHAP.

the *Style* of S. Mark xvi. 9—20 be indeed as utterly discordant from that of the rest of the Gospel as is commonly represented. We found, instead, the most striking resemblance . We also instituted a brief comparison between the two in order to discover whether the *Diction* of the one might not possibly be found as suggestive of *verbal* doubts as the diction of the other: and so we found it .—Let us for the third time draw the two extremities of this precious fabric into close proximity in order again to compare them. Nothing I presume can be fairer than to elect that, once more, our attention be chiefly directed to what is contained within the twelve verses (ver. 9—20) of S. Mark's *first* chapter which exactly correspond with the twelve verses of his *last* chapter (ver. 9—20) which are the subject of the present volume.

Now between these two sections of the Gospel, besides (1) the obvious *verbal* resemblance, I detect (2) a singular parallelism of *essential structure*. And this does not strike me the less forcibly because nothing of the kind was to have been *expected*.

(1.) On the verbal coincidences I do not propose to lay much stress. Yet are they certainly not without argumentative weight and significancy. I allude to the following:—

(*a*) [βαπτίζων, βάπτισμα (i. 4)— καὶ ἐβαπτίζοντο (i. 5)—ἐβάπτισα, βαπτίσει (i. 8)]—καὶ ἐβαπτίσθη (i. 9)

(*a*) βαπτισθείς (xvi. 16)

(*b*) [κηρύσσων, ἐκήρυσσε (i. 7)]

(*b*) ἐκήρυξαν (xvi. 20)

(*b* and *c*) κηρύσσων τὸ εὐαγγέλιον (i. 14)—[ἀρχὴ τοῦ εὐαγγελίου (i. 1)]

(*c*) κηρύξατε τὸ εὐαγγέλιον (xvi. 15)

(*c* and *d*) πιστεύετε ἐν τῷ εὐαγγελίῳ (i. 15)

(*d*) ἠπίστησαν (xvi. 11)—οὐδὲ ἐπίστευσαν (xvi. 13) — τὴν ἀπιστίαν, οὐκ ἐπίστευσαν (xvi. 14)—ὁ πιστεύσας, ὁ ἀπιστήσας (xvi. 16) — τοῖς πιστεύσασι (xvi. 17.)

Now this, to say the least, shews that there exists an unmistakable relation of sympathy between the first page of

S. Mark's Gospel and the last. The same doctrinal phraseology*,—the same indications of Divine purpose,—the same prevailing cast of thought is observed to occur in both. (i.) *A Gospel* to be everywhere *preached;*—(ii.) *Faith*, to be of all required;—(iii.) *Baptism* to be universally administered; ("one LORD, one Faith, one Baptism:")—Is not *this* the theme of the beginning of S. Mark's Gospel as well as of the end of it? Surely it is as if on comparing the two extremities of a chain, with a view to ascertaining whether the fabric be identical or not, it were discovered that those extremities are even meant *to clasp!*

(2.) But the *essential* parallelism between S. Mark xvi. 9 —20 and S. Mark i. 9—20 is a profounder phenomenon and deserves even more attention. I proceed to set down side by side, as before, what ought to require neither comment nor explanation of mine. Thus we find,—

(A) *in ch.* i. 9 *to* 11 :—Our LORD's Manifestation to the World (ἐπιφανεία) on His "coming up (ἀναβαίνων) out of the water" of Jordan : (having been "buried by Baptism," as the Apostle speaks :) when the Voice from Heaven proclaimed,—"Thou art My beloved SON in whom I am well pleased."

(A) *in ch.* xvi. 9 *to* 11 :— Our LORD's appearance to Mary Magdalene (ἐφάνη) after His Resurrection (ἀναστάς) from Death : (of which GOD had said, "Thou art My SON, this day have I begotten Thee." ——— 12 *to* 14 :—Two other Manifestations (ἐφανερώθη) to Disciples.

(B) ——— 12, 13 :—CHRIST's victory over Satan ; (whereby is fulfilled the promise "Thou shalt tread upon the lion and adder : the young lion and the dragon shalt Thou trample under feet.")

(B) ——— 17, 18 :—CHRIST's promise that "they that believe" "shall cast out devils" and "shall take up serpents:" (as [in S. Luke x. 19] He had given the Seventy "power to tread on serpents and scorpions, and over all the power of the Enemy.")

[(c) ——— 8 :—The Pentecostal Gift foretold : "He shall baptize you with the HOLY GHOST."]

(c) ——— 17 :— The chief Pentecostal Gift specified : "They shall speak with new tongues."

* My attention was first drawn to this by my friend, the Rev. W. Kay, D.D.

(D) *in ch.* i. 14, 15 :— Christ " comes into Galilee, preaching the Gospel .... and saying .... Repent ye, and believe the Gospel."

(E) ———— 15 : His announcement, that "The time is fulfilled, and the Kingdom of God is at hand."

(F) ———— 16 *to* 20 :—The four Apostles' Call to the Ministry: (which [S. Luke v. 8, 9] is miraculously attested.)

(D) *in ch.* xvi. 15, 16 :—He commands His Apostles to " go into all the world and preach the Gospel to every creature. He that believeth and is baptized shall be saved."

(E) ———— 19 :—S. Mark's record concerning Him, that " He was received up into Heaven, and sat on the right hand of God :" (where He must reign till He hath put all enemies under His feet.")

(F) ———— 20 :—The Apostles' Ministry, which is everywhere miraculously attested, —"The Lord working with them, and confirming the word by the signs that followed."

It is surely not an unmeaning circumstance, a mere accident, that the Evangelist should at the very outset and at the very conclusion of his Gospel, so express himself! If, however, it should seem to the Reader a mere matter of course, a phenomenon without interest or significancy,—nothing which I could add would probably bring him to a different mind.

(3.) Then, further : when I scrutinize attentively the two portions of Scripture thus proposed for critical survey, I am not a little struck by the discovery that the VIth Article of the ancient Creed of Jerusalem (A.D. 348) is found in the one : the Xth Article, in the other [d]. If it be a purely for-

---

[d] The Creed itself, ("ex variis Cyrillianarum Catacheseon locis collectum,") may be seen at p. 84 of De Touttée's ed. of Cyril. Let the following be compared :—

ἀνελήφθη εἰς τὸν οὐρανόν, καὶ ἐκάθισεν ἐκ δεξιῶν τοῦ Θεοῦ (ch. xvi. 19.)

'ΑΝΕΛΘΟΝΤΑ ΕΙΣ ΤΟΥΣ ΟΥΡΑΝΟΥΣ, ΚΑΙ ΚΑΘΙΣΑΝΤΑ 'ΕΚ ΔΕΞΙΩΝ ΤΟΥ ΠΑΤΡΟΣ (Art. VI.) This may be seen *in situ* at p. 224 c of Cyril.

βάπτισμα μετανοίας εἰς ἄφεσιν ἁμαρτιῶν (ch. i. 4.)

ΒΑΠΤΙΣΜΑ ΜΕΤΑΝΟΙΑΣ ΕΙΣ ΆΦΕΣΙΝ ΆΜΑΡΤΙΩΝ (Art. X.) This may be seen at p. 295 c of Cyril.

The point will be most intelligently and instructively studied in Professor Heurtley's little work *De Fide et Symbolo*, 1869, p. 9.

tuitous circumstance, that two cardinal verities like these,—(viz. "*He ascended into Heaven, and sat down at the Right Hand of God*,"—and "*One Baptism for the Remission of sins*,") should be found at either extremity of one short Gospel,—I will but point out that it is certainly one of a very remarkable series of fortuitous circumstances.—But in the thing to be mentioned next, there neither is, nor can be, any talk of fortuitousness at all.

(4.) Allusion is made to the diversity of Name whereby the Son of Man is indicated in these two several places of the Gospel; which constitutes a most Divine circumstance, and is profoundly significant. He who in *the first* verse (S. Mark i. 1) was designated by the joint title "'Ιησοῦς" and "Χριστός,"—here, in the last two verses (S. Mark xvi. 19, 20) is styled for the first and for the last time, "ὁ ΚΎΡΙΟΣ" —the LORD

And why? Because He who at His Circumcision was named "JESUS," (a Name which was given Him from *His Birth*, yea, and before His Birth); He who at His Baptism became "the CHRIST," (a Title which belonged to *His Office*, and which betokens His sacred *Unction*);—the same, on the occasion of His Ascension into Heaven and Session at the Right Hand of GOD,—when (as we know) "all power had been given unto Him in Heaven and in Earth" (S. Matth. xxviii. 18),—is designated by His Name of *Dominion*; "the LORD" JEHOVAH ... "Magnifica et opportuna appellatio!" —as Bengel well remarks.

But I take leave to point out that all this is what never either would or could have entered into the mind of a fabricator of a conclusion to S. Mark's unfinished Gospel. No inventor of a supplement, I say, *could* have planted his foot in this way in exactly the right place. The proof of my assertion is twofold :—

(*a*) First, because the present indication that the HOLY GHOST was indeed the Author of these last Twelve Verses is even appealed to by Dr. Davidson and his School, *as a proof of a spurious original.* Verily, such Critics do not recognise the token of the Divine Finger even when they *see* it!

(b) Next, as a matter of fact, we *have* a spurious Supplement to the Gospel,—the same which was exhibited above at p. 123-4 ; and which may here be with advantage reproduced in its Latin form :—" Omnia autem quaecumque praecepta erant illis qui cum Petro erant, breviter exposuerunt. Post haec et ipse IESUS adparuit, et ab oriente usque in occidentem misit per illos sanctam et incorruptam praedicationem salutis aeternae. Amen [f]."—Another apocryphal termination is found in certain copies of the Thebaic version. It occupies the place of ver. 20, and is as follows :—" Exeuntes terni in quatuor climata caeli praedicarunt Evangelium in mundo toto, CHRISTO operante cum iis in verbo confirmationem cum signis sequentibus eos et miraculis. Atque hoc modo cognitum est regnum Dei in terra tota et in mundo toto Israelis in testimonium gentium omnium harum quae exsistunt ab oriente ad occasum." It will be seen that the Title of *Dominion* (ὁ Κύριος—the LORD) is found in neither of these fabricated passages; but the Names of *Nativity* and of *Baptism* ('Ιησοῦς and Χριστός - JESUS and CHRIST) occur instead.

(ii.) Then further : — It is an extraordinary note of genuineness that such a vast number of minute but important facts should be found accumulated within the narrow compass of these twelve verses ; and should be met with *nowhere else*. The writer,—supposing that he had only S. Matthew's Gospel before him,—traverses (except in one single instance) *wholly new ground;* moves forward with unmistakable boldness and a rare sense of security; and wherever he plants his foot, it is to enrich the soil with fertility and beauty. But on the supposition that he wrote after S. Luke's and S. John's Gospel had appeared,—the marvel becomes increased an hundred-fold : for how then does it come to pass that he evidently draws his information from quite independent sources ? is not bound by any of their statements ? even seems *purposely* to break away from their guidance, and to adventure some extraordinary state-

---

[f] *Cod. Bobbiensis* (k): which however for "illis" has "et :" for "Petro," "puero :" and for "occidentem," "orientem." It also repeats "usque." I have ventured to alter "ab orientem" into " ab oriente."—Compare what is found in the Philoxenian margin, as given by White and Adler.

ment of his own,—which nevertheless carries the true Gospel savour with it; and is felt to be authentic from the very circumstance that no one would have ever dared to invent such a detail and put it forth on his own responsibility?

(iii.) Second to no indication that this entire section of the Gospel has a Divine original, I hold to be a famous expression which (like πρώτη σαββάτου) has occasioned general offence: I mean, the designation of Mary Magdalene as one "out of whom" the LORD "had cast seven devils;" and *that*, in immediate connexion with the record of her august privilege of being the first of the Human Race to behold His risen form. There is such profound Gospel significancy,—such sublime improbability,—such exquisite pathos in this record,—that I would defy any fabricator, be he who he might, to have achieved it. This has been to some extent pointed out already.

(iv.) It has also been pointed out, (but the circumstance must be by all means here insisted upon afresh,) that the designation (found in ver. 10) of the little company of our LORD's followers,—" τοῖς μετ' αὐτοῦ γενομένοις,"—is another rare note of veracious origin. No one but S. Mark,—or just such an one as he,—would or could have so accurately designated the little band of Christian men and women who, unconscious of their bliss, were "mourning and weeping" till after sunrise on the first Easter Day. The reader is reminded of what has been already offered on this subject, at p. 155-6.

(v.) I venture further to point out that no writer but S. Mark, (or such an one as he [h]), would have familiarly designated the Apostolic body as " αὐτοῖς τοῖς ἕνδεκα," in ver. 14. The phrase οἱ δώδεκα, he uses in proportion *far* oftener than any other two of the Evangelists [i]. And it is evident that the phrase οἱ ἕνδεκα soon became an equally recognised designation of the Apostolic body,—"from which Judas by transgression fell." Its familiar introduction into this place by the second Evangelist is exactly what one might have

---

[h] Consider S. Luke xxiv. 9: 33. Acts ii. 14.
[i] S. Matth. xxvi. 14, 29, 47.—S. Mark iv. 10: vi. 7: ix. 35: x. 32: xi. 11: xiv. 10, 17, 20, 43.—S. Luke viii. 1: ix. 1, 12: xviii. 31: xxii. 3, 47.—S. John vi. 37, 70, 71: xx. 24.

looked for, or at least what one is fully prepared to meet with, *in him*.

(vi.) I will close this enumeration by calling attention to an unobtrusive and unobserved verb in the last of these verses which (I venture to say) it would never have entered into the mind of any ordinary writer to employ in that particular place. I allude to the familiar word ἐξελθόντες.

The precise meaning of the expression,—depending on the known force of the preposition with which the verb is compounded,—can scarcely be missed by any one who, on the one hand, is familiar with the Evangelical method; on the other, is sufficiently acquainted with the Gospel History. Reference is certainly made to the final departure of the Apostolic body *out of the city of Jerusalem*[k]. And tacitly, beyond a question, there is herein contained a recollection of our SAVIOUR's command to His Apostles, twice expressly recorded by S. Luke, " that they should *not depart from Jerusalem*, but wait for the promise of the FATHER." "Behold," (said He,) "I send the promise of My FATHER upon you: but *tarry ye in the city of Jerusalem*, until ye be endued with power from on high [l]." ... After many days "*they went forth*," or "*out*." S. Mark, (or perhaps it is rather S. Peter,) expressly says so,—ἐξελθόντες. Aye, and *that* was a memorable "outgoing," truly! What else was its purpose but the evangelization of the World?

VII. Let this suffice, then, concerning the evidence derived from Internal considerations. But lest it should hereafter be reckoned as an omission, and imputed to me as a fault, that I have said nothing about the alleged *Inconsistency* of certain statements contained in these "Twelve Verses" with the larger notices contained in the parallel narratives of S. Luke and S. John,—I proceed briefly to explain *why* I am silent on this head.

1. I cannot see for whom I should be writing; in other

---

[k] Compare S. Luke xxii. 39; and especially S. John xviii. 1,—where the moment of departure *from the city* is marked: (for observe, they had left the house and the upper chamber at ch. xiv. 31). See also ch. xix. 17,—where the going *without the gate* is indicated: (for ἔξω τῆς πύλης ἔπαθε [Heb. xiii. 12.]) So Matth. xxvii. 32. Consider S. Luke xxi. 37.

[l] S. Luke xxiv. 49. Acts i. 4.

words,—what I should propose to myself as the end to be attained by what I wrote. For,

2. What would be gained by demonstrating,—(as I am of course prepared to do,)—that there is really *no inconsistency whatever* between anything which S. Mark here says, and what the other Evangelists deliver? I should have proved that,—(assuming the *other* Evangelical narratives to be authentic, i.e. historically true,)—the narrative before us cannot be objected to on the score of its not being authentic also. But *by whom* is such proof required?

(*a*) Not by the men who insist that errors are occasionally to be met with in the Evangelical narratives. In *their* estimation, *the genuineness of an inspired writing* is a thing not in the least degree rendered suspicious by the erroneousness of its statements. According to them, the narrative may exhibit inaccuracies and inconsistencies, and may yet be the work of S. Mark. If the inconsistencies be but "trifling," and the inaccuracies "minute,"—these "sound Theologians," (for so they style themselves ,) "have no dread whatever of acknowledging" their existence. Be it so. Then would it be a gratuitous task to set about convincing *them* that no inconsistency, no inaccuracy is discoverable within the compass of these Twelve concluding Verses.

(*b*) But neither is such proof required by faithful Readers; who, for want of the requisite Scientific knowledge, are unable to discern the perfect Harmony of the Evangelical narratives in this place. It is only one of many places where a primâ facie discrepancy, though it does not fail to strike, — yet (happily) altogether fails to distress them. Consciously or unconsciously, such readers reason with themselves somewhat as follows:—"GOD's Word, like all GOD's other Works, (and I am taught to regard GOD's Word as a very masterpiece of creative skill;)—the blessed Gospel, I say, is *full* of difficulties. And yet those difficulties are observed invariably to disappear under competent investigation. Can I seriously doubt that if sufficient critical skill were brought to bear on the highly elliptical portion of narrative contained in these Twelve Verses, it would present no exception to a rule which is observed to be else universal; and that any apparent inconsistency between S. Mark's statements in this place, and those of S. Luke and S. John, would also be found to be imaginary only?"

This then is the reason why I abstain from entering upon a prolonged Inquiry, which would in fact necessitate a discussion of *the Principles of Gospel Harmony*,—for which the present would clearly not be the proper place.

VIII. Let it suffice that, in the foregoing pages,—

1. I have shewn that the supposed argument from "Style," (in itself a highly fallacious test,) disappears under investigation.

It has been proved (pp. 142-5) that, on the contrary, the style of S. Mark xvi. 9—20 is exceedingly like the style of S. Mark i. 9—20; and therefore, that *it is rendered probable by the Style* that the Author of the beginning of this Gospel was also the Author of the end of it.

2. I have further shewn that the supposed argument from "Phraseology,"—(in itself, a most unsatisfactory test; and as it has been applied to the matter in hand, a very coarse and clumsy one;)—breaks down hopelessly under severe analysis.

Instead of there being twenty-seven suspicious circumstances in the Phraseology of these Twelve Verses, it has been proved (pp. 170-3) that in twenty-seven particulars there emerge *corroborative considerations.*

3. Lastly, I have shewn that a loftier method of Criticism is at hand; and that, tested by this truer, more judicious, and more philosophical standard, *a presumption* of the highest order is created *that these Verses must needs be the work of S. Mark.*

CHAPTER X.

THE TESTIMONY OF THE LECTIONARIES SHEWN TO BE ABSOLUTELY DECISIVE AS TO THE GENUINENESS OF THESE VERSES.

The Lectionary of the East shewn to be a work of extraordinary antiquity (275).—Proved to be older than any extant MS. of the Gospels, by an appeal to the Fathers (278).—In this Lectionary, (and also in the Lectionary of the West,) the last Twelve Verses of S. Mark's Gospel have, from the first, occupied a most conspicuous, as well as most honourable place, (284)—Now, this becomes the testimony of ante-Nicene Christendom in their favour (289)

I HAVE reserved for the last the testimony of THE LECTIONARIES, which has been hitherto all but entirely overlooked[a];—passed by without so much as a word of comment, by those who have preceded me in this inquiry. Yet is it, when rightly understood, altogether decisive of the question at issue. And why? Because it is not the testimony rendered by a solitary Father or by a solitary MS.; no, nor even the testimony yielded by a single Church, or by a single family of MSS. But it is *the united testimony of all the Churches.* It is therefore the evidence borne by a 'goodly fellowship of Prophets,' a 'noble army of Martyrs' indeed; as well as by *MSS. innumerable which have long since perished,* but which must of necessity once have been. And so, it comes to us like the voice of many waters: dates, (as I shall shew by-and-by,) from a period of altogether immemorial antiquity: is endorsed by the sanction of all the succeeding ages: admits of neither doubt nor evasion. This subject, in order that it may be intelligibly handled, will be

---

[a] The one memorable exception, which I have only lately met with, is supplied by the following remark of the thoughtful and accurate Matthaei, made in a place where it was almost safe to escape attention; viz. in a footnote at the very end of his *Nov. Test.* (ed. 1803), vol. i. p. 748.—" Haec lectio in Evangeliariis et Synaxariis omnibus ter notatur tribus maxime notabilibus temporibus. Secundum ordinem temporum Ecclesiae Graecae primo legitur κυριακῇ τῶν μυροφόρων, εἰς τὸν ὄρθρον. Secundo, τῷ ὄρθρῳ τῆς ἀναλήψεως. Tertio, ut ἑωθινὸν ἀναστάσιμον γ'. De hoc loco ergo vetustissimis temporibus nullo modo dubitavit Ecclesia."—Matthaei had slightly anticipated this in his ed. of 1788, vol. ii. 267.

most conveniently approached by some remarks which shall rehearse the matter from the beginning.

The Christian Church succeeded to the Jewish. The younger society inherited the traditions of the elder, not less as a measure of necessity than as a matter of right; and by a kind of sacred instinct conformed itself from the very beginning in countless particulars to its divinely-appointed model. The same general Order of Service went on unbroken,—conducted by a Priesthood whose spiritual succession was at least as jealously guarded as had been the natural descent from Aaron in the Church of the Circumcision [b]. It was found that "the Sacraments of the Jews are [but] types of ours [c]." Still were David's Psalms antiphonally recited, and the voices of "Moses and the Prophets" were heard in the sacred assemblies of GOD's people "every Sabbath day." Canticle succeeded to Canticle; while many a Versicle simply held its ground. The congenial utterances of the chosen race passed readily into the service of the family of the redeemed. Unconsciously perhaps, the very method of the one became adopted by the other: as, for example, the method of beginning a festival from the "Eve" of the preceding Day. The Synagogue-worship became transfigured; but it did not part with one of its characteristic features. Above all, the same three great Festivals were still retained which declare "the rock whence we are hewn and the hole of the pit whence we are digged:" only was it made a question, a controversy rather, whether Easter should or should not be celebrated *with the Jews* [d].

But it is the faithful handing on to the Christian community of *the Lectionary practice* of the Synagogue to which the reader's attention is now exclusively invited. That the Christian Church inherited from the Jewish the practice of reading a first and a second Lesson in its public assemblies, is demonstrable. What the Synagogue practice was in the time of the Apostles is known from Acts xiii. 15, 27. Justin

[b] Τὰς τῶν ἱερῶν ἀποστόλων διαδοχάς,—are *the first words* of the Ecclesiastical History of Eusebius.

[c] See the heading of 1 Cor. x. in our Authorized Version.

[d] See Bingham's *Origines*, Book xx. ch. v. §§ 2, 3, 4.

x.] *Lectionary-practice of the primitive Church.* 273

Martyr, (A.D. 150) describes the Christian practice in his time as precisely similar [e] : only that for "the Law," there is found to have been at once substituted "the Gospel." He speaks of the writings of "*the Apostles*" and of "the Prophets." Chrysostom has the same expression (for the two Lessons) in one of his Homilies [f]. Cassian (A.D. 400) says that in Egypt, after the Twelve Prayers at Vespers and at Matins, two Lessons were read, one out of the Old Testament and the other out of the New. But *on Saturdays and Sundays,* and the fifty days of Pentecost, both Lessons were from the New Testament,—one from the Epistles or the Acts of the Apostles; the other, from the Gospels [g]. Our own actual practice seems to bear a striking resemblance to that of the Christian Church at the earliest period: for we hear of (1) "Moses and the Prophets," (which will have been the carrying on of the old synagogue-method, represented by our first and second Lesson,)—(2) a lesson out of the "Epistles or Acts," together with a lesson out of the "Gospels [h]." It is, in fact, universally received that the Eastern Church has, from a period of even Apostolic antiquity, enjoyed a Lectionary,—or established system of Scripture lessons,—of her own. In its conception, this Lectionary is discovered to have been fashioned (as was natural) upon the model of the Lectionary of GOD's ancient people, the Jews: for it commences, as theirs did, *in the autumn,* (in September [i]) ; and

---

[e] Τῇ τοῦ ἡλίου λεγομένῃ ἡμέρᾳ, πάντων κατὰ πόλεις ἢ ἀγροὺς μενόντων ἐπὶ τὸ αὐτὸ συνέλευσις γίνεται, καὶ τὰ ἀπομνημονεύματα τῶν ἀποστόλων, ἢ τὰ συγγράμματα τῶν προφητῶν ἀναγινώσκεται, μέχρις ἐγχωρεῖ. Then came the Sermon,— then, all stood and prayed,—then followed Holy Communion.—*Apol.* i. c. 67, (*ed.* Otto, i. 158.)

[f] ὁ μάτην ἐνταῦθα εἰσελθὼν, εἰπὲ, τίς προφήτης, ποῖος ἀπόστολος ἡμῖν σήμερον διελέχθη, καὶ περὶ τίνων ;—(*Opp.* ix. p. 697 E. Field's text.)

[g] Cassian writes,—"Venerabilis Patrum senatus . . . . decrevit hunc numerum [*sc.* duodecim Orationum] tam in Vespertinis quam in Nocturnis conventiculis custodiri; quibus lectiones geminas adjungentes, id est, unam Veteris et aliam Novi Testamenti . . . . In die vero Sabbati vel Dominico utrasque de Novo recitant Testamento ; id est, unam de Apostolo vel Actibus Apostolorum, et aliam de Evangeliis. Quod etiam totis Quinquagesimae diebus faciunt hi, quibus lectio curae est, seu memoria Scripturarum."—*Instit.* lib. ii. c. 6. (*ed.* 1733, p. 18.)

[h] *Constitutiones Apostolicae,* lib. ii. c. 57, 59: v. 19: viii. 5.

[i] See Scrivener's *Introduction,* p. 74, and the reff. in note (k) overleaf.

prescribes two immovable "Lections" for every *Saturday* (as well as for every Sunday) in the year: differing chiefly in this,—that the prominent place which had been hitherto assigned to "the Law and the Prophets [k]," was henceforth enjoyed by the Gospels and the Apostolic writings. "Saturday-Sunday" lections—(σαββατοκυριακαί, for so these Lections were called,)—retain their place in the "Synaxarium" of the East to the present hour. It seems also a singular note of antiquity that the Sabbath and the Sunday succeeding it do as it were cohere, and bear one appellation; so that the week takes its name—*not* from the Sunday with which it commences [l], but—from the Sabbath-and-Sunday with which *it concludes*. To mention only one out of a hundred minute traits of identity which the public Service of the sanctuary retained:—Easter Eve, which from the earliest period to this day has been called "μέγα σάββατον [m]," is discovered to have borne the self-same appellation in the Church of the Circumcision [n].—If I do not enter more minutely into the structure of the Oriental Lectionary,—(some will perhaps think I have said too much, but the interest of the subject ought to be a sufficient apology,)—it is because further details would be irrelevant to my present purpose; which is only to call attention to the three following facts :

(I.) That the practice in the Christian Church of reading publicly before the congregation certain fixed portions of Holy Writ, according to an established and generally received rule, must have existed from a period long anterior to the date of any known Greek copy of the New Testament Scriptures.

(II.) That although there happens to be extant neither "Synaxarium," (i.e. Table of Proper Lessons of the Greek

---

[k] English readers may be referred to Horne's *Introduction*, &c. (*ed.* 1856.) vol. iii. p. 281-2. The learned reader is perhaps aware of the importance of the preface to Van der Hooght's *Hebrew Bible,* (*ed.* 1705) § 35 : in connexion with which, see vol. ii. p. 352 *b*.

[l] Thus, the κυριακή τῆς τυροφάγου is "Quinquagesima Sunday;" but *the week* of "the cheese-eater" is the week *previous*.

[m] See Suicer's *Thesaurus*, vol. ii. 920.

[n] "Apud Rabbinos, שַׁבָּת הַגָּדוֹל *Sabbathum Magnum.* Sic vocatur Sabbathum proximum ante Pascha."—Buxtorf, *Lexicon Talmud.* p. 2323.

x.] *established by an appeal to the Fathers.* 275

Church), nor "Evangelistarium," (i.e. Book containing the Ecclesiastical Lections *in extenso*), of higher antiquity than the viii[th] century,—yet that the scheme itself, as exhibited by those monuments,—certainly in every essential particular,—is older than any known Greek MS. which contains it, by *at least* four, in fact by full *five* hundred years.

(III.) Lastly, — That in the said Lectionaries of the Greek and of the Syrian Churches, the twelve concluding verses of S. Mark which are the subject of discussion throughout the present pages are observed *invariably* to occupy the same singularly conspicuous, as well as most honourable place.

I. The first of the foregoing propositions is an established fact. It is at least quite certain that in the iv[th] century (if not long before) there existed a known Lectionary system, alike in the Church of the East and of the West. Cyril of Jerusalem (A.D. 348,) having to speak about our LORD's Ascension, remarks that by a providential coincidence, on the previous day, which was Sunday, the event had formed the subject of the appointed lessons[o]; and that he had availed himself of the occasion to discourse largely on the subject.— Chrysostom, preaching at Antioch, makes it plain that, in

---

[o] Καὶ ἡ μὲν ἀκολουθία τῆς διδασκαλίας [cf. Cyril, p. 4, lines 16-7] τῆς πίστεως προέτρεπεν εἰπεῖν καὶ τὰ περὶ τῆς 'Αναλήψεως· ἀλλ' ἡ τοῦ Θεοῦ χάρις ᾠκονόμησε πληρέστατά σε ἀκοῦσαι, κατὰ τὴν ἡμετέραν ἀσθένειαν, τῇ χθὲς ἡμέρᾳ κατὰ τὴν Κυριακήν· κατ' οἰκονομίαν τῆς θείας χάριτος, ἐν τῇ Συνάξει τῆς τῶν ἀναγνωσμάτων ἀκολουθίας τὰ περὶ τῆς εἰς οὐρανοὺς ἀνόδου τοῦ Σωτῆρος ἡμῶν περιεχούσης· ἐλέγετο δὲ τὰ λεγόμενα, μάλιστα μὲν διὰ πάντας, καὶ διὰ τὸ τῶν πιστῶν ὁμοῦ πλῆθος· ἐξαιρέτως δὲ διά σε· ζητεῖται δὲ εἰ προσέσχες τοῖς λεγομένοις. Οἶδας γὰρ ὅτι ἡ ἀκολουθία τῆς Πίστεως διδάσκει σε πιστεύειν εἰς ΤΟΝ ἈΝΑΣΤΆΝΤΑ ΤΗ͂ ΤΡΊΤΗ͂ ἩΜΈΡΑ· ΚΑῚ ἈΝΕΛΘΌΝΤΑ ΕἸΣ ΤΟῪΣ ΟΥ̓ΡΑΝΟῪΣ, ΚΑῚ ΚΑΘΊΣΑΝΤΑ ἘΚ ΔΕΞΙΩ͂Ν ΤΟΥ͂ ΠΑΤΡΌΣ—μάλιστα μὲν οὖν μνημονεύειν σε νομίζω τῆς ἐξηγήσεως. πλὴν ἐν παραδρομῇ καὶ νῦν ὑπομιμνήσκω σε τῶν εἰρημένων. (Cyril. Hier. *Cat.* xiv. c. 24. *Opp.* p. 217 C, D.)—Of that Sermon of his, Cyril again and again reminds his auditory. Μέμνησο δὲ καὶ τῶν εἰρημένων μοι πολλάκις περὶ τοῦ, ἐκ δεξιῶν τοῦ Πατρὸς καθέζεσθαι τὸν Υἱόν,—he says, *ibid.* p. 219 B. A little lower down, Νῦν δὲ ὑμᾶς ὑπομνηστέον ὀλίγων, τῶν ἐκ πολλῶν εἰρημένων περὶ τοῦ, ἐκ δεξιῶν τοῦ Πατρὸς καθέζεσθαι τὸν Υἱόν.—*Ibid.* D.

From this it becomes plain *why Cyril nowhere quotes S. Mark* xvi. 19,—*or S. Luke* xxiv. 51,—*or Acts* i. 9. He must needs have enlarged upon those three *inevitable* places of Scripture, the day before.

the latter part of the iv[th] century, the order of the lessons which were publicly read in the Church *on Saturdays and Sundays* was familiarly known to the congregation: for he invites them to sit down, and study attentively beforehand, at home, the Sections (περικοπάς) of the Gospel which they were about to hear in Church[q].—Augustine is express in recording that in his time proper lessons were appointed for Festival days[r]; and that an innovation which he had attempted on Good Friday had given general offence[s].—Now by these few notices, to look no further, it is rendered certain that a Lectionary system of *some* sort must have been in existence at a period long anterior to the date of any copy of the New Testament Scriptures extant. I shall shew by-and-by that the fact is established by the Codices (B, ℵ, A, C, D) themselves.

But we may go back further yet; for not only Eusebius, but Origen and Clemens Alexandrinus, by their habitual use of the technical term for an Ecclesiastical Lection (περικοπή, ἀνάγνωσις, ἀνάγνωσμα,) remind us that the Lectionary practice of the East was already established in their days[t].

II. The Oriental Lectionary consists of "Synaxarion" and "Eclogadion," (or Tables of Proper Lessons from the Gospels and Apostolic writings daily throughout the year;)

---

[q] "Ὥστε δὲ εὐμαθέστερον γενέσθαι τὸν λόγον, δεόμεθα καὶ παρακαλοῦμεν, ὅπερ καὶ ἐπὶ τῶν ἄλλων γραφῶν πεποιήκαμεν, προλαμβάνειν, τὴν π ε ρ ι κ ο π ὴ ν τῆς γραφῆς ἣν ἂν μέλλωμεν ἐξηνεῖσθαι. — In Matth. *Hom.* i. (*Opp.* vii. 13 B.)— Κατὰ μίαν σαββάτων, ἢ καὶ κατὰ σάββατον, τὴν μέλλουσαν ἐν ὑμῖν ἀναγνωσθήσεσθαι τῶν εὐαγγελίων π ε ρ ι κ ο π ὴ ν, ταύτην πρὸ τούτων τῶν ἡμερῶν μετὰ χεῖρας λαμβάνων ἕκαστος οἴκοι καθήμενος ἀναγινωσκέτω." — In Joann. *Hom.* ix, (*Opp.* viii. 62 B.)

[r] It caused him (he says) to interrupt his teaching. " Sed quia nunc interposita est sollemnitas sanctorum dierum, quibus certas ex Evangelio lectiones oportet in Ecclesiâ recitari, quae ita sunt annuae ut aliae esse non possint; ordo ille quem susceperamus necessitate paullulum intermissus est, non amissus."— (*Opp.* vol. iii. P. ii. p. 825, *Prol.*)

[s] The place will be found quoted below, p. 202, note (o).

[t] See Suicer, (i. 247 and 9: ii. 673). He is much more full and satisfactory than Scholz, whose remarks, nevertheless, deserve attention, (*Nov. Test.* vol. i, Prolegg. p. xxxi.) See also above, p. 45, notes (r) and (s).

X.] *Difficulty of discovering particular proofs.* 277

together with "Menologion," (or Calendar of immovable Festivals and Saints' Days.) That we are thoroughly acquainted with all of these, as exhibited in Codices of the viii[th], ix[th] and x[th] centuries,—is a familiar fact; in illustration of which it is enough to refer the reader to the works cited at the foot of the page [u]. But it is no less certain that the scheme of Proper Lessons itself is of much higher antiquity.

1. The proof of this, if it could only be established by an induction of particular instances, would not only be very tedious, but also very difficult indeed. It will be perceived, on reflection, that even when the occasion of a Homily (suppose) is actually recorded, the Scripture references which it contains, apart from the Author's statement that what he quotes *had* formed part of that day's Service, creates scarcely so much as a presumption of the fact: while the correspondence, however striking, between such references to Scripture and the Lectionary as we have it, is of course no proof whatever that we are so far in possession of the Lectionary of the Patristic age. Nay, on famous Festivals,

---

[u] At the beginning of every volume of the first ed. of his *Nov. Test.* (Riga, 1788) Matthaei has laboriously *edited* the "Lectiones Ecclesiasticæ" of the Greek Church. See also his Appendices,—viz. vol. ii. pp. 272—318 and 322—363. His 2nd ed. (Wittenberg, 1803,) is distinguished by the valuable peculiarity of indicating the Ecclesiastical sections throughout, in the manner of an ancient MS.; and that, with extraordinary fulness and accuracy. His Συνα-ξάρια (i. 723—68 and iii. 1—24) though not intelligible perhaps to ordinary readers, are very important. He derived them from MSS. which he designates "B" and "H," but which are *our* "Evstt. 47 and 50,"—uncial Evangelistaria of the viii[th] century (See Scrivener's *Introd.* p. 214.)

Scholz, at the end of vol. i. of his N. T. p. 453—93, gives in full the "Synaxarium" and "Menologium" of Codd. K and M, (viii[th] or ix[th] century.) See also his vol. ii. pp. 456—69. Unfortunately, (as Scrivener recognises, p. 110,) all here is carelessly done,—as usual with this Editor; and therefore to a great extent useless. His slovenliness is extraordinary. The "Gospels of the Passion" (τῶν ἁγίων παθῶν), he entitles τῶν ἁγίων πάντων (p. 472); and so throughout.

Mr. Scrivener (*Introduction*, pp. 68—75,) has given by far the most intelligible account of this matter, by exhibiting *in English* the Lectionary of the Eastern Church, ("gathered chiefly from Evangelist. Arund. 547, Parham 18, Harl. 5598, Burney 22, and Christ's Coll. Camb."); and supplying the references to Scripture in the ordinary way. See, by all means, his *Introduction*, pp. 62—65: also, pp. 211—225.

the employment of certain passages of Scripture is, in a manner, inevitable[x], and may on no account be pressed.

2. Thus, when Chrysostom[y] and when Epiphanius[z], preaching on Ascension Day, refer to Acts i. 10, 11,—we do not feel ourselves warranted to press the coincidence of such a quotation with the Liturgical section of the day.—So, again, when Chrysostom preaches on Christmas Day, and quotes from S. Matthew ii. 1, 2[a]; or on Whitsunday, and quotes from S. John vii. 38 and Acts ii. 3 and 13;—though both places form part of the Liturgical sections for the day, no *proof* results therefrom that either chapter was actually used.

3. But we are not reduced to this method. It is discovered that nearly three-fourths of Chrysostom's Homilies on S. Matthew either begin at the first verse of *a known Ecclesiastical Lection;* or else at the first ensuing verse after the close of one. Thirteen of those Homilies in succession (the 63rd to the 75th inclusive) begin with *the first words of as many known Lections.* " Let us attend to this delightful section (περικοπή) which we never cease turning to,"—are the opening words of Chrysostom's 79th Homily, of which "the text" is S. Matth. xxv. 31, i.e. the beginning of the Gospel for Sexagesima Sunday.—Cyril of Alexandria's (so called) "Commentary on S. Luke" is nothing else but a series of short Sermons, for the most part delivered on *known Ecclesiastical Lections;* which does not seem to have been as yet observed.—Augustine (A.D. 416) says expressly that he had handled S. John's Gospel in precisely the same way [b].
—All this is significant in a high degree.

---

[x] Consider the following:—'Εν τῇ ἡμέρᾳ τοῦ σταυροῦ τὰ περὶ τοῦ σταυροῦ πάντα ἀναγινώσκομεν. ἐν τῷ σαββάτῳ τῷ μεγάλῳ πάλιν, ὅτι παρεδόθη ἡμῶν ὁ Κύριος, ὅτι ἐσταυρώθη, ὅτι ἀπέθανε τὸ κατὰ σάρκα, ὅτι ἐτάφη· τίνος οὖν ἕνεκεν καὶ τὰς πράξεις τῶν ἀποστόλων οὐ μετὰ τὴν πεντηκοστὴν ἀναγινώσκομεν, ὅτε καὶ ἐγένοντο, καὶ ἀρχὴν ἔλαβον;—Chrys. *Opp.* iii. 88.

Again:—εἰ γὰρ τότε ἤρξαντο ποιεῖν τὰ σημεῖα οἱ ἀπόστολοι, ἤγουν μετὰ τὴν κυρίου ἀνάστασιν, τότε ἔδει καὶ τὸ βιβλίον ἀναγινώσκεσθαι τοῦτο. ὥσπερ γὰρ τὰ περὶ τοῦ σταυροῦ ἐν τῇ ἡμέρᾳ σταυροῦ ἀναγινώσκομεν, καὶ τὰ ἐν τῇ ἀναστάσει ὁμοίως, καὶ τὰ ἐν ἑκάστῃ ἑορτῇ γεγονότα τῇ αὐτῇ πάλιν ἀναγινώσκομεν, οὕτως ἔδει καὶ τὰ θαύματα τὰ ἀποστολικὰ ἐν ταῖς ἡμέραις τῶν ἀποστολικῶν σημείων ἀναγινώσκεσθαι.—*Ibid.* p. 89 D.

[y] *Opp.* ii. 454 B, D.   [z] *Opp.* ii. 290 B.   [a] *Opp.* ii. 357 E.

[b] " Meminit sanctitas vestra Evangelium secundum Joannem ex ordine lectionum nos solere tractare." (*Opp.* iii. P. ii. 825 *Prol.*)

4. I proceed, however, to adduce a few distinct proofs that the existing Lectionary of the great Eastern Church,—as it is exhibited by Matthaei, by Scholz, and by Scrivener from MSS. of the viii[th] century,—and which is contained in Syriac MSS. of the vi[th] and vii[th]—must needs be in the main a work of extraordinary antiquity. And if I do not begin by insisting that at least one century more may be claimed for it by a mere appeal to the Hierosolymitan Version, it is only because I will never knowingly admit what may prove to be untrustworthy materials[c] into my foundations.

(*a*) "Every one is aware," (says Chrysostom in a sermon on our SAVIOUR's Baptism, preached at Antioch, A.D. 387,) "that this is called the Festival of the Epiphany. Two manifestations are thereby intended: concerning both of which *you have heard this day S. Paul discourse in his Epistle to Titus*[d]." Then follows a quotation from ch. ii. 11 to 13,—which proves to be the beginning of the lection for the day in the Greek Menology. In the time of Chrysostom, therefore, Titus ii. 11, 12, 13 formed part of one of the Epiphany lessons,—as it does to this hour in the Eastern Church. What is scarcely less interesting, it is also found to have been part of the Epistle for the Epiphany in the old Gallican Liturgy[e], the affinities of which with the East are well known.

(*b*) Epiphanius (speaking of the Feasts of the Church) says, that at the Nativity, a Star shewed that the WORD had become incarnate: at the "Theophania" (*our* "Epiphany") John cried, "Behold the Lamb of GOD," &c., and a Voice from Heaven proclaimed Him at His Baptism. Accordingly, S. Matth. ii. 1—12 is found to be the ancient lection for Christmas Day: S. Mark i. 9—11 and S. Matth. iii. 13—17 the lections for Epiphany. On the morrow, was read S. John i. 29—34.

(*c*) In another of his Homilies, Chrysostom explains with considerable emphasis the reason why the Book of the Acts was read publicly in Church during the interval between Easter and Pentecost; remarking, that it had been the

---

[c] See Scrivener's *Introduction*, p. 246.

[d] Chrysostom *Opp.* ii. 369 B, C.—Compare Scrivener, *ubi supra*, p. 75.

[e] *Ed.* Mabillon, p. 116.

liturgical arrangement of a yet earlier age [f].—After such an announcement, it becomes a very striking circumstance that Augustine also (A.D. 412) should be found to bear witness to the prevalence of the same liturgical arrangement in the African Church [g]. In the old Gallican Lectionary, as might have been expected, the same rule is recognisable. It ought to be needless to add that the same arrangement is obsérved universally to prevail in the Lectionaries both of the East and of the West to the present hour; although the fact must have been lost sight of by the individuals who recently, under pretence of "*making some advantageous alterations*" in our Lectionary, have constructed an entirely new one, —vicious in principle and liable to the gravest objections throughout,—whereby *this* link also which bound the Church of England to the practice of Primitive Christendom, has been unhappily broken; *this* note of Catholicity also has been effaced [h].

[f] *Opp.* vol. iii. p. 85 B: 88 A:— τίνος ἕνεκεν οἱ πατέρες ἡμῶν ἐν τῇ πεντηκοστῇ τὸ βιβλίον τῶν πράξεων ἀναγινώσκεσθαι ἐνομοθέτησαν.—τίνος ἕνεκεν τὸ βιβλίον τῶν πράξεων τῶν ἀποστόλων ἐν τῷ καιρῷ τῆς πεντηκοστῆς ἀναγινώσκεται.

[g] "Anniversariâ sollemnitate post passionem Domini nostis illum librum recitari." *Opp.* iii. (P. ii.) p. 337 G.

[h] I desire to leave in this place the permanent record of my deliberate conviction that the Lectionary which, last year, was hurried with such indecent haste through Convocation,—passed in a half-empty House by the casting vote of the Prolocutor,—and rudely pressed upon the Church's acceptance by the Legislature in the course of its present session,—is the gravest calamity which has befallen the Church of England for a long time past.

Let the history of this Lectionary be remembered.

Appointed (in 1867) for an *entirely* different purpose, (viz. the Ornaments and Vestments question,) 29 Commissioners (14 Clerical and 15 Lay) found themselves further instructed "to suggest and report *whether any and what alterations and amendments may be advantageously made* in the selection of Lessons to be read at the time of Divine Service."

Thereupon, these individuals,—(the Liturgical attainments of nine-tenths of whom it would be unbecoming in such an one as myself to characterise truthfully,)—at once imposed upon themselves the duty of inventing *an entirely new Lectionary* for the Church of England.

So to mutilate the Word of GOD that it shall henceforth be quite impossible to understand a single Bible story, or discover the sequence of a single connected portion of narrative,—seems to have been the guiding principle of their deliberations. With reckless eclecticism,—entire forgetfulness of the requirements of the poor brother,—strange disregard for Catholic Tradition and the

(*d*) The purely arbitrary arrangement, (as Mr. Scrivener phrases it), by which the Book of Genesis, instead of the Gospel, is appointed to be read [i] on the *week* days of Lent, is discovered to have been fully recognised in the time of Chrysostom. Accordingly, the two series of Homilies on the Book of Genesis which that Father preached, he preached in Lent [k].

(*e*) It will be seen in the next chapter that it was from a very remote period the practice of the Eastern Church to introduce into the lesson for Thursday in Holy-week, S. Luke's account (ch. xxii. 43, 44) of our LORD's "Agony and bloody Sweat," *immediately after S. Matth.* xxvi. 39. *That* is, no doubt, the reason why Chrysostom,—who has been suspected, (I think unreasonably,) of employing an Evangelistarium instead of a copy of the Gospels in the preparation of his Homilies, is observed to quote those same two verses in that very place in his Homily on S. Matthew [1]; which shews that the Lectionary system of the Eastern Church in this respect is at least as old as the iv[th] century.

(*f*) The same two verses used to be *left out* on the Tuesday after Sexagesima (τῇ ἡ τῆς τυροφάγου) for which day S. Luke xxii. 39—xxiii. 1, is the appointed lection. And *this* explains why Cyril (A.D. 425) in his Homilies on S. Luke, passes them by in silence [m].

But we can carry back the witness to the Lectionary practice of omitting these verses, at least a hundred years; for

claims of immemorial antiquity;—these Commissioners, (evidently unconscious of their own unfitness for their self-imposed task,) have given us a Lectionary which will recommend itself to none but the lovers of novelty,—the impatient, —and the enemies of Divine Truth.

That the blame, *the guilt* lies at the door of *our Bishops*, is certain; but the Church has no one but herself to thank for the injury which has been thus deliberately inflicted upon her. She has suffered herself to be robbed of her ancient birthright without resistance; without remonstrance; without (in her corporate capacity) so much as a word of audible dissatisfaction. *Can* it be right in this way to defraud those who are to come after us of their lawful inheritance? ... I am amazed and grieved beyond measure at what is taking place. At least, (as on other occasions,) *liberavi animam meam*.

[i] A trace of this remains in the old Gallican Liturgy,—pp. 137-8.
[k] Bingham, XIV. iii. 3.   [1] *Opp.* vol. vii. p. 791 B.
[m] See Dean Payne Smith's Translation, p. 863.

Cod. B, (evidently for that same reason,) *also* omits them, as was stated above, in p. 79. They are wanting also in the Thebaic version, which is of the iii[rd] century.

(*g*) It will be found suggested in the next chapter (page 218) that the piercing of our LORD's side, (S. John xix. 34), —thrust into Codd. B and ℵ immediately after S. Matth. xxvii. 49,—is probably indebted for its place in those two MSS. to the Eastern Lectionary practice. If this suggestion be well founded, a fresh proof is obtained that the Lectionary of the East was fully established in the beginning of the iv[th] century. But see Appendix (H).

(*h*) It is a remarkable note of the antiquity of that Oriental Lectionary system with which we are acquainted, that S. Matthew's account of the Passion (ch. xxvii. 1—61,) should be there appointed to be read *alone* on the evening of Good Friday. Chrysostom clearly alludes to this practice[n]; which Augustine expressly states was also the practice in his own day[o]. Traces of the same method are discoverable in the old Gallican Lectionary[p].

(*i*) Epiphanius, (or the namesake of his who was the author of a well-known Homily on Palm Sunday,) remarks that "yesterday" had been read the history of the rising of Lazarus[q]. Now S. John xi. 1—45 is the lection for the antecedent Sabbath, in all the Lectionaries.

(*k*) In conclusion, I may be allowed so far to anticipate what will be found fully established in the next chapter, as to point out here that since in countless places the text of our oldest Evangelia as well as the readings of the primitive Fathers exhibit unmistakable traces of the corrupting influence of the Lectionary practice, *that* very fact becomes irrefragable evidence of the antiquity of the Lectionary which is the occasion of it. Not only must it be more

---

[n] κατὰ τὴν μεγάλην τοῦ Πάσχα ἑσπέραν ταῦτα πάντα ἀναγινώσκεται.—Chrys. *Opp.* vii. 818 c.

[o] "Passio autem, quia uno die legitur, non solet legi nisi secundum Matthæum. Volueram aliquando ut per singulos annos secundum omnes Evangelistas etiam Passio legeretur. Factum est. Non audierunt homines quod consueverant, et perturbati sunt."—*Opp.* vol. v. p. 980 E.

[p] *Ed.* Mabillon, pp. 130-5.   [q] Epiph. *Opp.* ii. 152-3.

ancient than Cod. B or Cod. ℵ, (which are referred to the beginning of the iv[th] century), but it must be older than Origen in the iii[rd] century, or the Vetus Itala and the Syriac in the ii[nd]. And thus it is demonstrated, (1st) That fixed Lessons were read in the Churches of the East in the immediately post-Apostolic age; and (2ndly) That, wherever we are able to test it, the Lectionary of that remote period corresponded with the Lectionary which has come down to us in documents of the vi[th] and vii[th] century, and was in fact constructed in precisely the same way.

I am content in fact to dismiss the preceding instances with this general remark:—that a System which is found to have been fully recognised throughout the East and throughout the West in the beginning of the fourth century, *must of necessity have been established very long before.* It is as when we read of three British Bishops attending the Council at Arles, A.D. 314. The Church (we say) which could send out those three Bishops must have been *fully organized* at a greatly antecedent period.

4. Let us attend, however, to the great Festivals of the Church. These are declared by Chrysostom (in a Homily delivered at Antioch 20 Dec. A.D. 386) to be the five following:—(1) Nativity: (2) the Theophania: (3) Pascha: (4) Ascension: (5) Pentecost[r]. Epiphanius, his contemporary, (Bishop of Constantia in the island of Cyprus,) makes the same enumeration[s], in a Homily on the Ascension[t]. In the Apostolical Constitutions, the same five Festivals are enumerated[u]. Let me state a few Liturgical facts in connexion with each of these.

[r] Chrys. *Opp.* i. 497 c.   [s] Epiph. *Opp.* ii. 285-6.

[t] The learned reader will be delighted and instructed too by the perusal of both passages. Chrysostom declares that Christmas-Day is the greatest of Festivals; since all the others are but consequences of the Incarnation.

Epiphanius remarks with truth that Ascension-Day is the crowning solemnity of all: being to the others what a beautiful head is to the human body.

[u] *Constt. Apostt.* lib. viii. c. 33. After the week of the Passion and the week of (1) the Resurrection,—(2) Ascension-Day is mentioned;—(3) Pentecost;—(4) Nativity;—(5) Epiphany. [Note this clear indication that this viii[th] Book of the Constitutions was written or interpolated at a subsequent date to that commonly assigned to the work.]

It is plain that the preceding enumeration could not have been made at any earlier period : for the Epiphany of our SAVIOUR and His Nativity were originally but one Festival [y]. Moreover, the circumstances are well known under which Chrysostom (A.D. 386) announced to his Eastern auditory that in conformity with what had been correctly ascertained at Rome, the ancient Festival was henceforth to be disintegrated [z]. But this is not material to the present inquiry. We know that, as a matter of fact, "the Epiphanies" (for τὰ ἐπιφανία is the name of the Festival) became in consequence distributed over Dec. 25 and Jan. 5 : our LORD's *Baptism* being the event chiefly commemorated on the latter anniversary [a],—which used to be chiefly observed in honour of His *Birth* [b].—Concerning the Lessons for Passion-tide and Easter, as well as concerning those for the Nativity and Epiphany, something has been offered already; to which may be added that Hesychius, in the opening sentences of that "Homily" which has already engaged so much of our attention [c], testifies that the conclusion of S. Mark's Gospel was in his days, as it has been ever since, one of the lections for Easter. He begins by saying that the Evangelical narratives of the Resurrection were read on the Sunday night; and proceeds to reconcile *S. Mark's* with the rest.—Chrysostom once and again adverts to the practice of discontinuing the reading of the Acts after Pentecost [d],—which is observed to be also the method of the Lectionaries.

III. I speak separately of the Festival of the Ascension, for an obvious reason. It ranked, as we have seen, in the estimation of Primitive Christendom, with the greatest Festivals of the Church. Augustine, in a well-known passage, hints that it may have been of Apostolical origin [e]; so ex-

---

[y] Bingham's *Origines*, B. xx. c. iv. § 2.

[z] Chrys. *Opp.* ii. 355. (See the *Monitum*, p. 352.)

[a] Chrys. *Opp.* ii. 369 D.   [b] Epiphanius, Adv. Haer. LI, c. xvi. (*Opp.* i. 439 A.)   [c] See above, pp. 58-9 and 67.

[d] *Opp.* iii. 102 B. See Bingham on this entire subject,—B. xiv, c. iii.

[e] "Illa quae non scripta, sed tradita custodimus, quae quidem toto terrarum orbe observantur, datur intelligi vel ab ipsis Apostolis, vel plenariis Conciliis quorum in Ecclesia saluberrima authoritas, commendata atque statuta retineri. Sicut quod Domini Passio, et Resurrectio, et Ascensio in coelis, ut Adven-

ceedingly remote was its institution accounted in the days of the great African Father, as well as so entirely forgotten by that time was its first beginning. I have to shew that in the Great Oriental Lectionary (whether of the Greek or of the Syrian Church) the last Twelve Verses of S. Mark's Gospel occupy a conspicuous as well as a most honourable place. And this is easily done: for,

(*a*) The Lesson for Matins *on Ascension-Day* in the East, in the oldest documents to which we have access, consisted (as now it does) of *the last Twelve Verses*,—neither more nor less,—of S. Mark's Gospel. At the Liturgy on Ascension was read S. Luke xxiv. 36—53: but at Matins, S. Mark xvi. 9—20. The witness of the "Synaxaria" is constant to this effect.

(*b*) The same lection precisely was adopted among the Syrians by the Melchite Churches [f],—(the party, viz. which maintained the decrees of the Council of Chalcedon): and it is found appointed also in the " Evangeliarium Hierosolymitanum [g]." In the Evangelistarium used in the Jacobite, (i.e. the Monophysite) Churches of Syria, a striking difference of arrangement is discoverable. While S. Luke xxiv. 36— 53 was read at Vespers and at Matins on Ascension Day, *the last seven* verses of S. Mark's Gospel (ch. xvi. 14—20) were read *at the Liturgy* [h]. Strange, that the self-same Gospel should have been adopted at a remote age by some of the Churches of the West [i], and should survive in our own Book of Common Prayer to this hour!

(*c*) But S. Mark xvi. 9—20 was not only appointed by the Greek Church to be read upon Ascension Day. Those same twelve verses constitute the third of the xi " *Matin Gospels of the Resurrection*," which were universally held in high

tus de cœlo Spiritus Sancti anniversaria sollemnitate celebrantur."—*Ep.* ad Januarium, (*Opp.* ii. 124 B, C).

[f] " Lect. fer. quint., quae etiam Festum Adscensionis Dn̄i in caelos, ad mat. eadem ac lect. tert. Resurrect.; in Euchar. lect. sext. Resurrect."—But " Lect. γ Resurrectionis" is " Marc. xvi. 9—20:" " Lect. ς," " Luc. xxiv. 36—53." —See Dean Payne Smith's *Catalogus Codd. Syrr.* (1864) pp. 116, 127.

[g] See above, p. 34, note (e).   [h] R. Payne Smith's *Catal.* p. 148.

[i] *Hieronymi Comes*, (*ed.* Pamel. ii. 31.)—But it is not the Gallican. (*ed.* Mabillon, p. 155.) ... It strikes me as just possible that a clue may be in this way supplied to the singular phenomenon noted above at p. 118, line 22-8.

esteem by the Eastern Churches (Greek and Syrian [k]), and were read successively on Sundays at Matins throughout the year; as well as daily throughout Easter week.

(*d*) A rubricated copy of S. Mark's Gospel in Syriac*, *certainly older than* A.D. 583, attests that S. Mark xvi. 9—20 was the "Lection for the great First Day of the week," (μεγάλη κυριακή, i.e. Easter Day). Other copies almost as ancient † add that it was used "at the end of the Service at the dawn."

(*e*) Further, these same "Twelve Verses" constituted the Lesson at Matins for *the 2nd Sunday after Easter*,—a Sunday which by the Greeks is called κυριακὴ τῶν μυροφόρων, but with the Syrians bore the names of "Joseph and Nicodemus [1]." So also in the "Evangeliarium Hierosolymitanum."

(*f*) Next, in the Monophysite Churches of Syria, S. Mark xvi. 9—18 (or 9—20 [m]) was also read at Matins on *Easter-Tuesday* [n]. In the Gallican Church, the third lection for *Easter-Monday* extended from S. Mark xv. 47 to xvi. 11: for *Easter-Tuesday*, from xvi. 12 to the end of the Gospel [o]. Augustine says that in Africa also these concluding verses of S. Mark's Gospel used to be publicly read *at Easter tide* [p]. The same verses (beginning with ver. 9) are indicated in the oldest extant Lectionary of the Roman Church [q].

(*g*) Lastly, it may be stated that S. Mark xvi. 9—20 was with the Greeks the Gospel for the Festival of S. Mary Magdalene (ἡ μυροφόρος), July 22 [r].

---

[k] Εὐαγγέλια ἀναστάσιμα ἑωθινά. See Scrivener's *Introduction*, p. 72, and R. P. Smith's *Catal.* p. 127. See by all means, Suicer's *Thes. Eccl.* i. 1229.

* Dr. Wright's *Catal.* p. 70, N°. CX. (Addit. 14,464: *fol.* 61 *b*.)

† *Ibid.* N°. LXX (*fol.* 92 *b*), and LXXII (*fol.* 87 *b*).

[1] "Quae titulo Josephi et Nicodemi insignitur." (R. Payne Smith's *Catal.* p. 116.)—In the "Synaxarium" of Matthaei (*Nov. Test.* 1803, i. p. 731) it is styled K. τῶν μ. καὶ Ἰωσὴφ τοῦ δικαίου. [m] Adler's *N. T. Verss. Syrr.* p. 71.

[n] Dean Payne Smith's *Catal.* p. 146. [o] *Ed.* Mabillon, pp. 144-5.

[p] "Resurrectio Domini nostri I. C. ex more legitur his diebus [Paschalibus] ex omnibus libris sancti Evangelii." (*Opp.* v. 977 c)—"Quoniam hoc moris est .... *Marci Evangelium* est quod modo, cum legeretur, audivimus." "Quid ergo audivimus Marcum dicentem?" And he subjoins a quotation from S. Mark xvi. 12.—*Ibid.* 997 F, 998 B. [q] *Hieron. Comes* (ed. Pamel. ii. 27.)

[r] So Scrivener's *Introduction*, p. 75.—Little stress, however, is to be laid on Saint's Day lessons. In Matthaei's "Menologium" (*Nov. Test.* 1803, i. p. 765), I find that S. Luke viii. 1—4, or else S. John xx. 11—18 was the appointed Lection. See his note ([5]) at p. 750.

He knows wondrous little about this department of Sacred Science who can require to be informed that such a weight of *public* testimony as this to the last Twelve Verses of a Gospel is simply overwhelming. The single discovery that in the age of Augustine [385—430] this portion of S. Mark's Gospel was unquestionably read at Easter in the Churches of Africa, added to the express testimony of the Author of the 2nd Homily on the Resurrection, and of the oldest Syriac MSS., that they were also read by the Orientals at Easter in the public services of the Church, must be held to be in a manner decisive of the question.

Let the evidence, then, which is borne by Ecclesiastical usage to the genuineness of S. Mark xvi. 9—20, be summed up, and the entire case caused again to pass under review.

(1.) That Lessons from the New Testament were publicly read in the assemblies of the faithful according to a definite scheme, and on an established system, *at least* as early as the fourth century,—has been shewn to be a plain historical fact. Cyril, at Jerusalem,—(and by implication, his namesake at Alexandria,)—Chrysostom, at Antioch and at Constantinople,—Augustine, in Africa,—all four expressly witness to the circumstance. In other words, there is found to have been *at least at that time* fully established throughout the Churches of Christendom a Lectionary, which seems to have been essentially one and the same in the West[s] and in the East. That it must have been of even Apostolic antiquity may be inferred from several considerations. But that it dates its beginning from a period *anterior to the age of*

---

[s] Note, (in addition to all that has gone before,) that the Festivals are actually designated by their *Greek* names in the earliest Latin Service Books: not only "Theophania," "Epiphania," "Pascha," "Pentecostes," (the second, third and fourth of which appellations survive in the Church of the West, *in memoriam*, to the present hour;) but "Hypapante," which was the title bestowed by the Orientals in the time of Justinian, on Candlemas Day, (our Feast of the Purification, or Presentation of CHRIST in the Temple,) from the "Meeting" of Symeon on that occasion. Friday, or παρασκευή, was called "*Parasceve*" in the West. (Mab. *Lit. Gall.* p. 129.) So entire was the sympathy of the East with the West in such matters in very early times, that when Rome decided to celebrate the Nativity on the 25th December, Chrysostom (as we have been reminded) publicly announced the fact at Constantinople; and it was determined that in this matter East and West would walk by the same rule.

Eusebius,—which is the age of Codices B and ℵ,—at least admits of *no* controversy.

(2.) Next,—Documents of the vi[th] century put us in possession of the great Oriental Lectionary as it is found at that time to have universally prevailed throughout the vast unchanging East. In other words, several of the actual Service Books, in Greek and in Syriac[t], have survived the accidents of full a thousand years: and rubricated copies of the Gospels carry us back three centuries further. The entire agreement which is observed to prevail among these several documents,—added to the fact that when tested by the allusions incidentally made by Greek Fathers of the iv[th] century to what was the Ecclesiastical practice of their own time, there are found to emerge countless as well as highly significant notes of correspondence,—warrants us in believing, (in the absence of testimony of any sort to the contrary,) that the Lectionary we speak of differs in no essential respect from that system of Lections with which the Church of the iv[th] century was universally acquainted.

Nothing scarcely is more forcibly impressed upon us in the course of the present inquiry than the fact, that documents alone are wanting to make *that* altogether demonstrable which, in default of such evidence, must remain a matter of inevitable inference only. The forms we are pursuing at last disappear from our sight: but it is only the mist of the early morning which shrouds them. We still hear their voices: still track their footsteps: know that others still see them, although we ourselves see them no longer. We are sure that *there they still are*. Moreover they may yet reappear at any moment. Thus, there exist Syriac MSS. of the Gospels of the vii[th] and even of the vi[th] century, in which the Lessons are rubricated in the text or on the margin. A Syriac MS. (of part of the Old T.) is actually dated A.D. 464[u]. Should an Evangelium of similar date

---

[t] From Professor Wright's *Catalogue of Syriac MSS. in the British Museum* (1870) it appears that the oldest Jacobite Lectionary is dated A.D. 824; the oldest Nestorian, A.D. 862; the oldest Malkite, A.D. 1023. The respective numbers of the MSS. are 14,485; 14,492; and 14,488.—See his *Catalogue*, Part I. pp. 146, 178, 194.

[u] It is exhibited in the same glass-case with the Cod. Alexandrinus (A.)

ever come to light of which the rubrication was evidently by the original Scribe, the evidence of the Lectionaries would at once be carried back full three hundred years.

But in fact we stand in need of no such testimony. Acceptable as it would be, it is plain that it would add no strength to the argument whatever. We are already able to plant our footsteps securely in the iv[th] and even in the iii[rd] century. It is not enough to insist that inasmuch as the Liturgical method of Christendom was at least fully established in the East and in the West at the close of the iv[th] century, it therefore must have had its beginning at a far remoter period. Our two oldest Codices (B and א) bear witness throughout to the corrupting influence of a system which was evidently in full operation before the time of Eusebius. And even this is not all. The readings in Origen, and of the earliest versions of the Gospel, (the old Latin, the Syriac, the Egyptian versions,) carry back our evidence on this subject unmistakably to *the age immediately succeeding that of the Apostles.* This will be found established in the course of the ensuing Chapter.

Beginning our survey of the problem at the opposite end, we arrive at the same result; with even a deepened conviction that in its essential structure, the Lectionary of the Eastern Church must be of truly primitive antiquity: indeed that many of its leading provisions must date back almost,—nay *quite,*—to the Apostolic age. From whichever side we approach this question,—whatever test we are able to apply to our premisses,—our conclusion remains still the very same.

(3.) Into this Lectionary then,—so universal in its extent, so consistent in its witness, so Apostolic in its antiquity, —"*the* LAST TWELVE VERSES *of the Gospel according to S. Mark*" from the very first are found to have won for themselves not only an entrance, a lodgment, an established place; but, *the place of highest honour,*—an audience on two of the Church's chiefest Festivals.

The circumstance is far too important, far too significant to be passed by without a few words of comment.

For it is not here, (be it carefully observed,) as when

we appeal to some Patristic citation, that the recognition of a phrase, or a verse, or a couple of verses, must be accepted as a proof that the same ancient Father recognised the context also in which those words are found. Not so. *All the Twelve Verses in dispute are found in every known copy* of the venerable Lectionary of the East. *Those same Twelve Verses,*—neither more nor less,—*are observed to constitute one integral Lection.*

But even this is not all. The most important fact seems to be that to these Verses has been assigned a place of the highest possible distinction. It is found that, from the very first, S. Mark xvi. 9—20 has been everywhere, and by all branches of the Church Catholic, claimed for *two* of the Church's greatest Festivals,—Easter and Ascension. A more weighty or a more significant circumstance can scarcely be imagined. To suppose that a portion of Scripture singled out for such extraordinary honour by the Church universal is a spurious addition to the Gospel, is purely irrational; is simply monstrous. No unauthorized "fragment," however "remarkable," could by possibility have so established itself in the regards of the East and of the West, from the very first. No suspected "addition, placed here in very early times," would have been tolerated in the Church's solemn public Service six or seven times a-year. No. *It is impossible.* Had it been one short clause which we were invited to surrender: a verse: two verses: even three or four:— the plea being that (as in the case of the celebrated *pericopa de adulterâ*) the Lectionaries knew nothing of them:—the case would have been entirely different. But for any one to seek to persuade us that these Twelve Verses, which exactly constitute one of the Church's most famous Lections, are every one of them spurious:—that the fatal taint begins with the first verse, and only ends with the last:—*this* is a demand on our simplicity which, in a less solemn subject, would only provoke a smile. We are constrained to testify astonishment and even some measure of concern. Have the Critics then, (supposing them to be familiar with the evidence which has now been set forth so much in detail;)— Have the Critics then, (we ask) utterly taken leave of their senses? or do they really suppose that we have taken leave of ours?

It is time to close this discussion. It was declared at the outset that the witness of the Lectionaries to the genuineness of these Verses, though it has been generally overlooked, is the most important of any: admitting, as it does, of no evasion: being simply, as it is, decisive. I have now fully explained the grounds of that assertion. I have set the Verses, which I undertook to vindicate and establish, on a basis from which it will be found impossible any more to dislodge them. Whatever Griesbach, and Tischendorf, and Tregelles, and the rest, may think about the matter,— the Holy Eastern Church in her corporate capacity, has never been of their opinion. *They* may doubt. *The ante-Nicene Fathers* at least never doubted. If "the last Twelve Verses" of S. Mark were *deservedly* omitted from certain Copies of his Gospel in the iv[th] century, utterly incredible is it that these same TWELVE VERSES should have been disseminated, by their authority, throughout Christendom;— read, by their command, in all the Churches;—selected, by their collective judgment, from the whole body of Scripture for the special honour of being listened to once and again at EASTER time, as well as on ASCENSION-DAY.

CHAPTER XI.

THE OMISSION OF THESE TWELVE VERSES IN CERTAIN ANCIENT COPIES OF THE GOSPELS, EXPLAINED AND ACCOUNTED FOR.

The Text of our five oldest Uncials proved, by an induction of instances, to have suffered depravation throughout by the operation of the ancient Lectionary system of the Church (297).—*The omission of S. Mark's " last Twelve Verses," (constituting an integral Ecclesiastical Lection,) shewn to be probably only one more example of the same depraving influence* (304).

This solution of the problem corroborated by the language of Eusebius and of Hesychius (312); *as well as favoured by the " Western" order of the Gospels* (319).

I AM much mistaken if the suggestion which I am about to offer has not already presented itself to every reader of ordinary intelligence who has taken the trouble to follow the course of my argument thus far with attention. It requires no acuteness whatever,—it is, as it seems to me, the merest instinct of mother-wit,—on reaching the present stage of the discussion, to debate with oneself somewhat as follows :—

1. So then, the last Twelve Verses of S. Mark's Gospel were anciently often observed to be missing from the copies. Eusebius expressly says so. I observe that he nowhere says that *their genuineness* was anciently *suspected.* As for himself, his elaborate discussion of their contents convinces me that individually, he regarded them with favour. The mere fact,—(it is best to keep to his actual statement,)—that "the entire passage" was "not met with in all the copies," is the sum of his evidence: and two Greek manuscripts, yet extant, supposed to be of the ivth century (Codd. B and ℵ), mutilated in this precise way, testify to the truth of his statement.

2. But then it is found that these self-same Twelve Verses, —neither more nor less,—anciently constituted *an integral*

Ecclesiastical Lection; which lection,—inasmuch as it is found to have established itself in every part of Christendom at the earliest period to which liturgical evidence reaches back, and to have been assigned from the very first to two of the chiefest Church Festivals,—must needs be a lection of almost Apostolic antiquity. Eusebius, I observe, (see p. 45), designates the portion of Scripture in dispute by its technical name,—κεφάλαιον or περικοπή; (for so an Ecclesiastical lection was anciently called). Here then is a rare coincidence indeed. It is in fact simply unique. Surely, I may add that it is in the highest degree suggestive also. It inevitably provokes the inquiry,—Must not these two facts be not only connected, but even *interdependent?* Will not the omission of the Twelve concluding Verses of S. Mark from certain ancient copies of his Gospel, have been in some way *occasioned by the fact* that those same twelve verses constituted an integral Church Lection? How is it possible to avoid suspecting that the phenomenon to which Eusebius invites attention, (viz. that certain copies of S. Mark's Gospel in very ancient times had been mutilated from the end of the 8th verse onwards,) ought to be capable of illustration,—will have in fact *to be explained,* and in a word *accounted for,*—by the circumstance that at the 8th verse of S. Mark's xvi[th] chapter, one ancient Lection *came to an end,* and another ancient Lection *began?*

Somewhat thus, (I venture to think,) must every unprejudiced Reader of intelligence hold parley with himself on reaching the close of the preceding chapter. I need hardly add that I am thoroughly convinced he would be reasoning rightly. I am going to shew that the Lectionary practice of the ancient Church does indeed furnish a sufficient clue for the unravelment of this now famous problem: in other words, enables us satisfactorily to account for the omission of these Twelve Verses from ancient copies of the collected Gospels. But I mean to do more. I propose to make my appeal to documents which shall be observed to bear no faltering witness in my favour. More yet. I propose that Eusebius himself, the chief author of all this trouble, shall be brought back into Court and invited to resyllable his

Evidence; and I am much mistaken if even *he* will not be observed to let fall a hint that we have at last got on the right scent;—have accurately divined how this mistake took its first beginning;—and, (what is not least to the purpose,) have correctly apprehended what was his own real meaning in what he himself has said.

The proposed solution of the difficulty,—if not the evidence on which it immediately rests,—might no doubt be exhibited within exceedingly narrow limits. Set down abruptly, however, its weight and value would inevitably fail to be recognised, even by those who already enjoy some familiarity with these studies. Very few of the considerations which I shall have to rehearse are in fact unknown to Critics: yet is it evident that their bearing on the problem before us has hitherto altogether escaped their notice. On the other hand, by one entirely a novice to this department of sacred Science, I could scarcely hope to be so much as understood. Let me be allowed, therefore, to preface what I have to say with a few explanatory details which I promise shall not be tedious, and which I trust will not be found altogether without interest either. If they are anywhere else to be met with, it is my misfortune, not my fault, that I have been hitherto unsuccessful in discovering the place.

I. From the earliest ages of the Church, (as I shewed at page 192-5,) it has been customary to read certain definite portions of Holy Scripture, determined by Ecclesiastical authority, publicly before the Congregation. In process of time, as was natural, the sections so required for public use were collected into separate volumes: Lections from the Gospels being written out in a Book which was called "*Evangelistarium,*" (εὐαγγελιστάριον,)—from the Acts and Epistles, in a book called "*Praxapostolus,*" (πραξαπόστολος). These Lectionary-books, both Greek and Syriac, are yet extant in great numbers [b], and (I may remark in

---

[b] See the enumeration of Greek Service-Books in Scrivener's *Introduction,* &c. pp. 211—25. For the Syriac Lectionaries, see Dean Payne Smith's *Catalogue,* (1864) pp. 114-29-31-4-5-8: also Professor Wright's *Catalogue,* (1870) pp. 146 to 203.—I avail myself of this opportunity to thank both those learned Scholars for their valuable assistance, always most obligingly rendered.

passing) deserve a far greater amount of attention than has hitherto been bestowed upon them [c].

When the Lectionary first took the form of a separate book, has not been ascertained. That no copy is known to exist (whether in Greek or in Syriac) older than the viii[th] century, proves nothing. Codices in daily use, (like the Bibles used in our Churches,) must of necessity have been of exceptionally brief duration; and Lectionaries, more even than Biblical MSS. were liable to injury and decay.

II. But it is to be observed,—(and to explain this, is much more to my present purpose,)—that besides transcribing the Ecclesiastical lections into separate books, it became the practice at a very early period *to adapt copies of the Gospels to lectionary purposes.* I suspect that this practice began in the Churches of Syria; for *Syriac* copies of the Gospels (*at least* of the vii[th] century) abound, which have the Lections more or less systematically rubricated in the Text [d]. There is in the British Museum a copy of S. Mark's Gospel according to the Peshito version, *certainly written previous to* A.D. 583, which has at least five or six rubrics so inserted by the original scribe [e]. As a rule, in all later cursive Greek MSS., (I mean those of the xii[th] to the xv[th] century,) the Ecclesiastical lections are indicated throughout: while either at the summit, or else at the foot of the page, the formula with which the Lection was to be introduced is elaborately inserted; prefaced probably by a rubricated statement (not always very easy to decipher) of the occasion *when* the ensuing portion of Scripture was to be read. The ancients, to a far greater extent than ourselves [f], were accustomed,—

[c] "Evangelistariorum codices literis uncialibus scripti nondum sic ut decet in usum criticum conversi sunt." Tischendorf, quoted by Scrivener, [*Introduction to Cod. Augiensis,*—80 pages which have been sep\rately published and are *well* deserving of study,—p. 48,] who adds,—"I cannot even conjecture why an Evangelistarium should be thought of less value than another MS. of the same age."—See also Scrivener's *Introduction,* &c. p. 211.

[d] e.g. *Addit. MSS.* 12,141 : 14,449 : 14,450-2-4-5-6-7-8 : 14,461-3 : 17,113-4-5-6 :—(= 15 Codd. in all :) from p. 45 to p. 66 of Professor Wright's *Catalogue.*

[e] *Addit. MS.* 14,464. (See Dr. Wright's *Catalogue,* p. 70.)

[f] Add to the eight examples adduced by Mr. Scrivener from our Book of C. P., (*Introduction,* p. 11), the following :—Gospels for Quinquagesima,

(in fact, they made it *a rule*,)—to prefix unauthorized formulæ to their public Lections; and these are sometimes found to have established themselves so firmly, that at last they became as it were ineradicable; and later copyists of the fourfold Gospel are observed to introduce them unsuspiciously into the inspired text [g]. All that belongs to this subject deserves particular attention; because it is *this* which explains not a few of the perturbations (so to express oneself) which the text of the New Testament has experienced. We are made to understand how, what was originally intended only as a *liturgical note*, became mistaken, through the inadvertence or the stupidity of copyists, for a *critical suggestion*; and thus, besides transpositions without number, there has arisen, at one time, the insertion of something unauthorized into the text of Scripture,—at another, the omission of certain inspired words, to the manifest detriment of the sacred deposit. For although the *systematic* rubrication of the Gospels for liturgical purposes is a comparatively recent invention,—(I question if it be older in Greek MSS. than the xth century,)—yet will persons engaged in the public Services of God's House have been prone, from the very earliest age, to insert memoranda of the kind referred to, into the margin of their copies. In this way, in fact, it may be regarded as certain that in countless minute particulars

2nd S. after Easter, 9th, 12th, 22nd after Trinity, Whitsunday, Ascension Day, SS. Philip and James (see below, p. 220), All Saints.

[g] Thus the words εἶπε δὲ ὁ Κύριος (S. Luke vii. 31) which *introduce an Ecclesiastical Lection* (Friday in the iii[rd] week of S. Luke,) inasmuch as the words are found in *no* uncial MS., and are omitted besides by the Syriac, Vulgate, Gothic and Coptic Versions, must needs be regarded as a liturgical interpolation.—The same is to be said of ὁ Ἰησοῦς in S. Matth. xiv. 22,—words which Origen and Chrysostom, as well as the Syriac versions, omit; and which clearly owe their place in twelve of the uncials, in the Textus Receptus, in the Vulgate and some copies of the old Latin, to the fact that the Gospel for the ix[th] Sunday after Pentecost *begins at that place*.—It will be kindred to the present inquiry that I should point out that in S. Mark xvi. 9, Ἀναστὰς ὁ Ἰησοῦς is constantly met with in Greek MSS., and even in some copies of the Vulgate; and yet there can be *no* doubt that here also the Holy Name is an interpolation which has originated from the same cause as the preceding. The fact is singularly illustrated by the insertion of " ὁ ι̅σ̅ " in Cod. 267 (= Reg. 69,) *rubro* above *the same contraction* (for ὁ Ἰησους) in the text.

the text of Scripture has been depraved. Let me not fail to add, that by a judicious, and above all by an *unprejudiced* use of the materials at our disposal, it may, even at this distance of time, in every such particular, be successfully restored [h].

III. I now proceed to shew, by an induction of instances, that *even in the oldest copies in existence*, I mean in Codd. B, ℵ, A, C, and D, the Lectionary system of the early Church has left abiding traces of its operation. When a few such undeniable cases have been adduced, all objections grounded on *primâ facie* improbability will have been satisfactorily disposed of. The activity, as well as the existence of such a disturbing force and depraving influence, *at least* as far back as the beginning of the iv[th] century, (but it is in fact more ancient by full two hundred years,) will have been established: of which I shall only have to shew, in conclusion, that the omission of "the last Twelve Verses" of S. Mark's Gospel is probably but one more instance,— though confessedly by far the most extraordinary of any.

(1.) From Codex B then, as well as from Cod. A, the two grand verses which describe our LORD's "Agony and Bloody Sweat," (S. Luke xxii. 43, 44,) are missing. The same two verses are absent also from a few other important MSS., as well as from both the Egyptian versions; but I desire to fasten attention on the confessedly erring testimony in this place of Codex B. "Confessedly erring," I say; for the genuineness of those two verses is no longer disputed. Now, in every known Evangelistarium, the two verses here omitted by Cod. B follow, (the Church so willed it,) S. Matth. xxvi. 39, and are read as a regular part of the lesson for the Thursday in Holy Week [i]. Of course they are also *omitted* in the same Evangelistaria from the lesson for the Tuesday

---

[h] Not, of course, so long as the present senseless fashion prevails of regarding Codex B, (to which, if Cod. L. and Codd. 1, 33 and 69 are added, it is *only because they agree with B*), as an all but infallible guide in settling the text of Scripture; and quietly taking it for granted that *all the other MSS. in existence* have entered into a grand conspiracy to deceive mankind. Until this most uncritical method, this most unphilosophical theory, is unconditionally abandoned, progress in this department of sacred Science is simply impossible.

[i] See Matthaei's note on S. Luke xxii. 43, (*Nov. Test. ed.* 1803.)

after Sexagesima, (τῇ ἥ τῆς τυροφάγου, as the Easterns call that day,) when S. Luke xxii. 39—xxiii. 1 used to be read. Moreover, in all ancient copies of the Gospels which have been accommodated to ecclesiastical use, *the reader of S. Luke xxii. is invariably directed by a marginal note to leave out those two verses*, and to proceed *per saltum* from ver. 42 to ver. 45 [k]. What more obvious therefore than that the removal of the paragraph from its proper place in S. Luke's Gospel is to be attributed to nothing else but the Lectionary practice of the primitive Church? Quite unreasonable is it to impute heretical motives, or to invent any other unsupported theory, while this plain solution of the difficulty is at hand.

(2.) The same Cod. B., (with which Codd. א, C, L, U and Γ are observed here to conspire,) introduces the piercing of the SAVIOUR's side (S. John xix. 34) at the end of S. Matth. xxvii. 49. Now, I only do not insist that this must needs be the result of the singular Lectionary practice already described at p. 202, because a scholion in Cod. 72 records the singular fact that in the Diatessaron of Tatian, after S. Matth. xxvii. 48, was read ἄλλος δὲ λαβὼν λόγχην ἔνυξεν αὐτοῦ τὴν

---

[k] This will be best understood by actual reference to a manuscript. In Cod. Evan. 436 (Meerman 117) which lies before me, these directions are given as follows. After τὸ σὸν γενέσθω (i.e. the last words of ver. 42), is written ὑπέρβα εἰς τὸ τῆς γ́. Then, at the end of ver. 44, is written—ἄρξου τῆς γ́, after which follows the text καὶ ἀναστὰς, &c.

In S. Matthew's Gospel, at chap. xxvi, which contains the Liturgical section for Thursday in Holy Week (τῇ ἁγίᾳ καὶ μεγάλῃ έ), my Codex has been only imperfectly rubricated. Let me therefore be allowed to quote from Harl. MS. 1810, (our Cod. Evan. 113) which, at fol. 84, at the end of S. Matth. xxvi. 39, reads as follows, immediately after the words,—ἀλλ' ὡς σὺ :— $\frac{\ddot{π}}{γ}$ ※ (i.e. ὑπάντα.) But in order to explain what is meant, the above rubricated word and sign are repeated at foot, as follows :—※ ὑπάντα εἰς τὸ κατὰ Λουκὰν ἐν κεφαλαίῳ ρθ́. ὤφθη δὲ αὐτῷ ἄγγελος : εἶτα στραφεὶς ἐνταῦθα πάλιν, λέγε· καὶ ἔρχεται πρὸς τοὺς μαθητάς—which are the first words of S. Matth. xxvi. 40.

Accordingly, my Codex (No. 436, above referred to) immediately after S. Luke xxii. 42, *besides* the rubric already quoted, has the following : ἄρξου τῆς μεγάλης έ. Then come the two famous verses (ver. 43, 44); and, after the words ἀναστὰς ἀπὸ τῆς προσευχῆς, the following rubric occurs : ὑπάντα εἰς τὸ τῆς μεγάλης έ Ματθ. ἔρχεται πρὸς τοὺς μαθητάς.

[With the help of my nephew, (Rev. W. F. Rose, Curate of Holy Trinity, Windsor,) I have collated every syllable of Cod. 436. Its text most nearly resembles the Rev. F. H. Scrivener's l, m, n.]

πλευρὰν· καὶ ἐξῆλθεν ὕδωρ καὶ αἷμα. (Chrysostom's codex was evidently vitiated in *precisely* the same way.) This interpolation therefore *may* have resulted from the corrupting influence of Tatian's (so-called) "Harmony." See Appendix (H).

(3.) To keep on safe ground. Codd. B and D concur in what Alford justly calls the "grave error" of simply omitting from S. Luke xxiii. 34, our LORD's supplication on behalf of His murderers, (ὁ δὲ 'Ιησοῦς ἔλεγε, Πάτερ, ἄφες αὐτοῖς· οὐ γὰρ οἴδασι τί ποιοῦσι). They are not quite singular in so doing; being, as usual, kept in countenance by certain copies of the old Latin, as well as by both the Egyptian versions. How is this "grave error" in so many ancient MSS. to be accounted for? (for a "grave error," or rather "a fatal omission" it certainly is). Simply by the fact that in the Eastern Church the Lection for the Thursday after Sexagesima *breaks off abruptly, immediately before these very words,*—to recommence at ver. 44 [1].

(4.) Note, that at ver. 32, *the eighth "Gospel of the Passion" begins,*—which is the reason why Codd. B and א (with the Egyptian versions) exhibit a singular irregularity in that place; and why the Jerusalem Syriac introduces the established formula of the Lectionaries (σὺν τῷ 'Ιησοῦ) at the same juncture.

(If I do not here insist that the absence of the famous *pericopa de adulterâ* (S. John vii. 53—viii. 11,) from so many MSS., is to be explained in precisely the same way, it is only because the genuineness of that portion of the Gospel is generally denied; and I propose, in this enumeration of instances, not to set foot on disputed ground. I am convinced, nevertheless, that the first occasion of the omission of those memorable verses was the lectionary practice of the primitive Church, which, on Whitsunday, read from S. John vii. 37 to viii. 12, *leaving out the twelve verses* in question. Those verses, from the nature of their contents, (as Augustine declares,) easily came to be viewed with dislike or suspicion. The passage, however, is as old as the second century, for it is found in certain copies of the old Latin. Moreover Jerome deliberately gave it a place in the Vulgate. I pass on.)

---

[1] See by all means Matthaei's *Nov. Test.* (ed. 1803,) i. p. 491, and 492.

(5.) The two oldest Codices in existence,—B and ℵ,—stand all but alone in omitting from S. Luke vi. 1 the unique and indubitably genuine word δευτεροπρώτῳ; which is also omitted by the Peshito, Italic and Coptic versions. And yet, when it is observed that *an Ecclesiastical lection begins here*, and that the Evangelistaria (which *invariably* leave out such notes of time) simply drop the word,—only substituting for ἐν σαββάτῳ the more familiar τοῖς σάββασι,—every one will be ready to admit that if the omission of this word be not due to the inattention of the copyist, (which, however, seems to me not at all unlikely,) it is sufficiently explained by the Lectionary practice of the Church,—which may well date back even to the immediately post-Apostolic age.

(6.) In S. Luke xvi. 19, Cod. D introduces the Parable of Lazarus with the formula,—εἶπεν δὲ καὶ ἑτέραν παραβολήν; which is nothing else but a marginal note which has found its way into the text from the margin; being *the liturgical introduction of a Church-lesson*[n] which afterwards began εἶπεν ὁ Κύριος τὴν παραβολὴν ταύτην [o].

(7.) In like manner, the same Codex makes S. John xiv. begin with *the liturgical formula*,—(it survives in our Book of Common Prayer* to this very hour!)—καὶ εἶπεν τοῖς μαθηταῖς αὐτοῦ: in which it is countenanced by certain MSS. of the Vulgate and of the old Latin Version. Indeed, it may be stated generally concerning the text of Cod. D, that it bears marks *throughout* of the depraving influence of the ancient Lectionary practice. Instances of this, (in addition to those elsewhere cited in these pages,) will be discovered in S. Luke iii. 23: iv. 16 (and xix. 45): v. 1 and 17: vi. 37 (and xviii. 15): vii. 1: x. 1 and 25: xx. 1: in all but three of which, Cod. D is kept in countenance by the old Latin, often by the Syriac, and by other versions of the greatest antiquity. But to proceed.

(8.) Cod. A, (supported by Athanasius, the Vulgate, Gothic, and Philoxenian versions,) for καί, in S. Luke ix. 57,

---

[n] For the 5th Sunday of S. Luke.

[o] Such variations are quite common. Matthaei, with his usual accuracy, points out several: e.g. *Nov. Test.* (1788) vol. i. p. 19 (*note* 26), p. 23: vol. ii. p. 10 (*note* 12), p. 14 (*notes* 14 and 15), &c.   * SS. Philip and James.

reads ἐγένετο δέ,—which is the reading of the Textus Receptus. Cod. D, (with some copies of the old Latin,) exhibits καὶ ἐγένετο. All the diversity which is observable in this place, (and it is considerable,) is owing to the fact that *an Ecclesiastical lection begins here* [p]. In different Churches, the formula with which the lection was introduced slightly differed.

(9.) Cod. C is supported by Chrysostom and Jerome, as well as by the Peshito, Cureton's and the Philoxenian Syriac, and some MSS. of the old Latin, in reading ὁ Ἰησοῦς at the beginning of S. Matth. xi. 20. That the words have no business there, is universally admitted. So also is the cause of their interpolation generally recognized. *The Ecclesiastical lection* for Wednesday in the iv[th] week after Pentecost *begins at that place;* and begins with the formula,—ἐν τῷ καιρῷ ἐκείνῳ, ἤρξατο ὁ Ἰησοῦς ὀνειδίζειν.

(10.) Similarly, in S. Matth. xii. 9, xiii. 36, and xiv. 14, Cod. C inserts ὁ Ἰησοῦς; a reading which on all three occasions is countenanced by the Syriac and some copies of the old Latin, and on the last of the three, by Origen also. And yet there can be no doubt that it is only because *Ecclesiastical lections begin at those places* [q], that the Holy Name is introduced there.

(11.) Let me add that the Sacred Name is confessedly an interpolation in the six places indicated at foot,—its presence being accounted for by the fact that, in each, *an Ecclesiastical lection begins* [r]. Cod. D in one of these places, Cod. A in four, is kept in countenance by the old Latin, the Syriac, the Coptic and other early versions;—convincing indications of the extent to which the Lectionary practice of the Church had established itself so early as the second century of our æra.

Cod. D, and copies of the old Latin and Egyptian versions also read τοῦ Ἰησοῦ, (instead of αὐτοῦ,) in S. Mark xiv. 3; which is only because *a Church lesson begins there.*

[p] viz. σαββάτῳ θ: i.e. the ix[th] Saturday in S. Luke.—Note that Cod. A also reads ἐγένετο δέ in S. Lu. xi. 1.

[q] viz. Monday in the vth, Thursday in the vi[th] week after Pentecost, and the viii[th] Sunday after Pentecost.

[r] viz. S. Luke xiii. 2 : xxiv. 36. S. John i. 29 (ὁ Ἰωάννης): 44: vi. 14: xiii. 3,

(12.) The same Cod. D is all but unique in leaving out that memorable verse in S. Luke's Gospel (xxiv. 12), in which S.·Peter's visit to the Sepulchre of our risen LORD finds particular mention. It is only because that verse was claimed both as the *conclusion* of the iv[th] and also as the *beginning* of the vth Gospel of the Resurrection: so that the liturgical note ἀρχή stands at the beginning,—τέλος at the end of it. Accordingly, D is kept in countenance here only by the Jerusalem Lectionary and some copies of the old Latin. But what is to be thought of the editorial judgment which (with Tregelles) encloses this verse within brackets; and (with Tischendorf) *rejects it from the text altogether?*

(13.) Codices B, ℵ, and D are *alone* among MSS. in omitting the clause διελθὼν διὰ μέσου αὐτῶν· καὶ παρῆγεν οὕτως, at the end of the 59th verse of S. John viii. The omission is to be accounted for by the fact that just *there* the Church-lesson for Tuesday in the vth week after Easter *came to an end*.

(14.) Again. It is not at all an unusual thing to find in cursive MSS., at the end of S. Matth. viii. 13, (with several varieties), the spurious and tasteless appendix,—καὶ ὑποστρέψας ὁ ἑκατόνταρχος εἰς τὸν οἶκον αὐτοῦ ἐν αὐτῇ τῇ ὥρᾳ εὗρεν τὸν παῖδα ὑγιαίνοντα: a clause which owes its existence solely to the practice of ending the lection for the iv[th] Sunday after Pentecost in that unauthorized manner[s]. But it is not only in cursive MSS. that these words are found. *They are met with also in the Codex Sinaiticus* (ℵ): a witness at once to the inveteracy of Liturgical usage in the iv[th] century of our æra, and to the corruptions which the "Codex omnium antiquissimus" will no doubt have inherited from a yet older copy than itself.

—to which should perhaps be added xxi. 1, where B, ℵ, A, C (notD) read Ἰησοῦς.

[s] See by all means Matthaei's interesting note on the place,—*Nov. Test.* (1788) vol. i. p. 113-4. It should be mentioned that Cod. C (and four other uncials), together with the Philoxenian and Hierosolymitan versions, concur in exhibiting the same spurious clause. Matthaei remarks,—"Origenes (iv. 171 D) hanc pericopam haud adeo diligenter recensens terminat eum in γενηθήτω σοι." Will not the disturbing *Lectionary-practice* of his day sufficiently explain Origen's omission?

(15.) In conclusion, I may remark generally that there occur instances, again and again, of perturbations of the Text in our oldest MSS., (corresponding sometimes with readings vouched for by the most ancient of the Fathers,) which admit of no more intelligible or inoffensive solution than by referring them to the Lectionary practice of the primitive Church[t].

Thus when instead of καὶ ἀναβαίνων ὁ 'Ἰησοῦς εἰς 'Ἱεροσόλυμα (S. Matth. xx. 17), Cod. B reads, (and, is almost unique in reading,) Μέλλων δὲ ἀναβαίνειν ὁ 'Ἰησοῦς; and when Origen sometimes quotes the place in the same way, but sometimes is observed to transpose the position of the Holy Name in the sentence; when again six of Matthaei's MSS., (and Origen once,) are observed to put the same Name *after* 'Ἱεροσόλυμα : when, lastly, two of Field's MSS.[u], and one of Matthaei's, (and I dare say a great many more, if the truth were known,) omit the words ὁ 'Ἰησοῦς entirely:—*who* sees not that the true disturbing force in this place, from the ii[nd] century of our æra downwards, has been *the Lectionary practice of the primitive Church?*—the fact that *there* the lection for the Thursday after the viii[th] Sunday after Pentecost began?—And this may suffice.

IV. It has been proved then, in what goes before, more effectually even than in a preceding page[w], not only that Ecclesiastical Lections corresponding with those indicated in the "Synaxaria" were fully established in the immediately post-Apostolic age, but also that at that early period the Lectionary system of primitive Christendom had already exercised a depraving influence of a peculiar kind on the text of Scripture. Further yet, (and *this* is the only point I am now concerned to establish), that *our five oldest Copies of the Gospels*,—B and ℵ as well as A, C and D,—exhibit

[t] I recal S. John x. 29: xix. 13: xxi. 1;—but the attentive student will be able to multiply such references almost indefinitely. In these and similar places, while the phraseology is exceedingly simple, the variations which the text exhibits are so exceeding numerous,—that when it is discovered that *a Church Lesson begins in those places*, we may be sure that we have been put in possession of the name of the disturbing force.

[u] Viz. K and M. (Field's *Chrys.* p. 251.)—How is it that the readings of Chrysostom are made so little account of? By Tregelles, for example, why are they overlooked entirely?   [w] See above, p. 197 to 204.

not a few traces of the mischievous agency alluded to; errors, and especially *omissions*, which sometimes seriously affect the character of those Codices as witnesses to the Truth of Scripture.—I proceed now to consider the case of S. Mark xvi. 9—20; only prefacing my remarks with a few necessary words of explanation.

V. He who takes into his hands an ordinary cursive MS. of the Gospels, is prepared to find the Church-lessons regularly indicated throughout, in the text or in the margin. A familiar contraction, executed probably in vermillion $\overset{'\chi'}{\alpha\rho}$, ἀρ, indicates the "beginning" (ἀρχή) of each lection: a corresponding contraction $\overset{\epsilon'}{\tau}, \overset{\widehat{\epsilon}}{\tau'}, \tau\grave{\epsilon}:, \overset{\lambda}{\tau\epsilon}, \tau\epsilon\overset{o}{\lambda},$ indicates its "end" (τέλος.) Generally, these rubrical directions, (for they are nothing else,) are inserted for convenience into the body of the text,—from which the red pigment with which they are almost invariably executed, effectually distinguishes them. But all these particulars gradually disappear as recourse is had to older and yet older MSS. The studious in such matters have noticed that even the memorandums as to the "beginning" and the "end" of a lection are rare, almost in proportion to the antiquity of a Codex. When they do occur in the later uncials, they do not by any means always seem to have been the work of the original scribe; neither has care been always taken to indicate them in ink of a different colour. It will further be observed in such MSS. that whereas the sign where the reader is to begin is generally—(in order the better to attract his attention,)—inserted in *the margin* of the Codex, the note where he is to leave off, (in order the more effectually to arrest his progress,) is as a rule introduced *into the body of the text*[x]. In uncial MSS., however, all such symbols are not only rare, but (what is much to be noted) they are exceedingly irregular in their occurrence. Thus in Codex Γ, in the Bodleian Library, (a recently acquired uncial MS. of the Gospels, written A.D. 844), there occurs no indication of the "end" of a single lection in S. Luke's Gospel, until chap.

---

[x] e.g. in Cod. Evan. 10 and 270.

xvi. 31 is reached; after which, the sign abounds. In Codex L, the original notes of Ecclesiastical Lections occur at the following rare and irregular intervals: — S. Mark ix. 2: x. 46: xii. 40 (where the sign has lost its way; it should have stood against ver. 44): xv. 42 and xvi. 1 ʸ. In the *oldest* uncials, nothing of the kind is discoverable. Even in the Codex Bezæ, (vi[th] century,) not a single liturgical direction *coeval with the MS.* is anywhere to be found.

VI. And yet, although the practice of thus indicating the beginning and the end of a liturgical section, does not seem to have come into general use until about the xii[th] century; and although, previous to the ix[th] century, systematic liturgical directions are probably unknown ᶻ; the *need* of them must have been experienced by one standing up to read before the congregation, long before. The want of some reminder where he was to begin,—above all, of some hint where he was to leave off,—will have infallibly made itself felt from the first. Accordingly, there are not wanting indications that, occasionally, τελος (or το τελος) was written in the margin of Copies of the Gospels at an exceedingly remote epoch. One memorable example of this practice is supplied by the Codex Bezæ (D): where in S. Mark xiv. 41, instead of ἀπέχει. ἦλθεν ἡ ὥρα,—we meet with the unintelligible απεχει το τελος και η ωρα. Now, nothing else has here happened but that a marginal note, designed originally to indicate the end (το τελος) of the lesson for

---

ʸ In some cursive MSS. also, (which have been probably transcribed from ancient originals,) the same phenomenon is observed. Thus, in Evan. 265 (= Reg. 66), τελ only occurs, in S. Mark, at ix. 9 and 41 : xv. 32 and 41 : xvi. 8. Αρχ at xvi. 1. It is striking to observe that so little were these ecclesiastical notes (embedded in the text) understood by the possessor of the MS., that in the margin, over against ch. xv. 41, (where "τελ°:" stands *in the text,*) a somewhat later hand has written,— τε[λos] τ[ης] ὡρ[as]. A similar liturgical note may be seen over against ch. ix. 9, and elsewhere. Cod. 25 (=Reg. 191), at the end of S. Mark's Gospel, has *only two* notes of liturgical endings: viz. at ch. xv. 1 and 42.

ᶻ Among the *Syriac* Evangelia, as explained above (p. 215), instances occur of far more ancient MSS. which exhibit a text rubricated by the original scribe. Even here, however, (as may be learned from Dr. Wright's *Catalogue*, pp. 46 —66,) such Rubrics have been only *irregularly* inserted in the oldest copies.

the third day of the iind week of the Carnival, has lost its way from the end of ver. 42, and got thrust into the text of ver. 41,—to the manifest destruction of the sense[a]. I find D's error here is shared (*a*) by the Peshito Syriac, (*b*) by the old Latin, and (*c*) by the Philoxenian: venerable partners in error, truly! for the first two probably carry back this false reading to *the second century of our æra;* and so, furnish one more remarkable proof, to be added to the fifteen (or rather the forty) already enumerated (pp. 217-23), that the lessons of the Eastern Church were settled at a period long anterior to the date of the oldest MS. of the Gospels extant.

VII. Returning then to the problem before us, I venture to suggest as follows:—What if, at a very remote period, this same isolated liturgical note (το τελοc) occurring at S. Mark xvi. 8, (which *is* "the end" of *the Church-lection* for the iind Sunday after Easter,) should have unhappily suggested to some copyist,—καλλιγραφίας *quam vel Criticæ Sacræ vel rerum Liturgicarum peritior,*—the notion that *the entire " Gospel according to S. Mark,"* came to an end at verse 8? .... I see no more probable account of the matter, I say, than this:—That the mutilation of the last chapter of S. Mark has resulted from the fact, that some very ancient scribe *misapprehended the import of the solitary liturgical note* τελοc (or το τελοc) which he found at the close of verse 8. True, that he will have probably beheld, further on, several additional στίχοι. But if he did, how could he acknowledge the fact more loyally than by leaving (as the author of Cod. B is observed to have done) one entire column blank, before proceeding with S. Luke? He hesitated, all the same,

---

[a] Note, that the Codex from which Cod. D was copied will have exhibited the text thus,—απεχει το τελοc ηλθεν η ωρα,—which is the reading of Cod. 13 (= Reg. 50.) But the scribe of Cod. D, in order to improve the sense, substituted for ἦλθεν the word καί. Note the scholion [*Anon. Vat.*] in Possinus, p. 321:—ἀπέχει, τουτέστι, πεπλήρωται, τέλος ἔχει τὸ κατ' ἐμέ.

Besides the said Cod. 13, the same reading is found in 47 and 54 (in the Bodl.): 56 (at Linc. Coll.): 61 (i.e. Cod. Montfort.): 69 (i.e. Cod. Leicestr.): 124 (i.e. Cod. Vind. Lamb. 31): c^{scr} (i.e. Lambeth, 1177): 2^{pe} (i.e. the 2nd of Muralt's S. Petersburg Codd.); and Cod. 439 (i.e. Addit. Brit. Mus. 5107). All these eleven MSS. read ἀπέχει τὸ τέλος at S. Mark xiv. 41.

to transcribe any further, having before him, (as he thought,) an assurance that "THE END" had been reached at ver. 8.

VIII. That some were found in very early times eagerly to acquiesce in this omission: to sanction it: even to multiply copies of the Gospel so mutilated; (critics or commentators intent on nothing so much as reconciling the apparent discrepancies in the Evangelical narratives:)—appears to me not at all unlikely [b]. Eusebius almost says as much, when he puts into the mouth of one who is for getting rid of these verses altogether, the remark that "they would be in a manner superfluous *if it should appear that their testimony is at variance with that of the other Evangelists* [c]." (The ancients were giants in Divinity but children in Criticism.) On the other hand, I altogether agree with Dean Alford in thinking it highly improbable that the difficulty of harmonizing one Gospel with another in this place, (such as it is,) was the cause why these Twelve Verses were originally suppressed [d]. (1) First, because there really was no need to withhold more than three,—at the utmost, five of them,—if *this* had been the reason of the omission. (2) Next, because it would have

[b] So Scholz (i. 200) :— "Pericopa hæc *casu quodam* forsan exciderat a codice quodam Alexandrino; unde defectus iste in alios libros transiit. Nec mirum hunc defectum multis, immo in certis regionibus plerisque scribis arrisisse: confitentur enim ex ipsorum opinione Marcum Matthæo repugnare. Cf. maxime Eusebium ad Marinum," &c.

[c] περιττὰ ἂν εἴη, καὶ μάλιστα εἴπερ ἔχοιεν ἀντιλογίαν τῇ τῶν λοιπῶν εὐαγγελιστῶν μαρτυρίᾳ. (Mai, *Bibl. P.P. Nova*, vol. iv. p. 256.)

[d] Alford's N. T. vol. i. p. 433, (*ed.* 1868.)—And so Tischendorf, (ed. 8va. pp. 406-7.) "Talem dissentionem ad Marci librum tam misere mutilandum adduxisse quempiam, et quidem tanto cum successu, prorsus incredibile est, nec ullo probari potest exemplo."—Tregelles is of the same opinion. (*Printed Text*, pp. 255-6.)—Matthaei, a competent judge, seems to have thought differently. "Una autem causa cur hic locus omitteretur fuit quod Marcus in his repugnare ceteris videtur Evangelistis." The general observation which follows is true enough :—"Quæ ergo vel obscura, vel repugnantia, vel parum decora quorundam opinione habebantur, ea olim ab Criticis et interpretibus nonnullis vel sublata, vel in dubium vocata esse, ex aliis locis sanctorum Evangeliorum intelligitur." (*Nov. Test.* 1788, vol. ii. p. 266.) Presently, (at p. 270,)—"In summâ. Videtur unus et item alter ex interpretibus, qui hæc cæteris evangeliis repugnare opinebatur, in dubium vocasse. Hunc deinde plures temere secuti sunt, ut plerumque factum esse animadvertimus." Dr. Davidson says the same thing (ii. 116.) and, (what is of vastly more importance,) Mr. Scrivener also. (*Coll. Cod. Sin.* p. xliv.)

been easier far to introduce some critical correction of any supposed discrepancy, than to sweep away the whole of the unoffending context. (3) Lastly, because nothing clearly was gained by causing the Gospel to end so abruptly that every one must see at a glance that it had been mutilated. No. The omission having originated in a mistake, was perpetuated for a brief period (let us suppose) only through infirmity of judgment: or, (as I prefer to believe), only in consequence of the religious fidelity of copyists, who were evidently always instructed to transcribe exactly what they found in the copy set before them. The Church meanwhile in her corporate capacity, has never known anything at all of the matter,—as was fully shewn above in Chap. X.

IX. When this solution of the problem first occurred to me, (and it occurred to me long before I was aware of the memorable reading το τελοc in the Codex Bezæ, already adverted to,) I reasoned with myself as follows:—But if the mutilation of the second Gospel came about in this particular way, the MSS. are bound to remember *something* of the circumstance; and in ancient MSS., if I am right, I ought certainly to meet with *some* confirmation of my opinion. According to my view, at the root of this whole matter lies the fact that at S. Mark xvi. 8 a well-known Ecclesiastical lesson comes to an end. Is there not perhaps something exceptional in the way that the close of that liturgical section was anciently signified?

X. In order to ascertain this, I proceeded to inspect every copy of the Gospels in the Imperial Library at Paris[e]; and devoted seventy hours exactly, with unflagging delight, to the task. The success of the experiment astonished me.

1. I began with *our* Cod. 24 (= Reg. 178) of the Gospels: turned to the last page of S. Mark: and beheld, in a Codex of the xi[th] Century wholly devoid of the Lectionary apparatus which is sometimes found in MSS. of a similar date[f], at fol. 104, the word + τελοc + conspicuously written by the original scribe immediately after S. Mark xvi. 8, as

---

[e] I have to acknowledge very gratefully the obliging attentions of M. de Wailly, the chief of the Manuscript department.

[f] See above, p. 224.

well as at the close of the Gospel. *It occurred besides only at ch.* ix. 9, (the end of the lesson for the Transfiguration.) And yet there are *at least seventy* occasions in the course of S. Mark's Gospel where, in MSS. which have been accommodated to Church use, it is usual to indicate the close of a Lection. This discovery, which surprised me not a little, convinced me that I was on the right scent; and every hour I met with some fresh confirmation of the fact.

2. For the intelligent reader will readily understand that three such deliberate liturgical memoranda, occurring solitary in a MS. of this date, are to be accounted for only in one way. They infallibly represent a corresponding peculiarity in some far more ancient document. The fact that the word τελος is here (*a*) set down unabbreviated, (*b*) in black ink, and (*c*) as part of the text,—points unmistakably in the same direction. But that Cod. 24 is derived from a Codex of much older date is rendered certain by a circumstance which shall be specified at foot [g].

3. The very same phenomena reappear in Cod. 36 [h]. The sign + τελος +, (which occurs punctually at S. Mark xvi. 8 and again at v. 20,) is found besides in S. Mark's Gospel only at chap. i. 8 [i]; at chap. xiv. 31; and (+ τελος του κεφαλ/) at chap. xv. 24;—being on every occasion incorporated with the Text. Now, when it is perceived that in the second and third of these places, τελος has clearly lost its way,—appearing where *no* Ecclesiastical lection came to an end,—it will be felt that the MS. before us (of the xi[th] century) if it was not actually transcribed from,—must at least exhibit at second hand,—a far more ancient Codex [k].

---

[g] Whereas in the course of S. Matthew's Gospel, only two examples of + τελος + occur, (viz. at ch. xxvi. 35 and xxvii. 2,)—in the former case the note has entirely lost its way in the process of transcription; standing where it has no business to appear. *No* Liturgical section ends thereabouts. I suspect that the transition (ὑπέρβασις) anciently made at ver. 39, was the thing to which the scribe desired to call attention.

[h] = Coisl. 20. This sumptuous MS., which has not been adapted for Church purposes, appears to me to be the work of the same scribe who produced Reg. 178, (the codex described above); but it exhibits a different text. Bound up with it are some leaves of the LXX of about the viii[th] century.

[i] End of the Lection for the Sunday before Epiphany.

[k] In S. Matthew's Gospel, I could find τελος so written only twice,—viz.

4. *Only once more.*—Codex 22 (= Reg. 72) was never prepared for Church purposes. A rough hand has indeed scrawled indications of the beginnings and endings of a few of the Lessons, here and there; but these liturgical notes are no part of the original MS. At S. Mark xvi. 8, however, we are presented (as before) with the solitary note + τελοc +—, incorporated with the text. Immediately after which, (in writing of the same size,) comes a memorable statement[1] in red letters. The whole stands thus:—

φοβοῦντο γαρ + τέλοc+—
✣ ἔν τιcι τῶν ἀντιγράφων.
ἕωc ὧδε πληροῦται ὁ εὐ
αγγελιcτήc : ἐν πολλοῖc
δε. καὶ ταῦτα φέρεται +—
Ἀναcτὰc δὲ. πρωῒ πρώτη cαββάτων.

And then follows the rest of the Gospel; at the end of which, the sign + τελοc + is again repeated,—which sign, however, occurs *nowhere else* in the MS. *nor at the end of any of the other three Gospels.* A more opportune piece of evidence could hardly have been invented. A statement so apt and so significant was surely a thing rather to be wished than to be hoped for. For here is the liturgical sign τελοc not only occurring in the wholly exceptional way of which we have already seen examples, but actually followed by the admission that "In certain copies, *the Evangelist proceeds no further.*" The two circumstances so brought together seem exactly to bridge over the chasm between Codd. B and ℵ on the one hand,—and Codd. 24 and 36 on the other; and to supply us with precisely the link of evidence which we require. For observe:—During the first six centuries of our æra, no single instance is known of a codex in which τελοc is written at the end of a Gospel. The subscription of

at ch. ii. 23 and xxvi. 75: in S. Luke only once,—viz. at ch. viii. 39. These, in all three instances, are the concluding verses of famous Lessons,—viz. the Sunday after Christmas Day, the iii[rd] Gospel of the Passion, the vi[th] Sunday of S. Luke.

[1] This has already come before us in a different connection : (see p. 119): but it must needs be reproduced here; and *this* time, it shall be exhibited as faithfully as my notes permit.

S. Mark for instance is *invariably* either ΚΑΤΑ ΜΑΡΚΟΝ,—
(as in B and ℵ): or else ΕΥΑΓΓΕΛΙΟΝ ΚΑΤΑ ΜΑΡΚΟΝ,—
(as in A and C, and the other older uncials): *never* τελοc.
But here is a Scribe who first copies the *liturgical* note τελοc,
—and then volunteers the *critical* observation that "in some
copies of S. Mark's Gospel the Evangelist proceeds no further!" A more extraordinary corroboration of the view
which I am endeavouring to recommend to the reader's
acceptance, I really cannot imagine. Why, the ancient
Copyist actually comes back, in order to assure me that
the suggestion which I have been already offering in explanation of the difficulty, is the true one!

5. I am not about to abuse the reader's patience with
a prolonged enumeration of the many additional conspiring
circumstances,—insignificant in themselves and confessedly
unimportant when considered singly, but of which the cumulative force is unquestionably great,—which an examination of 99 MSS. of the Gospels brought to light[m]. Enough
has been said already to shew,

(1st.) That it must have been a customary thing, at
a very remote age, to write the word τελοc against S. Mark
xvi. 8, even when the same note was withheld from the
close of almost every other ecclesiastical lection in the
Gospel.

(2ndly.) That this word, or rather note, which no doubt

[m] (1) In Evan. 282 (written A.D. 1176),—a codex which *has been* adapted to
Lectionary purposes,—the sign τελ° and ϛ, strange to say, *is inserted into the
body of the Text, only at S. Mark* xv. 47 *and* xvi. 8.

(2) Evan. 268, (a truly superb MS., evidently left unfinished, the pictures
of the Evangelists only sketched in ink,) was never prepared for Lectionary
purposes; which makes it the more remarkable that, between ἐφοβοῦντο γάρ
and ἀναστάς, should be found inserted into the body of the text, τὲ. in gold.

(3) I have often met with copies of S. Matthew's, or of S. Luke's, or of
S. John's Gospel, unfurnished with a subscription in which τέλος occurs: but
scarcely ever have I seen an instance of a Codex where the Gospel *according
to S. Mark* was one of two, or of three from which it was wanting; much less
where it stood alone in that respect. On the other hand, in the following
Codices,—Evan. 10: 22: 30: 293,—S. Mark's is *the only Gospel of the Four*
which is furnished with the subscription, + τέλος τοῦ κατὰ Μάρκον εὐαγγελίου ∴
or simply + τέλος + ... In Evan. 282, S. Matthew's Gospel shares this
peculiarity with S. Mark's.

was originally written as a liturgical memorandum in the margin, became at a very early period incorporated with the text; where, retaining neither its use nor its significancy, it was liable to misconception, and may have easily come to be fatally misunderstood.

And although these two facts certainly prove nothing in and by themselves, yet, when brought close alongside of the problem which has to be solved, their significancy becomes immediately apparent: for,

(3rdly.) As a matter of fact, there are found to have existed before the time of Eusebius, copies of S. Mark's Gospel which *did* come to an end at this very place. Now, that *the Evangelist* left off there, no one can believe[n]. *Why*, then, did *the Scribe* leave off? But the Reader is already in possession of the reason why. A sufficient explanation of the difficulty has been elicited from the very MSS. themselves. And surely when, suspended to an old chest which has been locked up for ages, a key is still hanging which fits the lock exactly and enables men to open the chest with ease, they are at liberty to assume that the key *belongs* to the lock; is, in fact, the only instrument by which the chest may lawfully be opened.

XI. And now, in conclusion, I propose that we summon back our original Witness, and invite him to syllable his evidence afresh, in order that we may ascertain if perchance it affords any countenance whatever to the view which I have been advocating. Possible at least it is that in the Patristic record that copies of S. Mark's Gospel were anciently defective from the 8th verse onwards *some* vestige may be discoverable of the forgotten truth. Now, it has been already fully shewn that it is a mistake to introduce into this discussion any other name but that of Eusebius[o]. Do, then, the terms in which *Eusebius* alludes to this matter lend us any assistance? Let us have the original indictment read over to us once more: and *this* time we are bound to listen to every word of it with the utmost possible attention.

---

[n] "Nemini in mentem venire potest Marcum narrationis suae filum ineptissime abrupisse verbis—ἐφοβοῦντο γάρ."—Griesbach *Comment. Crit.* (ii. 197.) So, in fact, *uno ore* all the Critics.   [o] Chap. V.

XI.]   *resyllable his evidence.*   313

1. A problem is proposed for solution. "There are two ways of solving it," (Eusebius begins) :—ὁ μὲν γὰρ [τὸ κεφάλαιον αὐτὸ] τὴν τοῦτο φάσκουσαν περικοπὴν ἀθετῶν, εἴποι ἂν μὴ ἐν ἅπασιν αὐτὴν φέρεσθαι τοῖς ἀντιγράφοις τοῦ κατὰ Μάρκον εὐαγγελίου· τὰ γοῦν ἀκριβῆ τῶν ἀντιγράφων τὸ τέλος περιγράφει τῆς κατὰ τὸν Μάρκον ἱστορίας ἐν τοῖς λόγοις κ. τ. λ. οἷς ἐπιλέγει, " καὶ οὐδενὶ οὐδὲν εἶπον, ἐφοβοῦντο γάρ." Ἐν τούτῳ σχεδὸν ἐν ἅπασι τοῖς ἀντιγράφοις τοῦ κατά Μαρκον εὐαγγελίου περιγέγραπται τὸ τέλος.... Let us halt here for one moment.

2. Surely, a new and unexpected light already begins to dawn upon this subject! How is it that we paid so little attention before to the terms in which this ancient Father delivers his evidence, that we overlooked the import of an expression of his which from the first must have struck us as peculiar, but which *now* we perceive to be of paramount significancy? Eusebius is pointing out that *one* way for a man (so minded) to get rid of the apparent inconsistency between S. Mark xvi. 9 and S. Matth. xxviii. 1, would be for him to reject the entire " Ecclesiastical Lection[q]" in which S. Mark xvi. 9 occurs. Any one adopting this course, (he proceeds ; and it is much to be noted that Eusebius is throughout delivering the imaginary sentiments of another,—not his own :) Such an one (he says) "will say that it is *not met with in all* the copies of S. Mark's Gospel. The accurate copies, at all events,"—and then follows an expression in which this ancient Critic is observed ingeniously to accommodate his language to the phenomenon which he has to describe, so as covertly to insinuate something else. Eusebius employs an idiom (it is found elsewhere in his writings) sufficiently colourless to have hitherto failed to arouse attention; but of which it is impossible to overlook the actual design and import, after all that has gone before. He clearly *recognises the very phenomenon to which I have been calling*

---

[q] τὴν τοῦτο φάσκουσαν περικοπήν. The antecedent phrase, (τὸ κεφάλαιον αὐτό,) I suspect must be an explanatory gloss.

attention within the last two pages, and which I need not further insist upon or explain : viz. that *the words* το τέλος *were* in some very ancient (" *the accurate*") copies *found written after* ἐφοβοῦντο γάρ : although to an unsuspicious reader the expression which he uses may well seem to denote nothing more than that the second Gospel *generally came to an end* there.

3. And now it is time to direct attention to the important bearing of the foregoing remark on the main point at issue. The true import of what Eusebius has delivered, and which has at last been ascertained, will be observed really to set his evidence in a novel and unsuspected light. From the days of Jerome, it has been customary to assume that Eusebius roundly states that, in his time *almost all the Greek copies* were without our "last Twelve Verses" of S. Mark's Gospel[r] : whereas Eusebius really *does nowhere say so*. He expresses himself enigmatically, resorting to a somewhat unusual phrase[s] which perhaps admits of no exact English counterpart : but what he says clearly amounts to no more than this,—that "*the accurate* copies, at the words ἐφοβοῦντο γάρ, circumscribe THE END (το τέλος) of Mark's narrative :" that *there*, " in almost all the Copies of the Gospel according to Mark, is circumscribed THE END." He says no more. He does not say that *there* " is circumscribed *the Gospel.*" As for the twelve verses which follow, he merely declares that they were " *not met with in all* the copies ;" i.e. that *some* copies did not contain them. But this, so far from being

[r] " This then is clear," (is Dr. Tregelles' comment,) " that the greater part of the Greek copies had not the verses in question."—*Printed Text*, p. 247.

[s] Observe, the peculiarity of the expression in this place of Eusebius consists entirely in his introduction of the words τὸ τέλος. Had he merely said τὰ ἀκριβῆ τῶν ἀντιγράφων τὸ εὐαγγέλιον κατὰ Μάρκον περιγράφει ἐν τοῖς λόγοις κ. τ. λ. ..... Ἐν τούτῳ γὰρ σχεδὸν ἐν ἅπασι τοῖς ἀντιγράφοις περιγέγραπται τὸ κατὰ Μάρκον εὐαγγέλιον,—there would have been nothing extraordinary in the mode of expression. We should have been reminded of such places as the following in the writings of Eusebius himself:—'Ο Κλήμης ... εἰς τὴν Κομόδου τελευτὴν περιγράφει τοὺς χρόνους, (*Hist. Eccl.* lib. vi. c. 6.)—'Ιππόλυτος ... ἐπὶ τὸ πρῶτον ἔτος αὐτοκράτορος 'Αλεξάνδρου τοὺς χρόνους περιγράφει, (*Ibid.* c. 22. See the note of Valesius on the place.)—Or this, referred to by Stephanus (*in voce*),—'Ενὸς δ' ἔτι μνησθεὶς περιγράψω τὸν λόγον, (*Praep. Evang.* lib. vi. c. 10, [p. 280 c, *ed.* 1628].) But the substitution of τὸ τέλος for τὸ εὐαγγέλιον wants explaining ; and can be only satisfactorily explained in one way.

a startling statement, is no more than what Codd. B and א in themselves are sufficient to establish. In other words, Eusebius, (whose testimony on this subject as it is commonly understood is so extravagant [see above, p. 48-9,] as to carry with it its own sufficient refutation,) is found to bear consistent testimony to the two following modest propositions; which, however, are not adduced by him as reasons for rejecting S. Mark xvi. 9—20, but only as samples of *what might be urged* by one desirous of shelving a difficulty suggested by their contents;—

(1st.) That from *some* ancient copies of S. Mark's Gospel these last Twelve Verses were away.

(2nd.) That in *almost all* the copies,—(whether mutilated or not, he does not state,)—the words το τελοc were found immediately after ver. 8; which, (he seems to hint,) let those who please accept as evidence that there also is *the end of the Gospel.*

4. But I cannot dismiss the testimony of Eusebius until I have recorded my own entire conviction that this Father is no more an original authority here than Jerome, or Hesychius, or Victor. He is evidently adopting the language of some more ancient writer than himself. I observe that he introduces the problem with the remark that what follows is one of the questions " for ever mooted by every body [u]." I suspect (with Matthaei, [*suprà*, p. 66,]) that *Origen* is the *true* author of all this confusion. He certainly relates of himself that among his voluminous exegetical writings was *a treatise on S. Mark's Gospel* [x]. To Origen's works, Eusebius, (his

---

[u] Πάρειμι νῦν ... πρὸς τῷ τέλει τῶν αὐτῶν πάντοτε τοῖς πᾶσι ζητούμενα [sic].—Mai, vol. iv. p. 255.

[x] " Consentit autem nobis ad *tractatum quem fecimus de scripturâ* Marci."—Origen. (*Opp.* iii. 929 B.) *Tractat.* xxxv. *in Matth.* [I owe the reference to Cave (i. 118.) It seems to have escaped the vigilance of Huet.]—This serves to explain why Victor of Antioch's Catena on S. Mark was sometimes anciently attributed to Origen: as in Paris Cod. 703, [*olim* 2330, 958, and 1048 : also 18.] where is read (at fol. 247), Ὠριγένους πρόλογος εἰς τὴν ἑρμηνείαν τοῦ κατὰ Μάρκον εὐαγγελίου. Note, that Reg. 937 is but a (xvi[th] cent.) counterpart of the preceding; which has been transcribed [xviii[th] cent.] in Par. Suppl. Graec. 40.

Possevinus [*Apparat. Sac.* ii. 542,] (quoted by Huet, *Origeniana*, p. 274) states that there is in the Library of C. C. C., Oxford, a Commentary on S. Mark's Gospel by Origen. The source of this misstatement has been acutely

apologist and admirer,) is known to have habitually resorted; and, like many others, to have derived not a few of his notions from that fervid and acute, but most erratic intellect. Origen's writings in short, seem to have been the source of much, if not most of the mistaken Criticism of Antiquity. (The reader is reminded of what has been offered above at p. 96-7). And this would not be the first occasion on which it would appear that when an ancient Writer speaks of "*the accurate copies,*" what he actually *means* is *the text of Scripture which was employed or approved by Origen* [z]. The more attentively the language of Eusebius in this place is considered, the more firmly (it is thought) will the suspicion be entertained that he is here only reproducing the sentiments of another person. But, however this may be, it is at least certain that the precise meaning of what he says, has been hitherto generally overlooked. He certainly does *not* say, as Jerome, from his loose translation of the passage [a], evidently imagined,—"*om-*

---

pointed out to me by the Rev. W. R. Churton. James, in his "Ecloga Oxonio-Cantabrig.," (1600, lib. i. p. 49,) mentions "*Homiliae Origenis super Evangelio Marcae,* Stabat ad monumentum."—Read instead, (with Rev. H. O. Coxe, "Cat. Codd. MSS. C. C. C.;" [N°. 142, 4,]) as follows:—"Origenis presb. Hom. in istud Johannis, *Maria stabat ad monumentum,*" &c. But what actually led Possevinus astray, I perceive, was James's consummation of his own blunder in lib. ii. p. 49,—which Possevinus has simply appropriated.

[z] So Chrysostom, speaking of the reading Βηθαβαρά.

Origen (iv. 140) says that not only σχεδὸν ἐν πᾶσι τοῖς ἀντιγράφοις, but also that *apud Heracleonem,* (who wrote within 50 years of S. John's death,) he found Βηθανία written in S. John i. 28. Moved by *geographical* considerations, however, (as he explains,) for Βηθανία, Origen proposes to read Βηθαβαρά.—Chrysostom (viii. 96 D), after noticing the former reading, declares,—ὅσα δὲ τῶν ἀντιγράφων ἀκριβέστερον ἔχει ἐν Βηθαβαρά φησιν: but he goes on *to reproduce Origen's reasoning;*—thereby betraying himself.—The author of the Catena in Matth. (Cramer, i. 190-1) simply reproduces Chrysostom:—χρὴ δὲ γινώσκειν ὅτι τὰ ἀκριβῆ τῶν ἀντιγράφων ἐν Βηθαβαρὰ περιέχει. And so, other Scholia; until at last what was only due to the mistaken assiduity of Origen, became generally received as the reading of the "more accurate copies."

A scholium on S. Luke xxiv. 13, in like manner, declares that the true reading of that place is not "60" but "160,"—οὕτως γὰρ τὰ ἀκριβῆ περιέχει, καὶ ἡ Ὠριγένους τῆς ἀληθείας βεβαίωσις. Accordingly, *Eusebius* also reads the place in the same erroneous way.

[a] Jerome says of himself (*Opp.* vii. 537,)—" Non digne Græca in Latinum transfero: aut Græcos lege (si ejusdem linguae habes scientiam) aut si tantum

nibus Graeciae libris pene hoc capitulum in fine non habentibus:" but only,—"*non in omnibus Evangelii exemplaribus hoc capitulum inveniri;*" which is an entirely different thing. Eusebius adds,—" Accuratiora saltem exemplaria FINEM narrationis secundum Marcum circumscribunt in verbis ἐφοβοῦντο γάρ;"—and, " In hoc, fere in omnibus exemplaribus Evangelii secundum Marcum, FINEM circumscribi."—The point, however, of greatest interest is, that Eusebius here calls attention to the prevalence in MSS. of his time of the very *liturgical peculiarity* which plainly supplies the one true solution of the problem under discussion. His testimony is a marvellous corroboration of what we learn from Cod. 22, (see above, p. 230,) and, rightly understood, does not go a whit beyond it.

5. What wonder that Hesychius, because he adopted blindly what he found in Eusebius, should at once betray his author and exactly miss the point of what his author says? Τὸ κατὰ Μάρκον εὐαγγέλιον (so he writes) μέχρι τοῦ " ἐφοβοῦντο γάρ," ἔχει τὸ τέλος [b].

6. This may suffice concerning the testimony of Eusebius. —It will be understood that I suppose Origen to have fallen in with one or more copies of S. Mark's Gospel which exhibited *the Liturgical hint*, (τὸ τέλος,) conspicuously written against S. Mark xvi. 9. Such a copy may, or may not, have there terminated abruptly. I suspect however that it *did*. Origen at all events, (*more suo*,) will have remarked on the phenomenon before him; and Eusebius will have adopted his remarks,—as the heralds say, " with *a difference*,"—simply because they suited his purpose, and seemed to him ingenious and interesting.

7. For the copy in question,—(like *that* other copy of S. Mark from which the Peshito translation was made, and in which τὸ τέλος most inopportunely occurs at chap. xiv. 41,)—will have become the progenitor of several other copies (as Codd. B and ℵ); and some of these, it is pretty evident, were familiarly known to Eusebius.

Latinus es, noli de gratuito munere judicare, et, ut vulgare proverbium est: *equi dentes inspicere donati.*

[b] See above, pp. 57-9: also Appendix (C), § 2.

8. Let it however be clearly borne in mind that nothing of all this is in the least degree essential to my argument. Eusebius, (for aught that I know or care,) may be *solely* responsible for every word that he has delivered concerning S. Mark xvi. 9—20. Every link in my argument will remain undisturbed, and the conclusion will be still precisely the same, whether the mistaken Criticism before us originated with another or with himself.

XII. But *why*, (it may reasonably be asked,)—*Why* should there have been anything exceptional in the way of indicating the end of this particular Lection? *Why* should τέλος be so constantly found written after S. Mark xvi. 8?

I answer,—I suppose it was because the Lections which respectively ended and began at that place were so many, and were Lections of such unusual importance. Thus,— (1) On the 2nd Sunday after Easter, (κυριακή γ' τῶν μυροφόρων, as it was called,) at the Liturgy, was read S. Mark xv. 43 to xvi. 8; and (2) on the same day at Matins, (by the Melchite Syrian Christians as well as by the Greeks [d],) S. Mark xvi. 9—20. The severance, therefore, was at ver. 8. (3) In certain of the Syrian Churches the liturgical section for Easter Day was S. Mark xvi. 2—8 [e]: in the Churches of the Jacobite, or Monophysite Christians, the Eucharistic lesson for Easter-Day was ver. 1—8 [f]. (4) The second matin lesson of the Resurrection (xvi. 1—8) also ends,—and (5) the third (xvi. 9—20) begins, at the same place: and these two Gospels (both in the Greek and in the Syrian Churches) were in constant use not only at Easter, but throughout the year . (6) *That* same third matin lesson of the Resurrection was also the Lesson at Matins on Ascension-Day; as well in the Syrian [h] as in the Greek [i] Churches. (7) With

---

[d] R. Payne Smith's *Catal.* p. 116.   [e] See Adler's N. T. *Verss. Syrr.*, p. 70.   [f] R. Payne Smith's *Catal.* p. 146.

[h] R. Payne Smith's *Catal.* p. 117.

[i] Accordingly, in Cod. Evan. 266 (= Paris Reg. 67) is read, at S. Mark xvi. 8 (*fol.* 125), as follows:—ἐφοβοῦντο γάρ. [then, *rubro*,] τέλος τοῦ B' ἑωθίνου, καὶ τῆς κυριακῆς τῶν μυροφόρων. ἀρχή. [then the text:] 'Αναστάς κ.τ.λ. . . . After ver. 20, (at *fol.* 126 of the same Codex) is found the following concluding rubric:—τέλος τοῦ Γ' ἑωθίνου εὐαγγελίου.

In the same place, (viz. at the end of S. Mark's Gospel,) is found in another

the Monophysite Christians, the lection "feriae tertiae in albis, ad primam vesperam," (i.e. for the Tuesday in Easter-Week) was S. Mark xv. 37—xvi. 8: and (8) on the same day, at Matins, ch. xvi. 9—18 [k].—During eighteen weeks after Easter therefore, *the only parts* of S. Mark's Gospel publicly read were (*a*) the last thirteen [ch. xv. 43—xvi. 8], and (*b*) "*the last twelve*" [ch. xvi. 9—20] verses. Can it be deemed a strange thing that it should have been found *indispensable* to mark, with altogether exceptional emphasis, —to make it unmistakably plain,—where the former Lection came to an end, and where the latter Lection began [1]?

XIII. One more circumstance, and but one, remains to be adverted to in the way of evidence; and one more suggestion to be offered. The circumstance is familiar indeed to all, but its bearing on the present discussion has never been pointed out. I allude to the fact that anciently, in copies of the fourfold Gospel, *the Gospel according to S. Mark frequently stood last.*

This is memorably the case in respect of the Codex Bezae [vi]: more memorably yet, in respect of the Gothic version of Ulphilas (A.D. 360): in both of which MSS., the order of the Gospels is (1) S. Matthew, (2) S. John, (3) S. Luke, (4) S. Mark. This is in fact *the usual Western order.* Accordingly it is thus that the Gospels stand in the Codd. Vercellensis (*a*), Veronensis (*b*), Palatinus (*e*), Brixianus (*f*) of the old Latin version. But this order is not *exclusively* Western. It is found in Cod. 309. It is also observed in Matthaei's Codd. 13, 14, (which last is *our* Evan. 256), at Moscow. And

---

Codex (Evan. 7 = Paris Reg. 71,) the following rubric:—τέλος τοῦ τρίτου τοῦ ἑωθίνου, καὶ τοῦ ὄρθρου τῆς ἀναλήψεως.   [k] R. Payne Smith's *Catal.* p. 146.

[1] Cod. 27 (xi) is not provided with any lectionary apparatus, and is written continuously throughout: and yet at S. Mark xvi. 9 a fresh paragraph is observed to commence.

Not dissimilar is the phenomenon recorded in respect of some copies of the Armenian version. "The Armenian, in the edition of Zohrab, separates the concluding 12 verses from the rest of the Gospel ... Many of the oldest MSS., after the words ἐφοβοῦντο γάρ, put the final Εὐαγγέλιον κατὰ Μάρκον, and then give the additional verses with a new superscription." (Tregelles, *Printed Text*, p. 253)... We are now in a position to *understand* the Armenian evidence, which has been described above, at p. 36, as well as to estimate its exact value.

in the same order Eusebius and others of the ancients [m] are occasionally observed to refer to the four Gospels,—which induces a suspicion that they were not unfamiliar with it. Nor is this all. In Codd. 19 and 90 the Gospel according to S. Mark stands last; though in the former of these the order of the three antecedent Gospels is (1) S. John, (2) S. Matthew, (3) S. Luke *; in the latter, (1) S. John, (2) S. Luke, (3) S. Matthew. What need of many words to explain the bearing of these facts on the present discussion? Of course it will have *sometimes* happened that S. Mark xvi. 8 came to be written *at the bottom of the left hand page* of a MS.[n] And we have but to suppose that in the case of one such Codex the next leaf, which would have been *the last*, was missing, —(*the very thing which has happened in respect of one of the Codices at Moscow*[o])—and what else *could* result when a copyist reached the words,

ΕΦΟΒΟΥΝΤΟ ΓΑΡ. ΤΟ ΤΕΛΟC

but the very phenomenon which has exercised critics so sorely and which gives rise to the whole of the present discussion? The copyist will have brought S. Mark's Gospel to an end there, *of course*. What else could he possibly do? . . . . Somewhat less excusably was our learned countryman Mill betrayed into the statement, (inadvertently adopted by Wetstein, Griesbach, and Tischendorf,) that "the last verse of S. John's Gospel *is omitted* in Cod. 63:" the truth of the matter being (as Mr. Scrivener has lately proved) that *the*

[m] Euseb. apud Mai, iv. p. 264 = p. 287. Again at p. 289-90.—So also the author of the 2nd Homily on the Resurr. (Greg. Nyss. *Opp.* iii. 411-2.)— And see the third of the fragments ascribed to Polycarp. *Patres Apostol.*, (ed. Jacobson) ii. p. 515.

* I believe this will be found to be the *invariable* order of the Gospels *in the Lectionaries*.

[n] This is the case for instance in Evan. 15 (= Reg. 64). See *fol.* 98 *b*.

[o] I allude of course to Matthaei's Cod. g. (See the note in his *N. T.* vol. ix. p. 228.) Whether or no the learned critic was right in his conjecture "aliquot folia excidisse," matters nothing. *The left hand page ends at the words* ἐφοβοῦντο γάρ. Now, if τέλος had followed, how obvious would have been the inference that the Gospel itself of S. Mark had come to an end there!

Note, that in the Codex Bezæ (D), S. Mark's Gospel ends at ver. 15: in the Gothic Codex Argenteus, at ver. 11. The Codex Vercell. (*a*) proves to be imperfect from ch. xv. 15; Cod. Veron. (*b*) from xiii. 24; Cod. Brix.(*f*) from xiv. 70.

last leaf of Cod. 63,—on which the last verse of S. John's Gospel was demonstrably once written,—*has been lost* q.

XIV. To sum up.

1. It will be perceived that I suppose the omission of "the last Twelve Verses" of S. Mark's Gospel to have originated in a sheer error and misconception on the part of some very ancient Copyist. He *saw* το τελος written after ver. 8: he *assumed* that it was the Subscription, or at least that it denoted "the End," *of the Gospel*.

2. Whether certain ancient Critics, because it was acceptable to them, were not found to promote this mistake,—it is useless to inquire. That there may have arisen some old harmonizer of the Gospels, who, (in the words of Eusebius,) was disposed to "regard what followed as superfluous from its seeming inconsistency with the testimony of the other Evangelists [r];"—and that in this way the error became propagated;—is likely enough. But an error it most certainly was: and to that *error*, the *accident* described in the last preceding paragraph *would have* very materially conduced, and it may have very easily done so.

3. I request however that it may be observed that the "accident" is not *needed* in order to account for the "error." The mere presence of το τελος at ver. 8, so near the end of the Gospel, would be quite enough to occasion it. And we have seen that in very ancient times the word τελος frequently *did* occur in an altogether exceptional manner in that very place. Moreover, we have ascertained that its meaning was *not understood* by the transcribers of ancient MSS.

4. And will any one venture to maintain that it is to him a thing incredible that an intelligent copyist of the iii[rd] century, because he read the words το τελος at S. Mark xvi. 8, can have been beguiled thereby into the supposition that those words indicated "the End" of *S. Mark's Gospel?*— Shall I be told that, even if *one* can have so entirely overlooked the meaning of the liturgical sign as to suffer it to insinuate itself into his text , it is nevertheless so im-

---

[q] Scrivener, *Coll. Cod. Sin.* p. lix.   [r] See p. 227.

probable as to pass all credence that *another* can have supposed that it designated *the termination of the Gospel* of the second Evangelist?—For all reply, I take leave to point out that Scholz, and Tischendorf, and Tregelles, and Mai and the rest of the Critics have, *one and all, without exception, misunderstood the same word occurring in the same place, and in precisely the same way*.

Yes. The forgotten inadvertence of a solitary Scribe in the *second* or *third* century has been, *in the nineteenth*, deliberately reproduced, adopted, and stereotyped by every Critic and every Editor of the New Testament in turn.

What wonder,—(I propose the question deliberately,)— What wonder that an ancient Copyist should have been misled by a phenomenon which in our own days is observed to have imposed upon two generations of professed Biblical Critics discussing this very textual problem, and therefore fully on their guard against delusion[t]? To this hour, the illustrious Editors of the text of the Gospels are clearly, one and all, labouring under the grave error of supposing that "ἐφοβοῦντο γάρ + τέλος,"—(for which they are so careful to refer us to "Cod. 22,")—is an indication that *there*, by rights, comes *the "END" of the Gospel according to S. Mark*. They have failed to perceive that ΤΕΛCC in that place is only *a liturgical sign*,—the same with which (in its contracted form) they are sufficiently familiar; and that it serves no other purpose whatever, but to mark that *there* a famous *Ecclesiastical Lection* comes to an end.

With a few pages of summary, we may now bring this long disquisition to an end.

---

[t] So Scholz:—" hic [sc. 22] post γὰρ + τέλος; dein atramento rubro," &c. —Tischendorf,—" Testantur scholia . . . *Marci Evangelium* . . . versu 9 *finem habuisse*. Ita, ut de 30 fere Codd. certe tres videamus, 22 habet: ἐφοβουντο γαρ + τελος. εν τισι," &c.—Tregelles appeals to copies, "sometimes with τέλος interposed after ver. 8," (p. 254.)—Mai (iv. 256) in the same spirit remarks,— " Codex Vaticano-palatinus [220], ex quo Eusebium producimus, post octavum versum *habet quidem* vocem τέλος, ut alibi interdum observatum fuit; *sed tamen* ibidem eadem manu subscribitur incrementum cum progredientibus sectionum notis."

CHAPTER XII.

GENERAL REVIEW OF THE QUESTION: SUMMARY OF THE EVIDENCE; AND CONCLUSION OF THE WHOLE SUBJECT.

This discussion narrowed to a single issue (324).—That S. Mark's Gospel was imperfect from the very first, a thing altogether incredible (326):—But that at some very remote period Copies have suffered mutilation, a supposition probable in the highest degree (328).— Consequences of this admission (332).— Parting words (334)

THIS Inquiry has at last reached its close. The problem was fully explained at the outset [a]. All the known evidence has since been produced [b], every Witness examined [c]. Counsel has been heard on both sides. A just Sentence will assuredly follow. But it may not be improper that I should in conclusion ask leave to direct attention to the *single issue* which has to be decided, and which has been strangely thrust into the background and practically kept out of sight, by those who have preceded me in this Investigation. The case stands simply thus:—

It being freely admitted that, in the beginning of the iv[th] century, there must have existed Copies of the Gospels in which the last chapter of S. Mark extended no further than ver. 8, the Question arises,—*How is this phenomenon to be accounted for?* ... The problem is not only highly interesting and strictly legitimate, but it is even inevitable. In the immediately preceding chapter, I have endeavoured to solve it, and I believe in a wholly unsuspected way.

But the most recent Editors of the text of the New Testament, declining to entertain so much as the *possibility* that certain copies of the second Gospel *had experienced mutilation in very early times* in respect of these Twelve concluding

---

[a] Chap. I. and II.   Chap. IV, VI–X.   Chap. III, V, and VIII.

Verses, have chosen to occupy themselves rather with conjectures as to how it may have happened that S. Mark's Gospel *was without a conclusion from the very first.* Persuaded that no more probable account is to be given of the phenomenon than that *the Evangelist himself put forth a Gospel which* (for some unexplained reason) *terminated abruptly at the words* ἐφοβοῦντο γάρ (chap. xvi. 8),—they have unhappily seen fit to illustrate the liveliness of this conviction of theirs, by presenting the world with his Gospel mutilated in this particular way. Practically, therefore, the question has been reduced to the following single issue :—Whether of the two suppositions which follow is the more reasonable:

First,—That the Gospel according to S. Mark, as it left the hands of its inspired Author, *was in this imperfect or unfinished state;* ending abruptly at (what we call now) the 8th verse of the last chapter :—of which solemn circumstance, at the end of eighteen centuries, Cod. B and Cod. ℵ are the alone surviving Manuscript witnesses? . . . or,

Secondly,—That certain copies of S. Mark's Gospel *having suffered mutilation* in respect of their Twelve concluding Verses in the post-Apostolic age, Cod. B and Cod. ℵ are the only examples of MSS. so mutilated which are known to exist at the present day?

I. Editors who adopt the former hypothesis, are observed (*a*) to sever the Verses in question from their context [d] :—(*b*) to introduce after ver. 8, the subscription " ΚΑΤΑ ΜΑΡΚΟΝ [e] :" —(*c*) to shut up verses 9—20 within brackets [f]. Regarding them as "no integral part of the Gospel [g]," — "as an authentic anonymous addition to what Mark himself wrote down [h]," — a " remarkable Fragment," "placed as a completion of the Gospel in very early times [i] ;"—they consider themselves at liberty to go on to suggest that "the Evangelist may have been interrupted in his work :" at any rate,

---

[d] Tischendorf, Tregelles, Alford.

[e] Tregelles, Alford. [f] Alford.

[g] " Hæc non a Marco scripta esse argumentis probatur idoneis."—See the rest of Tischendorf's verdict, *suprà,* p. 10; and opposite, p. 245.

[h] Tregelles' *Account of the Printed Text,* p. 259.

[i] Alford's *New Test.* vol. i. *Proleg.* [p. 38] and p. 437.

that "something may have occurred, (as the death of
S. Peter,) to cause him to leave it unfinished [k]." But "the
most probable supposition" (we are assured) "is, that *the
last leaf of the original Gospel was torn away* [l]."

We listen with astonishment; contenting ourselves with
modestly suggesting that surely it will be time to conjecture
why S. Mark's Gospel was left by its Divinely inspired
Author in an unfinished state, when the fact has been established that it probably *was* so left. In the meantime, we
request to be furnished with some evidence of *that fact*.

But not a particle of Evidence is forthcoming. It is not
even pretended that any such evidence exists. Instead, we
are magisterially informed by "the first Biblical Critic in
Europe,"—(I desire to speak of him with gratitude and respect, but S. Mark's Gospel is a vast deal more precious to
me than Dr. Tischendorf's reputation,)—that "*a healthy piety
reclaims against the endeavours of those who are for palming
off as Mark's what the Evangelist is so plainly shewn* [where?]
to have known nothing at all about [m]." In the meanwhile, it
is assumed to be a more reasonable supposition,—(a) That
S. Mark published an imperfect Gospel; and that the Twelve
Verses with which his Gospel concludes were the fabrication of a subsequent age; than,—(β) That some ancient
Scribe having with design or by accident left out these
Twelve concluding Verses, copies of the second Gospel so
mutilated become multiplied, and in the beginning of the
iv[th] century existed in considerable numbers.

And yet it is notorious that very soon after the Apostolic
age, liberties precisely of this kind were freely taken with
the text of the New Testament. Origen (A.D. 185—254)
complains of the licentious tampering with the Scriptures
which prevailed in his day. "Men add to them," (he says)
"or *leave out,*—as seems good to themselves [n]." Dionysius
of Corinth, yet earlier, (A.D. 168—176) remarks that it was
no wonder his own writings were added to and *taken from,*
seeing that men presumed to deprave the Word of GOD

---

[k] So Norton, Tregelles, and others.

[l] This suggestion, which was originally Griesbach's, is found in Alford's *New Test.* vol. i. p. 433, (*ed.* 1868.)—See above, p. 12. The italics are not mine.

[m] Vide *suprà*, p. 10.   [n] *Opp.* vol. iii. p. 671.

in the same manner [o]. Irenæus, his contemporary, (living within seventy years of S. John's death,) complains of a corrupted Text [p]. We are able to go back yet half a century, and the depravations of Holy Writ become avowed and flagrant [q]. A competent authority has declared it "no less true to fact than paradoxical in sound, that *the worst corruptions to which the New Testament has been ever subjected* originated within a hundred years after it was composed [r]." Above all, it is demonstrable that Cod. B and Cod. ℵ abound in unwarrantable omissions very like the present[*]; omissions which only do not provoke the same amount of attention because they are of less moment. One such extraordinary depravation of the Text, *in which they also stand alone among MSS* and to which their patrons are observed to appeal with triumphant complacency, has been already made the subject of distinct investigation. I am much mistaken if it has not been shewn in my VIIth chapter, that the omission of the words ἐν Ἐφέσῳ from Ephes. i. 1, is just as unauthorized,—quite as serious a blemish,—as the suppression of S. Mark xvi. 9—20.

Now, in the face of facts like these, and in the absence of *any Evidence whatever* to prove that S. Mark's Gospel was imperfect from the first,—I submit that an hypothesis so violent and improbable, as well as so wholly uncalled for, is simply undeserving of serious attention. For,

(1st.) It is plain from internal considerations that the improbability of the hypothesis is excessive; "the contents of these Verses being such as to preclude the supposition that they were the work of a post-Apostolic period. The very difficulties which they present afford the strongest presumption of their genuineness." No fabricator of a supplement to S. Mark's Gospel would have ventured on introducing so many minute *seeming* discrepancies: and cer-

---

[o] Eusebius *Eccl. Hist.* iv. 23. Consider Rev. xxii. 18, 19.

[p] Note the remarkable adjuration of Irenæus, *Opp.* i. 821, preserved by Eusebius, *lib.* v. 20.—See Scrivener's *Introduction*, p. 383-4. Consider the attestations at the end of the account of Polycarp's martyrdom, *PP. App.* ii. 614-6.

[q] Allusion is made to the Gnostics Basilides and Valentinus; especially to the work of Marcion.

[r] Scrivener's *Introduction*, pp. 381—391.   [*] See Chap. VI.

tainly "his contemporaries would not have accepted and transmitted such an addition," if he had. It has also been shewn at great length that the Internal Evidence for the genuineness of these Verses is overwhelmingly strong [s]. But,

(2nd.) Even external Evidence is not wanting. It has been acutely pointed out long since, that the absence of a vast assemblage of various Readings in this place, is, in itself, a convincing argument that we have here to do with no spurious appendage to the Gospel [t]. Were this a deservedly suspected passage, it must have shared the fate of all other deservedly (or undeservedly) suspected passages. It never could have come to pass that the various Readings which these Twelve Verses exhibit would be *considerably fewer* than those which attach to the last twelve verses of any of the other three Gospels.

(3rd.) And then surely, if the original Gospel of S. Mark had been such an incomplete work as is feigned, the fact would have been notorious from the first, and must needs have become the subject of general comment [u]. It may be regarded as certain that so extraordinary a circumstance would have been largely remarked upon by the Ancients, and that evidence of the fact would have survived in a hundred quarters. It is, I repeat, simply incredible that Tradition would have proved so utterly neglectful of her office as to remain *quite* silent on such a subject, if the facts had been such as are imagined. Either Papias, or else John the Presbyter,—Justin Martyr, or Hegesippus, or one of the "Seniores apud Irenæum,"—Clemens Alexandrinus, or Tertullian, or Hippolytus,—if not Origen, yet at least Eusebius,—if not

---

[s] Chap. IX.

[t] "Ad defendendum hunc locum in primis etiam valet mirus Codicum consensus in vocabulis et loquendi formulis singulis. Nam in locis παρεγγράπτοις, etiam multo brevioribus, quo plures sunt Codices, eo plures quoque sunt varietates. Comparetur modo Act. xv. 18, Matth. viii. 13, et loca similia."— C. F. Matthaei's *Nov. Test.* (1788) vol. ii. p. 271.

[u] Speaking of the abrupt termination of the second Gospel at ver. 8, Dr. Tregelles asks,—"Would this have been transmitted as a fact by good witnesses, if there had not been real grounds for regarding it to be true?"— (*Printed Text*, p. 257.) Certainly not, we answer. But *where* are the "good witnesses" of the "transmitted fact?" *There is not so much as one.*

Eusebius, yet certainly Jerome,—*some* early Writer, I say, must *certainly* have recorded the tradition that S. Mark's Gospel, as it came from the hands of its inspired author, was an incomplete or unfinished work. The silence of the Ancients, joined to the inherent improbability of the conjecture,—(*that* silence so profound, *this* improbability so gross!) —is enough, I submit, *in the entire absence of Evidence on the other side*, to establish *the very contradictory* of the alternative which recent Critics are so strenuous in recommending to our acceptance.

(4th.) But on the contrary. We have indirect yet convincing testimony that the *oldest* copies of all *did contain* the Verses in question : while so far are any of the Writers just now enumerated from recording that these verses were absent from the early copies, that five out of those ten Fathers actually quote, or else refer to the verses in question in a way which shews that in their day they were the recognised termination of S. Mark's Gospel [y].

We consider ourselves at liberty, therefore, to turn our attention to the rival alternative. Our astonishment is even excessive that it should have been seriously expected of us that we could accept without Proof of any sort,—without a particle of Evidence, external, internal, or even traditional, —the extravagant hypothesis that S. Mark put forth an unfinished Gospel; when the obvious and easy alternative solicits us, of supposing,

II. That, at some period *subsequent* to the time of the Evangelist, certain copies of S. Mark's Gospel suffered that mutilation in respect of their last Twelve Verses of which we meet with *no trace whatever, no record of any sort, until the beginning of the fourth century*.

(i.) And the facts which *now* meet us on the very threshold, are in a manner conclusive: for if Papias and Justin Martyr [A.D. 150] do not refer to, yet certainly Irenæus [A.D. 185] and Hippolytus [A.D. 190—227] *distinctly quote* Six out of the Twelve suspected Verses,—which are also met with in the two oldest Syriac Versions, as well as in the old Latin Translation. Now the latest of these authorities is

[y] See Chap. III.

earlier by full a hundred years than *the earliest record* that the verses in question were ever absent from ancient MSS. At the eighth Council of Carthage, (as Cyprian relates,) [A.D. 256] Vincentius a Thiberi, one of the eighty-seven African Bishops there assembled, quoted the 17th verse in the presence of the Council.

(ii.) Nor is this all [z]. Besides the Gothic and Egyptian versions in the iv[th] century; besides Ambrose, Cyril of Alexandria, Jerome, and Augustine in the vth, to say nothing of Codices A and C;—the Lectionary of the Church universal, *probably from the second century of our æra*, is found to bestow its solemn and emphatic sanction on *every one* of these Twelve Verses. They are met with *in every MS. of the Gospels in existence*, uncial and cursive,—*except two*[a]; they are found *in every Version*; and are contained besides in *every known Lectionary*, where they are appointed to be read at Easter and on Ascension Day[b].

(iii.) Early in the iv[th] century, however, we are encountered by a famous place in the writings of Eusebius [A.D. 300—340], who, (as I have elsewhere explained,) is the *only* Father who delivers any independent testimony on this subject at all. What he says has been strangely misrepresented. It is simply as follows:—

(a) One, "Marinus," is introduced *quoting this part of S. Mark's Gospel without suspicion*, and enquiring, How its opening statement is to be reconciled with S. Matth. xxviii. 1 ? Eusebius, in reply, points out that a man whose only object was to get rid of the difficulty, might adopt the expedient of saying that this last section of S. Mark's Gospel "is *not found in all the copies:*" (μὴ ἐν ἁπᾶσι φέρεσθαι.) Declining, however, to act thus presumptuously in respect of anything claiming to be a part of Evangelical Scripture, (οὐδ' ὁτιοῦν τολμῶν ἀθετεῖν τῶν ὁπωσοῦν ἐν τῇ τῶν εὐαγγελίων γραφῇ φερομένων,)—he *adopts the hypothesis that the text is genuine*. Καὶ δὴ τοῦδε τοῦ μέρους συγχωρουμένου εἶναι ἀληθοῦς, he begins: and he enters at once without hesitation on an ela-

---

[z] See above, Chap. III. and IV.

[a] "Habent periocham hanc Codices Græci, si unum B excipias, omnes." (Scholz, adopting the statement of Griesbach.)—See above, p. 70.

[b] See above, Chap. X.

borate discussion to shew *how the two places may be reconciled*[d]. What there is in this to countenance the notion that in the opinion of Eusebius "the Gospel according to S. Mark originally terminated at the 8th verse of the last chapter,"— I profess myself unable to discover. I draw from his words the precisely opposite inference. It is not even clear to me that the Verses in dispute were absent from the copy which Eusebius habitually employed. He certainly quotes one of those verses once and again[e]. On the other hand, the express statement of Victor of Antioch [A.D. 450?] *that he knew of the mutilation, but had ascertained by Critical research the genuineness of this Section of Scripture, and had adopted the Text of the authentic "Palestinian" Copy*[f],— is more than enough to outweigh the faint presumption created (as some might think) by the words of Eusebius, that his own copy was without it. And yet, as already stated, there is nothing whatever to shew that Eusebius himself deliberately rejected the last Twelve Verses of S. Mark's Gospel. Still less does that Father anywhere say, or even hint, that in his judgment the original Text of S. Mark was without them. If he may be judged by his words, *he accepted them as genuine :* for (what is at least certain) he argues upon their contents at great length, and apparently without misgiving.

(*b*) It is high time however to point out that, after all, the question to be decided is, not *what Eusebius thought* on this subject, but what is historically probable. As a plain matter of fact, the sum of the Patristic Evidence against these Verses is the hypothetical suggestion of Eusebius already quoted; which, (after a fashion well understood by those who have given any attention to these studies), is observed to have rapidly propagated itself in the congenial soil of the vth century. And even if it could be shewn that Eusebius deliberately *rejected* this portion of Scripture, (which has never been done,)—yet, inasmuch as it may be regarded as certain that those famous codices in the library of his friend

---

[d] See   also Appendix (B).
[e] The reader is referred to Mai's *Nov. PP. Bibl.* vol. iv. p. 262, line 12 : p. 264 line 28 : p. 301, line 3—4, and 6—8.
[f]   also Appendix (E).

XII.]   *of S. Mark's Gospel suffered mutilation.*   331

Pamphilus at Cæsarea, to which the ancients habitually referred, *recognised it as genuine* ,—the only sufferer from such a conflict of evidence would surely be Eusebius himself: (not *S. Mark*, I say, but *Eusebius :*) who is observed to employ an incorrect text of Scripture on many other occasions; and must (in such case) be held to have been unduly partial to copies of S. Mark in the mutilated condition of Cod. B or Cod. ℵ. His words were translated by Jerome[h]; adopted by Hesychius[i]; referred to by Victor[j]; reproduced "with a difference" in more than one ancient scholion[k]. But they are found to have died away into a very faint echo when Euthymius Zigabenus[l] rehearsed them for the last time in his Commentary on the Gospels, A.D. 1116. Exaggerated and misunderstood, behold them resuscitated after an interval of seven centuries by Griesbach, and Tischendorf, and Tregelles and the rest: again destined to fall into a congenial, though very differently prepared soil; and again destined (I venture to predict) to die out and soon to be forgotten for ever.

(iv.) After all that has gone before, our two oldest Codices (Cod. B and Cod. ℵ) which alone witness to the truth of Eusebius' testimony as to the state of certain copies of the Gospels in his own day, need not detain us long. They are thought to be as old as the iv[th] century: they are certainly without the concluding section of S. Mark's Gospel. But it may not be forgotten that both Codices alike are disfigured throughout by errors, interpolations and omissions without number; that their testimony is continually divergent; and that it often happens that where they both agree they are both demonstrably in error[m]. Moreover, it is a highly significant circumstance that the Vatican Codex (B), which is the more ancient of the two, exhibits *a vacant column* at the end of S. Mark's Gospel,—*the only vacant column in the whole codex :* whereby it is shewn that the Copyist was aware of the existence of the Twelve concluding Verses of S. Mark's Gospel, even though he left them out : while the

[h] P. 51-7.   [i] P. 57-9.
[j] P. 59—66.   [k] P. 114—125.   [l] P. 68-9.
[m] Chap. VI.

original Scribe of the Codex Sinaiticus (א) is declared by Tischendorf to have actually *omitted the concluding verse of S. John's Gospel,*—in which unenviable peculiarity it stands alone among MSS.º

(I.) And thus we are brought back to the point from which we started. We are reminded that the one thing to be accounted for is *the mutilated condition of certain copies of S. Mark's Gospel in the beginning of the fourth century;* of which, Cod. B and Cod. א are the two solitary surviving specimens,—Eusebius, the one historical witness. We have to decide, I mean, between the *evidence* for this *fact,*—(namely, that within the first two centuries and a-half of our æra, the Gospel according to S. Mark *suffered mutilation;*)—and the *reasonableness* of the other *opinion,* namely, that S. Mark's *original autograph* extended no farther than ch. xvi. 8. All is reduced to this one issue; and unless any are prepared to prove that the Twelve familiar Verses (ver. 9 to ver. 20) with which S. Mark ends his Gospel *cannot* be his,—(I have proved on the contrary that he must needs be thought to have written them[p],)—I submit that it is simply irrational to persist in asseverating that the reason why those verses are not found in our two Codexes of the iv[th] century must be because they did not exist in the original autograph of the Evangelist. What else is this but to set unsupported *opinion,* or rather unreasoning *prejudice,* before the *historical evidence* of a *fact?* The assumption is not only gratuitous, arbitrary, groundless; but it is discountenanced by the evidence of MSS., of Versions, of Fathers, (Versions and Fathers much older than the iv[th] century:) is rendered in the highest degree improbable by every internal, every

---

º Will it be believed that Tischendorf accordingly rejects *that* verse also as spurious; and brings the fourth Gospel to an end at ver. 24, as he brings the second Gospel to an end at ver. 8? For my own part,—having (through the kindness and liberality of the Keeper of the Imperial MSS. at S. Petersburg, aided by the good offices of my friend, the Rev. A. S. Thompson, Chaplain at S. Petersburg,) obtained a photograph of the last page of S. John's Gospel,—I must be allowed altogether to call in question the accuracy of Dr. Tischendorf's judgment in this particular. The utmost which can be allowed is that the Scribe may have possibly changed his pen, or been called away from his task, just before bringing the fourth Gospel to a close.   [p] See Chap. IX.

XII.] *the re-establishment of S. Mark xvi. 9—20.* 333

external consideration: is condemned by *the deliberate judgment of the universal Church,*—which, in its corporate capacity, for eighteen hundred years, in all places, has not only solemnly accepted the last Twelve Verses of S. Mark's Gospel as genuine, but has even singled them out for special honour q.

(II.) Let it be asked in conclusion,—(for this prolonged discussion is now happily at an end,)—Are any inconveniences likely to result from a frank and loyal admission, (*in the absence of any Evidence whatever to the contrary,*) that doubtless the last Twelve Verses of S. Mark's Gospel are just as worthy of acceptation as the rest? It might reasonably be supposed, from the strenuous earnestness with which the rejection of these Verses is generally advocated, that some considerations must surely be assignable why the opinion of their genuineness ought on no account to be entertained. Do any such reasons exist? Are any inconveniences whatever likely to supervene?

No reasons whatever are assignable, I reply; neither are there *any* inconvenient consequences of any sort to be anticipated,—except indeed to the Critics: to whom, it must be confessed, the result proves damaging enough.

It will only follow,

(1st) That Cod. B and Cod. א must be henceforth allowed to be *in one more serious particular* untrustworthy and erring witnesses. They have been convicted, in fact, of bearing false witness in respect of S. Mark xvi. 9—20, where their evidence had been hitherto reckoned upon with the most undoubting confidence.

(2ndly) That the critical statements of recent Editors, and indeed the remarks of Critics generally, in respect of S. Mark xvi. 9—20, will have to undergo serious revision: in every important particular, will have to be unconditionally withdrawn.

(3rdly) That, in all future critical editions of the New Testament, these "Twelve Verses" will have to be restored to their rightful honours: never more appearing disfigured with brackets, encumbered with doubts, banished from their

q Chapter X.

context, or molested with notes of suspicion. On the contrary. A few words of caution against the resuscitation of what has been proved to be a "vulgar error," will have henceforth to be introduced *in memoriam rei*.

(4thly) Lastly, men must be no longer taught to look with distrust on this precious part of the Deposit; and encouraged to dispute the Divine sayings which it contains on the plea that *perhaps* they may not be Divine, after all; for that *probably* the entire section is not genuine. They must be assured, on the contrary, that these Twelve Verses are wholly undistinguishable in respect of genuineness from the rest of the Gospel of S. Mark; and it may not be amiss to remind them the Creed called the "Athanasian" speaks no other language than that employed by the Divine Author of our Religion and Object of our Faith. The Church warns her children against the peril incurred by as many as wilfully reject the Truth, in no other language but that of the Great Head of the Church. No person may presume to speak disparagingly of S. Mark xvi. 16, any more.

(III.) Whether,—after the foregoing exposure of a very prevalent and highly popular, but at the same time most calamitous misapprehension,—it will not become necessary for Editors of the Text of the New Testament to reconsider their conclusions in countless other places :—whether they must not be required to review their method, and to remodel their text throughout, now that they have been shewn the insecurity of the foundation on which they have so confidently builded, and been forced to reverse their verdict in respect of a place of Scripture where at least they supposed themselves impregnable ;—I forbear at this time to inquire.

Enough to have demonstrated, as I claim to have now done, that *not a particle of doubt*, that *not an atom of suspicion*, attaches to "THE LAST TWELVE VERSES OF THE GOSPEL ACCORDING TO S. MARK."

ΤΟ ΤΕΛΟC.

APPENDIX.

CONTENTS.

(A.) *On the Importance of attending to* Patristic Citations *of Scripture.—The correct Text of* S. LUKE ii. 14, *established* 337

(B.) EUSEBIUS "ad Marinum" *concerning the reconcilement of* S. Mark xvi. 9 *with* S. Matthew xxviii. 1 . . 345

(C.) *Proof that* HESYCHIUS *is a Copyist only in what he says concerning the end of S. Mark's Gospel* 347

(D.) *Some account of* VICTOR OF ANTIOCH's *Commentary on S. Mark's Gospel ; together with a descriptive enumeration of MSS. which contain Victor's Work* 349

(E.) *Text of the concluding Scholion of* VICTOR OF ANTIOCH's *Commentary on S. Mark's Gospel ; in which Victor bears emphatic Testimony to the Genuineness of "the last Twelve Verses"* 368

(F.) *On the relative antiquity of the* CODEX VATICANUS (B), *and the* CODEX SINAITICUS (א) 371

(G.) *On the (so-called)* "AMMONIAN" SECTIONS *and on the* EUSEBIAN CANONS : *a Dissertation. With some account of the Tables of Reference occasionally found in Greek and Syriac MSS.* 375

(H.) *On the Interpolation of the Text of* Codex B *and* Codex א, *at* S. Matthew xxvii. 48 *or* 49 393

POSTSCRIPT 399

L'ENVOY. 404

APPENDIX (A).

On the importance of attending to Patristic Citations of Scripture.— The correct Text of S. LUKE ii. 14, *established.*

IN Chapter III. the importance of attending to Patristic citations of Scripture has been largely insisted upon. The controverted reading of S. Luke ii. 14 supplies an apt illustration of the position there maintained, viz. that this subject has not hitherto engaged nearly as much attention as it deserves.

I. Instead of ἐν ἀνθρώποις εὐδοκία, (which is the reading of the "Textus receptus,") Lachmann, Tischendorf, Tregelles and Alford present us with ἐν ἀνθρώποις εὐδοκίας. Their authority for this reading is the consentient testimony of THE FOUR OLDEST MSS. WHICH CONTAIN S. Luke ii. 14 (viz. B, ℵ, A, D) : THE LATIN VERSIONS generally (*"in hominibus bonae voluntatis"*) ; and THE GOTHIC. Against these are to be set, COD. A (in the Hymn at the end of the Psalms); ALL THE OTHER UNCIALS; together with EVERY KNOWN CURSIVE MS. ; and EVERY OTHER ANCIENT VERSION in existence.

So far, the evidence of mere Antiquity may be supposed to preponderate in favour of εὐδοκίας : though no judicious Critic, it is thought, should hesitate in deciding in favour of εὐδοκία, even upon the evidence already adduced. The advocates of the popular Theory ask,—But *why* should the four oldest MSS., together with the Latin and the Gothic Versions, conspire in reading εὐδοκίας, if εὐδοκία be right? That question shall be resolved by-and-by. Let them in the mean time tell us, if they can,—How is it credible that, in such a matter as this, *every other MS. and every other Version in the world* should read εὐδοκία, if εὐδοκία be wrong? But the evidence of Antiquity has not yet been nearly cited. I proceed to set it forth in detail.

It is found then, that whereas εὐδοκίας is read by none, εὐδοκία is read by all the following Fathers:—

(1) ORIGEN, in three places of his writings, [i. 374 D: ii. 714 B: iv. 15 B,—A.D. 240.]

(2) The APOSTOLICAL CONSTITUTIONS, twice, [vii. 47: viii. 12 *ad fin.*,—IIIrd cent.]

(3) METHODIUS, [*Galland.* iii. 809 B,—A.D. 290.]

(4) EUSEBIUS, twice, [*Dem. Ev.* 163 c: 342 B,—A.D. 320.]

(5) APHRAATES THE PERSIAN, (for whose name [*suprà*, pp. 26-7] that of 'Jacobus of Nisibis' has been erroneously substituted), twice, [i. 180 and 385,—A.D. 337.]

(6) TITUS OF BOSTRA, twice, [*in loc.*, but especially in S. Luc. xix. 29 (*Cramer*, ii. 141, *line* 20),—A.D. 350.]

(7) GREGORY OF NAZIANZUS, [i. 845 c,—A.D. 360.]

(8) CYRIL OF JERUSALEM, [A.D. 370], as will be found explained below.

(9) EPIPHANIUS, [i. 154 D,—A.D. 375.]

(10) CHRYSOSTOM, four times, [vii. 311 B: 674 c: viii. 85 c: xi. 374 B expressly,—A.D. 400.]

(11) CYRIL OF ALEXANDRIA, in three places, [*Comm. on S. Luke*, pp. 12 and 16. Also *Opp.* ii. 593 A: vi. 398 c,—A.D. 420.]

(12) THEODORET, [*in Coloss.* i. 20,—A.D. 430.]

(13) THEODOTUS OF ANCYRA, [*Galland.* x. 446 B,—A.D. 430.]

(14) PROCLUS, Abp. of Constantinople, [*Gall.* x. 629 A,—A.D. 434.]

To which may be added the evidence of

(15) COSMAS INDICOPLEUSTES, four times repeated, [*Coll. Nov. PP.*, (Montfaucon,) ii. 152 A, 160 D, 247 E, 269 c,—A.D. 535.]

(16) EULOGIUS, Abp. of Alexandria, [*Gall.* xii. 308 E,—A.D. 581.]

(17) ANDREAS of Crete, twice, [*Gall.* xiii. 100 D, 123 c, —A.D. 635.]

Now, when it is considered that these seventeen Fathers of the Church[a] all concur in exhibiting the Angelic Hymn *as our own Textus Receptus exhibits it*,—(viz. ἐν ἀνθρώποις εὐδοκία,)—*who* does not see that the four oldest uncial autho-

---

[a] Pseudo-Gregory Thaumaturgus, Pseudo-Basil, Patricius, and Marius Mercator, are designedly omitted in this enumeration.

rities for εὐδοκίας are hopelessly outvoted by authorities yet older than themselves? Here is, to all intents and purposes, a record of what was once found in *two Codices of the* iii*rd century;* in *nine of the* iv*th;* in *three of the* v*th;*—added to the testimony of the two Syriac, the Egyptian, the Ethiopic, and the Armenian versions. In this instance therefore the evidence of Antiquity is even overwhelming.

Most decisive of all, perhaps, is the fact this was the form in which *the Churches of the East* preserved the Angelic Hymn in their private, as well as their solemn public Devotions. Take it, from a document of the vth century:—

ΔΟΞΑ ΕΝ ΥΨΙCΤΟΙC ΘΕΩ
ΚΑΙ ΕΠΙ ΓΗC ΕΙΡΗΝΗ
ΕΝ ΑΝΘΡΩΠΟΙC ΕΥΔΟΚΙΑ [b].

But the text of this Hymn, as a Liturgical document, at a yet earlier period is unequivocally established by the combined testimony of the Apostolical Constitutions (already quoted,) and of Chrysostom, who says expressly:—Εὐχαριστοῦντες λέγομεν, Δόξα ἐν ὑψίστοις Θεῷ, καὶ ἐπὶ γῆς εἰρήνη, ἐν ἀνθρώποις εὐδοκία. [*Opp.* xi. 347 B.] Now this incontestably proves that *the Church's established way of reciting the Angelic Hymn in the* iv*th century* was in conformity with the reading of the Textus Receptus. And this fact infinitely outweighs the evidence of any extant MSS. which can be named: for it is the consentient evidence of hundreds,—or rather of thousands of copies of the Gospels of a date anterior to A.D. 400, which have long since perished.

To insist upon this, however, is not at all my present purpose. About the true reading of S. Luke ii. 14, (which is *not* the reading of Lachmann, Tischendorf, Tregelles, Alford,) there is clearly no longer any room for doubt. It is perhaps one of the best established readings in the whole compass of the New Testament. My sole object is to call attention to the two following facts:—

(1) That *the four oldest Codices which contain S. Luke* ii. 14 (B, ℵ, A, D, A.D. 320—520), and two of the oldest Versions, conspire in exhibiting the Angelic Hymn *incorrectly.*

(2) That we are indebted to *fourteen of the Fathers* (A.D.

[b] Codex A,—ὕμνος ἑωθινός at the end of the Psalms.

240—434), and to the rest of the ancient Versions, for the true reading of that memorable place of Scripture.

II. Against all this, it is urged (by Tischendorf) that,—

1. IRENÆUS sides with the oldest uncials.—Now, the Greek of the place referred to is lost. A Latin translation is all that survives. According to *that* evidence, Irenæus, having quoted the place in conformity with the Vulgate reading (iii. c. x. § 41,—" *Gloria in excelsis* DEO *et in terra pax hominibus bonae voluntatis,*") presently adds,—" In eo quod dicunt, *Gloria in altissimis* DEO *et in terra pax*, eum qui sit altissimorum, hoc est, supercaelestium factor et eorum, quae super terram omnium conditor, his sermonibus glorificaverunt; qui suo plasmati, hoc est hominibus suam benignitatem salutis de caelo misit." (*ed.* Stieren, i. 459).—But it must suffice to point out (1) that these words really prove nothing: and (2) that it would be very unsafe to build upon them, even if they did; since (3) it is plain that the Latin translator exhibits the place in the Latin form most familiar to himself: (consider his substitution of "excelsis" for "altissimis.")

2. Next, ORIGEN is claimed on the same side, on the strength of the following passage in (Jerome's version of) his lost Homilies on S. Luke:—" Si scriptum esset, *Super terram pax*, et hucusque esset finita sententia, recte quaestio nasceretur. Nunc vero in eo quod additum est, hoc est, quod post pacem dicitur, *In hominibus bonae voluntatis*, solvit quaestionem. Pax enim quam non dat Dominus super terram, non est pax bonae voluntatis." (*Opp.* iii. p. 946.) "From this," (says Tischendorf, who is followed by Tregelles,) " it is plain that Origen regarded εὐδοκίας as the true reading; not εὐδοκία—which is now thrice found in his Greek writings."—But,

Is one here more struck with the unfairness of the Critic, or with the feebleness of his reasoning? For,—(to say nothing of the insecurity of building on a Latin Translation[c],

---

[c] The old Latin Interpreter of Origen's Commentary on S. Matthew seems to have found in Origen's text a quotation from S. Luke ii. 14 which is *not represented in the extant Greek text of Origen*. Here also we are presented with "hominibus *bonae voluntatis.*" (*Opp.* iii. 537 c). We can say nothing to such second-hand evidence.

especially in such a matter as the present,)—How can testimony like this be considered to outweigh the three distinct places in the original writings of this Father, where he reads not εὐδοκίας but εὐδοκία? Again. Why is a doubt insinuated concerning the trustworthiness of those three places, ("ut *nunc* reperitur,") where there really is *no* doubt? How is Truth ever to be attained if investigations like the present are to be conducted in the spirit of an eager partisan, instead of with the calm gravity of an impartial judge?

But I may as well state plainly that the context of the passage above quoted shews that Tischendorf's proposed inference is inadmissible. Origen is supposing some one to ask the following question:—"Since Angels on the night when CHRIST was born proclaimed 'on earth *Peace*,'—why does our SAVIOUR say, 'I am *not* come to send Peace upon earth, but a sword?.... Consider," (he proceeds) "whether the answer may not be this:"—and then comes the extract given above. Origen, (to express oneself with colloquial truthfulness,) is *at his old tricks*. He is evidently acquainted with the reading εὐδοκίας: and because it enables him to offer (what appears to him) an ingenious solution of a certain problem, he adopts it for the nonce: his proposal to take the words εἰρήνη εὐδοκίας together, being simply preposterous,—as no one ever knew better than Origen himself[d].

3. Lastly, CYRIL OF JERUSALEM is invariably cited by the latest Critics as favouring the reading εὐδοκίας. Those learned persons have evidently overlooked the candid acknowledgment of De Touttée, Cyril's editor, (p. 180, cf. bottom of p. 162,) that though *the MSS. of Cyril* exhibit εὐδοκία, yet in his editorial capacity he had ventured *to print* εὐδοκίας. This therefore is one more Patristic attestation to the trustworthiness of the Textus Receptus in respect of S. Luke ii. 14, which has been hitherto unaccountably lost sight of by Critics. (May I, without offence, remind Editors of Scripture that instead of *copying*, they ought in every instance *to verify* their references?)

[d] Consider his exactly similar method concerning Eph. i. 1. (*Suprà*, pp. 96—99.)

III. The history of this corruption of the Text is not hard to discover. It is interesting and instructive also.

(1.) In the immediately post-Apostolic age,—if not earlier still,—some Copyist will have omitted the ἐν before ἀνθρώποις. The resemblance of the letters and the similarity of the sound (ΕΝ, ΑΝ,) misled him:—

ΕΝΑΝΘΡΩΠΟΙC

Every one must see at a glance how easily the thing may have happened. (It is in fact precisely what *has* happened in Acts iv. 12; where, for ἐν ἀνθρώποις, D and a few cursive MSS. read ἀνθρώποις,—being countenanced therein by the Latin Versions generally, and by them only.)

(2.) The result however—(δόξα ἐν ὑψίστοις Θεῷ καὶ ἐπὶ γῆς εἰρήνη ἀνθρώποις εὐδοκία)—was obviously an impossible sentence. It could not be allowed to stand. And yet it was not by any means clear what had happened to it. In order, as it seems, to *force* a meaning into the words, some one with the best intentions will have put the sign of the genitive (c) at the end of εὐδοκία. The copy so depraved was destined to play an important part; for it became the fontal source of the Latin Version, which exhibits the place thus:—*Gloria in altissimis Deo, et in terra pax hominibus bonae voluntatis.* .... It is evident, by the way, (if the quotation from Irenæus, given above, is to be depended upon,) that Irenæus must have so read the place: (viz. εἰρήνη ἀνθρώποις εὐδοκίας.)

(3.) To restore the preposition (ἐν) which had been accidentally thrust out, and to obliterate the sign of the genitive (c) which had been without authority thrust in, was an obvious proceeding. Accordingly, *every Greek Evangelium extant* exhibits ἐν ἀνθρώποις: while *all but four* (B, ℵ, A, D) read εὐδοκία. In like manner, into some MSS. of the Vulgate (e.g. the *Cod. Amiatinus,*) the preposition ("in") has found its way back; but the genitive ("bonae voluntatis") has never been rectified in a single copy of the Latin version.—The Gothic represents a copy which exhibited ἐν ἀνθρώποις εὐδοκίας [e].

---

[e] From the Rev. Professor Bosworth.

The consequence is that a well-nigh untranslatable expression retains its place in the Vulgate to the present hour. Whether (with Origen) we connect εὐδοκίας with εἰρήνη,—or (with the moderns) we propose to understand "men of good pleasure,"—the result is still the same. The harmony of the three-part Anthem which the Angels sang on the night of the Nativity is hopelessly marred, and an unintelligible discord substituted in its place. Logic, Divinity, Documents are here all at one. The reading of Stephens is unquestionably correct. The reading of the latest Editors is as certainly corrupt. This is a case therefore where the value of Patristic testimony becomes strikingly apparent. It affords also one more crucial proof of the essential hollowness of the theory on which it has been recently proposed by Lachmann, Tischendorf, Tregelles and the rest to reconstruct the text of the New Testament.

To some, it may perhaps seem unreasonable that so many words should be devoted to the establishment of the text of a single place of Scripture,—depending, as that text does, on the insertion or the omission of a single letter. I am content to ask in reply,—*What* is important, if not the utterance of Heaven, when, at the laying of the corner-stone of the New Creation, "the Morning Stars sang together, and all the Sons of God shouted for joy?"

IV. Only one word in conclusion.

Whenever the time comes for the Church of England to revise her Authorized Version (1611), it will become necessary that she should in the first instance instruct some of the more judicious and learned of her sons carefully to revise the Greek Text of Stephens (1550). Men require to know precisely what it is they have to translate before they can pretend to translate it. As for supposing that Scholars who have been appointed to revise *a Translation* are competent at a moment's notice, as every fresh difficulty presents itself, to develope the skill requisite for revising *the original Text*,—it is clearly nothing else but supposing that experts in one Science can at pleasure shew themselves proficients in another.

But it so happens that, on the present occasion, that *other*

Science is one of exceeding difficulty. Revisionists *here* will find it necessary altogether to disabuse their minds of the *Theory* of Textual Criticism which is at present the dominant and the popular one,—and of which I have made it my business to expose the fallaciousness, in respect of several crucial texts, in the course of the present work.

I cannot so far forget the unhappy circumstances of the times as to close this note without the further suggestion, (sure therein of the approval of our trans-Atlantic brethren,) that, for a Revision of the Authorized Version to enjoy the confidence of the Nation, and to procure for itself acceptance at the hands of the Church,—it will be found necessary that the work should be confided to *Churchmen.* The Church may never abdicate her function of being "a Witness and a Keeper of Holy Writ." Neither can she, without flagrant inconsistency and scandalous consequence, ally herself in the work of Revision with the Sects. Least of all may she associate with herself in the sacred undertaking an Unitarian Teacher,—one who avowedly [see the letter of "One of the Revisionists, G. V. S.," in the "Times" of July 11, 1870] denies the eternal GODhead of her LORD. That the individual alluded to has shewn any peculiar aptitude for the work of a Revisionist; or that he is a famous Scholar; or that he can boast of acquaintance with any of the less familiar departments of Sacred Learning; is not even pretended. (It would matter nothing if the reverse were the case.) What else, then, is this but to offer a deliberate insult to the Majesty of Heaven in the Divine Person of Him who is alike the Object of the Everlasting Gospel, and its Author?

APPENDIX (B).

EUSEBIUS "ad Marinum" *concerning the reconcilement of* S. Mark xvi. 9 *with* S. Matthew xxviii. 1.

SUBJOINED is the original text of EUSEBIUS, taken from the "Quæstiones ad Marinum" published by Card. Mai, in his "Nova Patrum Bibliotheca" (Romae, 1847,) vol. iv. pp. 255-7.

I. Πῶς παρὰ μὲν τῷ Ματθαίῳ ὄψε σαββάτων φαίνεται ἐγεγερμένος ὁ Σωτήρ, παρὰ δὲ τῷ Μάρκῳ πρωῒ τῇ μιᾷ τῶν σαββάτων.

Τούτου διττὴ ἂν εἴη ἡ λύσις· ὁ μὲν γὰρ [τὸ κεφάλαιον αὐτὸ *del.**?*] τὴν τοῦτο φάσκουσαν περικοπὴν ἀθετῶν, εἴποι ἂν μὴ ἐν ἅπασιν αὐτὴν φέρεσθαι τοῖς ἀντιγράφοις τοῦ κατὰ Μάρκον εὐαγγελίου· τὰ γοῦν ἀκριβῆ τῶν ἀντιγράφων τὸ τέλος περιγράφει τῆς κατὰ τὸν Μάρκον ἱστορίας ἐν τοῖς λόγοις τοῦ ὀφθέντος νεανίσκου ταῖς γυναιξὶ καὶ εἰρηκότος αὐταῖς " μὴ φοβεῖσθε, Ἰησοῦν ζητεῖτε τὸν Ναζαρηνόν." καὶ τοῖς ἑξῆς, οἷς ἐπιλέγει· " καὶ ἀκούσασαι ἔφυγον, καὶ οὐδενὶ οὐδὲν εἶπον, ἐφοβοῦντο γάρ." Ἐν τούτῳ γὰρ σχεδὸν ἐν ἅπασι τοῖς ἀντιγράφοις τοῦ κατὰ Μάρκον εὐαγγελίου περιγέγραπται τὸ τέλος· τὰ δὲ ἑξῆς σπανίως ἔν τισιν ἀλλ' οὐκ ἐν πᾶσι φερόμενα περιττὰ ἂν εἴη, καὶ μάλιστα εἴπερ ἔχοιεν ἀντιλογίαν τῇ τῶν λοιπῶν εὐαγγελιστῶν μαρτυρίᾳ. ταῦτα μὲν οὖν εἴποι ἄν τις παραιτούμενος καὶ πάντῃ ἀναιρῶν περιττὸν ἐρώτημα. Ἄλλος δέ τις οὐδ' ὁτιοῦν τολμῶν ἀθετεῖν τῶν ὁπωσοῦν ἐν τῇ τῶν εὐαγγελίων γραφῇ φερομένων, διπλῆν εἶναί φησι τὴν ἀνάγνωσιν, ὡς καὶ ἐν ἑτέροις πολλοῖς, ἑκατέραν τε παραδεκτέαν ὑπάρχειν, τῷ μὴ μᾶλλον ταύτην ἐκείνης, ἢ ἐκείνην ταύτης, παρὰ τοῖς πιστοῖς καὶ εὐλαβέσιν ἐγκρίνεσθαι.

Καὶ δὴ τοῦδε τοῦ μέρους συγχωρουμένου εἶναι ἀληθοῦς, προσήκει τὸν νοῦν διερμηνεύειν τοῦ ἀναγνώσματος· εἰ γοῦν διέλοιμεν τὴν τοῦ λόγου διάνοιαν, οὐκ ἂν εὕροιμεν αὐτὴν ἐναντίαν τοῖς παρὰ τοῦ Ματθαίου ὀψὲ σαββάτων ἐγηγέρθαι τὸν Σωτῆρα λελεγμένοις· τὸ γὰρ " ἀναστὰς δὲ πρωῒ τῇ μιᾷ

* *Vid. suprà*, p. 233.

τοῦ σαββάτου" κατὰ τὸν Μάρκον, μετὰ διαστολῆς ἀναγνωσόμεθα· καὶ μετὰ τὸ ἀναστὰς δὲ, ὑποστίξομεν*· καὶ τὴν διάνοιαν ἀφορίζομεν τῶν ἑξῆς ἐπιλεγομένων. εἶτα τὸ μὲν ἀναστὰς ἂν, ἐπὶ τὴν παρὰ τῷ Ματθαίῳ ὀψέ σαββάτων. τότε γὰρ ἐγήγερτο· τὸ δὲ ἑξῆς ἑτέρας ὂν διανοίας ὑποστατικὸν, συνάψωμεν τοῖς ἐπιλεγομένοις· πρωῒ γὰρ τῇ μιᾷ τοῦ σαββάτου ἐφάνη Μαρίᾳ τῇ Μαγδαληνῇ. τοῦτο γοῦν ἐδήλωσε καὶ ὁ Ἰωάννης πρωῒ καὶ αὐτὸς τῇ μιᾷ τοῦ σαββάτου ὦφθαι αὐτὸν τῇ Μαγδαληνῇ μαρτυρήσας. οὕτως οὖν καὶ παρὰ τῷ Μάρκῳ πρωῒ ἐφάνη αὐτῇ. οὐ πρωῒ ἀναστὰς, ἀλλὰ πολὺ πρότερον κατὰ τὸν Ματθαῖον ὀψὲ τοῦ σαββάτου. τότε γὰρ ἀναστὰς ἐφάνη τῇ Μαρίᾳ, οὐ τότε ἀλλὰ πρωῒ. ὡς παρίστασθαι ἐν τούτοις καιροὺς δύο. τὸν μὲν γὰρ τῆς ἀναστάσεως τὸν ὀψὲ τοῦ σαββάτου, τὸν δὲ τῆς τοῦ Σωτῆρος ἐπιφανείας, τὸν πρωῒ, ὃν ἔγραψεν ὁ Μάρκος εἰπὼν (ὃ καὶ μετὰ διαστολῆς ἀναγνωστέον) ἀναστὰς δέ· εἶτα ὑποστίξαντες, τὸ ἑξῆς ῥητέον, πρωῒ τῇ μιᾷ τοῦ σαββάτου ἐφάνη Μαρίᾳ τῇ Μαγδαληνῇ, ἀφ᾽ ἧς ἐκβεβλήκει ἑπτὰ δαιμόνια.

II. Πῶς κατὰ τὸν Ματθαῖον ὀψὲ σαββάτων ἡ Μαγδαληνὴ τεθεαμένη τὴν ἀνάστασιν, κατὰ τὸν Ἰωάννην ἡ αὐτὴ ἑστῶσα κλαίει παρὰ τῷ μνημείῳ τῇ μιᾷ τοῦ σαββάτου.

Οὐδὲν ἂν ζητηθείη κατὰ τοὺς τόπους, εἰ τὸ ὀψὲ σαββάτων μὴ τὴν ἑσπερινὴν ὥραν τὴν μετὰ τὴν ἡμέραν τοῦ σαββάτου λέγεσθαι ὑπολάβοιμεν, ὥς τινες ὑπειλήφασιν, ἀλλὰ τὸ βραδὺ καὶ ὀψὲ τῆς νυκτὸς τῆς μετὰ τὸ σάββατον, κ.τ.λ.

---

* P.S. I avail myself of this blank space to introduce a passage from THEOPHYLACT (A.D. 1077) which should have obtained notice in a much earlier page:—'Ἀναστὰς δὲ ὁ Ἰησοῦς· ἐνταῦθα στίξον, εἶτα εἰπέ· πρωῒ πρώτῃ σαββάτου ἐφάνη Μαρίᾳ τῇ Μαγδαληνῇ. οὐ γὰρ ἀνέστη πρωῒ· (τίς γὰρ οἶδε πότε ἀνέστη;) ἀλλ᾽ ἐφάνη πρωῒ κυριακῇ ἡμέρᾳ (αὕτη γὰρ ἡ πρώτη τοῦ σαββάτου, τουτέστι, τῆς ἑβδομάδος,) ἣν ἄνω ἐκάλεσε μίαν σαββάτων· [*Opp.* vol. i. p. 263 c.]

It must be superfluous to point out that Theophylact also, —like Victor, Jerome, and Hesychius,—is here only reproducing Eusebius.

APPENDIX (C).

Proof that HESYCHIUS *is a copyist only in what he says concerning the end of S. Mark's Gospel.*

§ 1. It was confidently stated above (at p. 58) that HESYCHIUS, discussing the consistency of S. Matthew's ὀψὲ τῶν σαββάτων (chap. xxviii. 1), with the πρωὶ of S. Mark (chap. xvi. 9), is *a copyist* only; and that he copies from the "Quaestiones ad Marinum" of EUSEBIUS. The proof of that statement is subjoined. It should perhaps be explained that the extracts in the right-hand column have been dislocated in order to shew their close resemblance to what is set down in the left-hand column from Eusebius:—

(EUSEBIUS.)

τὸ ὀψὲ σαββάτων μὴ τὴν ἑσπερινὴν ὥραν τὴν μετὰ τὴν ἡμέραν τοῦ σαββάτου λέγεσθαι ὑπολάβοιμεν ....
ἀλλὰ τὸ βραδὺ καὶ ὀψὲ τῆς νυκτός.

οὕτω γὰρ καὶ ὀψὲ τῆς ὥρας εἰώθαμεν λέγειν, καὶ ὀψὲ τοῦ καιροῦ, καὶ ὀψὲ τῆς χρείας· οὐ τὴν ἑσπέραν δηλοῦντες, οὐδὲ τὸν μετὰ ἡλίου δυσμὰς χρόνον, τὸ δὲ σφόδρα βράδιον τούτῳ σημαίνοντες τῷ τρόπῳ·

ὅθεν ὥσπερ διερμηνεύων αὐτὸς ἑαυτὸν ὁ Ματθαῖος μετὰ τὸ ὀψὲ σαββάτων, ἐπήγαγε τῇ ἐπιφωσκούσῃ εἰς μίαν σαββάτων.
Ἔθος δὲ ὅλην τὴν ἑβδομάδα σάββατον καλεῖν.
λέγεται γοῦν παρὰ τοῖς Εὐαγγελισταῖς τῇ μιᾷ τῶν σαββάτων·
ἐν δὲ τῇ συνηθείᾳ, δευτέρα σαββάτων, καί τρίτη σαββάτων.

(EUSEBIUS ad Marinum, *apud* Mai, vol. iv. p. 257-8.)

(HESYCHIUS, or Severus.)

τὸ δὲ ὀψὲ σαββάτων οὐ τὴν ἑσπέραν τὴν μετὰ τὴν δύσιν τοῦ ἡλίου δηλοί. ...
ἀλλὰ .... τὸ βράδιον καὶ πολὺ διεστηκὸς. ...

καὶ γάρ που καὶ οὕτως ἡμῖν σύνηθες λέγειν, ὀψὲ τοῦ καιροῦ παραγέγονας· ὀψὲ τῆς ὥρας, ὀψὲ τῆς χρείας· οὐχὶ τὴν ἑσπέραν, καὶ τὸν μετὰ ἡλίου δυσμὰς χρόνον δηλοῦσιν· ἀλλὰ τὸ βράδιον, ... τὸν τρόπον τοῦτον μηνύουσι.

ὁ Ματθαῖος .... ὥσπερ ἑρμηνεύων ἑαυτὸν, ἐπήγαγε τῇ ἐπιφωσκούσῃ εἰς μίαν σαββάτων.
σάββατον δὲ τὴν πᾶσαν ἑβδομάδα καλεῖν Ἑβραίοις ἔθος.
αὐτίκα γοῦν οἱ εὐαγγελισταὶ τῇ μιᾷ τῶν σαββάτων φασί·
οὕτω δὴ καὶ ἐν τῇ συνηθείᾳ κεκχρήμεθα, δευτέραν σαββάτων, καὶ τρίτην σαββάτων.

(GREG. NYSS. [*vid. supra*, p. 39 to 41.] *Opp.* vol. iii. p. 402.

§ 2. Subjoined, in the right-hand column, is the original text of the passage of HESYCHIUS exhibited in English at p. 57. The intention of setting down the parallel passages from EUSEBIUS, and from VICTOR of Antioch, is in order to shew the sources from which Hesychius obtained his materials,—as explained at p. 58 :—

(EUSEBIUS.)
τὰ γοῦν ἀκριβῆ τῶν ἀντιγράφων τὸ τέλος περιγράφει τῆς κατὰ τὸν Μάρκον ἱστορίας ἐν τοῖς λόγοις κ.τ.λ. οἷς ἐπιλέγει· ... " καὶ οὐδενὶ οὐδὲν, εἶπον, ἐφοβοῦντο γάρ."
(EUSEBIUS ad Marinum, *apud* Mai, iv. p. 255.)

(VICTOR OF ANTIOCH.)
ἐπειδὴ δὲ ἔν τισι ... πρόσκειται ... " Ἀναστὰς" κ. τ. λ. δοκεῖ δὲ τοῦτο διαφωνεῖν τῷ ὑπὸ Ματθαίου εἰρημένῳ. ...

οὕτως ἀναγνωσόμεθα· " ' Ἀναστὰς δέ," καὶ ὑποστίξαντες ἐπάγωμεν, "πρωΐ τῇ μιᾷ τῶν σαββάτων ἐφάνη Μαρίᾳ τῇ Μαγδαληνῇ·" ἵνα τὸ μὲν " ἀναστὰς"—
(VICTOR ANTIOCH., ed. *Cramer*, vol. i. p. 444, line 19 to line 27.)

(HESYCHIUS, or Severus.)
ἐν μὲν οὖν τοῖς ἀκριβεστέροις ἀντιγράφοις τὸ κατὰ Μάρκον εὐαγγέλιον μεχρὶ τοῦ " ἐφοβοῦντο γάρ," ἔχει τὸ τέλος.

ἐν δέ τισι πρόσκειται καὶ ταῦτα. " Ἀναστὰς" κ.τ.λ. τοῦτο δὲ ἐναντίωσίν τινα δοκεῖ ἔχειν πρὸς τὰ ἔμπροσθεν εἰρημένα·
[τῆς γὰρ ὥρας τῆς νυκτὸς ἀγνώστου τυγχανούσης καθ᾽ ἣν ὁ Σωτὴρ ἀνέστη, πῶς ἐνταῦθα ἀναστῆναι " πρωΐ" γέγραπται; ἀλλ᾽ οὐδὲν ἐναντίον φανήσεται τὸ ῥητὸν, εἰ]

μετ᾽ ἐπιστήμης ἀναγνωσόμεθα· καὶ γὰρ ὑποστίξαι δεῖ συνετῶς· " Ἀναστὰς δέ," καὶ οὕτως ἐπαγάγειν, " πρωΐ πρώτῃ σαββάτων ἐφάνη πρῶτον Μαρίᾳ τῇ Μαγδαληνῇ." ἵνα τὸ μὲν " ἀναστὰς"

[ἔχῃ τὴν ἀναφορὰν συμφώνως τῷ Ματθαίῳ, πρὸς τὸν προλαβόντα καιρὸν, τὸ δὲ " πρωΐ" πρὸς τὴν τῆς Μαρίας γενομένην ἐπιφάνειαν ἀποδοθείη.]
(GREG. NYSS. *Opp.* vol. iii. p. 411, B, C, D: which may be also seen in Cramer's *Catenae*, [vol. i. p. 250, line 21 to line 33,] ascribed to "SEVERUS, Archbishop of Antioch," [*Ibid.* p. 243.])

APPENDIX (D).

Some account of VICTOR OF ANTIOCH'S *Commentary on S. Mark's Gospel; together with an enumeration of MSS. which contain Victor's Work.*

"APRÈS avoir examiné avec soin les MSS. de la Bibliothèque du Roi," (says the Père Simon in his *Hist. Crit. du N. T.* p. 79,) "j'ai réconnu que cet ouvrage" (he is speaking of the Commentary on S. Mark's Gospel popularly ascribed to Victor of Antioch,) "n'est ni d'Origéne, ni de Victor d'Antioche, ni de Cyrille, ni d'aucun autre auteur en particulier. C'est un recueil de plusieurs Pères, dont on a marqué les noms dans quelques exemplaires; et si ces noms ne se trouvent point dans d'autres, cela est assez ordinaire à ces recueils, qu'on appelle *chaînes*[a]." It will be seen from the notices of the work in question already offered, (*suprà*, p. 59 to p. 65,) that I am able to yield only a limited acquiescence in this learned writer's verdict. That the materials out of which VICTOR OF ANTIOCH constructed his Commentary are scarcely ever original,—is what no one will deny who examines the work with attention. But the Author of a compilation is an Author still; and to put Victor's claim to the work before us on a level with that of Origen or of Cyril, is entirely to misrepresent the case and hopelessly to perplex the question.

Concerning VICTOR himself, nothing whatever is known except that he was "a presbyter of Antioch." Concerning his Work, I will not here repeat what I have already stated elsewhere; but, requesting the Reader to refer to what was remarked at pp. 59 to 65, I propose to offer a few observations with which I was unwilling before to encumber the

---

[a] Kollar, (editing Lambecius,—iii. 159, 114,) expresses the same opinion.—Huet (*Origeniana*, lib. iii. c. 4, pp. 274-5,) has a brief and unsatisfactory dissertation on the same subject; but he arrives at a far shrewder conclusion.

text; holding it to be a species of duty for those who have given any time and attention to a subject like the present to contribute the result, (however slender and unsatisfactory it may prove,) to the common store. Let abler men enlarge the ensuing scanty notices, and correct me if in any respect I shall have inadvertently fallen into error.

1. There exists a Commentary, then, on S. Mark's Gospel, which generally claims on its front "VICTOR, PRESBYTER OF ANTIOCH," for its Author[b]. A Latin translation of this work, (not the original Greek,) was, in the first instance, published at Ingolstadt in 1580[c], by Theodore Peltanus. His Latin version found its way at once into "Bibliothecæ," (or Collections of Writings of the Fathers,) and has been again and again reprinted.

2. The Greek text of Victor was first published at Rome by Peter Possinus in 1673, from a MS. existing somewhere in Germany; which Bathazar Corderius had transcribed and presented to Possinus about thirty years before. Corderius gave Possinus at the same time his transcript of an anonymous Commentary on S. Mark preserved in the Vatican; and Possinus had already in his possession the transcript of a third Commentary on the same Evangelist (also anonymous) which he had obtained from the Library of Charles de Montchal, Abp. of Toulouse. These three transcripts Possinus published in a well-known volume. It is to be wished that he had kept them distinct, instead of to some extent blending their contents confusedly into one[d]. Still, the dis-

[b] The copies which I have seen, are headed,—ΒΙΚΤΟΡΟC (sometimes ΒΙΚΤѠΡΟC) ΠΡЄCΒΥΤЄΡΟΥ ΑΝΤΙΟΧЄΙΑC ЄΡΜΗΝЄΙΑ ЄΙC ΤΟ ΚΑΤΑ ΜΑΡΚΟΝ ЄΥΑΓΓЄΛΙΟΝ; or with words precisely to that effect. Very often no Author's name is given. Rarely is the Commentary assigned to Cyril, Origen, &c.— Vide infrà, N°. iii, xii, xiv, xix, xlviii. Also, N°. xlvii (comp. xxviii.)

[c] *Victoris Antiocheni in Marcum, et Titi Bostrorum Episcopi in Evangelium Lucae commentarii; ante hac quidem nunquam in lucem editi, nunc vero studio et operâ Theodori Peltani luce simul et Latinitate donati.* Ingolstad. 1580, 8vo. pp. 510.

[d] "Ex hoc ego, quasi metallo triplici, una conflata massa, inde annulos formavi, quos singulos Evangelici contextus articulis aptatos, inter seque morsu ac nexu mutuo commissos, in torquem producerem, quo, si possem consequi, sancto Evangelistae Marco decus et ornamentum adderetur."—*Præfatio*: from which the particulars in the text are obtained.

located paragraphs of Victor of Antioch are recognisable by the name of their author ("Victor Antiochenus") prefixed to each: while "Tolosanus" designates the Toulouse MS.: "Vaticanus" (or simply "Anonymus") the Vatican.

3. At the end of another century, (1775) C. F. Matthaei put forth at Moscow, with his usual skill and accuracy, a new and independent Edition of Victor's Commentary [e]: the text of which is based on four of the Moscow MSS. This work, which appeared in two parts, has become of extraordinary rarity. I have only just ascertained (June, 1871,) that one entire Copy is preserved in this country.

4. Lastly, (in 1840,) Dr. J. A. Cramer, in the first volume of his *Catenae* on the N. T., reproduced Victor's work from independent MS. sources. He took for his basis two Codices in the Paris Library, (No. 186 and No. 188), which, however, prove to have been anciently so exactly assimilated the one to the other [*infrà*, p. 279] as to be, in fact, but duplicates of one and the same original. Cramer supplemented their contents from Laud. Gr. 33, (in the Bodleian:) Coisl. 23: and Reg. 178 at Paris. The result has been by far the fullest and most satisfactory exhibition of the Commentary of Victor of Antioch which has hitherto appeared. Only is it to be regretted that the work should have been suffered to come abroad disfigured in every page with errors so gross as to be even scandalous, and with traces of slovenly editorship which are simply unintelligible. I cannot bring myself to believe that Dr. Cramer ever inspected the MSS. in the Paris Library in person. Else would the slender advantage which those abundant materials have proved to so learned and accomplished a scholar, be altogether unaccountable. Moreover, he is incorrect in what he says about them [f]: while his reasons for proposing to assign the work of Victor of Antioch to Cyril of Alexandria are undeserving of serious attention.

On a comparison of these four Editions of the same work, it is discovered that the Latin version of Peltanus (1580),

---

[e] ΒΙΚΤΩΡΟΣ πρεσβυτέρου Ἀντιοχείας καὶ ἄλλων τινῶν ἁγίων πατέρων ἐξήσησις εἰς τὸ κατὰ Μάρκον ἅγιον εὐαγγέλιον: *ex Codd. Mosqq. edidit* C. F. Matthæi, *Mosquae*, 1775.

[f] P. xxvii—xxviii.

represents the same Greek text which Possinus gave to the world in 1673. Peltanus translates very loosely; in fact he paraphrases rather than translates his author, and confesses that he has taken great liberties with Victor's text. But I believe it will be found that there can have been no considerable discrepancy between the MS. which Peltanus employed, and that which Possinus afterwards published.— Not so the text which Matthaei edited, which is in fact for the most part, (though not invariably,) rather an Epitome of Victor's Commentary. On the other hand, Cramer's text is more full than that of Possinus. There seem to be only a few lines in Possinus, here and there, which are not to be met with in Cramer; whereas no less than twenty-eight of Cramer's pages are not found in the work of Possinus. Cramer's edition, therefore, is by far the most complete which has hitherto appeared. And though it cries aloud for revision throughout; though many important corrections might easily be introduced into it, and the whole brought back in countless particulars more nearly to the state in which it is plain that Victor originally left it;— I question whether more than a few pages of *additional matter* could easily be anywhere recovered. I collated several pages of Cramer (Oct. 1869) with every MS. of Victor in the Paris Library; and all but invariably found that Cramer's text was fuller than that of the MS. which lay before me. Seldom indeed did I meet with a few lines in any MS. which had not already seen the light in Cramer's edition. One or other of the four Codices which he employed seems to fill up almost every hiatus which is met with in any of the MSS. of this Father.

For it must be stated, once for all, that an immense, and I must add, a most unaccountable discrepancy is observable between the several extant copies of Victor: yet not so much in respect of various readings, or serious modifications of his text; (though the transpositions are very frequent, and often very mischievous [g];) as resulting from the bound-

---

[g] To understand what is alluded to, the reader should compare the upper and the lower half of p. 442 in Cramer: noting that he has one and the same annotation before him; but diversely exhibited. (The lower part of the page

less license which every fresh copyist seems to have allowed himself chiefly in *abridging* his author.—To skip a few lines: to omit an explanatory paragraph, quotation, or digression: to pass *per saltum* from the beginning to the end of a passage: sometimes to leave out a whole page: to transpose: to paraphrase: to begin or to end with quite a different form of words;—proves to have been the rule. Two copyists engaged on the same portion of Commentary are observed to abridge it in two quite different ways. I question whether there exist in Europe three manuscripts of Victor which correspond entirely throughout. The result is perplexing in a high degree. Not unfrequently (as might be expected) we are presented with two or even three different exhibitions of one and the same annotation [h]. Meanwhile, as if to render the work of collation (in a manner) impossible,— (1) Peltanus pleads guilty to having transposed and otherwise taken liberties with the text he translated: (2) Possinus confessedly welded three codices into one: (3) Matthaei pieced and patched his edition out of four MSS.; and (4) Cramer, out of five.

The only excuse I can invent for this strange licentiousness on the part of Victor's ancient transcribers is this:— They must have known perfectly well, (in fact it is obvious,) that the work before them was really little else but a compilation; and that Victor had already abridged in the same merciless way the writings of the Fathers (Chrysostom chiefly) from whom he obtained his materials. We are to remember also, I suppose, the labour which transcription involved, and the costliness of the skins out of which ancient books were manufactured. But when all has been said, I must candidly admit that the extent of license which the ancients evidently allowed themselves quite perplexes me [i]. *Why*, for example, remodel the struc-

is taken from Cod. 178.) Besides transposing the sentences, the author of Cod. 178 has suppressed the reference to Chrysostom, and omitted the name of Apolinarius in line 10. (Compare Field's ed. of *Chrys.* iii. 529, top of the page.)

[h] Thus the two notes on p. 440 are found substantially to agree with the note on p. 441, which = Chrys. p. 527. See also *infrà*, p. 289.

[i] Let any one, with Mai's edition of the "Quaestiones ad Marinum" of Eu-

ture of a sentence and needlessly vary its phraseology? Never I think in my life have I been more hopelessly confused than in the *Bibliothèque*, while attempting to collate certain copies of Victor of Antioch.

I dismiss this feature of the case by saying that if any person desires a sample of the process I have been describing, he cannot do better than bestow a little attention on the "Preface" (ὑπόθεσις) at the beginning of Victor's Commentary. It consists of thirty-eight lines in Cramer's edition: of which Possinus omits eleven; and Matthaei also, eleven;—but *not the same eleven*. On the other hand, Matthaei[j] *prolongs* the Preface by eight lines. Strange to relate, the MS. from which Cramer professes to publish, goes on differently. If I may depend on my hasty pencilling, after ἐκκλησίαις [*Cramer*, i. p. 264, line 16,] Evan. 300, [= Reg. 186, *fol.* 93, line 16 from bottom] proceeds,—Κλήμης ἐν ἕκτῳ τῶν ὑποτυπώσεων, (thirty-one lines, ending) χαρακτὴρ ἐγένετο.

On referring to the work of Possinus, "Anonymus Vaticanus" is found to exhibit so admirable a condensation (?) of the ὑπόθεσις in question, that it is difficult to divest oneself of the suspicion that it must needs be an original and independent composition; the germ out of which the longer Preface has grown .... We inspect the first few pages of the Commentary, and nothing but perplexity awaits us at every step. It is not till we have turned over a few pages that we begin to find something like exact correspondence.

As for the Work,—(for I must now divest myself of the perplexing recollections which the hurried collation of so many MSS. left behind; and plainly state that, in spite of all, I yet distinctly ascertained, and am fully persuaded that the original work was *one*,—the production, no doubt, of "Victor, Presbyter of Antioch," as 19 out of the 52 MSS. declare):—For the Commentary itself, I say, Victor explains at the outset what his method had been. Having

---

sebius before him, note how mercilessly they are abridged, mutilated, amputated by subsequent writers. Compare for instance p. 257 with Cramer's "Catenae," i. p. 251-2; and this again with the "Catena in Joannem" of Corderius, p. 448-9.   [j] With whom, Reg. 177 and 703 agree.

failed to discover any separate exposition of S. Mark's Gospel, he had determined to construct one, by collecting the occasional notices scattered up and down the writings of Fathers of the Church [k]. Accordingly, he presents us in the first few lines of his Commentary (p. 266) with a brief quotation from the work of Eusebius "to Marinus, on the seeming inconsistency of the Evangelical accounts of the Resurrection;" following it up with a passage from "the vi[th] [vii[th]?] tome of Origen's Exegetics on S. John's Gospel." We are thus presented at the outset with *two* of Victor's favorite authorities. The work of Eusebius just named he was evidently thoroughly familiar with [l]. I suspect that he has many an unsuspected quotation from its pages. Towards the end of his Commentary, (as already elsewhere explained,) he quotes it once and again.

Of Origen also Victor was evidently very fond [m]: and his words on two or three occasions seem to shew that he had recourse besides habitually to the exegetical labours of Apolinarius, Theodore of Mopsuestia, and Titus of Bostra [n]. Passages from Cyril of Alexandria are occasionally met with [o]; and once at least (p. 370) he has an extract from Basil. The historian Josephus he sometimes refers to by name [p].

But the Father to whom Victor is chiefly indebted is Chrysostom,—whom he styles "the blessed John, Bishop of the Royal City;" (meaning Constantinople [q]). Not that

---

[k] p. 263, line 3 to 13, and in Possinus, p. 4.

[l] Eusebius is again quoted at p. 444, and referred to at p. 445 (line 23-5). See especially p. 446.

[m] What is found at p. 314 (on S. Mark v. 1,) is a famous place. (Cf. Huet's ed. ii. 131.) Compare also Victor's first note on i. 7 with the same edit. of Origen, ii. 125 C, D,—which Victor is found to have abridged. Compare the last note on p. 346 with Orig. i. 284 A. Note, that ἄλλος δέ φησι, (foot of p. 427) is also Origen. Cf. Possinus, p. 324.

[n] See pp. 408, 418, 442.

[o] e.g. the first note on p. 311; (comp. Possinus, p. 95): and the last note on p. 323; (comp. Poss. p. 123.) Compare also Cramer, p. 395 (line 16-22) with Poss. p. 249.—I observe that part of a note on p. 315 is ascribed by Possinus (p. 102) to Athanasius: while a scholium at p. 321 and p. 359, has no owner.

[p] e.g. p. 408, 411 (twice).

[q] In p. 418,—ὁ τῆς βασιλίδος πόλεως ἐπίσκοπος Ἰωάννης. For instances of

Victor, strictly speaking, *transcribes* from Chrysostom; at least, to any extent. His general practice is slightly to adapt his Author's language to his own purpose; sometimes, to leave out a few words; a paragraph; half a page[r]. Then, he proceeds to quote another Father probably; or, it may be, to offer something of his own. But he seldom gives any intimation of what it is he does: and if it were not for the occasional introduction of the phrase ὁ μέν φησι or ἄλλος δέ φησι[s], a reader of Victor's Commentary might almost mistake it for an original composition. So little pains does this Author take to let his reader know when he is speaking in his own person, when not, that he has not scrupled to retain Chrysostom's phrases ἐγὼ δὲ οἶμαι[t], &c. The result is that it is often impossible to know to *whose* sentiments we are listening. It cannot be too clearly borne in mind that ancient ideas concerning authorship differed entirely from those of modern times; especially when Holy Scripture was to be commented on.

I suspect that, occasionally, copyists of Victor's work, as they recognised a fragment here and there, prefixed to it

---

quotation from Chrysostom, comp. V. A. p. 315 with Chrys. pp. 398-9 : p. 376 with Chrys. pp. 227-8 : p. 420 with Chrys. p. 447, &c.

[r] Take for example Victor's Commentary on the stilling of the storm (pp. 312-3), which is merely an abridged version of the first part of Chrysostom's 28th Homily on S. Matthew (pp. 395-8); about 45 lines being left out. Observe Victor's method however. Chrysostom begins as follows :—'Ο μὲν οὖν Λουκᾶς, ἀπαλλάττων ἑαυτὸν τοῦ ἀπαιτηθῆναι τῶν χρόνων τὴν τάξιν, οὕτως εἶπεν. (Then follows S. Luke viii. 22.) καὶ ὁ Μάρκος ὁμοίως. Οὗτος δὲ οὐχ οὕτως· ἀλλὰ καὶ ἀκολουθίαν ἐνταῦθα διατηρεῖ. Victor, because he had S. Mark (not S. Matthew) to comment upon, begins thus :—'Ο μὲν Μάρκος ἀπαλλάττων ἑαυτὸν τοῦ ἀπαιτηθῆναι τῶν χρόνων τὴν τάξιν, οὕτως εἶπεν, ὁμοίως δὲ καὶ ὁ Λουκᾶς· ὁ δὲ Ματθαῖος οὐχ οὕτως· ἀλλὰ καὶ ἀκολουθίαν ἐνταῦθα διατηρεῖ.

[s] e.g. V. A. p. 422 (from ὁ μέν φησιν to ἄλλος δέ φησιν) = Chrys. p. 460. Observe the next paragraph also, (p. 423,) begins, ἄλλος φησιν.—So again, V. A. pp. 426-7 = Chrys. pp. 473-6 : where ἄλλος δέ φησι, at the foot of p. 427 introduces a quotation from Origen, as appears from Possinus, p. 324.—See also p. 269, line 1,—which is from Chrys. p. 130,—ἢ ὡς ὁ ἄλλος being the next words.—The first three lines in p. 316 = Chrys. p. 399. Then follows, ἄλλος δέ φησιν. See also pp. 392 : 407 (φασί τινες—ἕτερος δέ φησιν): pp. 415 and 433. After quoting Eusebius by name (p. 446-7), Victor says (line 3) ἄλλος δέ φησιν.

[t] e.g. V. A. p. 420 line 15, which = Chrys. p. 447.

the name of its author. This would account for the extremely partial and irregular occurrence of such notes of authorship; as well as explain why a name duly prefixed in one copy is often missing in another [u]. Whether Victor's Commentary can in strictness be called a "Catena," or not, must remain uncertain until some one is found willing to undertake the labour of re-editing his pages; from which, by the way, I cannot but think that some highly interesting (if not some important) results would follow.

Yet, inasmuch as Victor never, or certainly very seldom, prefixes to a passage from a Father *the name of its Author;* —above all, seeing that sometimes, at all events, he is original, or at least speaks in his own person;—I think the title of "Catena" inappropriate to his Commentary.

As favourable and as interesting a specimen of this work as could be found, is supplied by his annotation on S. Mark xiv. 3. He begins as follows, (quoting Chrysostom, p. 436): —"One and the same woman seems to be spoken of by all the Evangelists. Yet is this not the case. By three of them one and the same seems to be spoken of; not however by S. John, but another famous person,—the sister of Lazarus. This is what is said by John, the Bishop of the Royal City.—Origen on the other hand says that she who, in S. Matthew and S. Mark, poured the ointment in the house of Simon the leper was a different person from the sinner whom S. Luke writes about who poured the ointment on His feet in the house of the Pharisee.—Apolinarius [x] and Theodorus say that all the Evangelists mention one and the same person; but that John rehearses the story more accurately than the others. It is plain, however, that Matthew, Mark, and John speak of the same individual; for they relate that Bethany was the scene of the transaction; and this is *a village;* whereas Luke [viii. 37] speaks of some one else; for, 'Behold,' (saith he) 'a woman *in the city* which was *a sinner,*'" &c., &c.

[u] e.g. Theod. Mops., (p. 414,) which name is absent from Cod. Reg. 201:—Basil, (p. 370) whose name Possinus does not seem to have read:—Cyril's name, which Possinus found in a certain place (p. 311), is not mentioned in *Laud.* Gr. 33 *fol.* 100 *b*, at top, &c.

[x] So in the *Catena* of Corderius, *in S. Joannem,* p. 302.

But the most important instance by far of independent and sound judgment is supplied by that concluding paragraph, already quoted and largely remarked upon, at pp. 64-5; in which, after rehearsing all that had been said against the concluding verses of S. Mark's Gospel, Victor vindicates their genuineness by appealing in his own person to the best and the most authentic copies. The Reader is referred to Victor's Text, which is given below, at p. 288.

It only remains to point out, that since Chrysostom, (whom Victor speaks of as ὁ ἐν ἁγίοις, [p. 408,] and ὁ μακάριος, [p. 442,]) died in A.D. 407, it *cannot* be right to quote "401" as the date of Victor's work. Rather would A.D. 450 be a more reasonable suggestion: seeing that extracts from Cyril, who lived on till A.D. 444, are found here and there in Victor's pages. We shall not perhaps materially err if we assign A.D. 430—450 as Victor of Antioch's approximate date.

I conclude these notices of an unjustly neglected Father, by specifying the MSS. which contain his Work. Dry enough to ordinary readers, these pages will not prove uninteresting to the critical student. An enumeration of all the extant Codices with which I am acquainted which contain VICTOR OF ANTIOCH's Commentary on S. Mark's Gospel, follows:—

(i.) EVAN. 12 (= Reg. 230) *a most beautiful MS.*
The Commentary on S. Mark is here assigned to VICTOR by name; being a recension very like that which Matthaei has published. S. Mark's text is given *in extenso*.

(ii.) EVAN. 19 (= Reg. 189: anciently numbered 437 and 1880. Also 134 and 135. At back, 1603.) *A grand folio, well-bound and splendidly written. Pictures of the Evangelists in such marvellous condition that the very tools employed by a scribe might be reproduced. The ground gilded. Headings, &c. and words from Scripture all in gold.*
Here also the Commentary on S. Mark's Gospel is assigned to VICTOR. The differences between this text and that of Cramer (e.g. at fol. 320-3, 370,) are hopelessly numerous and complicated. There seem to have been extraordinary liberties taken with the text of this copy throughout.

(iii.) EVAN. 20 (= Reg. 188: anciently numbered 1883.) *A splendid folio,—the work of several hands and beautifully written.*
Victor's Commentary on S. Mark's Gospel is generally considered to be claimed for CYRIL of ALEXANDRIA by the following words:

ΥΠΟΘΕϹΙϹ ΕΙϹ ΤΟ ΚΑΤΑ ΜΑΡΚΟΝ ΑΓΙΟΝ ΕΥΑΓΓΕΛΙΟΝ ΕΚ ΤΗϹ ΕΙϹ ΑΥΤΟΝ ΕΡΜΗΝΕΙΑϹ ΤΟΥ ΕΝ ΑΓΙΟΙϹ ΚΥΡΙΛΛΟΥ ΑΛΕΞΑΝΔΡΕΙΑϹ.

The correspondence between Evan. 20 and Evan. 300 [*infrà*, N°. xiv], (= Reg. 188 and 186), is extraordinary[y]. In S. Mark's Gospel, (which alone I examined,) *every page begins with the same syllable, both of Text and Commentary*: (i.e. Reg. 186, fol. 94 to 197 = Reg. 188, fol. 87 to 140). Not that the number of words and letters in every line corresponds: but the discrepancy is compensated for by a blank at the end of each column, and at the foot of each page. Evan. 20 and Evan. 300 seem, therefore, in some mysterious way referable to a common original. The sacred Text of these two MSS., originally very dissimilar, has been made identical throughout; some very ancient (the original?) possessor of Reg. 188 having carefully assimilated the readings of his MS. to those of Reg. 186, the more roughly written copy; which therefore, in the judgment of the possessor of Reg. 188, exhibits the purer text. But how then does it happen that in both Codices alike, each of the Gospels (except S. Matthew's Gospel in Reg. 188,) ends with the attestation that it has been collated with approved copies? Are we to suppose that the colophon in question was added *after* the one text had been assimilated to the other? This is a subject which well deserves attention. The reader is reminded that these two Codices have already come before us at pp. 118-9,—where see the notes.

I proceed to set down some of the discrepancies between the texts of these two MSS.: in every one of which, Reg. 188 has been made conformable to Reg. 186:—

(COD. REG. 186.)	(COD. REG. 188.)
(1) Matth. xxvi. 70. αὐτῶν λέγων	αὐτῶν πάντων λέγων
(2) Mk. i. 2. ὡς	κάθως
(3) ,, 11. ᾧ	σοι
(4) ,, 16. βάλλοντας ἀμφίβληστρον	ἀμφιβάλλοντας ἀμφίβληστρον

[y] I believe it will be found that Cod. Reg. 186 corresponds *exactly* with Cod. Reg. 188: also that the contents of Cod. Reg. 201 correspond with those of Cod. Reg. 206; to which last two, I believe is to be added Cod. Reg. 187.

	(Cod. Reg. 186.)	(Cod. Reg. 188.)
(5)	Mk. ii. 21. παλαιῷ· εἰ δὲ μή γε αἱρεῖ ἀπ' αὐτοῦ τὸ πλήρωμα	παλαιῷ· εἰ δὲ μή, αἴρει τὸ πλήρωμα αὐτοῦ
(6)	,, iii. 10. ἐθεράπευεν	ἐθεράπευσεν
(7)	,, 17. τοῦ Ἰακώβου	Ἰακώβου.
(8)	,, 18. καὶ Ματθαῖον καὶ Θ.	καί Μ. τὸν τελώνην καὶ Θ.
(9)	,, vi. 9. μὴ ἐνδύσησθε	ἐνδέδυσθαι
(10)	,, 10. μένετε	μείνατε

In the 2nd, 3rd, and 6th of these instances, Tischendorf is found (1869) to adopt the readings of Reg. 188: in the last four, those of Reg. 186. In the 1st, 4th, and 5th, he follows neither.

(iv.) EVAN. 24 (= Reg. 178.) *A most beautifully written fol.*
Note, that this Codex has been mutilated at p. 70-1; from S. Matth. xxvii. 20 to S. Mark iv. 22 being away. It cannot therefore be ascertained whether the Commentary on S. Mark was here attributed to Victor or not. Cramer employed it largely in his edition of Victor (*Catenae*, vol. i. p. xxix,), as I have explained already at p. 271. Some notices of the present Codex are given above at p. 228-9.

(v.) EVAN. 25 (= Reg. 191: anciently numbered Colb. 2259: 1880. *Folio: grandly written.*
3)
No Author's name to the Commentary on S. Mark. The text of the Evangelist is given *in extenso.*

(vi.) EVAN. 34 (= Coisl. 195.) *A grand folio, splendidly written, and in splendid condition: the paintings as they came from the hand of the artist.*
At fol. 172, the Commentary on S. Mark is claimed for VICTOR. It will be found that Coisl. 23 (*infrà*, N°. ix.) and Coisl. 195 are derived from a common original; but Cod. 195 is the more perfect copy, and should have been employed by Cramer in preference to the other (*suprà*, p. 271.) There has been an older and a more recent hand employed on the Commentary.

(vii.) EVAN. 36 (= Coisl. 20.) *A truly sumptuous Codex.*
Some notices of this Codex have been given already, at p. 229. The Commentary on S. Mark is Victor's, but is without any Author's name.

(viii.) EVAN. 37 (= Coisl. 21.) *Fol.*
The Commentary on S. Mark is claimed for VICTOR at fol. 117. It seems to be very much the same recension which is exhibited by Coisl. 19 (*infrà*, N°. xviii.) and Coisl. 24 (*infrà*, N°. xi.) The Text is given *in extenso*: the Commentary, in the margin.

(ix.) EVAN. 39 (= Coisl. 23.) *A grand large fol. The writing singularly abbreviated.*
The Commentary on S. Mark is claimed for VICTOR: but is very dissimilar in its text from that which forms the basis of Cramer's editions. (See above, on N°. vi.) It is Cramer's "P." (See his *Catenae*, vol. i. p. xxviii; and *vide supra*, p. 271.)

(x.) EVAN. 40 (= Coisl. 22.)
No Author's name is prefixed to the Commentary (fol. 103); which is a recension resembling Matthaei's. The Text is *in extenso*: the Commentary, in the margin.

(xi.) EVAN. 41 (= Coisl. 24.) *Fol.*
This is a Commentary, not a Text. It is expressly claimed for VICTOR. The recension seems to approximate to that published by Matthaei. (See on N°. viii.) One leaf is missing. (See fol. 136 b.)

(xii.) EVAN. 50 (= Bodl. Laud. Graec. 33.) 4to. The Commentary here seems to be claimed for CYRIL OF ALEXANDRIA, but in the same unsatisfactory way as N°. iii and xiv. (See Coxe's *Cat.* i. 516.)

(xiii.) EVAN. 299 (= Reg. 177 : anciently numbered 2242^3).
The Commentary on S. Mark is Victor's, but is without any Author's name. The Text of S. Mark is given *in extenso*: Victor's Commentary, in the margin.

(xiv.) EVAN. 300 (= Reg. 186: anciently numbered 692, 750, and 1882.) *A noble Codex: but the work of different scribes. It is most beautifully written.*
At fol. 94, the Commentary on S. Mark is claimed for CYRIL OF ALEXANDRIA, in the same equivocal manner as above in N°. iii and xii. The writer states in the colophon that he had diversely found it ascribed to Cyril and to Victor. (ἐπληρώθη σὺν Θεῷ ἡ ἑρμηνεία τοῦ κατὰ Μάρκον ἁγίου εὐαγγελίου ἀπὸ φωνῆς, ἔν τισιν εὗρον Κυρίλλου Ἀλεξανδρέως, ἐν ἄλλοις δὲ Βίκτορος πρεσβυτέρου.)

See above, the note on Evan. 20 (N°. iii),—a MS. which, as already explained, has been elaborately assimilated to the present.

(xv.) EVAN. 301 (= Reg. 187: anciently numbered 504, 537 and 1879.) *A splendid fol. beautifully written throughout.*
The Commentary on S. Mark is here claimed for VICTOR.

(xvi.) EVAN. 309 (= Reg. 201 : anciently numbered 176 and 2423.) *A very interesting little fol.: very peculiar in its style. Drawings old and curious. Beautifully written.*
The Commentary is here claimed for VICTOR. This is not properly a text of the Gospel; but parts of the text interwoven with the Commentary. Take a specimen [z]: (S. Mark xvi. 8—20.)

Και εξελθουσαι εφυγον απο του μνημειου. ειχεν δε αυτας τρομος και εκστασις. εως δια των επακολουθουντων σημειων.

Over the text is written $\text{κ}\overset{M}{\text{ει}}$ (κειμένον i.e. *Text*) and over the Commentary $\overset{M}{\text{ερ}}$ (ἑρμηνεία, i.e. *Interpretation*.) See the next.

(xvii.) EVAN. 312 (= Reg. 206 : anciently numbered 968, 1058, 2283; and behind, 1604. Also A. 67.) *A beautiful little fol.*
Contains only the Commentary, which is expressly assigned to VICTOR. This Copy of Victor's Commentary is very nearly indeed a duplicate of Cod. 309, (N°. xvi.) both in its contents and in its method ; but it is less beautifully written.

(xviii.) EVAN. 329 (= Coisl. 19.) *A very grand fol.*
The Commentary on S. Mark is Victor's, but is without any Author's name. (See above, on N°. viii.)

(xix.) REG. 703, (anciently numbered 958 : 1048, and Reg. 2330: also No. 18.) *A grand large* 4to.
The Commentary is here claimed for ORIGEN. Such at least is probably the intention of the heading (in gold capital letters) of the Prologue :—

ΩΡΙΓΕΝΟΥΣ ΠΡΟΛΟΓΟΣ ΕΙΣ ΤΗΝ ΕΡΜΗΝΕΙΑΝ ΤΟΥ
ΚΑΤΑ ΜΑΡΚΟΝ ΕΥΑΓΓΕΛΙΟΥ.

See on this subject the note at foot of p. 235.

[z] Note, that this recurs at fol. 145 of a Codex at Moscow numbered 384 in the *Syr. Cat.*

(xx.) EVAN. 304 (= Reg. 194. Teller 1892.) The text of S. Mark is here interwoven with a Commentary which I do not recognise. But from the correspondence of a note at the end with what is found in Possinus, pp. 361—3, I am led to suspect that the contents of this MS. will be found to correspond with what Possinus published and designated as " Tolosanus."

(xxi.) EVAN. 77 (Vind. Ness. 114, Lambec. 29.) Victor's Commentary is here anonymous.

(xxii.) EVAN. 92 (which belonged to Faesch of Basle [see Wetstein's *Proleg.*], and which Haenel [p. 658 *b*] says is now in Basle Library). Wetstein's account of this Codex shews that the Commentary on S. Mark is here distinctly ascribed to VICTOR. He says, —" Continet Marcum et in eum *Victoris Antiocheni Commentarios*, foliis 5 mutilos. Item Scholia in Epistolas Catholicas," &c. And so Haenel.

(xxiii.) EVAN. 94 (As before, precisely; except that Haenel's [inaccurate] notice is at p. 657 *b*.) This Codex contains VICTOR of Antioch's Commentary on S. Mark, (which is evidently here also assigned to him *by name;*) and Titus of Bostra on S. Luke. Also several Scholia: among the rest, I suspect, (from what Haenel says), the Scholia spoken of *suprà*, p. 47, note (x).

(xxiv.) In addition to the preceding, and before mentioning them, Haenel says there also exists in the Library at Basle,— "VICTORIS Antiocheni Scholia in Evang. Marci: chart[a]."

(xxv.) EVAN. 108 (Vind. Forlos. 5. Koll. 4.) Birch (p. 225) refers to it for the Scholion given in the next article. (Append. E.)

(xxvi.) EVAN. 129 (Vat. 358.) ΒΙΚΟΡΟC π̅ρ̅ ΑΝΤΙΟ͞Χ ε͞ρ̅ ΕΙС ΚΑΤΑ Μ͞ΑΡΚΟΝ. The Commentary is written along the top and bottom and down the side of each page; and there are references (α', β', γ') inserted in the text to the paragraphs in the margin,—as in some of the MSS. at Paris. Prefixed is an exegetical apparatus by Eusebius, &c.

Note, that of these five MSS. in the Vatican, (358, 756, 757, 1229, 1445), the 3rd and 4th are without the prefatory section (beginning πολλῶν εἰς τὸ κατὰ Μ.)—All 5 begin, Μάρκος ὁ εὐαγγελιστής. In all but the 4th, the second paragraph begins σαφέστερον.

---

[a] *Catalogus Librorum MSS.* Lips. 1830, 4to, p 656 *b*.

The third passage begins in all 5, 'Ισοδυναμεῖ τοῦτο. Any one seeking to understand this by a reference to the editions of Cramer or of Possinus will recognise the truth of what was stated above, p. 274, line 24 to 27.

(xxvii.) EVAN. 137 (Vat. 756.) The Commentary is written as in Vat. 358 (N°. xxvi): but no Author's name is given.

(xxviii.) EVAN. 138 (Vat. 757.) On a blank page or fly-leaf at the beginning are these words:—ὁ ἀντίγραφος (sic) οὗτός ἐστιν ὁ Πέτρος ὁ τῆς Λαοδικείας ὅστις προηγεῖται τῶν ἄλλων ἐξηγητῶν ἐνταῦθα. (Comp. N°. xlvii.) The Commentary and Text are not kept distinct, as in the preceding Codex. Both are written in an ill-looking, slovenly hand.

(xxix.) EVAN. 143 (Vat. 1,229.) The Commentary is written as in Vat. 358 (N°. xxvi), but without the references; and no Author's name is given.

(xxx.) EVAN. 181 (Xavier, Cod. Zelada.) Birch was shewn this Codex of the Four Gospels in the Library of Cardinal Xavier of Zelada (*Prolegomena*, p. lviii) : "Cujus forma est in folio, pp. 596. In margine passim occurrunt scholia ex Patrum Commentariis exscripta."

(xxxi.) EVAN. 186 (Laur. vi. 18.) This Codex is minutely described by Bandini (*Cat.* i. 130), who gives the Scholion (*infra*, p. 388-9), and says that the Commentary is without any Author's name.

(xxxii.) EVAN. 194 (Laur. vi. 33.) Βίκτορος πρεσβυτέρου Ἀντιοχείας ἑρμηνεία εἰς τὸ κατὰ Μάρκον εὐαγγέλιον. (See the description of this Codex in Bandini's *Cat.* i. 158.)

(xxxiii.) EVAN. 195 (Laur. vi. 34.) This Codex seems to correspond in its contents with N°. xxxi. *suprà :* the Commentary containing the Scholion, and being anonymous. (See Bandini, p. 161.)

(xxxiv.) EVAN. 197 (Laur. viii. 14.) The Commentary, (which is Victor's, but has no Author's name prefixed,) is defective at the end. (See Bandini, p. 355.)

(xxxv.) EVAN. 210 (Venet. 27.) "Conveniunt initio Commentarii eum iis qui Victori Antiocheno tribuuntur, progressu autem discrepant." (Theupoli *Graeca D. Marci Bibl. Codd. MSS.* Venet. 1740.) I infer that the work is anonymous.

(xxxvi.) Venet. 495. "VICTORIS ANTIOCHENI Presbyteri expositio in Evangelium Marci, collecta ex divérsis Patribus." (I obtain this reference from the Catalogue of Theupolus.)

(xxxvii.) EVAN. 215 (Venet. 544.) I presume, from the description in the Catalogue of Theupolus, that this Codex also contains a copy of Victor's Commentary.

(xxxviii.) EVAN. 221 (Vind. Ness. 117, Lambec. 38). Kollar has a long note (B) [iii. 157] on the Commentary, which has no Author's name prefixed. Birch (p. 225) refers to it for the purpose recorded under N°. xxv.

(xxxix.) EVAN. 222 (Vind. Ness. 180, Lambec. 39.) The Commentary is anonymous. Birch refers to it, as before.

Add the following six MSS. at Moscow, concerning which, see Matthaei's Nov. Test. (1788) vol. ii. p. xii. :—

(xl.) EVAN. 237 (This is Matthaei's d or D [described in his *N. T.* ix. 242. Also *Vict. Ant.* ii. 137.] "SS. Synod. 42 :") and is one of the MSS. employed by Matthaei in his ed. of Victor.— The Commentary on S. Mark has no Author's name prefixed.

(xli.) EVAN. 238 (Matthaei's e or E [described in his *N. T.* ix. 200. Also *Vict. Ant.* ii. 141.] "SS. Synod. 48.") This Codex formed the basis of Matthaei's ed. of Victor, [See the *Not. Codd. MSS.* at the end of vol. ii. p. 123. Also *N. T.* ix. 202.] The Commentary on S. Mark is anonymous.

(xlii.) EVAN. 253 (Matthaei's 10 [described in his *N. T.* ix. 234.] It was lent him by Archbishop Nicephorus.) Matthaei says (p. 236) that it corresponds with a (our Evan. 259). No Author's name is prefixed to the Commentary on S. Mark.

(xliii.) EVAN. 255 (Matthaei's 12 [described in his *N.T.* ix. 222. Also *Vict. Ant.* ii. 133.] "SS. Synod. 139." The Scholia on S. Mark are here entitled ἐξηγητικαὶ ἐκλογαί, and (as in 14) are few in number. For some unexplained reason, in his edition of Victor of Antioch, Matthaei saw fit to designate this MS. as "B." [*N. T.* ix. 224 *note.*] .... See by all means, *infrà*, the "Postscript."

(xliv.) EVAN. 256 (Matthaei's 14 [described in his *N. T.* ix. 220.] "Bibl. Typ. Synod. 3.") The Commentary on S. Mark is here assigned to VICTOR, presbyter of Antioch; but the Scholia are said to be (as in "12" [N°. xxxix]) few in number.

(xlv.) EVAN. 259 (Matthaei's a or A [described in his *N. T.* ix. 237. Also *Vict. Ant.* ii. 128.] "SS. Synod. 45.") This is one of the MSS. employed by Matthaei in his ed. of Victor. No Author's name is prefixed to the Commentary.

(xlvi.) EVAN. 332 (Taurin. xx *b* iv. 20.) Victor's Commentary is here given anonymously. (See the Catalogue of Pasinus, P. i. p. 91.)

(xlvii.) EVAN. 353 (Ambros. M. 93): with the same Commentary as Evan. 181, (i.e. N°. xxx.)

(xlviii.) EVAN. 374 (Vat. 1445.) Written continuously in a very minute character. The Commentary is headed (in a later Greek hand) $+ \ \mathit{ἑρμηνεία \ Πέτρου \ Λαοδικείας \ εἰς \ τοὺς \ δ' \ ἁγ[ίους] \ εὐαγγελιστάς} \ +$. This is simply a mistake. No such Work exists: and the Commentary on the second Evangelist is that of Victor. (See N°. xxviii.)

(xlix.) EVAN. 428 (Monacensis 381. Augsburg 11): said to be duplicate of Evan. 300 (i.e. of N°. xiv.)

(l.) EVAN. 432 (Monacensis 99.) The Commentary contained in this Codex is evidently assigned to VICTOR.

(li.) EVAN. 7^{pe} (ix. 3. 471.) A valuable copy of the Four Gospels, dated 1062; which Edw. de Muralto (in his Catalogue of the Greek MSS. in the Imperial Library at S. Petersburg) says contains the Commentary of VICTOR ANT. (See Scrivener's *Introduction*, p. 178.)

(lii.) At Toledo, in the "Biblioteca de la Iglesia Mayor," Haenel [p. 885] mentions :—"VICTOR ANTIOCHENUS Comm. Graec. in iv. [?] Evangelia saec. xiv. membr. fol."

To this enumeration, (which could certainly be very extensively increased,) will probably have to be added the following :—

EVAN. 146 (Palatino-Vat. 5.)
EVAN. 233 (Escurial Y. ii. 8.)

EVAN. 373 (Vat. 1423.)
EVAN. 379 (Vat. 1769.)
EVAN. 427 (Monacensis 465, Augsburg 10.)

Middle Hill, Nº. 13,975,—a MS. in the collection of Sir Thomas Phillipps.

In conclusion, it can scarcely require to be pointed out that VICTOR's Commentary,—of which the Church in her palmiest days shewed herself so careful to multiply copies, and of which there survive to this hour such a vast number of specimens,—must needs anciently have enjoyed very peculiar favour. It is evident, in fact, that an Epitome of Chrysostom's Homilies on S. Matthew, together with *VICTOR's compilation on S. Mark*,—Titus of Bostra on S. Luke,—and a work in the main derived from Chrysostom's Homilies on S. John;—that these four constituted the established Commentary of ancient Christendom on the fourfold Gospel. Individual copyists, no doubt, will have been found occasionally to abridge certain of the Annotations, and to omit others: or else, out of the multitude of Scholia by various ancient Fathers which were evidently once in circulation, and must have been held in very high esteem,—(Irenæus, Origen, Ammonius, Eusebius, Apolinarius, Cyril, Chrysostom, the Gregorys, Basil, Theodore of Mopsuestia, and Theodore of Heraclea,) they will have introduced extracts according to their individual caprice. In this way, the general sameness of the several copies is probably to be accounted for, while their endless discrepancy in matters of detail is perhaps satisfactorily explained.

These last remarks are offered in the way of partial elucidation of the difficulty pointed out above, at pp. 272—4.

APPENDIX (E).

Text of the concluding Scholion of VICTOR OF ANTIOCH'S *Commentary on S. Mark's Gospel; in which Victor bears emphatic testimony to the genuineness of " the last Twelve Verses."*

I HAVE thought this very remarkable specimen of the method of an ancient and (as I think) unjustly neglected Commentator, deserving of extraordinary attention. Besides presenting the reader, therefore, with what seems to be a fair approximation to the original text of the passage, I have subjoined as many various readings as have come to my knowledge. It is hoped that they are given with tolerable exactness; but I have been too often obliged to depend on printed books and the testimony of others. I can at least rely on the readings furnished me from the Vatican.

The text chiefly followed is that of Coisl. 20, (in the Paris Library,—our EVAN. 36;) supplemented by several other MSS., which, for convenience, I have arbitrarily designated by the letters of the alphabet as under [a].

Εἰ δὲ καὶ τὸ "'Αναστὰς [b] δὲ πρωῒ πρώτῃ σαββάτου ἐφάνη πρῶτον Μαρίᾳ τῇ Μαγδαληνῇ," καὶ τὰ ἐξῆς ἐπιφερόμενα, ἐν τῷ κατὰ Μάρκον εὐαγγελίῳ παρὰ[c] πλείστοις ἀντιγράφοις οὐ κεῖνται[d], (ὡς νόθα γὰρ ἐνόμισαν αὐτά τινες εἶναι[e]) ἀλλ'

---

[a] *Reg.* 177 = A : 178 = B : 230 = C.—*Coisl.* 19 = D : 20 = E : 21 = F : 22 = G : 24 = H.—*Matthaei's* d *or* D = I : *his* e *or* E = J : *his* 12 = K : *his* a *or* A = L.—*Vat.* 358 = M : 756 = N : 757 = O : 1229 = P : 1445 = Q.— *Vind. Koll.* 4 *Forlos.* 5 = R.—*Xav. de Zelada* = S.—*Laur.* 18 = T : 34 = U.—*Venet.* 27 = V.—*Vind. Lamb.* 38 = W : 39 = X.

[b] So B—E (which I chiefly follow) begins,—Το δε αναστας.

[c] B begins thus,—Ει δε και το αναστας δε πρωι μετα τα επιφερομενα παρα. It is at this word (παρα) that most copies of the present scholion (A, C, D, F, G, H, I, J, K, L, M, N, O, P, Q, R, S, T, U, V, W, X) begin.

[d] So far (except in its opening phrase) E. But C, D, F, H, I, J, K, L, M, N, O, P, T, begin,—Παρα πλειστοις αντιγραφοις ου κεινται [I, ου κειται : J, ουκ ην δε] ταυτα τα [M, O, T om. τα] επιφερομενα εν [D, F, H om. εν] τῳ κατα Μαρκον [B, εν τω παροντι] ευαγγελιῳ.

[e] So I, J, K, L, and H. P proceeds,—ως νοθα νομισθεντα τισιν ειναι. But

[APP. E.] *Victor of Antioch's Scholion.* 369

ἡμεῖς ἐξ ἀκριβῶν ἀντιγράφων, ὡς ἐν πλείστοις εὑρόντες αὐτά [f], κατὰ τὸ Παλαιστιναῖον εὐαγγέλιον Μάρκου, ὡς ἔχει ἡ ἀλήθεια, συντεθείκαμεν [g] καὶ τὴν ἐν αὐτῷ ἐπιφερομένην δεσποτικὴν ἀνάστασιν, μετὰ τὸ " ἐφοβοῦντο γάρ [h]." τούτεστιν ἀπὸ τοῦ " ἀναστὰς δὲ πρωῒ πρώτῃ σαββάτου," καὶ καθ' ἑξῆς μέχρι τοῦ " διὰ τῶν ἐπακολουθούντων σημείων. Ἀμήν [i]."

More pains than enough (it will perhaps be thought) have been taken to exhibit accurately this short Scholion. And yet, it has not been without design (the reader may be sure) that so many various readings have been laboriously accumulated. The result, it is thought, is eminently instructive, and (to the student of Ecclesiastical Antiquity) important also.

For it will be perceived by the attentive reader that not more than two or three of the multitude of various readings afforded by this short Scholion can have possibly resulted from careless transcription [k]. The rest have been unmistakably occasioned by the merest licentiousness: every fresh Copyist evidently considering himself at liberty to take just whatever liberties he pleased with the words before

B, C, D, E, F, G, M, N, O, T exhibit,—ως νοθα νομισαντες αυτα τινες [B om. τινες] ειναι. On the other hand, A and Q begin and proceed as follows,—Παρα πλειστοις αντιγραφοις ταυτα τα [Q om. τα] επιφερομενα εν [A om. εν] τῳ κατα Μαρκον ευαγγελιῳ ως νοθα νομισαντες τινες [Q, τινας (a clerical error) : A om. τινες] ουκ εθηκαν.

[f] So B, except that it omits ως. So also, A, D, E, F, G, H, J, M, N, O, P, Q, T, except that they begin the sentence, ημεις δε.

[g] So D, E, F, G, H, J, M, N, O, P, T: also B and Q, except that they prefix και το κατα το Π. B is peculiar in reading,—ως εχει η αληθεια Μαρκου (transposing Μαρκου): while C and P read,—ομως ημεις εξ ακριβων αντιγραφων και πλειστων ου μην αλλα και εν τῳ Παλαιστιναιῳ ευαγγελιῳ Μαρκου ευροντες αυτα ως εχει η αληθεια συντεθεικαμεν.

[h] So all, apparently: except that P reads εμφερομενην for επιφερομενην ; and M, after αναστασιν inserts εδηλωσαμεν, with a point (.) before μετα : while C and P (after αναστασιν,) proceed,—και την [C, ειτα] αναληψιν και καθεδραν εκ δεξιων του Πατρος ῳ πρεπει η δοξα και η τιμη νυν και εις τους αιωνας. αμην. But J [and I think, H] (after γαρ) proceeds,—διο δοξαν αναπεμψωμεν τῳ αναστανι εκ νεκρων Χριστῳ τῳ Θεῳ ημων αμα τῳ αναρχῳ Πατρι και ζωοποιῳ Πνευματι νυν και αει και εις τους αιωνας των αιωνων. αμην,

[i] So B. All, except B, C, H, J, P seem to end at εφοβουντο γαρ.

[k] e.g. οὐκ ἦν δέ for οὐ κεῖται.

him. To amputate, or otherwise to mutilate; to abridge; to amplify; to transpose; to remodel;—this has been the rule with all. The *types* (so to speak) are reducible to two, or at most to three; but the varieties are almost as numerous as the MSS. of Victor's work.

And yet it is impossible to doubt that this Scholion was originally one, and one only. Irrecoverable perhaps, in some of its minuter details, as the actual text of Victor may be, it is nevertheless self-evident that *in the main* we are in possession of what he actually wrote on this occasion. In spite of all the needless variations observable in the manner of stating a certain fact, it is still unmistakably one and the same fact which is every time stated. It is invariably declared,—

(1.) That from certain copies of S. Mark's Gospel the last Twelve Verses had been LEFT OUT; and (2) That this had been done because their genuineness had been by certain persons suspected: but, (3) That the Writer, convinced of their genuineness, had restored them to their rightful place; (4) Because he had found them in accurate copies, and in the authentic Palestinian copy, which had supplied him with his exemplar.

It is obvious to suggest that after familiarizing ourselves with this specimen of what proves to have been the licentious method of the ancient copyists in respect of the text of an early Father, we are in a position to approach more intelligently the Commentary of Victor itself; and, to some extent, to understand how it comes to pass that so many liberties have been taken with it throughout. The Reader is reminded of what has been already offered on this subject at pp. 272-3.

APPENDIX (F).

On the Relative antiquity of the CODEX VATICANUS (B), *and the* CODEX SINAITICUS (ℵ).

I. "VIX differt aetate a Codice Sinaitico," says Tischendorf, (*ed. 8va,* 1869, p. ix,) speaking of the Codex Vaticanus (B). Yet does he perpetually designate his own Sinaitic Codex (ℵ) as "omnium antiquissimus." Now,

(1) The (all but unique) sectional division of the Text of Codex B,—confessedly the oldest scheme of chapters extant, is in itself a striking note of primitiveness. The author of the Codex knew nothing, apparently, of the Eusebian method. But I venture further to suggest that the following peculiarities in Codex ℵ unmistakably indicate for it a later date than Codex B.

(2) Cod. ℵ, (like C, and other later MSS.,) is broken up into short paragraphs throughout. The Vatican Codex, on the contrary, has very few breaks indeed: e.g. it is without break of any sort from S. Matth. xvii. 24 to xx. 17: whereas, within the same limits, there are in Cod. ℵ as many as *thirty* interruptions of the context. From S. Mark xiii. 1 to the end of the Gospel the text is absolutely continuous in Cod. B, except in *one* place: but in Cod. ℵ it is interrupted upwards of *fifty* times. Again: from S. Luke xvii. 11, to the end of the Gospel there is but *one* break in Cod. B. But it is broken into well nigh *an hundred and fifty* short paragraphs in Cod. ℵ.

There can be no doubt that the unbroken text of Codex B, (resembling the style of the papyrus of *Hyperides* published by Mr. Babington,) is the more ancient. The only places where it approximates to the method of Cod. ℵ, is where the Commandments are briefly recited (S. Matth. xix. 18, &c.), and where our LORD proclaims the eight Beatitudes (S. Matth. v.)

(3) Again; Cod. ℵ is prone to exhibit, on extraordinary occasions, *a single word* in a line, as at—

S. MATTH. xv. 30.   S. MARK x. 29.   S. LUKE xiv. 13.
ΧΩΛΟΥC   Η ΑΔΕΛΦΑC   ΠΤΩΧΟΥC
ΤΥΦΛΟΥC   Η ΠΑΤΕΡΑ   ΑΝΑΠΗΡΟΥC
ΚΥΛΛΟΥC   Η ΜΗΤΕΡΑ   ΧΩΛΟΥC
ΚΩΦΟΥC   Η ΤΕΚΝΑ   ΤΥΦΛΟΥC
                    Η ΑΓΡΟΥC

This became a prevailing fashion in the vi[th] century; e.g. when the Cod. Laudianus of the Acts (E) was written. The only trace of anything of the kind in Cod. B is at the Genealogy of our LORD.

(4) At the commencement of every fresh paragraph, the initial letter in Cod. ℵ *slightly projects into the margin,*— beyond the left hand edge of the column; as usual in all later MSS. This characteristic is only not undiscoverable in Cod. B. Instances of it there *are* in the earlier Codex; but they are of exceedingly rare occurrence.

(5) Further; Cod. ℵ abounds in such contractions as $\overline{ANOC}$, $\overline{OYNOC}$ (with all their cases), for ΑΝΘΡΩΠΟC, ΟΥΡΑΝΟC, &c. Not only $\overline{ΠΝΑ}$, $\overline{ΠΗΡ}$, $\overline{ΠΕΡ}$, $\overline{ΠΡΑ}$, $\overline{ΜΡΑ}$ (for ΠΝΕΥΜΑ, ΠΑΤΗΡ-ΤΕΡ-ΤΕΡΑ, ΜΗΤΕΡΑ), but also $\overline{CTPΘΗ}$, $\overline{ΙΗΛ}$, $\overline{ΙΗΛΗΜ}$, for CΤΑΥΡΩΘΗ, ΙCΡΑΗΛ, ΙΕΡΟΥCΑΛΗΜ.

But Cod. B, though familiar with $\overline{IC}$, and a few other of the most ordinary abbreviations, knows nothing of these compendia: which certainly *cannot* have existed in the earliest copies of all. Once more, it seems reasonable to suppose that their constant occurrence in Cod ℵ indicates for that Codex a date subsequent to Cod. B.

(6) The very discrepancy observable between these two Codices in their method of dealing with "the last twelve verses of S. Mark's Gospel," (already adverted to at p. 88,) is a further indication, and as it seems to the present writer a very striking one, that Cod. B is the older of the two. Cod. ℵ is evidently *familiar* with the phenomenon which *astonishes* Cod. B by its novelty and strangeness.

(7) But the most striking feature of difference, after all, is only to be recognised by one who surveys the Codices themselves with attention. It is *that* general air of primi-

tiveness in Cod. B which makes itself at once *felt*. The even symmetry of the unbroken columns;—the work of the *prima manus* everywhere vanishing through sheer antiquity; — the small, even, *square* writing, which partly recals the style of the Herculanean rolls; partly, the papyrus fragments of the *Oration against Demosthenes* (published by Harris in 1848):—all these notes of superior antiquity infallibly set Cod. B before Cod. א; though it may be impossible to determine whether by 50, by 75, or by 100 years.

II. It has been conjectured by one whose words are always entitled to most respectful attention, that Codex Sinaiticus may have been "one of the fifty Codices of Holy Scripture which Eusebius prepared A.D. 331, by Constantine's direction, for the use of the new Capital." (Scrivener's *Collation of the Cod. Sin.*, Introd. p. xxxvii-viii.)

1. But this, which is rendered improbable by the many instances of grave discrepancy between its readings and those with which Eusebius proves to have been most familiar, is made impossible by the discovery that it is without S. Mark xv. 28, which constitutes the Eusebian Section numbered "216" in S. Mark's Gospel. [Quite in vain has Tischendorf perversely laboured to throw doubt on this circumstance. It remains altogether undeniable,—as a far less accomplished critic than Tischendorf may see at a glance. Tischendorf's only plea is the fact that in Cod. M, (he might have added and in the Codex Sinaiticus, *which explains the phenomenon* in Cod. M), *against ver.* 29 is set the number, ("216,") instead of against ver. 28. But what then? Has not the number *demonstrably* lost its place? And is there not *still* one of the Eusebian Sections missing? And *which* can it *possibly* have been, if it was not S. Mark xv. 28?] Again. Cod. א, (like B, C, L, U, Γ, and some others), gives the piercing of the SAVIOUR'S side at S. Matth. xxvii. 49 : but if Eusebius had read that incident in the same place, he would have infallibly included S. John xix. 34, 35, with S. Matth. xxvii. 49, in his vii[th] Canon, where matters are contained which are common to S. Matthew and S. John, — instead of referring S. John xix. 31—37 to his x[th] Canon, which

specifies things peculiar to each of the four Evangelists. Eusebius, moreover, in a certain place (*Dem. Evan.* x. 8 [quoted by Tisch.]) has an allusion to the same transaction, and expressly says that it is recorded *by S. John.*

2. No inference as to the antiquity of this Codex can be drawn from the Eusebian notation of Sections in the margin: *that* notation having been confessedly added at a subsequent date.

3. On the other hand, the subdivision of Cod. ℵ into paragraphs, proves to have been made without any reference to the sectional distribution of Eusebius. Thus, there are in the Codex thirty distinct paragraphs from S. Matthew xi. 20 to xii. 34, inclusive; but there are comprised within the same limits only seventeen Eusebian sections. And yet, of those seventeen sections only nine correspond with as many paragraphs of the Codex Sinaiticus. This, in itself, is enough to prove that Eusebius knew nothing of the present Codex. His record is express:— ἐφ' ἑκάστῳ τῶν τεσσάρων εὐαγγελίων ἀριθμός τις πρόκειται κατὰ μέρος κ.τ.λ.

III. The supposed resemblance of the opened volume to an Egyptian papyrus,—when eight columns (σελίδες) are exhibited to the eye at once, side by side,—seems to be a fallacious note of high antiquity. If Cod. ℵ has four columns in a page,—Cod. B three,—Cod. A two,—Cod. C has only one. But Cod. C is certainly as old as Cod. A. Again, Cod. D, which is of the vi[th] century, is written (like Cod. C) across the page: yet was it "copied from an older model similarly divided in respect to the lines or verses,"—and therefore similarly written across the page. It is almost obvious that the size of the skins on which a Codex was written will have decided whether the columns should be four or only three in a page.

IV. In fine, nothing doubting the high antiquity of both Codices, (B and ℵ,) I am nevertheless fully persuaded that an interval of at least half a century,—if not of a far greater span of years,—is absolutely required to account for the marked dissimilarity between them.

APPENDIX (G).

On the so-called "Ammonian Sections" *and* "Eusebian Canons."

I. THAT the Sections (popularly miscalled "*Ammonian*") with which EUSEBIUS [A.D. 320] has made the world thoroughly familiar, and of which some account was given above (pp. 127-8), cannot be the same which AMMONIUS of Alexandria [A.D. 220] employed,—but must needs be the invention of EUSEBIUS himself,—admits of demonstration. On this subject, external testimony is altogether insecure*. The only safe appeal is to the Sections themselves.

1. The Call of the Four Apostles is described by the first three Evangelists, within the following limits of their respective Gospels:—S. Matthew iv. 18—22 : S. Mark i. 16—20 : S. Luke (with the attendant miraculous draught of fishes,) v. 1—11. Now, these three portions of narrative are observed to be dealt with in the sectional system of EUSEBIUS after the following extraordinary fashion : (the fourth column represents the Gospel according to S. John):—

(1.)	......	....	§ 29, (v. 1—3)	
(2.)	§ 20, (iv. 17, 18)	§ 9, (i. $14\frac{1}{2}$—16)		
(3.)	......	....	§ 30, (v. 4—7)	§219,(xxi. 1-6)
(4.)	......	....	§ 30 (v. 4—7)	§ 222, (xxi. 11)
(5.)	......	....	§ 31, (v. 8—$10\frac{1}{2}$)	
(6.)	§ 21, (iv. 19, 20)	§ 10, (i. 17,18)	§ 32, (v. $10\frac{1}{2}$, 11)	
(7.)	§ 22, (iv. 21, 22)	§ 11, (i. 19, 20)		

---

* Jerome evidently supposed that Ammonius was the author of *the Canons* as well:—" Canones quos *Eusebius* Caesariensis Episcopus *Alexandrinum secutus Ammonium* in decem numeros ordinavit, sicut in Graeco habentur expressimus." (*Ad Papam Damasum. Epist.*) And again : "*Ammonius* .... *Evangelicos Canones excogitavit* quos postea secutus est Eusebius Caesariensis." (*De Viris Illustr.* c. 55 [*Opp.* ii. 881.])

It will be perceived from this, that EUSEBIUS subdivides these three portions of the sacred Narrative into ten Sections ("§§;") — of which three belong to S. Matthew, viz. §§ 20, 21, 22 :—three to S. Mark, viz. §§ 9, 10, 11 :—four to S. Luke, viz. §§ 29, 30, 31, 32 : which ten Sections, EUSEBIUS distributes over four of his Canons: referring three of them to his IInd Canon, (which exhibits what S. Matthew, S. Mark, and S. Luke have in common); four of them to his VIth Canon, (which shews what S. Matthew and S. Mark have in common); one, to his IXth, (which contains what is common to S. Luke and S. John); two, to his Xth, (in which is found what is peculiar to each Evangelist.)

Now, the design which *EUSEBIUS* had in breaking up this portion of the sacred Text, (S. Matth. iv. 18—22, S. Mark i. 16—20, S. Luke v. 1—11,) after so arbitrary a fashion, into ten portions; divorcing three of those Sections from S. Matthew's Gospel, (viz. S. Luke's §§ 29, 30, 31); and connecting one of these last three (§ 30) *with two Sections* (§§ 219, 222) *of S. John;*—is perfectly plain. His object was, (as he himself explains,) to shew—not only (*a*) what S. Matthew has in common with S. Mark and S. Luke; but also (*b*) *what S. Luke has in common with S. John;*—as well as (*c*) what S. Luke has *peculiar to himself.* But, in the work of AMMONIUS, *as far as we know anything about that work*, all this would have been simply impossible. (I have already described his "Diatessaron," at pp. 126-7.) Intent on exhibiting the Sections of the other Gospels which correspond with the Sections of *S. Matthew*, AMMONIUS would not if he could,—(and he could not if he would,)—have dissociated from its context S. Luke's account of the first miraculous draught of fishes in the beginning of our LORD's Ministry, for the purpose of establishing its resemblance to S. John's account of the *second* miraculous draught of fishes which took place after the Resurrection, and is only found in S. John's Gospel. These Sections therefore are "EUSEBIAN," not AMMONIAN. They are *necessary,* according to the scheme of EUSEBIUS. They are not only unnecessary and even meaningless, but actually impossible, in the AMMONIAN scheme.

2. Let me call attention to another, and, as I think, a more convincing instance. I am content in fact to narrow the whole question to the following single issue:—Let me be shewn how it is rationally conceivable that AMMONIUS can have split up S. John xxi. 12, 13, into *three distinct Sections;* and S. John xxi. 15, 16, 17, into *six?* and yet, after so many injudicious disintegrations of the sacred Text, how it is credible that he can have made but *one* Section of S. John xxi. 18 to 25,—which nevertheless, from its very varied contents, confessedly requires even *repeated* subdivision? .... Why EUSEBIUS did all this, is abundantly plain. His peculiar plan constrained him to refer the *former* half of ver. 12,—the *latter* half of verses 15, 16, 17—to his IXth Canon, where S. Luke and S. John are brought together; (ἐν ᾧ οἱ δύο τὰ παραπλήσια εἰρήκασι) :—and to consign the *latter* half of ver. 12,—the *former* half of verses 15, 16, 17, —together with the whole of the *last eight verses* of S. John's Gospel, to his X[th] (or last) Canon, where what is peculiar to each of the four Evangelists is set down, (ἐν ᾧ περὶ τίνων ἕκαστος αὐτῶν ἰδίως ἀνέγραψεν.) But AMMONIUS, because he confessedly *recognised no such Canons,* was under no such constraint. He had in fact *no such opportunity.* He therefore simply *cannot* have adopted the same extraordinary sectional subdivision.

3. To state the matter somewhat differently, and perhaps to exhibit the argument in a more convincing form :—The Canons of EUSEBIUS, and the so-called "AMMONIAN SECTIONS,"—(by which, confessedly, nothing else whatever is *meant* but the Sections of *EUSEBIUS,*)—are discovered mutually to imply one another. Those Canons are without meaning or use apart from the Sections,—for the sake of which they were clearly invented. Those Sections, whatever convenience they may possess apart from the Canons, nevertheless are discovered to presuppose the Canons throughout: to be manifestly subsequent to them in order of time: to depend upon them for their very existence: in some places to be even unaccountable in the eccentricity of their arrangement, except when explained by the requirements of the *EUSEBIAN* Canons. I say—*That* particular sectional sub-

division, in other words, to which the epithet "AMMONIAN" is popularly applied,—(applied however without authority, and in fact by the merest license,)—proves on careful inspection to have been only capable of being devised by one *who was already in possession of the Canons of* EUSEBIUS. In plain terms, they are demonstrably *the work of* EUSEBIUS *himself*,—who expressly claims *The Canons* for his own (κανόνας δέκα τὸν ἀριθμὸν διεχάραξά σοι), and leaves it to be inferred that he is the Author of the Sections also. Wetstein (*Proleg.* p. 70,) and Bishop Lloyd (in the "Monitum" prefixed to his ed. of the Greek Test. p. x,) so understand the matter; and Mr. Scrivener (*Introduction*, p. 51) evidently inclines to the same opinion.

II. I desire, in the next place, to point out that a careful inspection of the Eusebian "Sections," (for Eusebius himself calls them περικοπαί, not κεφάλαια,) leads inevitably to the inference that they are only rightly understood when regarded in the light of "MARGINAL REFERENCES." This has been hitherto overlooked. Bp. Lloyd, in the interesting "Monitum" already quoted, remarks of the Eusebian Canons, —"quorum haec est utilitas, ut eorum scilicet ope quivis, nullo labore, Harmoniam sibi quatuor Evangeliorum possit conficere." The learned Prelate can never have made the attempt in this way "Harmoniam sibi conficere," or he would not have so written. He evidently did not advert to the fact that Eusebius refers his readers (in his IIIrd Canon) from S. John's account of the *Healing of the Nobleman's son* to the account given by S. Matthew and S. Luke of the *Healing of the Centurion's servant.* It is perfectly plain in fact that to enable a reader "to construct for himself *a Harmony of the Gospels*," was no part of Eusebius' intention; and quite certain that any one who shall ever attempt to avail himself of the system of Sections and Canons before us with that object, will speedily find himself landed in hopeless confusion [a].

[a] There was published at the University Press in 1805, a handsome quarto volume (pp. 216) entitled *Harmonia quatuor Evangeliorum juxta Sectiones Ammonianas et Eusebii Canones.* It is merely the contents of the X Canons

But in fact there is no danger of his making much progress in his task. His first discovery would probably be that S. John's weighty doctrinal statements concerning our LORD's *Eternal Godhead* in chap. i. 1—5 : 9, 10 : 14, are represented as parallel with the *Human Genealogy* of our SAVIOUR as recorded by S. Matthew i. 1—16, and by S. Luke iii. 23—38 :—the next, that the first half of the Visit of the Magi (S. Matthew ii. 1—6) is exhibited as corresponding with S. John vii. 41, 42.—Two such facts ought to open the eyes of a reader of ordinary acuteness quite wide to the true nature of the Canons of Eusebius. They are *Tables of Reference only*.

Eusebius has in fact himself explained his object in constructing them; which (he says) was twofold: (1st) To enable a reader to see at a glance, "*which* of the Evangelists have said *things of the same kind*," (τίνες τὰ παραπλήσια εἰρήκασι : the phrase occurs *four times* in the course of his short Epistle) : and (2ndly), To enable him to find out *where* they have severally done so : (τοὺς οἰκείους ἑκάστου εὐαγγελιστοῦ τόπους, ἐν οἷς κατὰ τῶν αὐτῶν ἠνέχθησαν εἰπεῖν ; Eusebius uses the phrase *twice*.) But this, (as all are aware) is precisely the office of (what are called) "Marginal References." Accordingly,

(*a.*) Whether referring *from* S. Matth. x. 40 (§ 98); S. Mark ix. 37 (§ 96); or S. Luke x. 16 (§ 116);—we find ourselves referred *to* the following *six* places of S. John,—v. 23 : xii. 44, 45 : xiii. 20 : xiv. 21 : xiv. 24, 25 : xv. 23 [b] (= §§ 40, 111, 120, 129, 131, 144 [b].) Again,

(*b.*) Whether we refer *from* S. Matth. xi. 27 (§§ 111, 112,) or S. Luke x. 22 (§ 119),—we find ourselves referred *to* the following *eleven* places of S. John,—i. 18 : iii. 35 : v. 37 : vi. 46 : vii. 28, 29 : viii. 19 : x. 15 : xiii. 3 : xv. 21 : xvi. 15 : xvii. 25 (§§ 8, 30, 44, 61, 76, 87, 90, 114, 142, 148, 154.)

(*c.*) So also, from S. Matthew's (xvi. 13—16), S. Mark's (viii. 27—29), and S. Luke's (ix. 18—20) account of S.

---

of Eusebius printed *in extenso*,—and of course is no "Harmony" at all. It would have been a really useful book, notwithstanding; but that the editor, strange to say, has omitted to number the sections.

[b] This last § according to *Tischendorf's* ed. of the Eusebian Canons.

Peter's Confession at Cæsarea Philippi, — we are referred to S. John i. 42, 43,—a singular reference; and to S. John vi. 68, 69.

(*d*.) From the mention of the last Passover by the three earlier Evangelists, (S. Matth. xxvi. 1, 2: S. Mark xiv. 1: S. Luke xxii. 1,) we are referred to S. John's mention of the *first* Passover (ii. 13 = § 20); and of the *second* (vi. 4 = § 48); as well as of the fourth (xi. 55 = § 96.)

(*e*.) From the words of Consecration at the Last Supper, as recorded by S. Matth. (xxvi. 16), S. Mark (xiv. 22), and S. Luke (xxii. 19),—we are referred to the four following Sections of our LORD'S Discourse in the Synagogue at Capernaum recorded by S. John, which took place a year before, —S. John vi. 35, 36: 48: 51: 55: (§§ 55, 63, 65, 67).

(*f*.) Nothing but the spirit in which "Marginal References" are made would warrant a critic in linking together three incidents like the following,—similar, indeed, yet entirely distinct: viz. S. Matth. xxvii. 34: S. Mark xv. 24: and S. John xix. 28, 29.

(*g*.) I was about to say that scarcely could such an excuse be invented for referring a Reader from S. Luke xxii. 32, to S. John xxi. 15, and 16, and 17 (= §§ 227, 228, 229,)— but I perceive that the same three References stand in the margin of our own Bibles. Not even the margin of the English Bible, however, sends a Reader (as the IXth Canon of Eusebius does) from our LORD'S eating "broiled fish and honeycomb," in the presence of the ten Apostles at Jerusalem on the evening of the first Easter-Day, (S. Luke xxiv. 41—43 (= § 341,)) to His feeding the seven Apostles with bread and fish at the Sea of Galilee many days after. (S. John xxi. 9, 10: 12: 13 = §§ 221, 223, 224.) — And this may suffice.

It is at all events certain that the correctest notion of the use and the value of the Eusebian Sections will be obtained by one who will be at the pains to substitute for *the Eusebian Numbers* in the margin of a copy of the Greek Gospels *the References* which these numbers severally indicate. It will then become plain that the system of Sections and Canons which Eusebius invented,—ingenious, interesting, and useful as it certainly is; highly important also, as being the known work of an illustrious Father of the Church, as well as most precious occasionally for critical purposes[c],—is nothing else but a clumsy substitute for what is achieved by an ordinary "Reference Bible":—participating in every inconvenience incidental to the unskilfully contrived apparatus with which English readers are familiar[d], and yet inferior in the following four respects:—

(1st.) The references of Eusebius, (except those found in Canon X.), require in every instance to be *deciphered*, before they can be verified; and they can only be deciphered by making search, (and sometimes laborious search,) in another part of the volume. They are not, in fact, (nor do they pretend to be,) references to the inspired Text at all; but only *references to the Eusebian Canons*.

(2ndly.) In their scope, they are of course strictly *confined to the Gospels*,—which most inconveniently limits their use, as well as diminishes their value. (Thus, by no possibility is Eusebius able to refer a reader from S. Luke xxii. 19, 20 to 1 Cor. xi. 23—25.)

(3rdly.) By the very nature of their constitution, reference even to *another part of the same Gospel* is impossible. (Euse-

---

[c] Thus, certain disputed passages of importance are proved to have been recognised at least *by Eusebius*. Our LORD'S Agony in the Garden for instance, (S. Luke xxii. 43, 44—wanting in Cod. B,) is by him numbered § 283: and that often rejected verse, S. Mark xv. 28, he certainly numbered § 216,—whatever Tischendorf may say to the contrary. (See p. 293.)

[d] It is obvious to suggest that, (1) whereas our Marginal References follow the order of the Sacred Books, they ought rather to stand in the order of their importance, or at least of their relevancy to the matter in hand:—and that, (2) actual Quotations, and even Allusions to other parts of Scripture when they are undeniable, should be referred to in some distinguishing way. It is also certain that, (3) to a far greater extent than at present, *sets* of References might be kept *together*; not scattered about in small parcels over the whole Book.—Above all, (as the point most pertinent to the present occasion,) (4) it is to be wished that *strictly parallel places* in the Gospels might be distinguished from those which are illustrative only, or are merely recalled by their similarity of subject or expression. All this would admit of interesting and useful illustration. While on this subject, let me ask,—Why is it no longer possible to purchase a Bible with References to the Apocrypha? *Who* does not miss the reference to "Ecclus. xliii. 11, 12" at Gen. ix. 14? *Who* can afford to do without the reference to "1 Macc. iv. 59" at S. John x. 22?

bius is unable, for example, to refer a reader from S. John xix. 39, to iii. 1 and vii. 50.)

But besides the preceding, which are disadvantages inherent in the scheme and inseparable from it, it will be found (4thly), That Eusebius, while he introduces not a few wholly undesirable references, (of which some specimens are supplied above), is observed occasionally to withhold references which cannot by any means be dispensed with. Thus, he omits to refer his reader from S. Luke's account of the visit to the Sepulchre (chap. xxiv. 12) to S. John's memorable account of the same transaction (chap. xx. 3—10) : *not* because he disallowed the verse in S. Luke's Gospel,—for in a certain place *he discusses its statements* [e].

III. It is abundantly plain from all that has gone before that the work of EUSEBIUS was entirely different in its structure and intention from the work of AMMONIUS. Enough, in fact, has been said to make it fully apparent that it is nothing short of impossible that there can have been any extensive correspondence between the two. According to EUSEBIUS, S. Mark has 21 Sections [f] *peculiar to his Gospel :* S. Luke, 72 : S. John, 97 [g]. According to the same EUSEBIUS, 14 Sections [h] are common to S. Luke and S. Mark *only :* 21, to S. Luke and S. John *only.* But those 225 Sections can have found *no place* in the work of AMMONIUS. And if, (in some unexplained way,) room *was* found for those parts of the Gospels, *with what possible motive can AMMONIUS have subdivided them into exactly* 225 *portions ?* It is nothing else but irrational to assume that he did so.

Not unaware am I that it has been pointed out by a most judicious living Critic as a " ground for hesitation before we ascribe the Sections as well as the Canons to Eusebius, that not a few ancient MSS. contain the former while they omit the latter [i]." He considers it to be certainly indicated thereby " that in the judgment of critics and transcribers,

---

[e] Mai, vol. iv. p. 287. See also p. 293. [f] Tischendorf says 19 only.
[g] Tischendorf says 96 only. [h] Tischendorf says 13 only.
[i] Scrivener specifies the following Codd. C, F, H, I, P, Q, R, W⁶, Y, Z, 54, 59, 60, 68, 440, i^scr, s^scr. Also D and K. (*Cod. Bezæ*, p. xx, and *Introd.* pp. 51, 2.) Add Evan. 117 : (but I think *not* 263.)

(whatever that judgment may be deemed worth,) the Ammonian Sections had a previous existence to the Eusebian Canons, as well as served for an independent purpose." But I respectfully demur to the former of the two proposed inferences. I also learn with surprise that "those who have studied them most, can the least tell what use the Ammonian Sections can serve, unless in connection with Canons of Harmony [k]."

However irregular and arbitrary these subdivisions of the Evangelical text are observed to be in their construction, their usefulness is paramount. They are observed to fulfil *exactly the same office* as our own actual division of the Text into 89 Chapters and 3780 Verses. Of course, 1165 subdivisions are (for certain purposes) somewhat less convenient than 3780;—but on the other hand, a place in the Gospels would be more easily discovered, I suspect, for the most part, by the employment of such a single set of consecutive numbers, than by requiring a Reader first to find the Chapter by its Roman numeral, and then the Verse by its Arabic figure. Be this as it may, there can be at least only one opinion as to the *supreme convenience to a Reader*, whether ancient or modern, of knowing that the copy of the Gospels which he holds in his hands is subdivided into exactly the same 1165 Sections as every other Greek copy which is likely to come in his way; and that, in every such copy, he may depend on finding every one of those sections invariably distinguished by the self-same number.

A Greek copy of the Gospels, therefore, having its margin furnished with the Eusebian *Sectional* notation, may be considered to correspond generally with an English copy merely divided into Chapters and Verses. The addition of the Eusebian *Canons* at the beginning, with numerical references thereto inserted in the margin throughout, does but superadd something analogous to the convenience of our *Marginal References*,—and may just as reasonably (or just as unreasonably) be dispensed with.

I think it not improbable, in fact, that in the preparation of a Codex, it will have been sometimes judged commercially

---

[k] Scrivener's *Introduction*, pp. 51 and 52 : *Cod. Bezæ*, p. xx. note [2.]

expedient to leave its purchaser to decide whether he would or would not submit to the additional expense (which in the case of illuminated MSS. must have been very considerable) of having the Eusebian Tables inserted at the commencement of his Book*,—without which *the References* thereto would confessedly have been of no manner of avail. In this way it will have come to pass, (as Mr. Scrivener points out,) that "not a few ancient MSS. contain the *Sections* but omit the *Canons.*" Whether, however, the omission of References to the Canons in Copies which retain in the margin the sectional numbers, is to be explained in this way, or not,— AMMONIUS, at all events, will have had no more to do with either the one or the other, than with our modern division into Chapters and Verses. It is, in short, nothing else but a "vulgar error" to designate the Eusebian Sections as the "Sections of AMMONIUS." The expression cannot be too soon banished from our critical terminology. Whether banished or retained, *to reason about* the lost work of AMMONIUS from the Sections of EUSEBIUS (as Tischendorf and the rest habitually do) is an offence against historical Truth which no one who values his critical reputation will probably hereafter venture to commit.

IV. This subject may not be dismissed until a circumstance of considerable interest has been explained which has already attracted some notice, but which evidently is not yet understood by Biblical Critics[1].

As already remarked, the necessity of resorting to the Eusebian Tables of Canons in order to make any use of a marginal reference, is a tedious and a cumbersome process; for which, men must have early sought to devise a remedy. They were not slow in perceiving that a far simpler expedient would be to note at the foot of every page of a Gospel *the numbers* of the Sections of that Gospel contained *in extenso* on the same page; and, parallel with those numbers, to exhibit the numbers of the corresponding Sections in the

---

* Evan. 263, for instance, has certainly *blank* Eusebian Tables at the beginning: the *frame* only. [1] See Scrivener's *Introduction*, p. 51 (note 2), —where Tregelles (in Horne's *Introd.* iv. 200) is quoted.

G.] *at the foot of the Gospels, explained.* 385

other Gospels. Many Codices, furnished with such an apparatus at the foot of the page, are known to exist [m]. For instance, in Cod. 262 (= Reg. 53, at Paris), which is written in double columns, at foot of the first page (*fol.* 111) of S. Mark, is found as follows:—

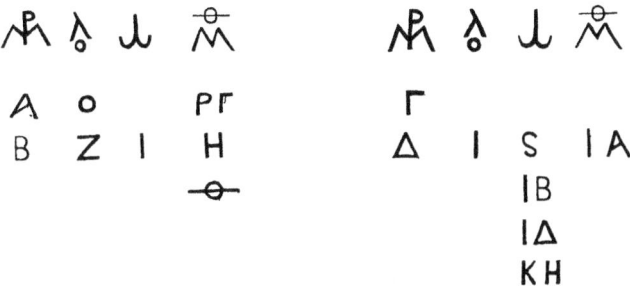

The meaning of this, every one will see who,—(remembering what is signified by the monograms MP, Λο, ΙΩ, ΜΘ,[n])—will turn successively to the IInd, the I[st], the VIth, and the I[st] of the Eusebian Canons. Translated into expressions more familiar to English readers, it evidently amounts to this: that we are referred,

(§ 1) From S. Mark i. 1, 2,—to S. Matth. xi. 10 : S. Luke vii. 27.
(§ 2) . . . . i. 3,—to S. Matth. iii. 3 : S. Luke iii. 3—6.
(§ 3) . . . . i. 4, 5, 6,—to S. Matth. iii. 4—6.
(§ 4) . . . . i. 7, 8,—to S. Matth. iii. 11 : S. Luke iii. 16 :
S. John i. 15, 26-27, 30-1 : iii. 28.

(I venture to add that any one who will compare the above with the margin of S. Mark's Gospel in a common English "reference Bible," will obtain a very fair notion of the convenience, and of the inconveniences of the Eusebian system. But to proceed with our remarks on the apparatus at the foot of Cod. 262.)

The owner of such a MS. was able to refer to parallel passages, (as above,) *by merely turning over the pages of his book.* E.g. The parallel places to S. Mark's § 1 (A) being § 70 of

[m] e.g. Codd. M, 262 and 264. (I saw at least one other at Paris, but I have not preserved a record of the number.) To these, Tregelles adds E ; (Scrivener's *Introduction*, p. 51, note [²].) Scrivener adds W[d], and Tischendorf T[b], (Scrivener's *Cod. Bezae*, p. xx.)

[n] The *order* of these monograms requires explanation.

S. Luke (O) and § 103 of S. Matthew (P Γ),—it was just as easy for him to find those two places as it is for us to turn to S. Luke vii. 27 and S. Matth. xi. 10: perhaps easier.

V. I suspect that this peculiar method of exhibiting the Eusebian references (Canons as well as Sections) at a glance, was derived to the Greek Church from the Syrian Christians. What is certain, a precisely similar expedient for enabling readers to discover *Parallel Passages* prevails extensively in the oldest Syriac Evangelia extant. There are in the British Museum about twelve Syriac Evangelia furnished with such an apparatus of reference [o]; of which a specimen is subjoined,—derived however (because it was near at hand) from a MS. in the Bodleian [p], of the vii[th] or viii[th] century.

From this MS., I select for obvious reasons the last page but one (*fol.* 82) of S. Mark's Gospel, which contains ch. xvi. 8—18. The Reader will learn with interest and surprise that in the margin of this page against ver. 8, is written in vermilion, *by the original scribe*, $\frac{281}{1}$: against ver. 9,—$\frac{282}{10}$: against ver. 10,—$\frac{283}{1}$: against ver. 11,—$\frac{284}{8}$: against ver. 12,—$\frac{285}{8}$: against ver. 13,—$\frac{286}{8}$: against ver. 14,—$\frac{287}{10}$: against ver. 15,—$\frac{288}{6}$: against ver. 16,—$\frac{289}{10}$: against ver. 19,—$\frac{290}{8}$. That these sectional numbers [q], with references to the Eusebian Canons subscribed, are no part of the (so-called) "*Ammonian*" system, will be recognised at a glance. According to *that* scheme, S. Mark xiv. 8 is numbered $\frac{233}{2}$. But to proceed.

---

[o] Addit. MSS. 14,449 : 14,450, and 1, and 2, and 4, and 5, and 7, and 8 : 14,463, and 9 : 17,113. (Dr. Wright's *Catalogue*, 4to. 1870.) Also Rich. 7,157. The reader is referred to Assemani; and to Adler, p. 52-3 : also p. 63.

[p] "Dawkins 3." See Dean Payne Smith's *Catalogue*, p. 72.

[q] It will be observed that, according to the Syrian scheme, *every verse* of S. Mark xvi, from ver. 8 to ver. 15 inclusive, constitutes an independent section (§§ 281—288) : ver. 16—18 another (§ 289); and verr. 19—20, another (§ 290), which is the last. The Greek scheme, as a rule, makes independent sections of verr. 8, 9, 14, 19, 20; but throws together ver. 10—11 : 12—13 : 15—16 : 17—18. (*Vide infrà*, p. 311.)

At the foot of the same page, (which is written in two columns), is found the following set of rubricated references to parallel places in the other three Gospels:—

[Syriac text in two columns]

The exact English counterpart of which,—(I owe it to the kind help of M. Neubauer, of the Bodleian),—is subjoined. The Reader will scarcely require to be reminded that the reason why §§ 282, 287, 289 do not appear in this Table is because those Sections, (belonging to the tenth Canon,) have nothing parallel to them in the other Gospels.

Luke	Matthew	Mark	‖	John	Luke	Matthew	Mark
391	...	286	‖	247	390	421	281
...	426	288	‖	247	390	421	283
			‖	...	391	...	284
			‖	...	393	...	285

The general intention of this is sufficiently obvious: but the Reader must be told that on making reference to S. MATTHEW'S Gospel, in this Syriac Codex, it is found that § 421 = chap. xxviii. 8; and § 426 = chap. xxviii. 19, 20:

That, in S. LUKE's Gospel,—§ 390 = chap. xxiv. 8—10: § 391 = chap. xxiv. 11; and § 393 = chap. xxiv. 13—17 [r]:

That, in S. JOHN's Gospel,—§ 247 = chap. xx. 17 ($\pi o\rho\epsilon \acute{u} o \upsilon$ down to $\Theta\epsilon\grave{o}\nu$ $\dot{\upsilon}\mu\hat{\omega}\nu$ [s].)

---

[r] Note that § $\frac{392}{9}$ = S. Luke xxiv. 12: § $\frac{394}{10}$ = ver. 18—34: § $\frac{395}{8}$ = ver. 35: § $\frac{396}{9}$ is incomplete. [Dr. Wright supplies the lacune for me, thus: § $\frac{396}{9}$ = ver. 36—41 (down to $\theta\alpha\upsilon\mu\alpha\zeta\acute{o}\nu\tau\omega\nu$): § $\frac{397}{9}$ = $\epsilon\hat{\iota}\pi\epsilon\nu$ $\alpha\dot{\upsilon}\tauo\hat{\iota}s$ down to the end of ver. 41: § $\frac{398}{9}$ = ver. 42: § $\frac{399}{9}$ = ver. 43: § $\frac{400}{10}$ = ver. 44—50: § $\frac{401}{8}$ = 51: § $\frac{402}{10}$ = ver. 52, 3.]

Critical readers will be interested in comparing, or rather contrasting, the Sectional system of a Syriac MS. with that which prevails in all Greek

So that, exhibited in familiar language, these Syriac *Marginal References* are intended to guide a Reader,

(§ 281) From S. Mark xvi. 8,—to S. Matth. xxviii. 8 : S. Luke xxiv. 8—10 : S. John xx. 17 (πορεύου to the end of the verse).
(§ 283) . . . . xvi. 10,—to the same three places.
(§ 284) . . . . xvi. 11,—to S. Luke xxiv. 11.
(§ 285) . . . . xvi. 12,—to S. Luke xxiv. 13—17,
(§ 286) . . . . xvi. 13,—to S. Luke xxiv. 11.
(§ 288) . . . . xvi. 15,—to S. Matth. xxiv. 19, 20.

Here then, although the Ten Eusebian Canons are faithfully retained, it is much to be noted that we are presented with *a different set of Sectional subdivisions*. This will be best understood by attentively comparing all the details which precede with the Eusebian references in the inner margin of a copy of Lloyd's Greek Testament.

But the convincing *proof* that these Syriac Sections are not those with which we have been hitherto acquainted from Greek MSS., is supplied by the fact that they are so many

Codices. S. John's § $\frac{248}{1}$ = xx. 18 : his § $\frac{249}{9}$ = ver. 19 to εἰρήνη ὑμῖν in ver. 21 : his § $\frac{250}{7}$ = ver. 21 (καθώς to the end of the verse) : his § $\frac{251}{10}$ = ver. 22 : his § $\frac{252}{7}$ = ver. 23 : his § $\frac{253}{[10]}$ = ver. 24-5 : his § $\frac{254}{[9]}$ = ver. 26-7 : his § $\frac{255}{10}$ = ver. 28 to the end of xxi. 4 : his § $\frac{256}{9}$ = xxi. 5 : his § $\frac{257}{9}$ = xxi. 6 (to εὑρήσετε) : his § $\frac{258}{9}$ = ver. 6, (ἔβαλον to the end) : his § $\frac{259}{[10]}$ = ver. 7, 8 : his § $\frac{260}{[9]}$ = ver. 9 : his § $\frac{261}{10}$ = ver. 10 : his § $\frac{262}{9}$ = ver. 11 : his § $\frac{263}{9}$ = first half of ver. 12 : his § $\frac{264}{10}$ is incomplete.

[But Dr. Wright, (remarking that in his MSS., which are evidently the correcter ones, $\frac{263}{10}$ stands opposite the middle of ver. 12 [οὐδεὶς δὲ ἐτόλμα], and $\frac{264}{9}$ opposite ver. 13 [ἔρχεται οὖν],) proceeds to supply the lacune for me, thus : § $\frac{264}{9}$ = ver. 13 : § $\frac{265}{10}$ = ver. 14-5 (down to φιλῶ σε· λέγει αὐτῷ) : § $\frac{266}{9}$ = βόσκε τὰ ἀρνία μου, (end of ver. 15) : § $\frac{267}{10}$ = ver. 16 (down to φιλῶ σε) : § $\frac{268}{9}$ = λέγει αὐτῷ, Ποίμαινε τὰ πρόβατά μου (end of ver. 16) : § $\frac{269}{10}$ = ver. 17 (down to φιλῶ σε) : § $\frac{270}{9}$ = λέγει αὐτῷ ὁ Ἰ., β. τὰ π. μου (end of ver. 17) : § $\frac{271}{10}$ = ver. 18 to 25.]

more *in number*. The sum of the Sections in each of the Gospels follows; for which, (the Bodleian Codex being mutilated,) I am indebted to the learning and obligingness of Dr. Wright[t]. He quotes from "the beautiful MS. Addit. 7,157, written A.D. 768[u]." From this, it appears that the Sections in the Gospel according to,—

S. MATTHEW, (instead of being from 359 to 355,) are 426 : (the last Section, $\S\frac{426,}{6}$ consisting of ver. 19, 20.)

S. MARK, (. . . . . 241 to 233,) . . 290: (the last Section, $\S\frac{290,}{8}$ consisting of ver. 19, 20.)

S. LUKE, (. . . . . 349 to 342,) . . 402: (the last Section, $\S\frac{402,}{10}$ consisting of ver. 52, 53.)

S. JOHN, (. . . . . 232,) . . 271: (the last Section, $\S\frac{271,}{10}$ consisting of ver. 18—25.)

The sum of the Sections therefore, in *Syriac* MSS. instead of being between 1181 and 1162[v], is found to be invariably 1389.

But here, the question arises,—Did the Syrian Christians then retain the Ten Tables, dressing their contents afresh, so as to adapt them to their own ampler system of sectional subdivision ? or did they merely retain the elementary principle of referring each Section to one of Ten Canons, but substitute for the Eusebian Tables a species of harmony, or apparatus of reference, at the foot of every page?

The foregoing doubt is triumphantly resolved by a reference to Assemani's engraved representation, on xxii Copper Plates, of the X Eusebian Tables from a superb Syriac Codex (A.D. 586) in the Medicean Library[w]. The student who

[t] " I have examined for your purposes, Add. 14,449; 14,457; 14,458; and 7,157. The first three are N[os]. lxix, lxx, and lxxi, in my own Catalogue: the last, a Nestorian MS., is N°. xiii in the old Catalogue of Forshall and Rosen (London, 1838). All four agree in their numeration."

[u] See the preceding note.—Availing myself of the reference given me by my learned correspondent, I read as follows in the Catalogue:—" Inter ipsa textus verba, numeris viridi colore pictis, notatur Canon harmoniae Eusebianae, ad quem quaevis sectio referenda est. Sic, { [i.e. 1] indicat canonem in quo omnes Evangelistae concurrunt," &c. &c.

[v] Suidas [A.D. 980], by giving 236 to S. Mark and 348 to S. Luke, makes the sum of the Sections in Greek Evangelia 1,171.

[w] This sheet was all but out of the printer's hands when the place in vol. i.

inquires for Assemani's work will find that the numbers in the last line of each of the X Tables is as follows:—

	Matthew	Mark	Luke	John
Canon i	421	283	390	247
—— ii	416	276	383	...
—— iii	134	...	145	178
—— iv	394	212	...	223
—— v	319	...	262	...
—— vi	426	288	...	...
—— vii	425	...	...	249
—— viii	...	290	401	...
—— ix	...	...	399	262
—— x	424	289	402	271

The Syrian Church, therefore, from a period of the remotest antiquity, not only subdivided the Gospels into a far greater number of Sections than were in use among the Greeks, but also habitually employed Eusebian Tables which —identical as they are in *appearance* and in *the principle* of their arrangement with those with which Greek MSS. have made us familiar,—yet differ materially from these as to *the numerical details* of their contents.

Let abler men follow up this inquiry to its lawful results. When the extreme antiquity of the Syriac documents is considered, may it not almost be made a question whether Eusebius himself put forth the larger or the smaller number of Sections? But however *that* may be, more palpably precarious than ever, I venture to submit, becomes the confident assertion of the Critics that, "just as EUSEBIUS found these Verses [S. Mark xvi. 9—20] absent in his day from the best and most numerous [*sic*] copies, *so was also the case with AMMONIUS* when he formed his Harmony in the preceding century"[x]. To speak plainly, the statement is purely mythical.

VI. Birch [*Varr. Lectt.* p. 226], asserts that in the best Codices, the Sections of S. Mark's Gospel are not numbered beyond ch. xvi. 8. Tischendorf prudently adds, "*or* ver. 9:"

---

of Assemani's *Bibliotheca Medicea*, (fol. 1742,) was shewn me by my learned friend, P. E. Pusey, Esq., of Ch. Ch.—Dr. Wright had already most obligingly and satisfactorily resolved my inquiry from the mutilated fragments of the Canons, as well as of the Epistle to Carpianus in Add. 17,213 and 14,450.

[x] Dr. Tregelles. (*Vide suprà*, pp. 125-6.) And so, Tischendorf.

but to introduce *that* alternative is to surrender everything. I subjoin the result of an appeal to 151 Greek Evangelia. There is written opposite to,

ver. 6, .. § 232, in 3 Codices, (viz. A, U, 286)
— 8, .. § 233, .. 34 ...... (including L, S)[y]
— 9, (?) § 234, .. 41 ...... (including Γ, Δ, Π)[z]
— 10, (?) § 235, .. 4 ...... (viz. 67, 282, 331, 406)
— 12, (?) § 236, .. 7 .... (the number assigned by Suidas)[a]
— 14, (?) § 237, .. 12 ...... (including Λ)[b]
— 15, .. § 238, .. 3 ...... (viz. Add. 19,387: 27,861, Ti^2)
— 17, .. § 239, .. 1 ...... (viz. G)
— 19, .. § 240, .. 10 .... (including H, M, and the Codices from which the Hharklensian Revision, A.D. 616, was made)[c]
— 20, .. § 241, .. 36 ...... (including C, E, K, V)[d]

Thus, it is found that 114 Codices sectionize the last Twelve Verses, against 37 which close the account at ver. 8, or sooner. I infer—(*a*) That the reckoning which would limit the sections to precisely 233, is altogether precarious; and—(*b*) That the sum of the Sections assigned to S. Mark's Gospel by Suidas and by Stephens (viz. 236) is arbitrary.

VII. To some, it may not be unacceptable, in conclusion, to be presented with the very words in which Eusebius explains how he would have his Sections and Canons used. His language requires attention. He says:—

Εἰ οὖν ἀναπτύξας ἕν τι τῶν τεσσάρων εὐαγγελίων ὁποιονδήποτε, βουληθείης ἐπιστῆναί τινι ᾧ βούλει κεφαλαίῳ, καὶ γνῶναι τίνες τὰ παραπλήσια εἰρήκασι, καὶ τοὺς οἰκείους ἐν

---

[y] The others are 11, 14, 22, 23, 28, 32, 37, 40, 45, 52, 98, 113, 115, 127, 129, 132, 133, 134, 137, 169, 186, 188, 193, 195, 265, 269, 276, 371. Add. 18,211, Cromwell 15, Wake 12 *and* 27.

[z] The others are 5, 6, 9, 12, 13, 15, 24, 29, 54 [more §§ ?], 65, 68, 111, 112, 114, 118, 157, 183, 190, 202, 263, 268, 270, 273, 277, 278, 284, 287, 294, 414, 438, 439. Rich 7,141. Add. 17,741 *and* 17,982. Cromw. 16. Canonici 36 *and* 112. Wake 21. [a] Viz. 184, 192, 264, h^{scr}, Add. 11,836. Ti^1. Wake 29.

[b] The others are 10, 20, 21, 36, 49, 187, 262, 266, 300, 364. Rawl. 141.

[c] *Vide suprà*, p. 33. Assemani, vol. i. p. 28. (Comp. Adler, p. 53.) The others are 8, 26, 72, 299, 447. Bodl. Miscell. 17. Wake 36.

[d] The others are 7, 27, 34, 38, 39, 46, 74, 89, 105, 116, 117, 135, 179, 185, 194, 198, 207, 212, 260, 261, 267, 275, 279, 293, 301, 445, k^{scr}. Add. 22,740. Wake 22, 24, 30; *and* 31 in which, ver. 20 is numbered смв.

ἑκάστῳ τόπους εὑρεῖν ἐν οἷς κατὰ τῶν αὐτῶν ἠνέχθησαν, ἧς ἐπέχεις περικοπῆς ἀναλαβὼν τὸν προκείμενον ἀριθμὸν, ἐπιζητήσας τὲ αὐτὸν ἔνδον ἐν τῷ κανόνι ὃν ἡ διὰ τοῦ κινναβάρεως ὑποσημείωσις ὑποβέβληκεν, εἴσῃ μὲν εὐθὺς ἐκ τῶν ἐπὶ μετώπου τοῦ κανόνος προγραφῶν, ὁπόσοι καὶ τίνες τὰ παραπλήσια εἰρήκασιν· ἐπιστήσας δὲ καὶ τοῖς τῶν λοιπῶν εὐαγγελίων ἀριθμοῖς τοῖς ἐν τῷ κανόνι ᾧ ἐπέχεις ἀριθμῷ παρακειμένοις, ἐπιζητήσας τὲ αὐτοὺς ἔνδον ἐν τοῖς οἰκείοις ἑκάστου εὐαγγελίου τόποις, τὰ παραπλήσια λέγοντας εὑρήσεις.

Jerome,—who is observed sometimes to exhibit the sense of his author very loosely,—renders this as follows:—

"Cum igitur aperto Codice, verbi gratia, illud sive illud Capitulum scire volueris cujus Canonis sit, statim ex subjecto numero doceberis; et recurrens ad principia, in quibus Canonum est distincta congeries, eodemque statim Canone ex titulo frontis invento, illum quem quærebas numerum, ejusdem Evangelistæ, qui et ipse ex inscriptione signatur, invenies; atque e vicino ceterorum tramitibus inspectis, quos numeros e regione habeant, annotabis. Et cum scieris, recurres ad volumina singulorum, et sine mora repertis numeris quos ante signaveras, reperies et loca in quibus vel eadem, vel vicina dixerunt."

This may be a very masterly way of explaining the use of the Eusebian Canons. But the points of the original are missed. What Eusebius actually says is this:—

"If therefore, on opening any one soever of the four Gospels, thou desirest to study any given Section, and to ascertain which of the Evangelists have said things of the same kind; as well as to discover the particular place where each has been led [to speak] of the same things;—note the number of the Section thou art studying, and seek that number in the Canon indicated by the numeral subscribed in vermilion. Thou wilt be made aware, at once, from the heading of each Canon, how many of the Evangelists, and which of them, have said things of the same kind. Then, by attending to the parallel numbers relating to the other Gospels in the same Canon, and by turning to each in its proper place, thou wilt discover the Evangelists saying things of the same kind."

APPENDIX (H).

On the Interpolation of the text of CODEX B *and* CODEX ℵ *at*
S. MATTHEW xxvii. 48 *or* 49.

IT is well known that our two oldest Codices, Cod. B and Cod. ℵ, (see above, p. 80,) exhibit S. Matthew xxvii. 49, as follows. After σωσων [*Cod. Sinait.* σωσαι] αυτον, they read:—

(COD. B.)

αλλος δε λαβω̄
λογχην ενυξεν αυτου
την πλευραν και εξηλ
θεν υδωρ και αιμα

(COD. ℵ.)

αλλος
δε λαβων λογχη̄
ενυξεν αυτου τη̄
πλευραν και εξηλ
θεν υδωρ και αι
μα

Then comes, ο δε ῑς παλιν κραξας κ.τ.λ. The same is also the reading of Codd. C, L, U, Γ: and it is known to recur in the following cursives,—5, 48, 67, 115, 127[a].

Obvious is it to suspect with Matthaei, (ed. 1803, vol. i. p. 158,) that it was the Lectionary practice of the Oriental Church which occasioned this interpolation. In S. John xix. 34 occurs the well-known record,—ἀλλ' εἶς τῶν στρατιωτῶν λόγχῃ αὐτοῦ τὴν πλευρὰν ἔνυξε, καὶ εὐθὺς ἐξῆλθεν αἷμα καὶ ὕδωρ: and it was the established practice of the Easterns, in the Ecclesiastical lection for Good Friday, (viz. S. Matth. xxvii. 1—61,) *to interpose S. John* xix. 31 *to* 37 between the 54th and the 55th verses of S. Matthew. This will be found alluded to above, at p. 202 and again at pp. 218-9.

[a] But Cod. U inserts ευθεως before εξηλθεν; and (at least two of the other Codices, viz.) 48, 67 read αιμα και υδωρ.

After the pages just quoted were in type, while examining Harl. MS. 5647 in the British Museum, (*our* Evan. 72,) I alighted on the following Scholion, which I have since found that Wetstein duly published; but which has certainly not attracted the attention it deserves, and which is incorrectly represented as referring to the end of S. Matth. xxvii. 49. It is *against ver.* 48 that there is written in the margin,—

(H^b Ὅτι εἰς τὸ καθ' ἱστορίαν εὐαγγέλιον Διαδώρου καὶ Τατιανοῦ καὶ ἄλλων διαφόρων ἁγίων πατέρων· τοῦτο πρόσκειται :

(Η Ἄλλος δὲ λαβὼν λόγχην ἔνυξεν αὐτοῦ τὴν πλευρὰν καὶ ἐξῆλθεν ὕδωρ καὶ αἷμα : τοῦτο λέγει καὶ ὁ Χρυσόστομος.

This writer is perfectly correct in his statement. In Chrysostom's 88th Homily on S. Matthew's Gospel, (*Opp.* vii, 825 c : [vol. ii, p. 526, *ed.* Field.]) is read as follows :— Ἐνόμισαν Ἠλίαν εἶναι, φησὶ, τὸν καλούμενον, καὶ εὐθέως ἐπότισαν αὐτὸν ὄξος : (which is clearly meant to be a summary of the contents *of ver.* 48 : then follows) ἕτερος δὲ προσελθών λόγχῃ αὐτοῦ τῆν πλευρὰν ἔνυξε. (Chrysostom quotes no further, but proceeds,—Τί γένοιτ' ἂν τούτων παρανομώτερον, τί δὲ θηριωδέστερον, κ.τ.λ.)

I find it impossible on a review of the evidence to adhere to the opinion I once held, and have partially expressed above, (viz. at p. 202,) that the Lectionary-practice of the Eastern Church was the occasion of this corrupt reading in our two oldest uncials. A corrupt reading it undeniably is; and the discredit of exhibiting it, Codd. B, ℵ, (not to say Codd.

---

^b Σημείωσις is what we call an "Annotation." [On the sign in the text, see the Catalogue of MSS. in the Turin Library, P. i. p. 93.] On the word, and on σημειοῦσθαι, (consider 2 Thess. iii. 14,) see the interesting remarks of Huet, *Origeniana*, iii. § i. 4. (at the end of vol. iv. of Origen's *Opp.* p. 292-3.)—Eusebius (*Hist. Eccl.* v. 20) uses σημείωσις in this sense. (See the note of Valesius.) But it is plain from the rendering of Jerome and Rufinus (*subscriptio*), that it often denoted a "signature," or signing of the name. Eusebius so employs the word in *lib.* v. 19 *ad fin.*

C, L, U, Γ,) must continue to sustain. That Chrysostom and Cyril also employed Codices disfigured by this self-same blemish, is certain. It is an interesting and suggestive circumstance. Nor is this all. Severus[e] relates that between A.D. 496 and 511, being at Constantinople, he had known this very reading strenuously discussed: whereupon had been produced a splendid copy of S. Matthew's Gospel, traditionally said to have been found with the body of the Apostle Barnabas in the Island of Cyprus in the time of the Emperor Zeno (A.D. 474—491); and preserved in the palace with superstitious veneration in consequence. It contained no record of the piercing of the SAVIOUR's side: nor (adds Severus) does any ancient Interpreter mention the transaction in that place,—except Chrysostom *and Cyril of Alexandria;* into whose Commentaries it has found its way.— Thus, to Codices B, ℵ, C and the copy familiarly employed by Chrysostom, has to be added the copy which Cyril of Alexandria[d] employed; as well as evidently sundry other Codices extant at Constantinople about A.D. 500. That the corruption of the text of S. Matthew's Gospel under review is ancient therefore, and was once very widely spread, is certain. The question remains,—and this is the only point to be determined,—How did it *originate?*

Now it must be candidly admitted, that if the strange method of the Lectionaries already explained, (viz. of interposing seven verses of S. John's xix[th] chapter [ver. 31—7] between the 54th and 55th verses of S. Matth. xxvii,) really were the occasion of this interpolation of S. John xix. 34 after S. Matth. xxvii. 48 or 49,—two points would seem to call for explanation which at present remain unexplained: First, (1) Why does *only that one verse* find place in the interpolated copies? And next, (2) How does it come to pass

---

[e] He was Patriarch of Antioch, A.D. 512-9. — The extract (made by Petrus junior, Monophysite Patriarch of Antioch, A.D. 578,) purports to be derived from the 26th Epistle, (Book 9,) which Severus addressed to Thomas Bp. of Germanicia after his exile. See Assemani, *Bibl. Orient.* vol. ii. pp. 81-2.

[d] I cannot find the place in Cyril. I suppose it occurs in a lost Commentary of this Father,—whose Works by the way are miserably indexed.

that *that* one verse is exhibited in so very depraved and so peculiar a form? For, to say nothing of the inverted order of the two principal words, (which is clearly due to 1 S. John v. 6,) let it be carefully noted that the substitution of ἄλλος δὲ λαβὼν λόγχην, for ἀλλ᾽ εἷς τῶν στρατιωτῶν λόγχῃ of the Evangelist, is a tell-tale circumstance. The turn thus licentiously given to the narrative clearly proceeded from some one who was bent on weaving incidents related by different writers into a connected narrative, and who was sometimes constrained to take liberties with his Text in consequence. (Thus, S. Matthew having supplied the fact that "ONE OF THEM ran, and *took a sponge*, and filled it with vinegar, and put it on a reed, and gave Him to drink," S. John is made to say, "AND ANOTHER—*took a spear*.") Now, this is exactly what Tatian is related by Eusebius to have done: viz. "after some fashion of his own, to have composed out of the four Gospels one connected narrative [e]."

When therefore, (as in the present Scholion,) an ancient Critic who appears to have been familiarly acquainted with the lost "Diatessaron" of Tatian, comes before us with the express declaration that in that famous monument of the primitive age (A.D. 173), S. John's record of the piercing of our SAVIOUR's side was thrust into S. Matthew's History of the Passion in this precise way and in these very terms,—(for, "Note," he says, "That into the Evangelical History of Diodorus, of Tatian, and of divers other holy Fathers, is introduced [here] the following addition: 'And another took a spear and pierced His side, and there came out Water and Blood.' This, Chrysostom also says"),—it is even unreasonable to seek for any other explanation of the vitiated text of our two oldest Codices. Not only is the testimony to the critical fact abundantly sufficient, but the proposed solution of the difficulty, in itself the reverse of improbable,

---

[e] Ὁ μέντοι γε πρότερος αὐτῶν [viz. the sect of the Severiani] ἀρχηγὸς ὁ Τατιανὸς συνάφειάν τινα καὶ συναγωγὴν οὐκ οἶδ᾽ ὅπως τῶν εὐαγγελίων συνθεὶς, τὸ διὰ τεσσάρων τοῦτο προσωνόμασεν. Ὃ καὶ παρά τισιν εἰσέτι νῦν φέρεται. The next words are every way suggestive. Τοῦ δὲ ἀποστόλου φασὶ τολμῆσαί τινας αὐτὸν μεταφράσαι φωνὰς, ὡς ἐπιδιορθούμενον αὐτῶν τὴν τῆς φράσεως σύνταξιν.—Eusebius, *Hist. Eccl.* iv. 29, § 4.

is in the highest degree suggestive as well as important. For,—May we not venture to opine that the same καθ' ἱστορίαν εὐαγγέλιον,—as this Writer aptly designates Tatian's work,—is responsible for not a few of the *monstra potius quam variae lectiones* [f] which are occasionally met with in the earliest MSS. of all? And,—Am I not right in suggesting that the circumstance before us is *the only thing we know for certain* about the text of Tatian's (miscalled) "Harmony?"

To conclude.—That the "Diatessaron" of Tatian, (for so, according to Eusebius and Theodoret, Tatian himself styled it,) has long since disappeared, no one now doubts [g]. That Eusebius himself, (who lived 150 years after the probable date of its composition,) had never seen it, may I suppose be inferred from the terms in which he speaks of it. Jerome does not so much as mention its existence. Epiphanius, who is very full and particular concerning the heresy of Tatian, affords no indication that he was acquainted with his work. On the contrary. "The Diatessaron Gospel," (he remarks in passing,) "which some call the Gospel according to the Hebrews, is said to have been the production of this writer [h]." The most interesting notice we have of Tatian's work is from the pen of Theodoret. After explaining that Tatian the Syrian, originally a Sophist, and next a disciple of Justin Martyr [A.D. 150], after Justin's death aspired to being a heretical leader,—(statements which are first found in Irenæus,)—Theodoret enumerates his special tenets. "This man" (he proceeds) "put together the so-called *Diatessaron Gospel*,—from which he cut away the genealogies, and whatever else shews that the LORD was born of the seed of David. The book was used not only by those who favoured Tatian's opinions, but by the orthodox as well; who, unaware of the mischievous spirit in which the work had been executed, in their simplicity used the book as an epitome. *I myself found upwards of two hundred such copies honourably preserved in the Churches of this place*," (Cyrus in Syria namely, of which Theodoret was made

---

[f] See, for example, the readings of B or ℵ, or both, specified from p. 80 to p. 86.   [g] *Vid. suprà*, p. 129, note (g).   [h] *Opp.* vol. i. p. 391 D.

Bishop, A.D. 423,)—"all of which I collected together, and put aside; substituting the Gospels of the Four Evangelists in their room ⁱ."

The diocese of Theodoret (he says) contained eight hundred Parishes [k]. It cannot be thought surprising that a work of which copies had been multiplied to such an extraordinary extent, and which was evidently once held in high esteem, should have had *some* influence on the text of the earliest Codices; and here, side by side with a categorical statement as to one of its licentious interpolations, we are furnished with documentary proof that many an early MS. also was infected with the same taint. To assume that the two phenomena stand related to one another in the way of cause and effect, seems to be even an inevitable proceeding.

I will not prolong this note by inquiring concerning the "Diodorus" of whom the unknown author of this scholion speaks: but I suppose it was *that* Diodorus who was made Bishop of Tarsus in A.D. 378. He is related to have been the preceptor of Chrysostom; was a very voluminous writer; and, among the rest, according to Suidas, wrote a work "on the Four Gospels."

Lastly,—How about the singular introduction *into the Lection for Good-Friday* of this incident of the piercing of the REDEEMER's side? Is it allowable to conjecture that, indirectly, the Diatessaron of Tatian may have been the occasion of *that* circumstance also; as well as of certain other similar phenomena in the Evangeliaria?

---

[i] *Haeret. Fab.* lib. i. c. xx. (*Opp.* iv. 208.)

[k] Clinton, F. R. ii. *Appendix*, p. 473, quoting Theodoret's "Ep. 113, p. 1190. [*al.* vol. iii. p. 986-7]."

POSTSCRIPT.

(PROMISED AT p 129)

I PROCEED to fulfil the promise' made at p. 51.—C. F. Matthaei (*Nov. Test.*, 1788, vol. iii. p. 269) states that in one of the MSS. at Moscow occurs the following "Scholion of EUSEBIUS:—κατὰ Μάρκον μετὰ τὴν ἀνάστασιν οὐ λέγεται ὦφθαι τοῖς μαθηταῖς." On this, Griesbach remarks (*Comm. Crit.* ii. 200),—" quod scribere non potuisset si pericopam dubiam agnovisset:" the record in S. Mark xvi. 14, being express, —Ὕστερον ἀνακειμένοις αὐτοῖς τοῖς ἔνδεκα ἐφανερώθη. The epigrammatic smartness of Griesbach's dictum has recommended it to Dr. Tregelles and others who look unfavourably on the conclusion of S. Mark's Gospel; and to this hour the Scholion of Matthaei remains unchallenged.

But to accept the proposed inference from it, is impossible. It ought to be obvious to every thoughtful person that problems of this class will not bear to be so handled. It is as if one were to apply the rigid mathematical method to the ordinary transactions of daily life, for which it is clearly unsuitable. Before we move a single step, however, we desire a few more particulars concerning this supposed evidence of Eusebius.

Accordingly, I invoked the good offices of my friend, the Rev. W. G. Penny, English Chaplain at Moscow, to obtain for me *the entire context* in which this "Scholion of Eusebius" occurs: little anticipating the trouble I was about to give him. His task would have been comparatively easy had I been able to furnish him (which I was not) with the exact designation of the Codex required. At last by sheer determination and the display of no small ability, he discovered the place, and sent me a tracing of the whole page: viz. fol. 286 (the last ten words being overleaf) of Matthaei's "12," ("Synod. 139,") our EVAN. 255.

It proves to be the concluding portion of Victor's Commentary, and to correspond with what is found at p. 365 of

Possinus, and p. 446-7 of Cramer: except that after the words "ἀποκυλίσειε τὸν λίθον :· ⌢," and before the words "ἄλλος δέ φησιν" [Possinus, *line* 12 *from bottom:* Cramer, *line* 3 *from the top*], is read as follows:—

σχὄ΄ κατὰ Μάρκον· μετὰ τὴν ἀνάστασιν οὐ λέγεται ὦφθαι
εὖσε τοῖς μαθηταῖς: κατὰ Ματθαῖον· μετὰ τὴν ἀνάστασιν τοῖς
βίου μαθηταῖς ὤφθη ἐν τῇ Γαλιλαίᾳ :·   ⌢
κατὰ Ἰωάννην· ἐν αὐτῇ τῇ ἡμέρᾳ τῆς ἀναστάσεως τῶν
θυρῶν κεκλεισμένων ὁ Ἰησοῦς μέσος τῶν μαθητῶν μὴ
παρόντος τοῦ Θωμᾶ ἔστη· καὶ μεθ᾽ ἡμέρας πάλιν ὀκτὼ
συμπαρόντος καὶ τοῦ Θωμᾶ. μετὰ ταῦτα πάλιν ἐφάνη
αὐτοῖς ἐπὶ τῆς θαλάσσης τῆς Τιβεριάδος :·   · ·
κατὰ Λουκᾶν· ὤφθη Κλεόπᾳ σὺν τῷ ἑταίρῳ αὐτοῦ αὐτῇ
τῇ ἡμέρᾳ τῆς ἀναστάσεως· καὶ πάλιν ὑποστρέψασιν εἰς
Ἱερουσαλὴμ ὤφθη τῇ αὐτῇ ἡμέρᾳ συνηγμένων τῶν λοιπῶλ
μαθητῶν· καὶ ὤφθη Σίμωνι· καὶ πάλιν ἐξήγαγεν αὐτοὺς
εἰς Βηθανίαν καὶ διέστη ἀπ᾽ αὐτῶν.

But surely no one who considers the matter attentively, will conceive that he is warranted in drawing from this so serious an inference as that Eusebius disallowed the last Section of S. Mark's Gospel.

(1.) In the first place, we have already [*suprà*, p. 44] heard Eusebius elaborately discuss the Section in question. That he allowed it, is therefore *certain*.

(2.) But next, this σχόλιον εὐσεβίου at the utmost can only be regarded as a general summary of what Eusebius has somewhere delivered concerning our LORD's appearances after His Resurrection. *As it stands*, it clearly is not the work of Eusebius.

(3.) And because I shall be reminded that such a statement cannot be accepted on my own mere 'ipse dixit,' I proceed to subjoin the original Scholion of which the preceding is evidently only an epitome. It is found in three of the Moscow MSS., (our Evan. 239, 259, 237,) but without any Author's name:—

Δεικνὺς δὲ ὁ εὐαγγελιστής, ὅτι μετὰ τὴν ἀνάστασιν οὐκέτι συνεχῶς αὐτοῖς συνῆν, λέγει, τοῦτο ἤδη τρίτον τοῖς μαθηταῖς ὤφθη ὁ Κύριος μετὰ τὴν ἀνάστασιν· οὐ τοῦτο λέγων, ὅτι μόνον τρίτον, ἀλλὰ τὰ τοῖς ἄλλοις παραλελειμμένα λέγων, τοῦτο ἤδη πρὸς τοῖς ἄλλοις τρίτον ἐφανερώθη τοῖς μαθηταῖς. κατὰ μὲν γὰρ τὸν Ματθαῖον, ὤφθη αὐτοῖς ἐν τῇ Γαλιλαίᾳ μόνον· κατὰ δὲ τὸν Ἰωάννην, ἐν αὐτῇ τῇ ἡμέρᾳ τῆς ἀναστάσεως, τῶν θυρῶν κεκλεισμένων, μέσος αὐτῶν ἔστη, ὄντων ἐν Ἱερουσαλὴμ, μὴ παρόντος ἐκεῖ Θωμᾶ. καὶ πάλιν μεθ᾽ ἡμέρας ὀκτὼ, παρόντος καὶ τοῦ Θωμᾶ, ὤφθη αὐτοῖς, ἤδη κεκλεισμένων τῶν θυρῶν. μετὰ ταῦτα ἐπὶ τῆς θαλάσσης τῆς Τιβεριάδος ἐφάνη αὐτοῖς, οὐ τοῖς ιᾱ ἀλλὰ μόνοις ζ. κατὰ δὲ Λουκᾶν ὤφθη Κλεόπᾳ σὺν τῷ ἑταίρῳ αὐτοῦ, αὐτῇ τῇ ἡμέρᾳ τῆς ἀναστάσεως. καὶ πάλιν ὑποστρέψασιν εἰς Ἱερουσαλὴμ αὐτῇ τῇ ἡμέρᾳ, συνηγμένων τῶν μαθητῶν, ὤφθη Σίμωνι. καὶ πάλιν ἐξαγαγὼν αὐτοὺς εἰς Βηθανίαν, ὅτε καὶ διέστη ἀναληφθεὶς ἀπ᾽ αὐτῶν· ὡς ἐκ τούτου παρίστασθαι ζ. εἶναι τὰς εἰς τοὺς μαθητὰς μετὰ τὴν ἀνάστασιν γεγονυίας ὀπτασίας τοῦ Σωτῆρος ἡμῶν Ἰησοῦ Χριστοῦ. μίαν μὲν παρὰ τῷ Ματθαίῳ, τρεῖς δὲ παρὰ τῷ Ἰωάννῃ, καὶ τρεῖς τῷ Λουκᾷ ὁμοίως *.

(4.) Now, the chief thing deserving of attention here,—the *only* thing in fact which I am concerned to point out,—is the notable circumstance that the supposed dictum of Eusebius,—("quod scribere non potuisset si pericopam dubiam agnovisset,")—*is no longer discoverable*. To say that 'it has disappeared,' would be incorrect. In the original document *it has no existence*. In plain terms, the famous "σχόλιον εὐσεβίου" proves to be every way a figment. It is a worthless interpolation, thrust by some nameless scribe into his abridgement of a Scholion, of which Eusebius (as I shall presently shew) *cannot* have been the Author.

(5.) I may as well point out *why* the person who wrote the longer Scholion says nothing about S. Mark's Gospel. It is because there was nothing for him to say.

* Quoted by *Matthaei, N. T.* (1788) vol. ix. p. 228, *from* g, n, d.

He is enumerating our LORD's *appearances to His Disciples* after His Resurrection; and he discovers that these were exactly seven in number: *one* being peculiar to S. Matthew,—*three*, to S. John,—*three*, to S. Luke. But because, (as every one is aware), there exists *no* record of an appearance to the Disciples *peculiar* to S. Mark's Gospel, the Author of the Scholion is silent concerning S. Mark *perforce*.

.... How so acute and accomplished a Critic as Matthaei can have overlooked all this: how he can have failed to recognise the identity of his longer and his shorter Scholion: how he came to say of the latter, "conjicias ergo Eusebium hunc totum locum repudiasse;" and, of the former, "ultimam partem Evangelii Marci videtur tollere [a]:" lastly, how Tischendorf (1869) can write,—" est enim ejusmodi ut ultimam partem evangelii Marci, de quo quaeritur, excludat [b]:"—I profess myself unable to understand.

(6.) The epitomizer however, missing the point of his Author,—besides enumerating *all* the appearances of our SAVIOUR which S. Luke anywhere records,—is further convicted of having injudiciously *invented* the negative statement about S. Mark's Gospel which is occasioning us all this trouble.

(7.) And yet, by that unlucky sentence of his, he certainly did not mean what is commonly imagined. I am not concerned to defend him: but it is only fair to point out that, to suppose he intended *to disallow the end of S. Mark's Gospel*, is altogether to misapprehend the gist of his remarks, and to impute to him a purpose of which he clearly knew nothing. Note, how he throws his first two statements into a separate paragraph; contrasts, and evidently *balances* one against the other: thus,—

κατὰ Μάρκον, μετὰ τὴν ἀνάστασιν οὐ λέγεται ὦφθαι,—
κατὰ Ματθαῖον μετὰ τὴν ἀνάστασιν ὤφθη,— τοῖς μαθηταῖς ἐν τῇ Γαλιλαίᾳ.

Perfectly evident is it that the 'plena locutio' so to speak, of the Writer would have been somewhat as follows:—

'[The first two Evangelists are engaged with our SAVIOUR'S appearance to His Disciples *in Galilee*: but] by

---

[a] *Ibid.*, ii. 69, and ix. 228.   [b] *Nov. Test.* (1869), p. 404.

S. Mark, He is *not*—by S. Matthew, He *is*—related to have been actually *seen* by them there.

'[The other two Evangelists relate the appearances *in Jerusalem :* and] according to S. John, &c. &c.

'According to S. Luke,' &c. &c.

(8.) And on passing the "Quaestiones ad Marinum" of Eusebius under review, I am constrained to admit that the Scholion before us is just such a clumsy bit of writing as an unskilful person might easily be betrayed into, who should attempt to exhibit in a few short sentences the substance of more than one tedious disquisition of this ancient Father [c]. Its remote parentage would fully account for its being designated "*σχόλιον εὐσεβίου,*" all the same.

(9.) Least of all am I concerned to say anything more about the longer Scholion; seeing that S. Mark is not so much as mentioned in it. But I may as well point out that, *as it stands*, Eusebius cannot have been its Author: the proof being, that whereas the Scholion in question is a note on S. John xxi. 12, (as Matthaei is careful to inform us,)— its opening sentence is derived *from Chrysostom's Commentary on that same verse* in his 87th Homily on S. John [d].

(10.) And thus, one by one, every imposing statement of the Critics is observed hopelessly to collapse as soon as it is questioned, and to vanish into thin air.

So much has been offered, only because of the deliberate pledge I gave in p. 51.—Never again, I undertake to say, will the "Scholion of Eusebius" which has cost my friend at Moscow, his Archimandrites, and me, so much trouble, be introduced into any discussion of the genuineness of the last Twelve Verses of the Gospel according to S. Mark. As the oversight of one (C. F. Matthaei) who was singularly accurate, and towards whom we must all feel as towards a Benefactor, let it be freely forgiven as well as loyally forgotten!

---

[c] Let the reader examine his "Quaestio ix," (Mai, vol. iv. p. 293-5): his "Quaestio x," (p. 295, last seven lines). See also p. 296, line 29—32.

[d] See Chrys. *Opp.* vol. viii. p. 522 C:—ὅτι δὲ οὐδὲ συνεχῶς ἐπεχωρίαζεν, οὐδὲ ὁμοίως, λέγει ὅτι τρίτον τοῦτο ἐφάνη αὐτοῖς, ὅτε ἐγέρθη ἐκ νεκρῶν.

L'ENVOY

As one, escaped the bustling trafficking town,
Worn out and weary, climbs his favourite hill
And thinks it Heaven to see the calm green fields
Mapped out in beautiful sunlight at his feet:
Or walks enraptured where the fitful south
Comes past the beans in blossom; and no sight
Or scent or sound but fills his soul with glee:—
So I,—rejoicing once again to stand
Where Siloa's brook flows softly, and the meads
Are all enamell'd o'er with deathless flowers,
And Angel voices fill the dewy air.
Strife is so hateful to me! most of all
A strife of words about the things of GOD.
Better by far the peasant's uncouth speech
Meant for the heart's confession of its hope.
Sweeter by far in village-school the words
But half remembered from the Book of Life,
Or scarce articulate lispings of the Creed.

And yet, three times that miracle of Spring
The grand old tree that darkens Exeter wall
Hath decked itself with blossoms as with stars,
Since I, like one that striveth unto death,
Find myself early and late and oft all day
Engaged in eager conflict for GOD's Truth;
GOD's Truth, to be maintained against Man's lie.
And lo, my brook which widened out long since
Into a river, threatens now at length
To burst its channel and become a sea.

O Sister, who ere yet my task is done
Art lying (my loved Sister!) in thy shroud
With a calm placid smile upon thy lips
As thou wert only "taking of rest in sleep,"
Soon to wake up to ministries of love,—
Open those lips, kind Sister, for my sake
In the mysterious place of thy sojourn.
(For thou must needs be with the bless'd,—yea, where
The pure in heart draw wondrous nigh to GOD,)
And tell the Evangelist of thy brother's toil;
Adding (be sure!) "He found it his reward,
Yet supplicates thy blessing and thy prayers,
The blessing, saintly Stranger, of thy prayers,
Sure at the least unceasingly of mine!"

One other landed on the eternal shore!
One other garnered into perfect peace!
One other hid from hearing and from sight! . . .
O but the days go heavily, and the toil
Which used to seem so pleasant yields scant joy.
There come no tokens to us from the dead:
Save—it may be—that now and then we reap
Where not we sowed, and *that* may be from *them,*
Fruit of their prayers when we forgot to pray!
Meantime there comes no message, comes no word:
Day after day no message and no sign:
And the heart droops, and finds that it was Love
Not Fame it longed for, lived for: only Love.

CANTERBURY.

Thinking that all readers of this book may not
have access to Dr. F. H. Scrivener's excellent INTRODUCTION TO THE CRITICISM OF
THE NEW TESTAMENT, we are appending a
few pages from the Third Edition.

You will note that he thinks that Burgon has a
"brilliant monograph," in this book, and concludes that he is quite unanswerable. This is
true because of the evidence involved, indeed,
but it must not be forgotten that all the critics
were content to misstate the evidence, and it
was Dean Burgon who played the scholar by a
laborious search into the true evidence.

Although many men have pronounced judgment
on the New Testament Text in the past century
of 'progress,' few of them actually have played the scholar by examining the evidence, and
none have matched Dr. Scrivener and Burgon,
unless it be Tischendorf. (Jay Green, Editor)

(11). MARK xvi. 9—20. In Chapter I. we engaged to defend the authenticity of this long and important passage, and
that without the slightest misgiving (p. 7). Dean Burgon's
brilliant monograph, "The Last Twelve verses of the Gospel
according to S. Mark vindicated against recent objectors and
established" (Oxford and London, 1871), has thrown a stream
of light upon the controversy, nor does the joyous tone of
his book misbecome one who is conscious of having triumphantly maintained a cause which is very precious to him. We
may fairly say that his conclusions have in no essential point
been shaken by the elaborate and very able counter-plea of Dr
Hort (*Notes*, pp. 28—51). This whole paragraph is set apart
by itself in the critical editions of Tischendorf and Tregelles.
Besides this, it is placed within double brackets by Westcott
and Hort, and followed by the wretched supplement derived from
Cod. L (*vide infra*), annexed as an alternative reading (αλλωc).
Out of all the great manuscripts, the two oldest (אB) stand

alone in omitting ver. 9—20 altogether[1]. Cod. B, however, betrays consciousness on the scribe's part that something is left out, inasmuch as after ἐφοβοῦντο γάρ ver. 8, a whole column is left perfectly blank (*the only blank one in the whole volume*[2]), as well as the rest of the column containing ver. 8, which is usual in Cod. B at the end of every book of Scripture (*see* p. 104). No such peculiarity attaches to Cod. ℵ. The testimony of L, that close companion of B, is very suggestive. Immediately after ver. 8 the copyist breaks off; then in the same hand (for all corrections in this manuscript seem *primâ manu: see* p. 133), at the top of the next column we read...φερετε που και ταυτα+...πάντα δὲ τα παρηγγελμενα τοῖς περι τον πετρον συντομωσ ἐξηγγιλαν+μετα δὲ ταῦτα καὶ αὐτος ὁ ισ̄, ἀπο ἀνατολησ καὶ ἀχρι δυσεωσ ἐξαπεστιλεν δι αὐτων το ἱερον καὶ ἀφθαρτον κηρυγμα+ τησ αἰωνιου σωτηριασ+ ...εστην δε και ταῦτα φερομενα μετα το ἐφοβουντο γαρ+... Ἀναστὰσ δὲ πρωϊ πρωτη σαββατȣ+ κ.τ.λ., ver. 9, ad fin. capit. (Burgon's *facsimile*, facing his p. 113: our *facsimile* No. 21): as if vv. 9—20 were just as little to be regarded as the trifling apocryphal supplement[3] which precedes them. Besides these, the twelve verses are omitted in none but some old Armenian codices[4] and two of the Æthiopic, *k* of the Old Latin, and an Arabic Lectionary [IX] No. 13, examined by Scholz in the Vatican. The Old Latin Codex *k* puts in their room a corrupt and careless version of the subscription in L ending with σωτηρίας (*k* adding *amen*): the same subscription being appended to the end of the Gospel in the two Æthiopic manuscripts, and (with ἀμήν) in the margin

---

[1] I have ventured but slowly to vouch for Tischendorf's notion, that six leaves of Cod. ℵ, *that containing* Mark xvi. 2—Luke i. 56 *being one of them*, were written by the scribe of Cod. B. On mere identity of handwriting and the peculiar shape of certain letters who shall insist? Yet there are parts of the case, apparently unnoticed by Tischendorf himself (*see* p. 92, note), which I know not how to answer, and which have persuaded even Dr Hort. Having now arrived at this conclusion our inference is simple and direct, that at least in these leaves, Codd. ℵB make but one witness, not two.

[2] The cases of Nehemiah, Tobit, and Daniel, in the Old Testament portion of Cod. B, are obviously in no wise parallel in regard to their blank columns.

[3] Of which supplement Dr Hort says unexpectedly enough "In style it is unlike the ordinary narratives of the Evangelists, but comparable to the four introductory verses of S. Luke's Gospel " (*Introduction*, p. 298).

[4] We ought to add that some Armenian codices which contain the paragraph have the subscription "Gospel after Mark" at the end of ver. 8 as well as of ver. 20, as though their scribes, like Cod. L's, knew of a double ending to the Gospel.

of 274 and the Philoxenian. Not unlike is the marginal note in *Hunt.* 17 or Cod. 1 of the Memphitic, translated by Bp Lightfoot above, p. 379. Of cursive Greek manuscripts 137. 138, which Birch had hastily reported as marking the passage with an asterisk, each contains the marginal annotation given below, which claims the passage as genuine, 138 with no asterisk at all, 137 (like 36 and others) with an ordinary mark of reference from the text to the note, where (of course) it is repeated[1]. Other manuscripts contain marginal scholia respecting it, of which the following is the substance. Cod. 199 has τέλος[2] after ἐφοβοῦντο γάρ and before Ἀναστὰς δέ, and in the same hand as τέλος we read, ἔν τισι τῶν ἀντιγράφων οὐ κεῖται ταῦτα, ἀλλ᾽ ἐνταῦθα καταπαύει. The kindred Codd. 20. 215. 300 (but after ver. 15, not ver. 8) mark the omission in some (τισὶ) copies, adding ἐν δὲ τοῖς ἀρχαίοις πάντα ἀπαράλειπτα κεῖται, and these had been corrected from Jerusalem copies (*see* pp. 154 and note, 182). Cod. 573 (*see* p. 239) has for a subscription ἐγράφη καὶ ἀντεβλήθη ὁμοίως ἐκ τῶν ἐσπουδασμένων κεφαλαίοις σλζ´: where Burgon, going back to S. Matthew's Gospel (*see* p. 154, note) infers that the old Jerusalem copies must have contained our twelve verses. Codd. 15. 22 conclude at ἐφοβοῦντο γάρ, then add in red ink that in some copies the Evangelist ends here, ἐν πολλοῖς δὲ καὶ ταῦτα φέρεται, affixing vv. 9—20. In Codd. 1. 205 (in its duplicate 206 also), 209 is the same notice, ἄλλοις standing for πολλοῖς in 206, with the additional assertion that Eusebius "canonised" no further than ver. 8, a statement which is confirmed by the absence of the Ammonian and Eusebian numerals beyond that verse in ℵALSU and at least eleven cursives, with *am. fuld. ing.* of the Vulgate. It would be no marvel if Eusebius, the author of this harmonising system (*see* pp. 56, &c.), had consistently acted upon his own rash opinion respecting the paragraph, an opinion which we shall

[1] Burgon (*Guardian*, July 12, 1882) speaks of seven manuscripts (Codd. 538, 539 being among them) wherein these last twelve verses begin on the right hand of the page. This would be more significant if a space were left, as is not stated, at the foot of the preceding page. In Cod. 550 the first letter α is small, but covers an abnormally large space.

[2] Of course no notice is to be taken of τέλος after ἐφοβοῦντο γάρ, as the end of the ecclesiastical lesson is all that is intimated (*see* p. 72 note, and p. 73). The grievous misstatements of preceding critics from Wetstein and Scholz down to Tischendorf, have been corrected throughout by means of Burgon's laborious researches (*Burgon*, pp. 114—123).

have to notice presently, and such action on his part would have added nothing to the strength of the adverse case. But it does not seem that he really did so. These numerals appear in most manuscripts, and in all parts of them, with a good deal of variation which we can easily account for. In the present instance they are annexed to ver. 9 and the rest of the passage in Codd. CEKVΠ, and (with some changes) in GHMΓΔΛ and many others : in Cod. 566 the concluding sections are there (σλδ ver. 11, σλε ver. 12, σλς ver. 14) without the canons. In their respective margins the annotated codices 12 (of Scholz), 24. 36. 37. 40. 41. 108. 129. 137. 138. 143. 181. 186. 195. 210. 221. 222. 237. 238. 255. 259. 299. 329. 374 (twenty-four in all), present in substance[1] the same weighty testimony in favour of the passage : παρὰ πλείστοις ἀντιγράφοις οὐ κεῖται (thus far also Cod. 119, adding only ταῦτα, ἀλλ' ἐνταῦθα καταπαύει) ἐν τῷ παρόντι εὐαγγελίῳ, ὡς νόθα νομίσαντες αὐτὰ εἶναι· ἀλλὰ ἡμεῖς ἐξ ἀκριβῶν ἀντιγράφων ἐν πλείστοις εὑρόντες αὐτὰ καὶ κατὰ τὸ Παλαιστιναῖον εὐαγγέλιον Μάρκου, ὡς ἔχει ἡ ἀλήθεια, συντεθείκαμεν καὶ τὴν ἐν αὐτῷ ἐπιφερομένην δεσποτικὴν ἀνάστασιν. Now this is none other than an extract from Victor of Antioch's [v] commentary on S. Mark, which they all annex in full to the sacred text, and which is expressly assigned to that Father in Codd. 12. 37. 41. Yet these very twenty-four manuscripts have been cited by critical editors as adverse to the authenticity of a paragraph which their scribes never dreamt of calling into question, but had simply copied Victor's decided judgment in its favour. His appeal to the famous Palestine codices which had belonged to Origen and Pamphilus (*see* pp. 53 and note, 512) is found in twenty-one of them: possibly these documents are akin to the Jerusalem copies mentioned in Codd. Evan. Λ. 20. 164. 262. 300, &c. (*see* p. 585).

All other codices, e.g. ACD (which is defective from ver. 15, *primâ manu*) EF^wGH (begins ver. 14) KMSUVXΓΔΠ. 33. 69, the Peshito, Jerusalem and Curetonian Syriac (which last, by a singular happiness, contains vv. 17—20, though no other part of

---

[1] The minute variations between these several codices are given by Burgon (Appendix E, pp. 288—90). Cod. 255 contains a scholion imputed to Eusebius, from which Griesbach had drawn inferences which Burgon (*Last Twelve Verses*, &c. Postscript pp. 319—23) has shown to be unwarranted by the circumstances of the case.

S. Mark), the Philoxenian *text*, the Thebaic (only ver. 20 is preserved), the Memphitic and Æthiopic (with the exceptions before named, pp. 584—5), the Gothic (to ver. 12), the Vulgate, all extant Old Latins except *k* (though *a. primâ manu* and *b.* are defective), the Georgian (*see* p. 411), the printed Armenian, its later manuscripts, and all the lesser versions (Arabic, &c.) agree in maintaining the paragraph. It is cited, possibly by Papias, unquestionably by Irenæus (both in Greek and Latin) and by Justin Martyr as early as the second century; by Hippolytus (see Tregelles, *An Account of the Printed Text*, p. 252) and apparently by Celsus in the third; by Aphraates (in a Syriac Homily dated A.D. 337), Cyril of Jerusalem[1], Epiphanius, Ambrose, Augustine, Chrysostom, &c. in the fourth. Add to this, what has been so forcibly stated by Burgon (*ubi supra*, p. 205), that in the Calendar of Greek Church lessons, which existed certainly in the fourth century, very probably much earlier, the disputed verses were honoured by being read as a special matins service for Ascension Day (*see* p. 79), and as the Gospel for S. Mary Magdalene's Day, July 22 (p. 86); as well as by forming the third of the eleven εὐαγγέλια ἀναστάσιμα ἑωθινά, the preceding part of the chapter forming the second (p. 83): so little were they suspected as of even doubtful authenticity[2].

The earliest objector to ver. 9—20 we know of was Eusebius (*Quæst. ad Marin.*), who tells that they were not ἐν ἅπασι τοῖς ἀντιγράφοις, but after ἐφοβοῦντο γάρ that τὰ ἑξῆς are found σπανίως ἔν τισιν, yet not in τὰ ἀκριβῆ: language which Jerome (*see* p. 516) *twice* echoes and almost exaggerates by saying "in

---

[1] It is surprising that Dr Hort, who lays very undue stress upon the silence of certain early Christian writers that had no occasion for quoting the twelve verses in their extant works, should say of Cyril of Jerusalem, who lived about A.D. 349, that his "negative evidence is peculiarly cogent" (*Notes*, p. 37). To our mind it is not at all negative. Preaching on a Sunday, he reminds his hearers of a sermon he had delivered the day before, and which he would have them keep in their thoughts. One of the topics he briefly recalls is the article of the Creed τὸν καθίσαντα ἐκ δεξιῶν τοῦ πατρός. He must inevitably have used Mark xvi. 19 in his Saturday's discourse.

[2] Nor were these verses used in the Greek Church only. Ver. 9—20 comprised the Gospel for Easter Monday in the old Spanish or Mozarabic Liturgy, for Easter Tuesday among the Syrian Jacobites, for Ascension Day among the Armenians. Ver. 12—20 was the Gospel for Ascension Day in the Coptic Liturgy (Malan, *Original Documents*, IV. p. 63): ver. 16—20 in the old Latin *Comes*.

raris fertur Evangeliis, omnibus Graeciae libris paene hoc capitulum fine non habentibus." A second cause with Eusebius for rejecting them is μάλιστα εἴπερ ἔχοιεν ἀντιλογίαν τῇ τῶν λοιπῶν εὐαγγελιστῶν μαρτυρίᾳ[1]. The language of Eusebius has been minutely examined by Dean Burgon, who proves to demonstration that all the subsequent evidence which has been alleged against the passage, whether of Severus, or Hesychius, or any other writer down to Euthymius Zigabenus in the twelfth century, is a mere echo of the doubts and difficulties of Eusebius, if indeed he is not retailing to us at second-hand one of the fanciful Biblical speculations of Origen (see pp. 509, 512—3).

With regard to the argument against these twelve verses arising from their alleged difference in style from the rest of the Gospel, I must say that the same process might be applied—and has been applied—to prove that S. Paul was not the writer of the Pastoral Epistles (to say nothing of that to the Hebrews), S. John of the Apocalypse, Isaiah and Zechariah of portions of those prophecies that bear their names. Every one used to literary composition may detect, if he will, such minute variations as have been made so much of in this case[2], either in his own writings, or in those of the authors he is most familiar with.

Persons who, like Eusebius, devoted themselves to the pious

---

[1] To get rid of one apparent ἀντιφωνία, that arising from the expression πρωΐ τῇ μιᾷ τοῦ σαββάτου (sic), ver. 9, compared with ὀψὲ σαββάτων Matth. xxviii. 1, Eusebius proposes the plan of setting a stop between Ἀναστὰς δέ and πρωΐ, so little was he satisfied with rudely expunging the whole clause. Hence Cod. E puts a red cross after δέ: Codd. 20. 22. 34. 72. 193. 196. 199. 271. 345. 405. 411. 456, have a colon: Codd. 332. 339. 340. 439, a comma (Burgon, Guardian, Aug. 20, 1873).

[2] The following peculiarities have been noticed in these verses: ἐκεῖνος used absolutely, ver. 10, 11, 13; πορεύομαι ver. 10, 12, 15; τοῖς μετ' αὐτοῦ γενομένοις ver. 10; θεάομαι ver. 11, 14; ἀπιστέω ver. 11, 16; μετὰ ταῦτα ver. 12: ἕτερος ver. 12; παρακολουθέω ver. 17; ἐν τῷ ὀνόματι ver. 17; κύριος for the Saviour, ver. 19, 20; πανταχοῦ, συνεργοῦντος, βεβαιόω, ἐπακολουθέω ver. 20, all of them as not found elsewhere in S. Mark. A very able and really conclusive plea for the genuineness of the paragraph, as coming from that Evangelist's pen, appeared in the Baptist Quarterly, Philadelphia, July 1869, bearing the signature of Professor J. A. Broadus, of South Carolina. Unfortunately, from the nature of the case, it does not admit of abridgement. Burgon's ninth chapter (pp. 136—190) enters into full details, and amply justifies his conclusion that the supposed adverse argument from phraseology "breaks down hopelessly under severe analysis."

task of constructing harmonies of the Gospels, would soon perceive the difficulty of adjusting the events recorded in ver. 9—20 to the narratives of the other Evangelists. Alford regards this inconsistency (more apparent than real, we believe) as "a valuable testimony to the antiquity of the fragment" (N. T. *ad loc.*): we would go further, and claim for the harder reading the benefit of any critical doubt as to its genuineness (Canon I. p. 493). The difficulty was both felt and avowed by Eusebius, and was recited after him by Severus of Antioch or whoever wrote the scholion attributed to him. Whatever Jerome and the rest may have done, these assigned the ἀντιλογία, the ἐναντίωσις they thought they perceived, as a reason (not the first, nor perhaps the chief, but still as a reason) for supposing that the Gospel ended with ἐφοβοῦντο γάρ. Yet in the balance of probabilities, can anything be more unlikely than that S. Mark broke off so abruptly as this hypothesis would imply, while no ancient writer has noticed or seemed conscious of any such abruptness[1]? This fact has driven those who reject the concluding verses to the strangest fancies ;—namely, that, like Thucydides, the Evangelist was cut off before his work was completed, or even that the last leaf of the original Gospel was torn away.

We emphatically deny that such wild surmises [2] are called

[1] "Can any one, who knows the character of the Lord and of His ministry, conceive for an instant that we should be left with nothing but a message baulked through the alarm of women" (Kelly, *Lectures Introductory to the Gospels*, p. 258). Even Dr Hort can say "It is incredible that the Evangelist deliberately concluded either a paragraph with ἐφοβοῦντο γάρ, or the Gospel with a petty detail of a secondary event, leaving his narrative hanging in the air" (*Notes*, p. 46).

[2] When Burgon ventures upon a surmise, one which is probability itself by the side of those we have been speaking of, Professor Abbot (*ubi supra*, p. 197) remarks upon it that "With Mr Burgon a conjecture seems to be a demonstration." We will not be deterred by dread of any such reproach from mentioning his method of accounting for the absence of these verses from some very early copies, commending it to the reader for what it may seem worth. After a learned and exhaustive proof that the Church lessons, as we now have them, existed from very early times (*Twelve verses*, pp. 191—211), and noting that an important lesson ended with Mark xvi. 8 (*see* p. 83); he supposes that τέλος, which would stand at the end of such a lesson (*see* p. 72, and note), misled some scribe who had before him an *exemplar* of the Gospels whose last leaf (containing Mark xvi. 9—20, or according to Codd. 20. 215. 300 only ver. 16 —20, *see* p. 585) was lost, as it might easily be in those older manuscripts wherein S. Mark stood last

for by the state of the evidence in this case. All opposition to the authenticity of the paragraph resolves itself into the allegations of Eusebius and the testimony of אB. Let us accord to these the weight which is their due: but against their verdict we can appeal to the reading of Irenæus and of both the elder Syriac translations in the second century; of nearly all other versions; and of all extant manuscripts excepting two. So powerfully is it vouched for, that many of those who are reluctant to recognise S. Mark as its author, are content to regard it notwithstanding as an integral portion of the inspired record originally delivered to the Church[1].

Besides the foregoing attestation of approval by the accomplished Dr. Scrivener, we thought you would also find the testimony of two more scholars most interesting too.

Dr. Christopher Wordsworth, Bishop of Lincoln— a distinguished textual critic in his own right— has no hesitation in recommending Burgon's book.

Dr. F. C. Cook, in several places expressed very strong approval. The following excerpt is only the portion of his REVISED VERSION OF THE FIRST THREE GOSPELS wherein he shows that he counts this effort of Burgon unanswerable.

All three men were contemporaries of Burgon.

---

[1] Dr Hort, however, while he admits the possibility of the leaf containing ver. 9—20 having been lost in some very early copy, which thus would become the parent of transcripts having a mutilated text (*Notes*, p. 49), rather inconsistently arrives at the conclusion that the passage in question "manifestly cannot claim any apostolic authority; but it is doubtless founded on some tradition of the apostolic age" (*ibid*. p. 51).

[2] Dr Hort will hardly find many friends for his division (*Notes*, p. 56)

Δόξα ἐν ὑψίστοις θεῷ καὶ ἐπὶ γῆς,
Εἰρήνη ἐν ἀνθρώποις εὐδοκίας.

[3] I am loth to sully with a semblance of unseasonable levity a page which is devoted to the vindication of the true form of the Angelic Hymn, and must ask the student to refer for himself to the 470th number of the *Spectator*, where what we will venture to call a precisely parallel case exercises the delicate humour

Here is the remark by Dr. Wordsworth, taken from Page 154 of his NEW TESTAMENT, 1872 edition.

> To those who lay stress on this argument let me commend a careful perusal of chapter ix. (pp. 136—190) of the Rev. *J. W. Burgon's* masterly vindication of the genuineness of these twelve verses (Oxford, 1871).

Here are pages 122-3 of Canon Cook's book:

The arguments urged, with great ability, and, I would not use the word offensively, but I must say with remarkable subtlety, by Dr. Hort, could not here be fully discussed without breaking the thread of my own reasoning, in which I deal only with positive facts and broad statements; and presently I shall have occasion to revert to those arguments which appear to me to demand serious attention; but I will at once press upon all inquirers this general statement.

Dr. Hort does not impugn the fact, which of itself would seem to most inquirers conclusive, that with the exception of א, B, L, every ancient manuscript, of all recensions and of all ages, has the contested verses; nor again that א is the only manuscript which omits them without any indication of a hiatus; nor, though he notices, does he give any satisfactory reason for the very instructive fact that B leaves a blank space, contrary to its unvarying usage, thus proving decisively that the transcriber had a concluding portion before him.

Nor again does he deny that all ancient Versions, some of them 100 or 200 years earlier than the most ancient MS., have the missing passage; a very singular fact is passed over *sub silentio*, that the MSS. include those which are most commonly found on the side of B; and that whereas two very ancient Versions, the Syriac of Cureton and the Sahidic, are grievously mutilated, each preserves just enough of the missing verses to prove their existence and their reception.

Nor again does he deal fully, I venture to say fairly, with the patristic evidence. He relies chiefly on negative evidence, which is universally admitted to be a very insecure foundation for unfavourable judgment in the face of clear positive testimony; and he is far from putting before his readers the enormous weight which attaches to the distinct attestation of Irenæus in the passage which I have quoted above (see p. 38), an attestation which, whether we consider the position, character, and age of the writer, or the peculiar force of his statement—not an *obiter dictum*, but applying to the whole structure of the second Gospel—ought to suffice to raise the question far above the range of controversy. Nothing indeed can be more striking than the contrast between the hesitating, varying, uncertain words of Eusebius, on the one hand, uttered with an avowed intention of meeting a difficulty, and on the other the plain, strong, clear words of the great pupil of Polycarp, speaking in the name of the Church, and resting on the authority of what all then admitted to be the Petrine Gospel.

For these and other points I would simply refer to the unanswered and unanswerable arguments of Dean Burgon in his palmary work, and to the decisive judgment of Dr. Scrivener, who *without any hesitation* maintains the authenticity of the whole passage.